C000056462

ATLAS

LONDON, NEW YORK
MUNICH, MELBOURNE, DELHI

LONDON, NEW YORK
MUNICH, MELBOURNE, DELHI

FOR THE THIRD EDITION
Senior Cartographic Manager David Roberts
Senior Cartographic Editors Roger Bullen, Simon Mumford
Database Editors Cambridge International Reference on Current Affairs (CIRCA)
Systems Co-ordinator Philip Rowles
Production Melanie Dowland
3D Globes Planetary Visions Ltd., London

FOR PREVIOUS EDITIONS
Cartographic Director Andrew Heritage
Cartography Encompass Graphics Limited, Rob Stokes, Iorwerth Watkins
Project Editor Sam Atkinson   **Art Editor** Karen Gregory

First published in Great Britain in 2001 by
Dorling Kindersley Limited, 80 Strand, London WC2R 0RL
A Penguin Company
Third Edition 2007
Previously published as the Ultimate Pocket Book of the World Atlas & Factfile
Copyright © 1996, 1998, 2001, 2003, 2004, 2005, 2007
Dorling Kindersley Limited, London

See our complete catalogue at
www.dk.com

*All rights reserved. No part of this publication may be reproduced, stored in a retrieval system,
or transmitted in any form or by any other means, electronic, mechanical, photocopying, recording
or otherwise, without the written permission of the copyright owner.*
A CIP catalogue record for this book is available from the British Library

ISBN: 978-1-4053-2034-4

Printed and bound in Singapore by Star Standard

For the very latest information, visit:
www.dk.com and click on the Maps & Atlases icon

Key to map symbols

ELEVATION

6000m / 19,686ft
4000m / 13,124ft
2000m / 6562ft
1000m / 3281ft
500m / 1640ft
250m / 820ft
100m / 328ft
0
Below sea level

▲   Mountain

•   Depression

BORDERS

▬▬▬▬   Full international

━ ━ ━ ━   Disputed *de facto*

• • • • • •   Territorial claim

×–×–×–×   Cease-fire line

⋯⋯⋯⋯   Undefined

────   State / Province

DRAINAGE FEATURES

──────   River

──────   Seasonal river

⊥⊥⊥⊥⊥⊥   Canal

⬭   Lake

⬭   Seasonal lake

SETTLEMENTS

●   Capital city

◎   Major town

○   Minor town

•   Major port

COMMUNICATIONS

──────   Major road

──────   Rail

✈   International airport

◆   Insight; facts, figures and amazing information from around the world

NAVIGATOR

	120	
122	128–29	130
	136	

The navigator device can be used to quickly move around the atlas. Using this example, the next map to the north of page 128 can be found on page 120.

4

Atlas contents

North & Central America 16-17

Africa 50-51

South America 38-39

Europe 62-63

North & West Asia 94-95

South & East Asia 106-107

Australasia & Oceania 124-125

Country factfiles 138-359

See overleaf for contents

6
Factfile contents

Factfile contents

The Political World

Svalbard (Norway)

Jan Mayen (Norway)

Franz Josef Land

Severnaya Zemlya

New Siberian Islands

Novaya Zemlya

ICELAND

DENMARK

RUSSIAN FEDERATION

Faeroe Islands (Denmark)

IRELAND

UNITED KINGDOM

NORWAY

SWEDEN

FINLAND

ESTONIA

LATVIA

LITHUANIA

BELARUS

POLAND

NETH.

BELGIUM

LUXEMBOURG

SWITZERLAND

FRANCE

ANDORRA

SPAIN

PORTUGAL

MONACO

ITALY

UKRAINE

MOLDOVA

ROM.

BULG.

ALB.

MAC.

GREECE

TURKEY

CYPRUS

MALTA

TUNISIA

GEORGIA

ARMENIA

AZ.

AZER.

SYRIA

LEBANON

ISRAEL

IRAQ

JORDAN

KAZAKHSTAN

UZBEK.

KYRG.

TURKMEN.

TAJ.

AFGH.

IRAN

KUWAIT

BAHRAIN

QATAR

U.A.E.

SAUDI ARABIA

MONGOLIA

CHINA

NEPAL

BHUTAN

N. KOREA

S. KOREA

JAPAN

PAKISTAN

INDIA

MYANMAR (BURMA)

LAOS

TAIWAN

MOROCCO

WESTERN SAHARA (disputed)

ALGERIA

LIBYA

EGYPT

NIGER

CHAD

SUDAN

ERITREA

YEMEN

OMAN

DJIBOUTI

ETHIOPIA

SOMALIA

BANGLADESH

SRI LANKA

MALDIVES

Northern Mariana Islands (USA)

Guam (USA)

THAI.

CAMB.

VIETNAM

PHILIPPINES

BRUNEI

MALAYSIA

MICRONE.

PALAU

CAPE VERDE

MAURITANIA

MALI

SENEGAL

GAMBIA

GUINEA-BISSAU

GUINEA

BURKINA

SIERRA LEONE

LIBERIA

CÔTE D'IVOIRE

GHANA

TOGO

BENIN

NIGERIA

CAMEROON

C.A.R.

UGANDA

KENYA

RWANDA

BURUNDI

TANZANIA

SINGAPORE

INDONESIA

PAPUA NEW GUINEA

EAST TIMOR

SAO TOME & PRINCIPE

EQ. GUINEA

GABON

CONGO

DEM. REP. CONGO

Cabinda (Angola)

ANGOLA

ZAMBIA

MALAWI

SEYCHELLES

COMOROS

ATLANTIC OCEAN

Tropic of Capricorn

NAMIBIA

ZIMB.

BOTS.

SOUTH AFRICA

SWAZILAND

LESOTHO

MOZAMBIQUE

MADAGASCAR

MAURITIUS

INDIAN OCEAN

French Southern & Antarctic Territories (France)

AUSTRALIA

Key to Numbers
1. Germany
2. Liechtenstein
3. Czech Republic
4. Austria
5. Slovakia
6. Hungary
7. Slovenia
8. Croatia
9. Bosnia & Herzegovina
10. Serbia
11. Montenegro
12. San Marino
13. Vatican City

SOUTHERN OCEAN

ANTARCTICA

The Political World

CONTINENTAL KEY

- North & Central America
- South America
- Africa
- Europe
- NW/SE Asia
- Australasia & Oceania

ARCTIC OCEAN

Greenland *(Denmark)*

Arctic Circle

Alaska *(US)*

C A N A D A

Aleutian Islands (US)

ATLANTIC OCEAN

PACIFIC OCEAN

UNITED STATES OF AMERICA

Bermuda *(UK)*

Midway Islands *(US)*

Puerto Rico *(US)*
ST KITTS & NEVIS
ANTIGUA & BARBUDA

Hawaii *(US)*

MEXICO

DOM. REP.
BAHAMAS
BELIZE CUBA

Tropic of Cancer
DOMINICA
ST LUCIA
BARBADOS
ST VINCENT &
THE GRENADINES

MARSHALL ISLANDS

WALLIS & FUTUNA *(France)*
Palmyra Atoll *(US)*

GUATEMALA
EL SALVADOR
HONDURAS
NICARAGUA
PANAMA

JAMAICA
HAITI
COSTA RICA
VENEZUELA
COLOMBIA

GRENADA
TRINIDAD & TOBAGO
French Guiana *(France)*

NAURU
TUVALU

KIRIBATI

Tokelau *(NZ)*

Galapagos Islands *(Ecuador)*

GUYANA
SURINAME

Equator

SOLOMON ISLANDS
VANUATU

Cook Islands *(NZ)*

French Polynesia *(France)*

ECUADOR

PERU

B R A Z I L

FIJI

Niue *(NZ)*

Pitcairn Islands *(UK)*

BOLIVIA

TONGA

American Samoa *(US)*

CHILE

PARAGUAY

Tropic of Capricorn

New Caledonia *(France)*

SAMOA

P A C I F I C

URUGUAY

NEW ZEALAND

O C E A N

ARGENTINA

CHILE

Falkland Islands *(UK)*

South Georgia &
South Sandwich Islands
(UK)

A N T A R C T I C A

Antarctic Circle

The Physical World

ARCTIC

Spitsbergen
Franz Josef Land
Severnaya Zemlya
New Siberian Islands
Laptev Sea
Khrebet Cherskiy

Greenland Sea
Novaya Zemlya
Kara Sea
Yenisey
Lena

Arctic Circle
Denmark Strait
Norwegian Sea
Barents Sea
Ob

Iceland
Scandinavia
Sea of Okh

British Isles
North European Plain
Siberia
Lake Baikal
Amur
Sakh

North Sea
Baltic Sea
Volga
Ural Mountains
Altai Mountains
Gobi
Manchurian Plain
Hokk

Bay of Biscay
EUROPE
ASIA
Lake Balkhash
Tien Shan
Yellow River
Sea of Japan (East Sea)
Honsh

Azores
Iberian Peninsula
Alps
Danube
Black Sea
Caucasus
Caspian Sea
Aral Sea
Iranian Plateau
Hindu Kush
Plateau of Tibet
Himalayas
Yangtze
East China Sea
Kyushu

Madeira
Anatolia
Mediterranean Sea
Syrian Desert
Zagros Mts
Thar Desert
Mount Everest 29,035ft (8850m)
Taiwan

Canary Islands
Atlas Mts
Tropic of Cancer
Sahara
Sahel
Nile
Arabian Peninsula
Ganges
Deccan
Bay of Bengal
South China Sea
Philippi
Sea
Me

Cape Verde Islands
AFRICA
Lake Chad
Ethiopian Highlands
Horn of Africa
Arabian Sea
Sri Lanka
Philippine Islands

Niger
Equator
Gulf of Guinea
Congo
Congo Basin
Great Rift Valley
Lake Victoria 19,340ft (5895m)
Somali Basin
Seychelles
Sumatra
Malay Peninsula
Borneo
Celebes
Java Sea
East Indies
New Guine

ATLANTIC
OCEAN
Kilimanjaro
INDIAN
Java
Timor Sea

Angola Basin
Zambezi
Namib Desert
Mauritius
Réunion
OCEAN
Great Sandy Desert

Tropic of Capricorn
Kalahari Desert
Mozambique Channel
Madagascar
AUSTRALIA
Nullarbor Plain
Darling

Cape Basin
Cape of Good Hope
Southwest Indian Ridge
Ninetyeast Ridge
Southeast Indian Ridge
Tasmania

Mid-Atlantic Ridge
Kerguelen
South Indian Basin

SOUTHERN

Antarctic Circle

ANTARCTICA

OCEAN

East Siberian Sea

Beaufort Sea

Ellesmere Island

Queen Elizabeth Islands

Greenland

Baffin Bay

Baffin Island

Chukchi Sea

Brooks Range

Arctic Circle

Bering Strait

Mackenzie

Great Bear Lake

Bering Sea

Mount McKinley (Denali) 20,322ft (6194m)

Great Slave Lake

Hudson Bay

Labrador Sea

Coast Mountains

Rocky Mountains

Gulf of Alaska

NORTH AMERICA

Aleutian Islands

Vancouver Island

Coast Ranges

Great Plains

Great Lakes

Appalachian Mts

Grand Banks of Newfoundland

Northwest Pacific Basin

North American Basin

Mid-Atlantic Ridge

Mississippi

Hawaiian Islands

Polynesia

Mid-Pacific Mountains

Gulf of Mexico

Tropic of Cancer

West Indies

ATLANTIC

Micronesia

Caribbean Sea

PACIFIC

Galapagos Islands

OCEAN

Solomon Islands

Equator

OCEAN

Amazon

Coral Sea

Fiji

New Caledonia

Peru Basin

Amazon Basin

SOUTH AMERICA

Brazil Basin

Andes

East Pacific Rise

Easter Island

Cerro Aconcagua 22,831ft (6959m)

Gran Chaco

Tropic of Capricorn

Tasman Sea

Southwest Pacific Basin

Pampas

Argentine Basin

South Island

North Island

Patagonia

New Zealand

Falkland Islands

South Georgia

Cape Horn

Tierra del Fuego

South Sandwich Islands

Drake Passage

OCEAN

Antarctic Peninsula

Antarctic Circle

−2 −1 0 +1 +2 +3 +4 +5 +6 +7 +8 +9 +

ARCTIC

+7

0

+1

+10

1

+3

0

+1

+2

+5

+7

+10

0

+3

+4

+8

+9

+10

0

+2

+6

+1

+2

+4

+10

−1

0

+5

+9

0

+2

+4

+3½

+4½

+5¾ +6

−1

+2

+3

+5

+6

+8

−1

+1

+5½

−1

+4

+6

ATLANTIC OCEAN

Greenwich Meridian

+2 +3

+4

+6½

+8

+8

+9½

+8

+2

+3

+6½

+1

+10

INDIAN OCEAN

0

+5

+5 +5

+10

| 11:00 | 12:00 | 13:00 | 14:00 | 15:00 | 16:00 | 17:00 | 18:00 | 19:00 | 20:00 | 21:00 | 22 |

Time zones

The World's Regions

North & Central America

ATLANTIC
OCEAN

St Pierre & Miquelon (France)

Sargasso Sea

Bermuda (UK)

British Virgin Islands (UK)
Virgin Islands (US)
Anguilla (UK)
ST KITTS & NEVIS
ANTIGUA & BARBUDA
Guadeloupe (France)
DOMINICAN REPUBLIC
Puerto Rico (US)
Montserrat (UK)
DOMINICA
Martinique (France)
ST LUCIA
BARBADOS
ST VINCENT & THE GRENADINES
GRENADA
TRINIDAD & TOBAGO
Netherlands Antilles (Neth.)
Aruba (Neth.)

Turks & Caicos Islands (UK)

BAHAMAS

HAITI

CUBA

JAMAICA

Cayman Islands (UK)

SOUTH
AMERICA

Andes

Equator

Gulf of Mexico

BELIZE
GUATEMALA
HONDURAS
EL SALVADOR
NICARAGUA
COSTA RICA
PANAMA

UNITED STATES
OF AMERICA

Great Lakes
Lake Superior
Lake Huron
Lake Michigan
Lake Ontario
Lake Erie
Appalachian Mountains
Ohio
Missouri
Mississippi
Arkansas
Plains
Great Plains

MEXICO

Sierra Madre Occidental

Rio Grande

Mount Whitney
14,495ft (4418m) ▲
Death Valley
-282ft (-86m)
Colorado

Tropic of Cancer

PACIFIC
OCEAN

Clipperton Island (French Polynesia)

Galápagos Islands (Ecuador)

Equator

0 km   1000
0 miles   1000

Western Canada & Alaska

RUSSIAN
FEDERATION

Wrangel I.

ARCTI

OCEA

◆ In 1867 William Henry Seward negotiated
the purchase of Alaska from Russia for
the price of $7,200,000, which amounted
to around two cents per acre (0.4 hectares).

Attu I.

*Bering
Sea*

Bering Strait

Arctic Circle

Brooks Range

Prudhc
Bay

Rat Is.

Aleutian Islands

St. Lawrence I.

Nunivak I.

Yukon

ALASKA
(part of USA)

180°

Mt McKinley
20,322ft (6194m) ▲

Alaska Range

Fairbanks

Umnak I.
Dutch Harbor
Unalaska I.

Anchorage

YUKON
TERRITO

Kodiak I. •Kodiak

Valdez
Cordova

◆ The Aleutian Islands span some 1200 miles
(1800 km) and by crossing the 180° line of
longitude, form both the most easterly
and westerly extents of the USA.

Gulf
of
Alaska

WHITEHORSE

Ru

JUNEAU

PACIFIC

OCEAN

Ketchikan

Prince Rupert

Queen Charlotte Is.

*Queen Charlotte
Sound*

◆ On July 9, 1958 a massive landslide
dropped 40 million cubic yards
(30.6 million cu m) of rock into Lituya Bay
creating a wave 1720 ft (524 m) high.

160°

Port Hardy
Vancouver I.

0 km   400

0 miles   400

140°

VICTOR

A   B   C   D

Greenland
(Danish external
territory)

◇ Despite an area of 769,900 sq miles
(1,994,000 sq km) the northerly
province of Nunavut has only
13 miles (21 km) of highway.

Queen Elizabeth Islands

Ellesmere
Island

Axel
Heiberg
Island

Baffin Bay

Davis Strait

Bathurst I.

Melville
Island

Devon
Island

Lancaster Sound

Resolute

Viscount
Melville
Sound

Somerset
Island

Banks
Island

Prince
of
Wales I.

Baffin Island

Amundsen
Gulf

Victoria
Island

King
William I.

Arctic Circle

IQALUIT

eaufort
Sea

Beaufort
Sea

Kugluktuk

NUNAVUT

Hudson Strait

60°

eat Bear L.

Great Bear L.

Southampton I.

uvik

NORTHWEST

ERRITORIES

TERRITORIES

YELLOWKNIFE

Mackenzie

Great Slave L.

Rankin
Inlet

Hudson
Bay

QUEBEC

Hay River

Fort Smith

Duburnt

Churchill

St. John

ALBERTA

Fort
McMurray

L. Athabasca

MANITOBA

C A N A D A

ONTARIO

Grande Prairie

SASKATCHEWAN

Flin
Flon

Thompson

Leduc

Red Deer

Saskatchewan

Prince
Albert

Saskatoon

Yorkton

L. Winnipeg

◇ Some 7% of Canada's 3.5 million sq
miles (9.2 million sq km) land area is
devoted to grain production yielding
around 26 million tons (tonnes) of
wheat every year.

Calgary

REGINA

Brandon

WINNIPEG

Lethbridge

Estevan

U S A

100°

80°

Eastern Canada

NUNAVUT

Southampton I.

Salisbury I.
Nottingham I.

Coats I.

Ivujivik

Mansel I.

Hudson
Bay

Péninsu
d'Unga

MANITOBA

◆ The largest hydroelectric complex
in Canada at James Bay produces
over 16,000 megawatts of power.

Inukjuak

L. Mi

Belcher Is.
(Nunavut)

Kuujjuarapik

◆ The Trans-Canada Highway, running
from St John's in the east to
Victoria in the west, is
4860 miles (7820 km) long.

Winisk

James
Bay

Severn

Attawapiskat

Akimiski I.
(Nunavut)

C

A

N

A

Winisk

Attawapiskat

Albany

L. Seul

O N **T** A **R** I **O**

Moosonee

Qu

Eastm

L. Mistassi

Kenora

Armstrong

Lake
of the
Woods

L. Nipigon

Cochrane

Rés. Go

Thunder Bay

MINNESOTA

Lake Superior

Wawa

Timmins

◆ Lake Superior is the largest freshwater
lake in the world covering an area
of 32,150 sq miles (83,268 sq km).

Sault
Sainte Marie

Sudbury

North Bay

Ottawa

OTTAWA

WISCONSIN

Lake
Michigan

Lake
Huron

Peterborough

Lake

Oshawa

Kings

UNITED STATES

MICHIGAN

TORONTO

Ontario

N

Kitchener

Hamilton

OF AMERICA

London

IOWA

Windsor

Lake Erie

St. Catharines

ILLINOIS

INDIANA

OHIO

PENNSYLVANIA

Baffin I.

Hudson Strait

Akpatok I. (Nunavut)

Ungava Bay

Labrador Sea

Canada has the world's longest coastline (including those of 52,455 islands) with a total length of 151,394 miles (243,638 km).

A T L A N T I C

O C E A N

• Kuujjuaq

• Nain

Hopedale
Makkovik

Schefferville

Labrador

NEWFOUNDLAND & LABRADOR

• Cartwright

Smallwood Reservoir

Réservoir aniapiscau

Strait of Belle Isle

Newfoundland

D
E C
A

Réservoir Manicouagan

Havre-Saint-Pierre

Île d'Anticosti

• Gander

Grand Falls

Corner Brook

ST JOHN'S

Sept-Îles

Gulf of St. Lawrence

Channel-Port-aux-Basques

C. Race

L. Saint-Jean

St. Lawrence

Gaspé

St Pierre & Miquelon
(French territorial collectivity)

Jonquière

Chicoutimi

Bathurst

PRINCE EDWARD ISLAND

NEW BRUNSWICK

Moncton

• Sydney

Cabot Strait

QUÉBEC

FREDERICTON

CHARLOTTETOWN

Trois-Rivières

MAINE

Saint John

NOVA SCOTIA

Sherbrooke

Dartmouth

Montréal

HALIFAX

Yarmouth

NEW HAMPSHIRE

A T L A N T I C

VERMONT

O C E A N

MASSACHUSETTS

The Bay of Fundy has the world's highest tidal range with water's rising 20-50ft (5-15m) every high tide.

RHODE ISLAND

CONNECTICUT

0 km   300

0 miles   300

USA: The Northeast

The Chicago River originally flowed into Lake Michigan, but was reversed in 1900 by the completion of a canal.

NAVIGATOR
20
24 | 22 - 23 | 48
30

NADA

QUEBEC

St Lawrence

NEW BRUNSWICK

MAINE

Presque Isle

Calais

Bay of Fundy

NOVA SCOTIA

◆ Around 40 million gallons (180 million litres)
of water plunge over the 190 ft (58 m)
drop of Niagara Falls every minute.

Ogdensburg

Burlington
MONTPELIER

Watertown

Rutland

Lake Ontario

Utica

Syracuse

Buffalo   Rochester

ALBANY

NEW YORK

Niagara Falls

Elmira   Binghamton

Springfield

HARTFORD

Williamsport

Scranton

NNSYLVANIA

Appalachian

tsburg

HARRISBURG

Gettysburg

Philadelphia

mberland

Baltimore

Arlington

ANNAPOLIS

WASHINGTON, D.C.

Fredericksburg

Charlottesville

RICHMOND

VIRGINIA

Roanoke

Danville

NORTH CAROLINA

AUGUSTA
Lewiston

Portland

Gulf of Maine

CONCORD

Manchester

BOSTON

Worcester   Cape Cod

MASSACHUSETTS

PROVIDENCE

RHODE ISLAND

CONNECTICUT

New Haven   Long Island

Newark

New York

Allentown

TRENTON

NEW JERSEY

Wilmington

DOVER   Atlantic City

DELAWARE

MARYLAND

Chesapeake Bay

Newport News

Norfolk

◆ In 1626 the Dutch bought Manhattan Island
from the local Indians for a collection of
trinkets that, legend has it, were
worth around $25.

ATLANTIC

OCEAN

◆ The Pentagon building in Arlington, Virginia,
has nearly 68,000 miles (110,000 km) of
telephone lines, enough to go around the
circumference of the earth almost three times.

0 km   200
0 miles   200

USA: Central States

At 20,016 ft (6104 m), or almost 4 miles (6 km) in length, the Fort Peck Dam is the largest earth-filled hydraulic dam in the US.

The Great Salt Lake is a remnant of the prehistoric Lake Bonneville, which once covered almost 20,000 square miles (51,800 sq km) of western Utah.

The world's largest organism is a 200 acre (81 hectares) grove of aspen trees in Utah. Derived from a single tree it has hundreds of suckers growing from its root system.

CANADA

ANITOBA

ONTARIO

MINNESOTA

Lake of the Woods

Lake Superior

Grand Forks

Virginia

DAKOTA

Moorhead

Duluth

Fargo

Brainerd

◆ *Access to the St Lawrence Seaway via the Great Lakes makes Duluth the most westerly Atlantic port in the US, some 1100 miles (1770 km) from the Atlantic ocean.*

Aberdeen

St Cloud

WISCONSIN

MICHIGAN

DAKOTA

Minneapolis

SAINT PAUL

PIERRE

Watertown

Mitchell

Rochester

Lake Michigan

Sioux Falls

Mason City

Missouri

Dubuque

OHIO

Sioux City

IOWA

Cedar Rapids

ASKA

DES MOINES

Davenport

INDIANA

orth

Columbus

Council Bluffs

ILLINOIS

Omaha

Burlington

atte

Platte

LINCOLN

◆ *Between 1950 and 1994 Kansas suffered over 2000 tornadoes, claiming around 200 lives and causing in excess of $1.2 billion damage.*

Hastings

Kirksville

Mississippi

St Joseph

kley

Kansas City

Independence

Hays

Missouri

SAINT LOUIS

Kansas City

TOPEKA

JEFFERSON CITY

Ohio

KANSAS

MISSOURI

KENTUCKY

Pratt

Wichita

Springfield

Dodge City

Arkansas

Ozark Plateau

TENNESSEE

OKLAHOMA

ARKANSAS

0 km   200

0 miles   200

Hells Canyon is the deepest in the US, with cliffs up to 7900 ft (2408 m) high.

At Black Rock Desert on October 15, 1997, ThrustSSC, driven by Andy Green, became the first land vehicle to break the sound barrier by achieving a speed of 763 mph (1228 km/h).

Death Valley is not only the lowest point in North America at 282 ft (86 m) below sea level, it is also the hottest, with a maximum air temperature of 134°F (57°C) recorded in 1913.

The Golden Gate Bridge, completed in 1937, has 80,000 miles (129,000 km) of wire in its two main cables, weighing a total of 22,200 tons (tonnes).

UTAH

NEVADA

ARIZONA

MEXICO

CALIFORNIA

Sierra Nevada

Coast Ranges

Ranges

PACIFIC OCEAN

Lake Mead

Colorado

Colorado

Las Vegas

Death Valley

86m

Mojave Desert

Barstow

Lancaster

Pasadena

San Bernardino

Riverside

Palm Springs

Santa Ana

Salton Sea

Oceanside

San Diego

Chula Vista

Los Angeles

Long Beach

Huntington Beach

Santa Catalina I.

San Clemente I.

San Nicolas I.

Santa Rosa I.

Santa Barbara

Oxnard

Channel Islands

Mojave

Bakersfield

Visalia

Mt Whitney 4418m

Fresno

Merced

Modesto

Stockton

Salinas

Monterey

Santa Cruz

San Jose

Berkeley

Oakland

San Francisco

SACRAMENTO

Santa Rosa

Ukiah

Redding

Chico

Yuba City

Sukanville

Reno

Sparks

Fallon

Pyramid Lake

Lake Tahoe

CARSON CITY

Hawthorne

Tonopah

Bishop

Ely

San Joaquin Valley

San Luis Obispo

Truckee

0 km   200

0 miles   200

USA: The Southwest

◇ The Colorado River has cut down some 6242 ft (2000 m) into the Colorado Plateau to form the Grand Canyon, exposing rock strata over 2 billion years old.

◇ Meteor Crater was formed when a meteor about 150 ft (46 m) across struck the desert at about 40,000 mph (64,372 km/h) creating a bowl shaped depression 4,150 ft (1,265 m) wide and 570 ft (174 m) deep.

◇ The first atomic bomb was tested at Trinity Site near Alamogordo on July 16, 1945 yielding an explosive force equivalent to 20,000 tons (tonnes) of TNT from around 2.2 lbs (1 kg) of plutonium-239.

NEVADA · UTAH · COLORADO · L. Powell · Grand Canyon · Painted Desert · Farmington · Rio Grande · L. Mead · Colorado Plateau · Los Alamos · SANTA FE · Gallup · Flagstaff · Albuquerque · Pecos · Prescott · CALIFORNIA · Colorado · ARIZONA · NEW MEXICO · Glendale · Scottsdale · PHOENIX · Mesa · Sonoran · Yuma · Desert · Casa Grande · Alamogordo · Roswell · Tucson · Las Cruces · Artesia · Carlsbad · Douglas · El Paso · Golfo de California · Baja California · Rio Grande · PACIFIC OCEAN · MEXI

0 km 200
0 miles 200

K A N S A S

OKLAHOMA

Ponca City
Enid
Tulsa
Broken Arrow

Borger
Pampa
OKLAHOMA CITY
Shawnee

Amarillo

Norman

Arkansas

A R K A N S A S

anadian

Red River

Lawton

Vernon

Red River

lovis

Wichita Falls
Denton
Paris

Lubbock

Fort Worth
Arlington
Dallas
Longview

Brownfield

Abilene

Tyler

Hobbs

Sweetwater

Brazos

Jacksonville

Big Spring

Waco

Toledo Bend Res.

Odessa
Midland
San Angelo

Colorado

T E X A S

Neches

Pecos

L O U I S I A N A

Bryan

Beaumont

*Edwards
Plateau*

L. Travis
AUSTIN

Houston

Port Arthur

Pasadena

Del Rio

San Antonio

San Antonio

Texas City
Galveston
Freeport

Eagle Pass

Victoria

C O

Corpus Christi

Laredo
Kingsville

Padre Island

Rio Grande

Brownsville

G u l f

o f

M e x i c o

◆ On January 10, 1901
the Lucas Gusher blew
oil 100 ft (30 m) into the
air, flowing at 100,000
barrels a day until it was
eventually capped nine
days later.

USA: The Southeast

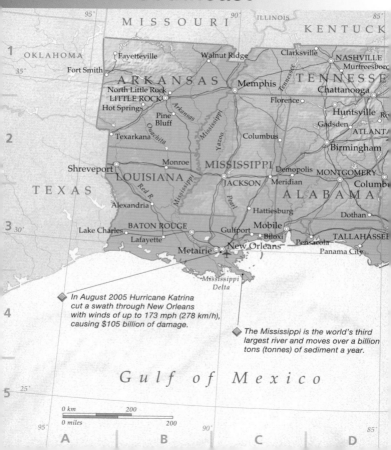

In August 2005 Hurricane Katrina cut a swath through New Orleans with winds of up to 173 mph (278 km/h), causing $105 billion of damage.

The Mississippi is the world's third largest river and moves over a billion tons (tonnes) of sediment a year.

VIRGINIA

Kingsport

Winston-Salem
Durham
Greensboro RALEIGH
Roanoke

Knoxville
Asheville Gastonia
NORTH CAROLINA
Charlotte
Fayetteville
Havelock
Cape Hatteras

Greenville
Spartanburg
Wilmington

COLUMBIA
Florence
Cape Fear
SOUTH CAROLINA

Athens
Augusta
L. Marion

Macon
Charleston

GEORGIA
Savannah

Albany
Brunswick

Valdosta

Jacksonville

FLORIDA
Daytona Beach

Orlando
Cape Canaveral
Melbourne

Tampa
Clearwater
St Petersburg
L. Okeechobee
West Palm Beach

Fort Myers
The Everglades
Pompano Beach
Fort Lauderdale
Miami Beach
Miami
Grand Bahama I.

BAHAMAS

Key West
Florida Keys
Straits of Florida
New Providence
Andros I.

ATLANTIC

OCEAN

The carnivorous Venus's-flytrap plant, found only on the wet coastal plains of North and South Carolina, can count. They require two separate stimuli on trigger hairs before the trap is sprung to avoid "false alarms" caused by raindrops, twigs, etc.

Lake Okeechobee is actually a shallow, slow moving river, 150 miles (240 km) long and 50 miles (80 km) wide, flowing southward at the rate of 6 inches (15 cm) a day.

E   F   G   H

◆ Large examples of the Saguaro cactus, found in the Altar Desert, can take nearly 150 years to grow to their full height of around 50 ft (16 m), and can hold several tons (tonnes) of water.

◆ Gray whales have one of the longest migrations of any mammal, traveling some 12,500 miles (20,000 km) every year from the Arctic Ocean to their winter breeding grounds in the Golfo de California.

◆ The cliff divers of Acapulco must time their dive from the 125 ft (38 m) cliff at La Quebrada to coincide with the incoming swells to avoid being dashed on the rocks in the shallow inlet.

Map labels:

NEW MEXICO
ARIZONA
UNITED
Mexicali
Tijuana
Ensenada
Desierto de Altar
Ciudad Juárez
Rio Grande
30°
I. Ángel de la Guarda
Hermosillo
Chihuahua
Sierra Madre
I. Cedros
Baja California
Golfo de California
Conchos
25°
Ciudad Obregón
Gómez Palacio
Torreón
Los Mochis
Culiacán
Durango
La Paz
Fresnillo
Zacatecas
Tropic of Cancer
Mazatlán
Sierra Madre Occidental
Aguascalientes
Islas Marías
Tepic
Guadalajara
Puerto Vallarta
L. de Chapala
20°
PACIFIC
OCEAN
Islas Revillagigedo
(part of Mexico)

0 km   200
0 miles   200

115°   110°   105°

A   B   C   D

STATES OF AMERICA   LOUISIANA

Mississippi

TEXAS

Rio Grande

◆ In spring 2001, the Rio Grande stopped flowing into the Gulf of Mexico for the first time in recorded history, allowing illegal immigrants to simply walk into the US.

Nuevo Laredo

Monclova

Reynosa

Monterrey   Matamoros

Saltillo

G u l f

o f

M e x i c o

Tropic of Cancer

Ciudad Victoria

◆ It is thought that "The Ballgame," a ritual sport played by Maya and Aztec civilizations, and a forerunner of soccer, often ended with the losing team being sacrificed.

Cancún

San Luis
Potosí   Tampico
Ciudad Valles   Mérida

Río Verde   *Isla Cozumel*

Dolores Hidalgo

León   Poza Rica   *Bahía de Campeche*   Campeche   Yucatan Peninsula

Irapuato   Querétaro   Tulancingo

Morelia   Pachuca   Xalapa

Cuernavaca   MEXICO   Veracruz   Villahermosa

Uruapan   CITY   Puebla   Coatzacoalcos   BELIZE

Tehuacán   Minatitlán

Balsas   Oaxaca   Tuxtla

Sierra Madre del Sur   GUATEMALA

Acapulco   15°   HONDURAS

Golfo de Tehuantepec   Tapachula

EL SALVADOR

Central America

MEXICO

Belize City
BELMOPAN
Flores
San Ignacio
BELIZE
Islas de la Bahía

Usumacinta

GUATEMALA
Huehuetenango
Quezaltenango
Cobán
Lago de Izabal
Puerto Barrios
Gulf of Honduras
Puerto Cortés
Trujillo
Zacapa
San Pedro Sula
La Ceiba
GUATEMALA CITY
Santa Rosa de Copán
HONDURAS
Escuintla
Comayagua
La Esperanza
Juticalpa
Patuca
TEGUCIGALPA
Santa Ana
SAN SALVADOR
San Miguel
EL SALVADOR
Choluteca
Somoto
Jinotega
Gulf of Fonseca
Estelí
Matagalpa
Chinandega
Corinto
León
Juigalpa
NICARAGUA
Coc

P A C I F I C

MANAGUA
Granada
Lago de Nicaragua
Rivas
San Ju

O C E A N

◇ Unique freshwater species of shark and swordfish have
evolved in the long period since Lake Nicaragua was cut
off from the Pacific Ocean by a belt of volcanic cones.

Península de Nicoya
Liberia
Puntarenas
Alajuela
SAN JOSÉ

◇ The strongest living creature is the Rhinoceros Beetle
found in the jungles of Costa Rica, which can support
up to 850 times it's own body weight, equivalent to
a human carrying about 70 tons (tonnes).

0 km   200
0 miles   200

The Blue Hole in Lighthouse Reef, a submerged cave some 1000 ft (300 m) in diameter and 400 ft (120 m) deep, was originally explored by Jacques Cousteau, co-inventor of the aqualung.

Greater Antilles

80°

75°

HAITI

JAMAICA

*Islas Santanilla
(part of Honduras)*

*Bajo Nuevo .
(part of Colombia)*

15°

. *Cayos Miskitos*

C a r i b b e a n

Mosquito Coast

. *I. de Providencia
(part of Colombia)*

S e a

. *I. de San Andrés
(part of Colombia)*

Islas del Maíz

Bluefields

Gatun Locks on the Panama Canal are 110 ft (33 m) wide and 1000 ft (303 m) long, took four years to build and required 2 million cubic yards (1.5 million cu m) of concrete.

COSTA
RICA

Limón

Cartago

Cordillera de Talamanca

Colón

10°

PANAMA

*Gulf
of
Darien*

Penonomé

PANAMA CITY

*Panama
Canal*

David

*Isla del
Rey*

COLOMBIA

*Golfo
de
Chiriquí*

Santiago

Chitré

Las Tablas

*Golfo
de
Panamá*

80°

75°

E

F

G

H

Gulf of Mexico

UNITED STATES OF AMERICA

Grand Bahama I. • Freeport

Great Abaco

1 25°

85° 80° 75°

Tropic of Cancer

Straits of Florida

B A H A M A S

New Providence

NASSAU •

Eleuthera I.

Andros I.

Cat I.

Santaren Channel

Great Exuma I.

Long I.

Mayaguana

HAVANA • • Matanzas

Pinar del Río

Santa Clara

Acklins I.

2 20°

Cienfuegos

Isla de la Juventud

C U B A

Camagüey

Holguín

Great Inagua

Yucatan Channel

G r e a t e r

Bayamo

Guantánamo

Cap-Haïtien

Cayman Islands
(UK dependent territory)

George Town

Santiago de Cuba

Gonaïves

HAITI

PORT-AU-PRINCE •

◆ The Bee Hummingbird, found in Cuba, is the smallest bird in the world. An adult male measures around 2.2 inches (5.7 cm) from beak to tail and weighs about 0.06 oz (1.6 gms).

Montego Bay

KINGSTON •

Jérémie

Jacm

JAMAICA

Navassa Island
(US unincorporated territory)

A n t i

3

HONDURAS

4 15°

C a r i b b e a n

S e a

N I C A R A G U A

5 10°

0 km 200
0 miles 200

85° 80° 75°

COLOMBIA

A B C D

ATLANTIC

OCEAN

Tropic of Cancer

◆ With an area of only 37 sq miles (96 sq km), the island of
St. Maarten/St. Martin is the smallest landmass in the world to
be divided between two countries. Its dual owners are the Dutch
and French, who have shared the island for almost 350 years.

Leeward Islands

Monte Cristi
•Puerto Plata
•Santiago

urks &
aicos Islands
UK dependent
erritory)

DOMINICAN REPUBLIC

La Romana

**SANTO
DOMINGO**

Virgin Islands
*(US unincorporated
territory)*

San Juan

Puerto Rico
*(US commonwealth
territory)*

Charlotte
Amalie

British Virgin
Islands
*(UK dependent
territory)*

•Road
Town

Anguilla
(UK dependent territory)
•The Valley

Barbuda

Antigua

**ANTIGUA
& BARBUDA**

•**ST JOHN'S**

BASSETERRE

ST KITTS & NEVIS

Montserrat
(UK dependent territory)

•Plymouth

Guadeloupe
*(French overseas
department)*

Basse-Terre•

DOMINICA

ROSEAU

Martinique
*(French overseas
department)*

Fort-de-France•

ST LUCIA

CASTRIES

◆ The deadliest volcanic eruption
of the 20th century took place on
May 8, 1902 when Mount Pelee
erupted on Martinique killing
30,000 people, around 15%,
of the island's population.

**ST VINCENT &
THE GRENADINES**

KINGSTOWN

BARBADOS

•**BRIDGETOWN**

Aruba
*(autonomous part
of Netherlands)*

•Oranjestad

Lesser Antilles

Netherlands Antilles
*(autonomous part
of Netherlands)*

Willemstad•

GRENADA

•**ST GEORGE'S**

Tobago•

**TRINIDAD
& TOBAGO**

Isla de Margarita

VENEZUELA

•**PORT-OF-SPAIN**

San Fernando•

Lesser Antilles

Windward Islands

ATLANTIC
OCEAN

Equator

Caribbean Sea

Greater Antilles

Hispaniola

Jamaica

Puerto
Rico

Lesser Antilles

Trinidad

*(claimed by
Venezuela)*

VENEZUELA

GUYANA

SURINAME

French
Guiana
(France)

*(claimed by
Suriname)*

Guiana Highlands

Tumuc Humac
Mountains

Orinoco

Caroní

COLOMBIA

Meta

Rio Negro

Represa
Balbina

A m a z o n

Amazon

B a s i n

B R A Z I L

Cauca

Magdalena

Putumayo

Içá

Juruá

Napo

Marañón

Ucayali

Madeira

Purus

Juruá

Tapajós

Xingu

Tocantins

Araguaia

Serra do Cachimbo

Serra Formosa

Serra do Rondônia

Planalto de
Mato Grosso

Chapada dos Parecis

Planalto
da
Borborema

São Francisco

Serra de
Sobradinho

Brazilian Highlands

Represa de
Sobradinho

BOLIVIA

P E R U

A n d e s

Mato Grosso

Beni

Altiplano

Lake
Titicaca

ECUADOR

Chimborazo ▲
20,702ft (6310m)

Equator

Tropic of Capricorn

ATLANTIC
OCEAN

Serra do Mar

Serra Geral

Lagoa dos Patos

Mirim Lagoon

PARAGUAY

Gran Chaco

Pilcomayo

Paraguay

Paraná

Uruguay

Uruguay

Paraná

URUGUAY

Río de la Plata

Mesopotamia

Pampas

Bahía Blanca

Colorado

Golfo San Matías

Península Valdés

Río Negro

Gulf of San Jorge

Chubut

Bahía Grande

Deseado

Chico

A R G E N T I N A

Cordillera

Cerro Ojos
del Salado
(22,572ft)
6880m

Cerro Aconcagua
22,835ft
6959m

Atacama

CHILE

Isla de Chiloé

Patagonia

Strait of
Magellan

Tierra del Fuego

Cape Horn

Drake Passage

West Falkland

East Falkland

Falkland Islands
(UK)

Scotia Sea

South Georgia
(UK)

South Sandwich
Islands
(UK)

South Orkney Islands

South Shetland Islands

ANTARCTICA

PACIFIC
OCEAN

Isla San Ambrosio
(Chile)

Isla San Félix
(Chile)

Islas Juan Fernández
(Chile)

Tropic of Capricorn

0 km   1000

0 miles   1000

Northern South America

Caribbean Sea

PANAMA

PACIFIC OCEAN

Ríohacha
Santa Marta
Barranquilla
Cartagena
Valledupar

Gulf of Venezuela
Coro
Maicao
Maracaibo
Cabimas
CARACA
Maracay

Ciudád Ojeda
Lago de Maracaibo
Barquisimeto
Valencia
Acarigua
San Juan de los Morros
Sincelejo
Montería
Mérida
Guanare
Barinas
Valera

Cúcuta
San Cristóbal
San Fernando

Cauca
Magdalena

Bucaramanga
Barrancabermeja
Arauca
Arauca
VEN
Puerto Carreño

Bello
Medellín
Itagüí
Quibdó
Manizales
Pereira
Armenia
Ibagué
Tunja
Yopal
Meta

BOGOTÁ
Villavicencio
Guaviare

Buenaventura
Cali
Popayán
Neiva
San José del Guaviare

COLOMBIA

Orinoco

Pasto
Tulcán
Ibarra
Esmeraldas
Mocoa
Florencia

Mitú

0° Equator
QUITO
Aguarico

Manta
Santo Domingo de los Colorados
Ambato
Riobamba
Guayaquil
Milagro
Cuenca
Golfo de Guayaquil
Machala
Loja

ECUADOR

Putumayo
Caquetá

PERU

◇ The first coffee seedlings were brought to Colombia in 1804 by Jesuit Missionaries; today Columbia produces over a million tons (tonnes) of coffee beans every year.

◇ Nestling between snow capped peaks, at 9350 ft (2850 m) Quito is the second highest capital in the world.

GRENADA

Antilles

Isla de Margarita
Carúpano

TRINIDAD
& TOBAGO

ATLANTIC
OCEAN

Cumaná

Barcelona
Maturín

The Serpent's Mouth

El Tigre
Tucupita

Orinoco
a n o s

Ciudad Bolívar

Ciudad Guayana

◆ The Guyana shield is one of the
Earth's oldest surfaces, formed
around 4 billion years ago.
(claimed by Venezuela)

*Embalse
de Guri*

Z U E L A

Cuyuni

GEORGETOWN

New Amsterdam

Nieuw
Amsterdam

Caura

*Salto
Ángel*

Bartica

Rockstone

PARAMARIBO

St.-Laurent-
du-Maroni

Sinnamary

Caroní

GUYANA

Linden

W.J. van
Blommesteinmeer

Kourou

Paragua

G u i a n a

SURINAME

French
Guiana
*(French overseas
department)*

CAYENNE

Orinoco

H i g h l a n d s

Essequibo

Courantyne

Marowijne

◆ Angel Falls
(Salto Ángel)
plunge 3121 ft
(951 m) to form
the world's
highest waterfall.

Acarai Mts.

*(claimed by
Suriname)*

(claimed by Suriname)

◆ The European Space Agency launch
facility at Kourou takes advantage
of the Earth's spin near the
Equator to gain 10 percent
more payload than an equivalent
launch at Cape Canaveral in the US.

Equator

A m a z o n

B   R   A   Z   I   L

B a s i n

Amazon

◆ 2.47 acres (one hectare) of Amazon rain forest
can contain more than 750 types of trees and
1500 plant species, amounting to around
900 tons (tonnes) of living plant material.

0 km   200

0 miles   200

Peru, Bolivia & North Brazil

VENEZUELA

COLOMBIA

GUYANA

Boa Vista

Guiana

Equator

ECUADOR

Rio Negro

Amazon

Represa Balbina

Manaus

Putumayo

Napo

Amazon

Iquitos

Jurua

Amazon Basin

Marañón

Moyobamba

Tarapoto

Piura

Chiclayo

Ucayali

Saña

B

Purus

R

A

Trujillo

Pucallpa

Porto Velho

Chimbote

Huaraz

Huánuco

Rio Branco

Huacho

Huánuco

Madre de Dios

Riberalta

La Oroya

Puerto Maldonado

Guapore

Callao

Beni

LIMA

Huancayo

P

Trinidad

PACIFIC

Ayacucho

E

Pisco

Cusco

R

B O L I V I A

OCEAN

Ica

U

Nazca

Puno

LA PAZ

Arequipa

Lake Titicaca

Cochabamba

Montero

◆ *Lake Titicaca is the largest lake in South America at 3220 sq miles (8340 sq km) and with an altitude of 12,500 ft (3810 m) it is also the world's highest navigable lake.*

Tacna

Oruro

Lago Poopó

SUCRE

Santa Cruz

Puerto Suárez

Potosí

PARAGUAY

BOLIVIA'S TWO CAPITALS
La Paz - legislative and administrative capital
Sucre - legal capital

Uyuni

Tupiza

Tarija

CHILE

ARGENTINA

French Guiana
(French overseas department)

I g h l a n d s

TRINAME

Macapá

Ilha Caviana de Fora

ATLANTIC

Amazon

Santarém

Ilha de Marajó

Belém

OCEAN

Equator

São Luís

Paranaíba

Fortaleza

San Fernando
de Noronha
(part of Brazil)

Mossoró

*Represa de
Tucuruí*

Imperatriz

Teresina

Natal

Carolina

Campina
Grande

João
Pessoa

Z I L

Juàzeiro do Norte

Recife

*Represa de
Sobradinho*

São Francisco

Juàzeiro

Maceió

Xingu

Araguaia

Tocantins

Aracaju

10°

eles Pires

M a t o   G r o s s o

Taguatinga

Feira de Santana

B r a z i l i a n

Salvador

Cuiabá

Anápolis

BRASÍLIA

Itabuna

Goiânia

H i g h l a n d s

Vitória da Conquista

Montes Claros

Governador Valadares

Uberlândia

Uberaba

Divinópolis

Belo Horizonte

Campo
Grande

Ribeirão Preto

Vitória

Paraná

Marília

Nova

Campos

20°

Campinas

Iguaçu

Juiz de Fora

Londrina

Sorocaba

Taubaté

Rio de Janeiro

Tropic of Capricorn

30°

São Paulo

The Amazon River is 4195 miles (6751 km) long with
a peak flow of 7 million cubic feet (198,229 cu m) of
water entering the Atlantic Ocean every second.

50°

40°

E

F

G

H

1

2

3

4

Paraguay, Uruguay & South Brazil

BOLIVIA

B R A

General Eugenio A. Garay

Campo Grande

São José do Rio Preto

Fuerte Olimpo

Presidente Prudente

Marília

Baur

Mariscal Estigarribia

Dourados

Ourinhos

P A R A G U A Y

Tropic of Capricorn

Pozo Colorado

Concepción

Londrina

Maringá

Coronel Oviedo

Ciudad del Este

Ponta Grossa

ASUNCIÓN

Villarrica

Guarapuava

Curitiba

Lambaré

Caazapá

Joinville

San Juan Bautista

◆ Formed by river deposits washed
down from the Andes and Brazilian
Shield, the Gran Chaco is virtually
free of stones. It is composed of
sand and silt sediments that are
up to 10,000 ft (3050 m) thick.

Pilar

Encarnación

Pelotas

Blumenau

Erechim

Florianópolis

Lajes

◆ The Itaipú hydroelectric scheme is
able to produce more power than
10 average nuclear reactors; it supplies
24% of the electrical power consumption
of Brazil and 95% for Paraguay.

Passo Fundo

Carazinho

Caxias do Sul

São Borja

Santa Maria

Canoas

Uruguaiana

Porto Alegre

A R G E N T I N A

Artigas

Rivera

Bagé

Lagoa dos Patos

Salto

Tacuarembó

Pelotas

Melo

Rio Grande

Paysandú

URUGUAY

Mirim Lagoon

Fray Bentos

Mercedes

Durazno

Chuy

Trinidad

Las Piedras

San Carlos

MONTEVIDEO

Río de la Plata

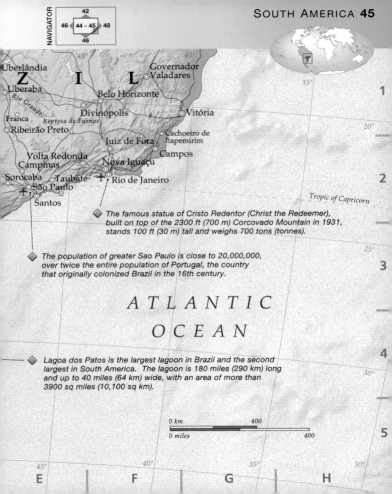

Uberlândia

Z   I   L

Governador
Valadares

Uberaba

Belo Horizonte

Rio Grande

Divinópolis

Vitória

Franca

Represa de Furnas

Ribeirão Preto

Cachoeiro de
Itapemirim

Juiz de Fora

Campos

Volta Redonda

Nova Iguaçu

Campinas

Sorocaba

Taubaté

Rio de Janeiro

São Paulo

Santos

◈ The famous statue of Cristo Redentor (Christ the Redeemer),
built on top of the 2300 ft (700 m) Corcovado Mountain in 1931,
stands 100 ft (30 m) tall and weighs 700 tons (tonnes).

Tropic of Capricorn

◈ The population of greater Sao Paulo is close to 20,000,000,
over twice the entire population of Portugal, the country
that originally colonized Brazil in the 16th century.

A T L A N T I C

O C E A N

◈ Lagoa dos Patos is the largest lagoon in Brazil and the second
largest in South America. The lagoon is 180 miles (290 km) long
and up to 40 miles (64 km) wide, with an area of more than
3900 sq miles (10,100 sq km).

0 km   400

0 miles   400

45°   40°   35°   30°

E   F   G   H

Southern South America

BRAZIL

BRAZIL

PARAGUAY

URUGUAY

BUENOS AIRES

The world's tallest, active volcano is the Guallatiri volcano in northern Chile. It stands 19,918 ft (6071 m) tall, and last erupted in 1987.

The driest place on earth is the Atacama Desert in Chile with an average rainfall of 0.004 inches (0.1 mm) per year. Until recently some places had received no rain for over 400 years.

Tropic of Capricorn

Paraná

Paraguay

Posadas

Formosa

Corrientes

Bermejo

Resistencia

Vera

Salado

Paraná

Santa Fe

Concordia

Gualeguaychú

La Plata

Río de la

Junín

Dolores

BOLIVIA

Pilcomayo

Gran
Chaco

San Salvador
de Jujuy

San Miguel
de Tucumán

Salta

Santiago
del Estero

*Laguna Mar
Chiquita*

Córdoba

Río
Cuarto

Paraná

Rosario

ARGENTINA

Pampas

Olavarría

PERU

Desierto de Atacama

Arica

Chuquicamata

Calama

Tocopilla

Iquique

Antofagasta

Chañaral

Copiapó

Vallenar

La Rioja

San Juan

Villa Mercedes

Santa Rosa

La Serena

Coquimbo

Illapel

*Cerro
Aconcagua
22,831 ft
(6960 m)*

Mendoza

Godoy Cruz

SANTIAGO

Rancagua

CHILE

La Ligua

Viña del Mar

Valparaíso

San Antonio

Pichilemu

Talca

Curicó

Linares

San Fernández

Talcahuano

*Islas
Juan Fernández
(to Chile)*

PACIFIC

OCEAN

Tropic of Capricorn

A T L A N T I C

O C E A N

A group of 150 Welsh settlers arrived
in Patagonia on July 28, 1865 seeking
a new life away from cultural and
religious oppression in the UK;
Today the area has one of the largest
Welsh populations outside of Wales.

Falkland Islands
(UK dependent territory)

Stanley
East
Falkland

West
Falkland

The Strait of Magellan was named after
Ferdinand Magellan who passed through
the straits during the first circumnavigation
of the globe in 1520. Of the 5 vessels and
270 men that set out only one ship and 17
survivors returned to Spain after the 3 year
voyage. Magellan himself was killed
in the Philippines.

Mar del Plata

Necochea

Bahía Blanca

Bahía Blanca

Colorado

Río Negro

Viedma

Península
Valdés

Rawson

Trelew

Comodoro Rivadavia

Caleta Olivia

Puerto
Deseado

Puerto San Julián

Puerto
Deseado

Río Gallegos

Chubut

Lago
Musters

P a t a g o n i a

Deseado

Cabo de Hornos
(Cape Horn)

San Antonio
Oeste

Neuquén

Zapala

San Carlos
de Bariloche

Esquel

Lago Buenos Aires
Chile Chico

Cochrane

El Calafate

Puerto
Natales

Tierra
del Fuego

Ushuaia

Punta Arenas

Porvenir

Strait of
Magellan

Concepción

Temuco

Valdivia

Osorno

Puerto Montt

Castro

Isla de Chiloé

Archipiélago
de los Chonos

Puerto Aisén

Coyhaique

Isla
Wellington

P A C I F I C

O C E A N

0 km   400

0 miles   400

5

6

7

8

A   B   C   D   E

40°

50°

40°

50°

60°

70°

80°

The Atlantic Ocean

ARCTIC OCEAN

Ellesmere I.

Baffin I.

Baffin Bay

Davis Strait

Hudson Bay

Great Lakes

St Lawrence

Grand Banks

Newfoundland Basin

New York

NORTH AMERICA

Gulf of Mexico

Tropic of Cancer

Mississippi

West Indies

Caribbean Sea

Sargasso Sea

Bermuda (UK)

Labrador Sea

Greenland (Denmark)

Greenland Sea

Denmark Strait

Iceland

Jan Mayen (Norway)

Faeroe Is. (Denmark)

Svalbard (Norway)

Barents Sea

Arctic Circle

Scandinavia

Baltic Sea

North Sea

British Isles

EUROPE

Rotterdam

Alps

Danube

Black Sea

Red Sea

Nile

Tropic of Cancer

Port Said

Mediterranean Sea

Atlas Mts.

Gibraltar

AFRICA

Sahara

Azores (Portugal)

Madeira (Portugal)

Canary Is. (Spain)

CAPE VERDE

Cape V.

Lake

Niger

Bissau

Mid-Atlantic Ridge

The North Atlantic Deep Water Current is an oceanic "river" that carries around twenty times more water than all the rivers of the world put together.

The Gulf Stream travels across the Atlantic Ocean at up to 110 miles (170 km) a day.

E

D

C

B

A

1

2

3

4

More large rivers drain into the Atlantic, than any other ocean, including the Amazon, Congo and Mississippi. These three alone deposit around 4560 tonnes of sediment per sq mile per year.

Africa

ATLANTIC OCEAN

Caspian Sea

Black Sea

Caucasus

EUROPE

ASIA

Iberian Peninsula

Mediterranean Sea

Sicily

Cyprus

Syrian Desert

The Gulf

Tropic of Cancer

Arabian Peninsula

Red Sea

Gulf of Aden

SOMALILAND (not internationally recognized)

SOMALIA

DJIBOUTI

ERITREA

Ethiopian Highlands

ETHIOPIA

Shebele

Lake Turkana

UGANDA

SUDAN

Blue Nile

White Nile

Sudd

Nile

EGYPT

Libyan Desert

CHAD

Tibesti

CENTRAL AFRICAN REPUBLIC

Uele

CAMEROON

LIBYA

S a h a r a

TUNISIA

Atlas Mountains

Ahaggar

NIGER

NIGERIA

Niger

EQUATORIAL GUINEA

Gulf of Guinea

MOROCCO

Ceuta (Spain)

Melilla (Spain)

ALGERIA

MALI

S a h e l

BENIN

TOGO

GHANA

BURKINA

CÔTE D'IVOIRE (IVORY COAST)

Niger

Madeira (Portugal)

Islas Canarias (Spain)

WESTERN SAHARA (disputed)

Tropic of Cancer

MAURITANIA

SENEGAL

Senegal

GAMBIA

GUINEA-BISSAU

GUINEA

SIERRA LEONE

LIBERIA

E

D

C

B

A

1

2

3

4

40°

20°

0°

20°

40°

Tropic of Capricorn

COMOROS

Mayotte
(France)

MADAGASCAR

Mozambique Channel

INDIAN

OCEAN

DEM. REP. BURUNDI 19,341ft (5895m)

CONGO

TANZANIA

Lake Nyasa

MALAWI

Lake
Tanganyika

ZAMBIA

Zambezi

MOZAMBIQUE

ANGOLA

ZIMBABWE

SWAZILAND

Bié
Plateau

BOTSWANA

LESOTHO

Kalahari
Desert

NAMIBIA

Orange River

SOUTH
AFRICA

Cabinda
(Angola)

Namib Desert

Cape of
Good Hope

ATLANTIC

OCEAN

Ascension I.
(St Helena)

St Helena
(UK)

Tropic of Capricorn

Gough Island
(Tristan da Cunha)

Tristan da Cunha
(St Helena)

0 km   1000

0 miles   1000

ATLANTIC
OCEAN

SPAIN

1

20° 10° 0°

◇ On March 27, 1977, two Boeing 747s
carrying 583 passengers and crew collided
on the runway at Los Rodeos Airport in
the world's worst ever air disaster.

ALGIERS
Mostaganem
Tanger Ceuta (Spain) Oran
Tetouan Melilla Sidi Bel
Kénitra (Spain) Abbès
RABAT Fès Tlemcen
Casablanca Oujda Laghou
Khouribga
Safi Beni Figuig Ghard
Essaouira Mellal Er Rachidia Béchar
Marrakech Agadir **MOROCCO**

Madeira
(Portugal)

2

30°

Islas Canarias
(Spain)

La Palma Tenerife Lanzarote
Gran Fuerte-
Canaria ventura Tan-Tan

Atlas Mountai

Grand Erg
Occidental

3

LAÂYOUNE
Smara Tindouf I-n-Sal

**WESTERN
SAHARA**
(disputed territory under
Moroccan occupation)

Reggane

A L G E R

Tropic of Cancer

Ad Dakhla

◇ The region of Tidikelt
in Algeria once went
for ten years without
a drop of rain.

S a

4

20°

Lagouira

◇ The Sahara desert covers an area of
around 3,565,600 sq miles (9,234,904 sq km),
an area roughly the size of Europe.

5

M A U R I T A N I A

0 km 400

0 miles 400

M A L I

10°

A B C D

10°

I T A L Y

Sicily

20°

G R E E C E

Crete

Annaba ✈ Bizerte

TUNIS

Constantine

Sétif

Batna

Biskra   Gafsa

Chott
Melghir

Tozeur

Médenine

TUNISIA

Touggourt

Ouargla

Grand Erg
Oriental

Kairouan

Sousse

MALTA

Mediterranean
Sea

Sfax

Gabès

Zuwārah
Az Zāwiyah

✈ **TRIPOLI**

Al Khums

Gharyān   Mişrātah

Yafran

Surt

Khalīj Surt

◆ The hottest place on earth is Al 'Aziziyah,
Libya, where on September 13, 1922, an air
temperature of 136°F (57°C) was recorded.

Al Baydā'   Darnah

Banghāzī ✈   Tubruq

Al Marj

Ajdābiyā

30°

E G Y P T

Great
Sand
Sea

I A

L I B Y A

Tassili-n-Ajjer

Ahaggar

Tamanrasset

a   r   a

Birāk

● Sabhā

Awbārī

Murzuq

L i b y a n

Al Kufrah

Tropic of Cancer

D e s e r t

Tibesti

20°

◆ Libyan oil is especially prized because
of its low sulfur content, which means
it produces much less pollution than
other fuel oil.

N I G E R

C H A D

10°

20°

1

2

3

4

5

E

F

G

H

Northeast Africa

When first opened in 1869, the Suez Canal consisted of a channel 26 ft (8 m) deep and 200 to 300 ft (60 to 90 m) wide at the surface. Construction involved the excavation and dredging of 97 million cubic yards (74 million cubic metres) of material.

For thousands of years the Nile has supported cultivation in the Aswan region, despite it being one of the driest places on Earth, with an average of only 0.02 inches (0.5 mm) of rain per year.

IRAN
IRAQ
SYRIA
JORDAN
ISRAEL
LEBANON
CYPRUS
The Gulf
Tropic of Cancer

SAUDI ARABIA

YEMEN
Gulf of Aden
Boosaaso

DJIBOUTI
DJIBOUTI
Aseb

ERITREA
Massawa
ASMARA
Mek'ele
Dese

Red Sea

(administered by Sudan)

Teseney
Himora
Bahir Dar
Gonder

Mediterranean Sea

Alexandria
Nile Delta
Port Said
Ismā'līya
Suez Canal
Suez
Sinai
Port Sudan

CAIRO
El Gîza
Beni Suef
El Mînya
Asyût
Sohâg
Qena
Luxor
Isna
Idfu
El Khârga
Aswân

Hurghada

Nubian Desert

Kassala
Gedaref
Atbara

Blue Nile

EGYPT

Lake Nasser
(administered by Egypt)
Wadi Halfa
Dongola

Omdurman
KHARTOUM
Wad Medani
El Obeid
Dilling
Kadugli

White Nile

Monkhafad
el Qattâra
-436ft (-133m)

Libyan Desert

LIBYA

Tropic of Cancer

CHAD

El Geneina
Nyala
El Fasher

Darfur

SUDAN

The Somali language did not become a written language until 1972.

The shortest war on record, between Britain and Zanzibar in 1896, lasted just 38 minutes.

The Great Rift Valley is one of the most extensive rifts on the Earth's surface extending from Jordan southward through eastern Africa to Mozambique. The system is some 4,000 miles (6,400 km) long and averages 30–40 miles (48–64 km) wide.

West Africa

0 km 400

0 miles 400

Tropic of Cancer

◆ Mauritania and Madagascar are the only countries in the world not to use a decimal-based currency. The basic unit of currency, the ouguiyal, is divided into five khoums.

WESTERN SAHARA
(disputed territory under Moroccan occupation)

Bîr Mogreïn

'Erg Iguïdi

Kâgret

El Hank

Fdérik Zouérat

Ouarâne

Nouâdhibou

Choûm

Atâr

El Mreyyé

S

Akchâr

Akjoujt

CAPE VERDE

Ilhas de Barlavento

Santo Antão

São Vicente

São Nicolau

Santiago

Fogo

Maio

Boa Vista

Sal

Ilhas de Sotavento

PRAIA

A T L A N T I C

O C E A N

NOUAKCHOTT

M A U R I T A N I A

Rkíz

Aleg

Kiffa

Aoukâr

S

Saint Louis

Senegal

Kaédi

Nioro

SENEGAL

DAKAR

Mbaké

Diourbel

Kaolack

Kayes

Ségou

Bay

S

BANJUL

GAMBIA

Bignona

Gambia

BAMAKO

◆ Gambia is only around 20 miles (32 km) wide and 300 miles (483 km) long; its unusual shape and size are down to territorial compromises arising from 19th-century Anglo-French rivalry in western Africa.

BISSAU

GUINEA-BISSAU

Boké

Gaoual

Labé

Niger

Bougouni

Bo

Dioula

Siguiri

G U I N E A

Odienné

Kindia

Kankan

CÔTE D'IVOIRE (IVORY COAS

CONAKRY

SIERRA LEONE

FREETOWN

◆ Monrovia, named after the fifth US President James Monroe, was founded in 1830 by the American Colonization Society as a settlement for freed American slaves.

Bo

Tubmanburg

LIBERIA

YAMOUSSOUKRO

La

MONROVIA

Buchanan

Zwedru

Cagn

◆ A Ruppell's Griffen Vulture collided with a commercial airliner at 37,000 ft (11,277 m) above Côte d'Ivoire to earn the posthumous distinction of the highest flying bird ever recorded.

Harper

Abid

A   B   C   D

0°   10°

A L G E R I A   L I B Y A

◆ In the late 1960s and early 1970s a series of
catastrophic droughts caused the Sahara Desert
to advance southward up to 60 miles (100 km) into
the Sahel region. The loss of human life by starvation
and disease was estimated in 1973 to be 100,000.

Tropic of Cancer

aoudenni

a   h   a   r   a   Ténéré   a   Tibesti
du
Tafassâsset   20°

Erg-n-Sâkâne

Tessalit   Assamakka

Araouane   Azaouâd   Adrar des   Massif   Ténéré
Ifôghas   de l'Aïr

M A L I   Grand Erg de Bilma   C H A D

aguibine   Tombouctou   Gao   Agadez
Lac   Ansongo
Niangay
opti   Hombori   N I G E R   21

a   h   Tahoua   l   Zinder   Nguigmi
e   Maradi   Gouré   Lake Chad
BURKINA   NIAMEY   3
OUAGADOUGOU   Sokoto   Katsina   Hadejia
oudougou   Fada-   Gusau   Kano   Maiduguri
Ngourma   Zaria
Kandi   Kumo
BENIN   Kainji   Kaduna   Jos
Wa   Natitingou   Reservoir   N I G E R I A   Plateau   Congola   10°
Tamale   Sokodé   Ilorin   Niger   Benue
GHANA   ABUJA   4
mani   Oyo   Ogbomosho   C.A.R.
Umasi   Lake   Abomey   Ede   Gotel
Nsawam   Volta   Ibadan   Benin   Enugu   Mountains
amankese   LOMÉ PORTO-   Lagos   City
ACCRA   NOVO   Sapele   Onitsha
Bight of Benin   Aba   Calabar   5
Gulf of Guinea   Port Harcourt
Mouths of the Niger   CAMEROON
◆ Lake Volta is one of the largest man-made   EQUATORIAL
lakes in the world covering 3283 sq miles   GUINEA   10°
(8502 sq km), or 3.6% of Ghana's area
E   0°   F   10°   G   H

Central Africa

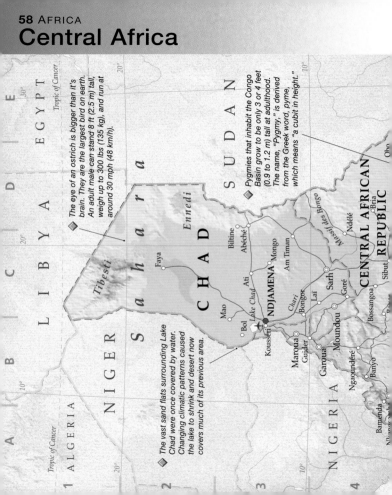

The eye of an ostrich is bigger than it's brain. They are the largest bird on earth. An adult male can stand 8 ft (2.5 m) tall, weigh up to 300 lbs (135 kg), and run at around 30 mph (48 km/h).

Pygmies that inhabit the Congo Basin grow to be only 3 or 4 feet (0.9 to 1.2 m) tall at adulthood. The name, "Pygmy," is derived from the Greek word, pyme, which means "a cubit in height."

The vast sand flats surrounding Lake Chad were once covered by water. Changing climatic patterns caused the lake to shrink and desert now covers much of its previous area.

Tropic of Cancer

ALGERIA

LIBYA

EGYPT

NIGER

NIGERIA

CHAD

SUDAN

CENTRAL AFRICAN REPUBLIC

Sahara

Tibesti

Ennedi

Faya

Mao

Bol

Lake Chad

Kousséri

NDJAMENA

Ati

Biltine

Abéché

Mongo

Am Timan

Charri

Bongor

Laï

Goré

Sarh

Massif des Bongo

Ndélé

Bria

Sibut

Bossangoa

Moundou

Garoua

Guider

Maroua

Ngaoundéré

Banyo

Bamenda

Oko

Southern Africa

Cabinda
(Angola)
Cabinda

Uíge

Lucapa

Ambriz

N'Dalatando

Saurimo

LUANDA

Malanje

Ndola
Mufulira

Sumbe

A N G O L A

Chingola

Lobito
Benguela

Kuito

Kitwe
Luanshya

A T L A N T I C

Huambo

Zambezi

Z A M B I A

Lubango

Menongue

O C E A N

Namibe
Tombua

N'Giva

LUSAKA

Choma

◆ The Okavango River pours
some 14.4 billion cubic yards
(11 billion cu m) of water into
the Okavango Delta each year.
It drains away through a maze of
lagoons, channels, and islands
covering around 5800 sq miles
(15,000 sq km) before eventually
disappearing into the sands of the
Kalahari Desert to the south.

Cunene

Rundu

Livingstone

Cubango

Zambezi

Lake
Kariba

Cuando

Victoria
Falls

Chitungwi

Etosha
Pan

Tsumeb

Okavango

ZIMBA

Grootfontein

Okavango Delta

Namib Desert

N A M I B I A

Maun

Bulawayo

Ghanzi

Francistown

WINDHOEK

B O T S W A N A

Swakopmund

Kalahari

Mahalapye

Limpopo

Walvis Bay

Rehoboth

GABORONE

TSHWA

Desert

Lobatse

(PRETORI

Mmabatho

◆ The Kalahari Desert is the largest
continuous sand surface in the world.
Iron oxide gives a distinctive red
color to the sand, which is over
200 ft (60 m) deep in places.

Keetmanshoop

Soweto
Johannesburg

Tropic of Capricorn

Lüderitz

Karasburg

Vaal

Kroons

Kimberley

MASER

Orange R.

BLOEMFONTEIN

LESOTHO

SOUTH AFRICA'S THREE CAPITALS

Tshwane (Pretoria) - administrative capital
Cape Town - legislative capital
Bloemfontein - financial capital

S O U T H

Middelburg

A F R I C A

Beaufort West

East
Londo

Bellville

Drakensberg

CAPE TOWN

George

Port
Elizabeth

Cape of Good Hope

0 km   400

0 miles   400

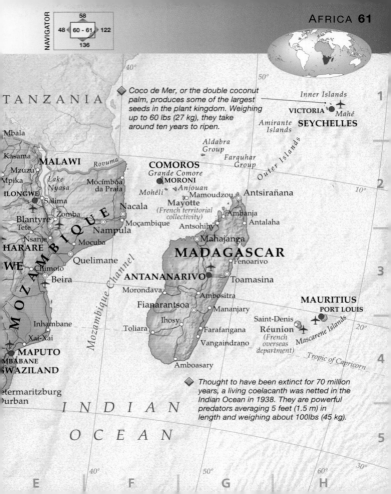

TANZANIA

Mbala

Kasama

MALAWI

Mzuzu   *Rovuma*

Mpika   *Lake   Mocímboa*
         Nyasa   *da Praia*

ILONGWE   Salima

Blantyre   Zomba

Tete   Nacala

Nsanje   Nampula

Mocuba

HARARE

WE

Chimoio   Quelimane

Beira

Inhambane

Xai-Xai

MAPUTO

MBABANE

SWAZILAND

etermaritzburg
Durban

MOZAMBIQUE

Mozambique Channel

◆ Coco de Mer, or the double coconut
palm, produces some of the largest
seeds in the plant kingdom. Weighing
up to 60 lbs (27 kg), they take
around ten years to ripen.

Inner Islands

VICTORIA • *Mahé*

*Amirante   **SEYCHELLES***
Islands

Aldabra
Group
Farquhar
Group

COMOROS
Grande Comore
● **MORONI**

Mohéli   *Anjouan*
Mamoudzou   • Antsirañana
Mayotte
(French territorial   Ambanja
collectivity)   Antalaha
Moçambique   Antsohihy
● Mahajanga

MADAGASCAR

Penoarivo

ANTANANARIVO ✈   • Toamasina

Morondava   • Ambositra

Fianarantsoa   Mananjary

Ihosy   Saint-Denis   **MAURITIUS**
                        PORT LOUIS
Toliara   Farafangana   **Réunion**
                        (French
         Vangaindrano   *overseas*
                        department)   *Mascarene Islands*

Amboasary   *Tropic of Capricorn*

◆ Thought to have been extinct for 70 million
years, a living coelacanth was netted in the
Indian Ocean in 1938. They are powerful
predators averaging 5 feet (1.5 m) in
length and weighing about 100lbs (45 kg).

INDIAN

OCEAN

Europe

Arctic Circle

Limit of winter pack ice

20°

40°

60°

0°

1

0 km   800

0 miles   800

ICELAND

Norwegian Sea

Lofo

Faeroe Islands
(Denmark)

40°

2

Shetland Islands

Outer
Hebrides

*British
Isles*

Orkney
Islands

N
O
R

Vänern

Vät

Ireland

Isle of Man
(to UK)

IRELAND

Britain

North
Sea

DENMARK

40°

3

*Celtic
Sea*

**UNITED
KINGDOM**

NETHERLANDS

Nor

English Channel

Channel Is
(UK)

Seine

BELGIUM

GERMANY

LUX.

**CZECH
REPUBLI**

A T L A N T I C

O C E A N

Bay of Biscay

FRANCE

Loire

Rhine

Massif
Central

SWITZ.

Rhône

Garonne

LIECH.

AUSTRI

S

4

▲ Mont Blanc
15,771ft 4807m

Po

SLOVEN

PORTUGAL

Duero

Iberian

Ebro

Pyrenees

MONACO

**SAN
MARINO**

CROA

**BOSN
& HE**

Tagus

SPAIN

ANDORRA

Corsica

ITALY

Madeira
(to Portugal)

Peninsula

Guadalquivir

Balearic Islands

**VATICAN
CITY**

Strait of Gibraltar

Gibraltar
(UK)

Sardinia

M e d i t e r r a n e

*Tyrrhenian
Sea*

5

20°

*Canary Islands
(to Spain)*

A t l a s   M o u n t a i n s

A F R I C A

0°

Sicily

MALTA

| A | B | C | D |

Barents Sea
North Cape
Ostrov Kolguyev

Arctic Circle

Ob

Irtysh

Ural Mountains

FINLAND

Kola
Peninsula

White
Sea

Gulf of Bothnia

Northern Dvina

Lake Onega

R U S S I A N

Lake
Ladoga

Åland

F E D E R A T I O N

ESTONIA

Baltic Sea

LATVIA

European Plain

LITHUANIA

RUSS.
FED.

Central
Russian
Upland

BELARUS

Volga Uplands

Volga

Ural

Aral Sea

Syr Darya

POLAND

Pripet
Marshes

Dnieper Lowlands

Bug

Don

Vistula

UKRAINE

Dnieper

Carpathian Mountains

Dniester

Ural

Amu Dary

SLOVAKIA

Caspian Sea

MOLDOVA

Sea of
Azov

HUNGARY

Crimea

Caucasus

ROMANIA

El'brus
18,510ft
(5642m)

Black Sea

SERBIA

Balkan
Mountains

BULGARIA

MACED.

TURKEY

ALBANIA

Anatolia

A S I A

Zagros Mountains

Aegean
Sea

GREECE

Euphrates

Tigris

Peloponnese

S e a

Crete

Cyprus

Danube

Dniester

The North Atlantic

◆ At 840,000 sq miles (2,175,600 sq km), Greenland is the largest island in the world. However, 650,000 sq miles (1,638,400 sq km) of this is a massive ice sheet so heavy that the central land area has sunk to form to a basin more than 1000 ft (300 m) below sea level.

◆ The Jakobshavn Glacier, often moving 100 feet (30 m) a day, is among the world's fastest glaciers, and calves around 1350 icebergs every year.

Arctic Circle

N U N A V U T

Devon Island

Ellesmere Island

Nares Strait

Qaanaaq

Hudson Bay

Innaanganeq

Knud Rasmussen Land

Savissivik

Qimusseriarsuaq

Baffin Bay

Kullorsuaq

C A N A D A

Péninsule d'Ungava

Baffin Island

Hudson Strait

QUEBEC

Davis Strait

Limit of summer pack ice

Qeqertarsuaq

Qeqertarsuaq

Qasigiannguit

Frobisher Bay

Cumberland Sound

Sisimiut

Greenland
(Danish external territory)

Ungava Bay

Kong Frederik IX Land

Maniitsoq

NUUK

Kong Christian IX Land

Gunnbjørn Fjeld 3700m

Paamiut

Ammassalik

Ivittuut

Denmark

NEWFOUNDLAND & LABRADOR

Labrador Sea

Qaqortoq

Kong Frederik VI Kyst

Limit of winter pack ice

Nanortalik

Faxaf

Nunap Isua (Kap Farvel)

ATLANTIC OCEAN

0 km   800

0 miles   800

With temperatures ranging from 59° F (15° C) in the summer to -40° F (-40° C) in the winter, vegetation on Svalbard consists mostly of lichens and mosses; the only trees are the tiny polar willow and the dwarf birch.

Greenland's deeply indented coastline is 24,430 miles (39,330 km) long, a distance roughly equivalent to the Earth's circumference at the Equator.

Even though only one twentieth of Iceland's potential geothermal power has been harnessed, around 89% of houses are heated geothermally.

ARCTIC OCEAN

Barents Sea

RUSSIAN FEDERATION

Arctic Circle

◆ The North Cape Current warms the northern coasts of Norway, Finland, and Russia's Kola Peninsula with water temperatures of 39–54° F (4–12° C), allowing this area of the Barents Sea to remain free of pack ice throughout the winter.

Vardø
Kirkenes

Nordkapp (North Cape)

Hammerfest

Sodankylä
Kuusamo
Kuhmo
Kajaani
Pielinen

F I N L A N D

Deatnu
Ounasjoki
Kemijärvi
Oulujärvi
Iisalmi
Jakobstad

Kemijoki
Rovaniemi
Oulujoki
Oulu

◆ The sun is continuously visible from late May to late July in Tromsø because of its position well north of the Arctic Circle.

Tromsø

Tornio
Kemi

Kokkola

Muonionjoki
Tornionjoki

Luleå
Piteå
Skellefteå
Umeå

Harstad
Narvik
Lofoten

L A P L A N D

Kiruna
Gällivare

Vesterålen

Bodø

S W E D E N

Mo i Rana

Norwegian Sea

◆ Scandinavia is still recovering from the last ice age, when the land was depressed 2000 ft (600 m) by the weight of the ice. Today the earth's crust is "rebounding" at the rate of 0.3 inches (9 mm) a year in the Gulf of Bothnia.

Ångermanälven

Steinkjer

Trondheimsfjorden
Trondheim

Dovrefjell

Arctic Circle

0 km 200
0 miles 200

LATVIA

BELARUS

ESTONIA

The sauna is a Finnish institution with some 2 million sauna facilities to serve a population of just 5 million.

LITHUANIA

KALININGRAD
(part of Russian Federation)

Baltic Sea

POLAND

Gulf of Finland

HELSINKI
Espoo

Johsun
Varkaus
Saimaa
Imatra
Kouvola
Vantaa·Kotka
Lappeenranta
Hämeenlinna
Riihimäki
Tampere
Seinäjoki
Jyväskylä
Vaasa
Pori
Rauma
Turku
Åland
Mariehamn

D

Sundsvall
Östersund
Örnsköldsvik

Gulf of Bothnia

STOCKHOLM
Västerås
Uppsala
Gävle
Falun
Borlänge
Örebro
Nyköping
Norrköping
Linköping
Visby
Gotland

E

M
S

Ljusnan

Vänern
Karlstad
Skövde
Vättern
Jönköping
Borås
Öland
Kalmar
Karlskrona
Kristianstad
Växjö
Bornholm
Rønne

Lillehammer
Hamar
Gjøvik
Mjøsa
Hermansverk

OSLO
Fredrikstad
Moss
Halden
Drammen
Kongsberg
Porsgrunn
Arendal
Trollhättan
Göteborg
Halmstad
Helsingborg
Malmö
Helsingør

O

N

Setesdal
Kristiansand
Skagerrak

Bergen
Haugesund
Stavanger
Ålesund
Sognefjorden

Hjørring
Frederikshavn
Aalborg
Randers
Århus
Jylland
Silkeborg
Herning
Vejle
Esbjerg
DENMARK
Odense
COPENHAGEN
Aabenraa
Sjælland
Nykøbing

GERMANY

The 10 mile (16 km) bridge and tunnel link across the Øresund sound is one of the largest infrastructure projects in European history. It connects the Danish capital Copenhagen to the Swedish port of Malmo.

55°
60°
25°
20°
15°
10°
55°
5
6
7
8

The Low Countries

THE NETHERLANDS'S TWO CAPITALS

Amsterdam - Capital
The Hague - Seat of Government

◆ The Netherlands is the lowest country in the world. It is estimated that 30 percent of the land is below sea level with the lowest point some 23 ft (6.7 m) below sea level.

◆ The inner city of Amsterdam is divided by its network of canals into some 90 "islands" linked together by approximately 1300 bridges and viaducts.

◆ The port of Rotterdam, combined with Europoort (which handles vessels too large to reach Rotterdam), is the largest in the world in terms of capacity, handling around 325 million tons (tonnes) of cargo every year.

GERMANY

NETHERLANDS

North Sea

AMSTERDAM

THE HAGUE

Rotterdam

Delfzijl
Emmen
Groningen
Almelo
Hengelo
Enschede
Assen
Heerenveen
Apeldoorn
Deventer
Arnhem
Nijmegen
Meppel
Zwolle
Amersfoort
Ede
Utrecht
Oss
's-Hertogenbosch
Tilburg
Breda
Leeuwarden
Hoorn
Lelystad
Purmerend
Hilversum
Zoetermeer
Gouda
Dordrecht
Roosendaal
Alkmaar
Den Helder
Haarlem
Leiden
Delft

Schiermonnikoog
Ameland
Terschelling
Vlieland
Texel
Waddenzee
Waddeneilanden

IJsselmeer
IJssel
Lek
Waal
BergseMa

53°
52°
52°

GERMANY

BELGIUM

LUXEMBOURG

FRANCE

BRUSSELS

LUXEMBOURG

Belgium and the Netherlands have an underground boundary that differs from the surface boundary shown on maps. In 1950, the two countries agreed to move the underground boundary so as not to divide coal mines between the two countries.

On August 23, 1914 three weeks after Britain entered World War I, the 70,000 strong British Expeditionary Force encountered the advancing German army for the first time at the battle of Mons.

Echternach is the home of the only religious dancing procession remaining in the Western world. Every year since the 15th century thousands of pilgrims have marched down the streets of the town performing a ritual dance involving specific movements, music, and prayers.

0 km 50
0 miles 50

The British Isles

Midges have the fastest wing-beat of any insect, and are able to flap their wings at around 63,000 beats per minute.

After the surrender of the German fleet in 1918 and its internment in Scapa Flow, over 50 ships were scuttled by the German crews on June 21, 1919, to prevent them falling into British hands.

With a depth of 788 ft (240 m) and a length of about 23 miles (36 km), Loch Ness contains the largest volume of fresh water in Great Britain.

The Giant's Causeway comprises approximately 37,000 dark basalt polygonal columns packed together; they were formed by volcanic activity some 55 million years ago.

North Sea

ATLANTIC

OCEAN

Faroe Islands

Lerwick

Shetland Islands

Orkney Islands

Kirkwall

Thurso

Newcastle upon Tyne

Sunderland

Aberdeen

Dundee

Perth

EDINBURGH

Elgin

Inverness

Moray Firth

Firth of Forth

Stirling

Forth

SCOTLAND

Grampian Mts.

Ben Nevis

4406 ft (1343 m)

Loch Ness

Ullapool

Fort William

Loch Linnhe

Oban

Glasgow

Greenock

Ayr

Southern Uplands

Dumfries

Stranraer

The Minch

Isle of Skye

Mull

Islay

Isle of Arran

Iona

Isle of Lewis

Stornoway

The Little Minch

North Uist

South Uist

Barra

Outer Hebrides

UNITED KINGDOM

NORTHERN

Londonderry

Seven percent of Ireland's barley crop goes into the production of Guinness stout.

The River Severn has the second highest tidal range in the world, as much as 50 ft (15 m), often giving rise to a tidal bore. In September 1996 one such wave carried a surfer for 5.7 miles (9 km).

France, Andorra & Monaco

Work began on the 31-mile (50-km) Channel Tunnel in 1987. Earth was removed at the rate of 2400 tons (tonnes) a day until completion, seven years later. Around 10.5 million cu yards (8 million cu m) had been excavated.

Champagne bottles are placed neck down into a freezing brine bath (bac à glace), freezing only the bottle's neck to form a plug that keeps the wine – and the bubbles – in the bottle while sediments are removed.

On July 1, 1916, the British suffered 58,000 casualties on the opening day of the Somme Offensive. Five months later, after advancing only a few miles, there had been 420,000 British, 200,000 French, and 500,000 German casualties.

ITALY

Mont Blanc 15,771ft (4807m)

Chambéry
Grenoble
Annecy
Villeurbanne
Lyon
St-Étienne
Le Puy
Valence
Mâcon
Roanne
Vichy
Clermont-Ferrand
St-Chamond

Limoges
Massif Central
Aurillac
Mende
Rodez
Millau

MONACO
MONACO
Nice
Cannes
Côte d'Azur
Ligurian Sea

Bastia

Corse (Corsica)
Ajaccio

Sardinia

Provence
Aix-en-Provence
Avignon
Arles
Îles d'Hyères
Toulon
Marseille
Nîmes
Béziers
Montpellier
Narbonne
Perpignan
Golfe du Lion

Mediterranean Sea

Saintes
Angoulême
Périgueux
Dordogne
Cahors
Montauban
Albi
Toulouse
Carcassonne
Auch
Agen
Garonne
Tarbes
Pau
Mont-de-Marsan
Bayonne
Bordeaux

Bay of Biscay

SPAIN

Pyrenees

ANDORRA
ANDORRA LA VELLA

Balearic Islands

◆ One of history's great leaders, Napoleon Bonaparte was born on August 15, 1769, at Ajaccio in Corsica.

◆ The word denim comes from "de Nîmes," this being the town where the fabric was originally produced.

◆ The lowest point in Andorra is Riu Runer at 2756 ft (840m) above sea level.

◆ The Tour de France bicycle race is typically held over some 20 day-long stages covering around 2200 miles (3600 km) for the coveted yellow jersey.

0 km   100
0 miles   100

A   B   C   D   E

5

6

7

8

Spain & Portugal

ATLANTIC

OCEAN

0 km   100
0 miles   100

10°   5°

Ferrol   Avilés   Gijon
A Coruña (La Coruña)   (Xixón)
Galicia   Oviedo
Santiago de Compostela   Lugo   *Cordillera Cantábrica*
                                    León
Pontevedra
Vigo   Ourense   *Emb. de   Palencia
        (Orense)   Ricobayo*   Valladolid
Viana do Castelo   Chaves   Bragança   *Duero*
Póvoa de Varzim   Braga   Zamora
Matosinhos   Guimarães   Vila Real   **S**   **P**
Porto   *Douro*   Salamanca
Vila Nova de Gaia   *Ávila*
Aveiro   Viseu

◆ Port has been produced in the Duoro
Valley under strict regulation since the
1750s. Brandy is added to the grape
juice to fortify and strengthen
the wine.

Coimbra   Covilhã   *Sistema Central*
Figueira da Foz
PORTUGAL   Plasencia
Castelo Branco   *Tagus*
Caldas da Rainha   *Tagus*
                    Cáceres
Sintra   Santarém   Portalegre
Cascais   Mérida   *Guadiana*
LISBON   Badajoz
Setúbal
Alcácer do Sal
                    Beja   *Sierra Morena*
◆ Portugal is one of the world's largest   Córdoba
producers of cork and has regulations   Sines
protecting cork trees dating back to 1320.   *Guadalquivir*
                Sevilla
        Algarve   *Guadiana*   *Andalucía*
    Lagos   Faro Olhão   Huelva   Antequera
Cabo de São Vicente   Málaga

El Puerto de Santa María   Marbella
    Cádiz   Gibraltar
◆ Gibraltar was seized by a combined Anglo-Dutch fleet   Algeciras   (UK)
under Admiral Rooke in 1704. British sovereignty was   Ceuta (Spa
then formalized in 1713 by the Treaty of Utrecht, and
Gibraltar eventually became a British colony in 1830.   MOROCCO

40°

35°

10°   5°

A   B   C   D

Bay of Biscay

F R A N C E

0°

5°

Santander

Bilbao   Donostia-San Sebastián

Vitoria-Gasteiz

Golfe du Lion

1

Miranda de Ebro   Pamplona (Iruña)   ANDORRA

Burgos   Logroño   Huesca   Figueres

Soria   *Pyrenees*   Girona (Gerona)

Cataluña   *Costa Brava*

Sistema   Lleida   Terrassa   Mataró

Zaragoza   Sabadell

Ibérico   Reus   Tarragona   Barcelona

...AIN   N   Tortosa   L'Hospitalet de Llobregat

2

egovia   ◇ Work continues on the Sagrada Família,
Gaudí's unfinished cathedral. Begun in
1882 the masterpiece is still
without a roof.

MADRID   Teruel

Getafe   Cuenca

...oledo

40°

Castellón
de la Plana   Palma   *Menorca*

3

Júcar   Valencia   *Mallorca*

Albacete   Gandía   Ibiza   *Islas Baleares*
(Balearic Islands)

...udad Real   *País Valenciano*   Elda   Formentera

Cieza   Benidorm   ◇ Seat of many great civilizations
throughout history, the name
Mediterranean translates as
"sea between the lands."

...én   *Segura*   Alicante (Alacant)

...ranada   Murcia   Elche (Elx)   *Costa Blanca*

4

...erra Nevada   Lorca

Cartagena

Motril   Almería

...osta del Sol

M e d i t e r r a n e a n   S e a

A L G E R I A

5

0°

5°

E   F   G   H

Germany & The Alpine States

The Kiel Canal is one of the busiest in the world, with around 45,000 ships a year passing between the Baltic and the North Sea

Early in the morning of Sunday, August 13, 1961, work began on the Berlin Wall, which would eventually run for 66 miles (107 km) between east and west Berlin, cutting through 192 streets.

The German Bundestag, or Parliament, based in Berlin, has 672 members and is the world's largest elected legislative body.

North Sea

SWEDEN

Baltic Sea

Bornholm (Denmark)

DENMARK

Jylland

Sjælland

Fyn

Falster

North Frisian Islands

Flensburg
Neumünster
Kiel
Lübeck
Rostock
Stralsund
Greifswald
Rügen
Wismar
Schwerin
Neubrandenburg
Hamburg
Lüneburg
Müritz
BERLIN
Potsdam
Frankfurt an der Oder
Cottbus
Dresden
Leipzig
Gera
Halle
Dessau
Magdeburg
Salzgitter
Braunschweig
Wolfsburg
Hannover
Hildesheim
Göttingen
Kassel
Paderborn
Bielefeld
Hamm
Bremen
Oldenburg
Osnabrück
Cuxhaven
Bremerhaven
Emden
Münster
Dortmund
Bochum
Recklinghausen
Essen
Duisburg
Düsseldorf
Wuppertal
Leverkusen

G E R M A N Y

POLAND

NETHERLANDS

Elbe
Saale
Ems
Spree
Weser
Mecklenburger Bucht
Fehmarn Belt

HUNGARY

CZECH REPUBLIC

BELGIUM

FRANCE

ITALY

CROATIA

SLOVENIA

AUSTRIA

SWITZERLAND

LIECHTENSTEIN

Erzgebirge

Bohemian Forest

Fränkische Alb

Schwäbische Alb

Bodensee

Berner Alpen

Gulf of Venice

Koblenz

Wiesbaden
Mainz

Frankfurt am Main
Offenbach
Darmstadt Würzburg
Mannheim
Heidelberg
Karlsruhe
Pforzheim
Heilbronn
Stuttgart
Reutlingen
Ulm

Freiburg im Breisgau

Kaiserslautern

Saarbrücken

LUX.

Mosel

Rhine

Neckar

Erlangen
Nürnberg
Regensburg
Landshut
Ingolstadt
Augsburg
München

Donau

Inn

Salzburg

Hallein

Krems an
der Donau
Linz
Wels

Enns

Hollabrunn

VIENNA
Baden
Wiener
Neustadt

Eisenstadt
Neusiedler
See

Mur

Leoben
Kapfenberg

Graz

Judenburg

Klagenfurt
Villach

Maribor
Celje

Sava

LJUBLJANA

Kranj

Koper

Drau

Mur

Salzach

Inn

Bregenz
VADUZ

Chur
Rhine

Bellinzona
Lugano
Lake Maggiore

Lake Constance

St Gallen

Zürich
Zug
Luzern

BERN

Basel

Delémont

Biel

Lausanne

Yverdon

Genève

Lake Geneva

Lake Neuchâtel

Schaffhausen

Innsbruck

Matterhorn
14,692ft (4478m)

Thuner See

Brienzer See

Lake Lucerne

Monthey

Gotthard

Bavarian Alps

◆ At 528 ft (161 m) the spire of
Ulm Cathedral is the tallest
in the world.

◆ The glass roof over the Olympic stadium in München
(Munich) measures 914,940 sq ft (85,000 sq m) making
it the biggest structure of its kind in the world.

◆ Born in Salzburg on January 27,
1756, Wolfgang Amadeus Mozart
was already writing music by the
age of five, and at eleven he
produced his first opera.

◆ St Gothard tunnel is 10.14 miles
(16.32 km) long, making it the
second longest road tunnel
in the world.

0 km   100

0 miles   100

50°

45°

5°

10°

15°

A   B   C   D   E

5

6

7

8

CZECH REPUBLIC

SLOVAKIA

HUNGARY

GERMANY

AUSTRIA

SLOVENIA

CROATIA

BOSNIA & HERZEGOVINA

FRANCE

SWITZERLAND

LIECHTENSTEIN

In April 1998 a violin made by Italian master Stradivari at Cremona in around 1680 sold at Christie's in London for £947,500.

San Marino formed in AD 301 is the oldest, and, at 24 sq mi (61 sq km), one of the smallest, republics in the world.

Adriatic Sea

Aosta

Torino

Novara

Monza

Milano

Bergamo

Brescia

Cremona

Lago di Como

Lago Maggiore

Lake Maggiore

San Remo

Savona

Genova

Golfo di Genova

Alessandria

Piacenza

Parma

Reggio nell'Emilia

Modena

La Spezia

Viareggio

Pisa

Livorno

Isola d'Elba

Arcipelago Toscano

Corsica (part of France)

Ligurian Sea

Bolzano

Alpi

Dolomitiche

Trento

Lago di Garda

Udine

Treviso

Piave

Mestre

Venezia

Gulf of Venice

Vicenza

Verona

Mantova

Padova

Adige

Trieste

Po Delta

Po

Ferrara

Ravenna

Bologna

Rimini

Forlì

Prato

Firenze

Arno

Toscana

Siena

Grosseto

Lago Trasimeno

Arezzo

SAN MARINO

Ancona

Ascoli Piceno

Pescara

L'Aquila

Perugia

Foligno

Terni

Tevere

Viterbo

ROME

VATICAN CITY

ITALY

Appennino

45°

15°

10°

A B C D E

1 2 3 4

Gulf of Otranto
Bari
Brindisi
Altamura
Lecce
Gallipoli
Potenza
Taranto
Golfo di Taranto
Benevento
Salerno
Napoli
Torre del Greco
Golfo di Gaeta
Isola di Capri
Golfo di Salerno

Crotone
Catanzaro
Ionian Sea
Cosenza
Calabria
Isola Stromboli
Isola Lipari
Isola Vulcano
Reggio di Calabria
Stretto di Messina
Messina
Isole Eolie
Isola d'Ustica
Palermo
Cefalù
Sicilia (Sicily)
Catania
Siracusa
Trapani
Caltanissetta
Ragusa
Isole Egadi
Marsala
Agrigento
Isola di Pantelleria

Strait of Sicily
Malta Channel
Gozo
VALLETTA
MALTA
Isole Pelagie

Tyrrhenian Sea

Sardegna (Sardinia)
Vittoria
Nuoro
Oristano
Alghero
Iglesias
Cagliari

Mediterranean Sea

TUNISIA

The medical school at Salerno is the oldest in Europe, established during the 11th and 12th centuries.

Mt Etna began some 300,000 years ago as a submarine volcano and has since grown to a cone with a base 30 miles (48 km) wide and 10,958 ft (3340 m) high.

The George cross that appears on the Maltese flag was awarded to the islanders by King George VI of Britain for their heroism during World War II.

0 km   100
0 miles   100

BELARUS

LATVIA

LITHUANIA

SWEDEN

Baltic Sea

DENMARK

Bornholm
(part of Denmark)

Pomeranian Bay

Zalew
Szczeciński

Gulf
of
Danzig

Courland Lagoon

KALININGRAD
(part of Russian
Federation)

◆ *Warsaw was home to the world's first public library, opened in 1747.*

◆ *Hitler's demand in 1939 that Gdansk be returned to German control precipitated the invasion of Poland which ultimately led to World War II.*

◆ *In November 1989 the so-called "Velvet Revolution" saw Czechoslovakia split into the Czech Republic and Slovakia.*

GERMANY

POLAND

M a z u r y

WARSAW

Białystok

Lublin

Ostrowiec
Świętokrzyski

Olsztyn

Ostrołęka

Radom

Kielce

Elbląg

Płock

Gdynia
Gdańsk

Grudziądz

Toruń

Bydgoszcz

Włocławek

Łódź

Słupsk

Koszalin

Piła

Czluchów

Notéc

Kalisz

Wrocław

Poznań

Szczecin

Gorzów
Wielkopolski

Zielona
Góra

Legnica

Wisła

Narew

Bug

Wisła

Warta

Odra

Warta

Notéc

Odra

Bornholm

Zalew
Szczeciński

0 km   100

0 miles   100

25°

15°

20°

25°

55°

55°

55°

A   B   C   D   E

1

2

3

UKRAINE

Carpathian Mts.

Laborec

Rzeszów
Kraków Tarnów
Bielsko-Biała
Wodzisław
Śląski
Rybnik

Prešov
Poprad Košice

Nyíregyháza
Debrecen

ROMANIA

Mures

udeten Mts.

Ostrava

Žilina
Martin

Trenčín

SLOVAKIA

Ružomberok
Banská
Bystrica
Lučenec Ózd

Miskolc

Tisza

Szolnok

Kecskemét

Békéscsaba
Szeged

SERBIA

Elbe
Kladno
PRAGUE
Plzeň
Pardubice
CZECH REPUBLIC

Olomouc

Morava
Brno

Nitra
Piešťany
Trnava
Váh

BRATISLAVA

BUDAPEST

Danube

Danube

Jihlava

Tábor

Stratonice
České
Budějovice

AUSTRIA

Sopron

Szombathely

Zalaegerszeg

Nagykanizsa

Győr
Tatabánya

Székesfehérvár

Veszprém
Balaton

Drava

HUNGARY

Great Hungarian Pln

Szekszárd
Baja

Pécs
Kaposvár

Plain

SLOVENIA

ITALY

CROATIA

BOSNIA -
HERZEGOVINA

Adriatic
Sea

ROMANIA

◆ Built in 1357, Charles Bridge was the
only crossing point of the Vltava in
Prague until the 19th century.

◆ With a surface area of around
231 sq mi (598 sq km) Lake Balaton
has an average depth of only 11 ft (3.25 m).

◆ The Great Hungarian Plain (Alföld) stretches south from Budapest
to the borders of Croatia and Serbia and east to Ukraine and
Romania. It covers an area of 20,000 sq miles (51,800 sq km)
and is almost completely flat.

Southeast Europe

At 11:15 am, on June 28, 1914, Archduke Francis Ferdinand and his wife were shot dead by Gavrilo Princip in Sarajevo. This single act precipitated World War I, which eventually lead to the death of almost 9 million troops.

Born in Zagreb in 1892, Marshall Tito was the president of the former Yugoslavia from 1953 until his death in 1980.

The Danube forms all or part of the border between nine different European nations; Germany, Austria, Slovakia, Hungary, Croatia, Serbia, Romania, Bulgaria, and the Ukraine.

SLOVAKIA

AUSTRIA

HUNGARY

ROMANIA

BUL

SLOVENIA

CROATIA

ZAGREB

Samobor

Karlovac

Ogulin

Gospić

Rijeka

Pula

Cres

Krk

Pag

Zadar

Dugi Otok

Šibenik

Split

Brač

Makarska

Knin

Bihać

Prijedor

Banja Luka

Ključ

Sana

Una

Sisak

Koprivnica

Varaždin

Čakovec

Bjelovar

Virovitica

Nova Gradiška

Slavonski Brod

Đakovo

Osijek

Drava

BOSNIA &
HERZEGOVINA

Rep. Srpska

Doboj

Modriča

Bosanski Šamac

Tuzla

Zvornik

Srebrenica

Zenica

Fojnica

SARAJEVO

Fed. Bosna
i Hercegovina

Konjic

Livno

Mostar

Dinaric Alps

Dinara

Drina

Loznica

Šabac

Vukovar

Sombor

Subotica

Kanjiža

Bačka Topola

Vojvodina

Novi Sad

Zrenjanin

Vršac

Pančevo

BELGRADE

Smederevo

SERBIA

Kragujevac

Čačak

Kraljevo

Morava

Kopaonik

Kruševac

Aleksinac

Niš

Zaječar

Danube

ROMANIA

Danube

◆ Macedonia's capital, Skopje, was hit by a devastating earthquake in 1963. Around 80% of the city's buildings were damaged or destroyed and over 1000 people killed.

◆ Under an extreme communist regime between 1944 and 1991, Albania was for many years the only officially atheist state in the world.

◆ European eels migrate thousands of miles from their birthplace in the Sargasso Sea to live most of their 10-year lives in Lake Ohrid, before returning to the Atlantic to spawn and die.

The Mediterranean

UNITED
KINGDOM *Thames* NETHERLANDS **GERMAN**
BELGIUM **LUX.**
English Channel *Rhine*

50° *Seine* E U

Loire **FRANCE** **SWITZ.** LIECH.
Danube

0 km 400 *L. Geneva*
0 miles 400

A *T* *L* *A* *N* *T* *I* *C*

Bay
of
Biscay *Dordogne* *Massif* *Central* *Rhône* *Po* SA
MARI
Apennin

O *C* *E* *A* *N* *Garonne* Marseille Genoa *Apennin*
MONACO
Livorno

Pyrenees *Golfe* VATICAN
du CITY
ANDORRA *Lion* *Corsica*

Ebro Barcelona

PORTUGAL **SPAIN** *Balearic Is.* *Sardinia* *Tyrrher*
Sea

40° *Tagus*
Iberian Valencia *M* *e* *d* *i* *t*
Peninsula

Guadalquivir

Gibraltar Algiers Tunis
(UK) Gibraltar Oran *Tell Atlas*
Strait of Gibraltar **TUNISI**

Madeira Sfax
(Portugal) **MOROCCO** *Atlas Mountains* Trip

30° **ALGERIA** *Chott el Jerid*

Grand Erg
Canary Is. *Occidental* *Grand Erg*
(Spain) *Oriental*

A **F** **R** **I**

S *a* *h* *a*

A B C D E

POLAND

CZECH REP.

USTRIA

SLOVAKIA

HUNGARY

Hungarian Plain

SLOVENIA

CROATIA

BOS. & HERZ.

SERBIA

Dinaric Alps

ITALY

MONTENEGRO

ALBANIA

Naples

Sicily

Ionian Sea

MALTA

UKRAINE

Dnieper

Carpathians

MOLDOVA

ROMANIA

Danube

BULGARIA

Balkan Mts.

Rhodope Mts.

MACEDONIA

Pindus Mts.

Aegean Sea

Lesbos

GREECE

Piraeus

Peloponnese

Kos

Rhodes

Crete

Danube Delta

Adriatic Sea

Sea of Azov

Crimea

RUSSIAN FEDERATION

Black Sea

Bosporus

GEORGIA

Caucasus Mts.

TURKEY

Anatolia

Taurus Mts.

Izmir

Lake Van

Cyprus

× × ×

SYRIA

LEBANON

Haifa

ISRAEL

Anti-Lebanon

Euphrates

Tigris

IRAQ

Syrian Desert

ASIA

Gulf of Sirte

rranean

Sea

Nile Delta

Port Said

Suez Canal

JORDAN

Nile

SAUDI ARABIA

L I B Y A

C

a

r

a

E G Y P T

Libyan Desert

Arabian Peninsula

Red Sea

Bulgaria & Greece

Sofia's skyline is dominated by the gold domes of the Alexander Nevski Memorial Church, which took craftsmen and artists some thirty years to build between 1882 and 1912.

Built between 447 and 438 BCE, the Parthenon survived almost unscathed for over 2000 years until, in 1687, a gunpowder magazine beneath the building exploded causing considerable damage.

ROMANIA

BULGARIA

Black Sea

Dobrich

Varna

Razgrad

Shumen

Ruse

Santimbu

Burgas

Pleven

Loveech

Gabrovo

Shliven

Yambol

Vratsa

Stara Zagora

Kazanlăk

Balkan Mountains

Plovdiv

Pernik

SOFIA

Yazovir Iskăr

Pazardzhik

Velingrad

Khaskovo

Orestiáda

TURKEY

Komotini

Rhodope Mountains

Xánthi

Blagoevgrad

Petrich

Dráma

Kavála

Alexandroúpoli

Marmara Denizi

Mítilni

Lésvos

Sanothráki

Thracian Sea

Thásos

Sérres

Akrotírio Pínes

Akrotírio Drépano

Límnos

Kilkís

Stýmonas

Vardar

Thessaloníki

Kalamariá

Thermaïkós Kólpos

Akrotírio Palioúri

Vóreies Sporádes

Katerini

Kozáni

Véroia

Flórina

MACEDONIA

Lake Ohrid

Lake Prespa

ALBANIA

Ioánnina

Tríkala

Lárisa

Pindus

Pineiós

Kardítsa

Vólos

GREECE

Kérkyra

Préveza

25°

20°

Olt

Danube

Danube

Vidin

Maritsa

Tundzha

Maritsa

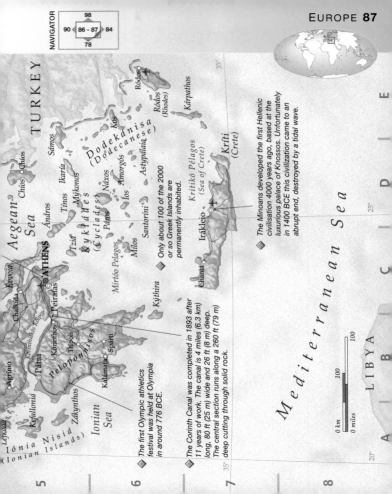

TURKEY

Aegean Sea

ATHENS

Chalkída

Évvoia

Ándros

Tziá

Kýklades
(Cyclades)

Mýkonos

Tínos

Ikaría

Sámos

Chíos · Chíos

Náxos

Páros

Íos

Amorgós

Dodekánisa
(Dodecanese)

Astypálaia

Kos

Kárpathos

Ródos

Ródos
(Rhodes)

Santoríni

Mílos

Mirtóo Pélagos

Kýthira

Kritikó Pélagos
(Sea of Crete)

Chaniá

Iráklejo

Kríti
(Crete)

◆ Only about 100 of the 2000
or so Greek Islands are
permanently inhabited.

◆ The Minoans developed the first Hellenic
civilisation 4000 years ago, based at the
luxurious palace of Knossos. Unfortunately
in 1400 BCE this civilization came to an
abrupt end, destroyed by a tidal wave.

Ágrínio

Lefkáda

Kefalloniá

Pátra

Korinthiakós Kólpos

Kórinthos · Peiraiás

Trípoli

Pelopónnisos

Spárti

Kalamáta

Zákynthos

Iónia Nisiá
(Ionian Islands)

Ionian
Sea

◆ The first Olympic athletics
festival was held at Olympia
in around 776 BCE.

◆ The Corinth Canal was completed in 1893 after
11 years of work. The canal is 4 miles (6.3 km)
long, 80 ft (25 m) wide and 26 ft (8 m) deep.
The central section runs along a 260 ft (79 m)
deep cutting through solid rock.

Mediterranean Sea

LIBYA

0 km   100
0 miles   100

35°

25°

20°

5   6   7   8

The Baltic States & Belarus

◆ Rich oil shale deposits in northern Estonia are quarried, crushed, and heated to produce almost 7,000 barrels of oil a day.

◆ Low salinity and the shallow coastal waters cause pack ice to accumulate at the head of the Gulf of Bothnia and off Finland during most winters; occasionally the ice becomes banked up in pressure ridges that are almost 50 ft (15 m) high.

RUSSIAN

FINLAND

SWEDEN

Gulf of Bothnia

Gotland

BALTIC SEA

Gulf of Finland

Narva Bay

Kohtla-Järve
Narva

Lake
Peipus

Lake
Pskov

Loksa

Rakvere

TALLINN

Paldiski

Tapa
Paide

Viru

Tartu

Võru

ESTONIA

Hiiumaa

Haapsalu

Vōrtsu

Pärnu

Viljandi

Valga

LATVIA

Virtsu

Gulf of
Riga

Bārtnieku
Ezers

Valmiera

Cēsis

Madona

Rēzekne

Saaremaa

Kuressaare

Kolka

Talsi

RIGA

Ogre

Jelgava

Jēkabpils

Daugavpils

Navapolask

Western Dvina

Venta

Saldus

Dobele

Biržai

Talsi

Ventspils

Kuldīga

Venta

Mažeikiai

Radviliškis

Šiauliai

Panevėžys

Utena

Ukmergė

Nēris

LITHUANIA

Liepāja

Kretinga

Plunge

Telšiai

Kelmė

Tauragė

Jurbarkas

Kaunas

Marijampolė

Klaipėda

Šilutė

Nemunas

Courland
Lagoon

Gusev

KALININGRAD
(part of Russian
Federation)

Kaliningrad

Chernyakhovsk

Mariampole

Formed in 1945 from the northern half of German East Prussia, and ceded to Russia under the Potsdam agreement, Kaliningrad oblast became a true enclave, completely separated from the rest of Russia, when Lithuania and Belarus achieved their independence in 1991.

Covering an area of approximately 104,000 sq miles (270,000 sq km) Pripet Marshes are the largest area of marshland in Europe.

Following the break up of the Soviet Union the Commonwealth of Independent States was established on December 8, 1991 by a treaty signed at Minsk, with the intent of coordinating the foreign policies of the newly independent former Soviet republics.

Ukraine, Moldova & Romania

◆ On April 25, 1986, engineers accidentally initiated an uncontrolled chain reaction in the number 4 reactor of the Chornobyl' nuclear power plant. The resulting explosion released 8 tons (tonnes) of radioactive material in the world's worst ever nuclear accident.

◆ Vlad Dracula or Vlad the Impaler was the real life prince upon whom Bram Stoker based his famous Count Dracula. Dracula was born in Transylvania in 1431 in the town of Sighisoara.

POLAND

BELARUS

Pripet

Pripet Marshes

Kovel

Luts'k

Korosten

Rivne

L'viv

Zhytomyr

SLOVAKIA

Ternopil'

U K R

Ivano-Frankivs'k

Khmel'-nyts'kyy

Vinnyts

Uzhhorod

Kam''yanets-Podil's'kyy

Chernivtsi

Dniester

HUNGARY

Satu Mare

Suceava

Botoşani

Ribnita

Bălţi

MOLDOVA

Baia Mare

Oradea

Dej

Transylvania

Cluj-Napoca

Piatra-Neamţ

Dubăsari

Iaşi

CHIŞINĂ

Arad

Târgu Mureş

Bacău

Tiraspol

Alba Iulia

Sighisoara

Tighina (Bendery)

Timişoara

Deva

R O M A N I A

Basarabeasca

Reşiţa

Sibiu

Carpaţii Meridionali

Focşani

Braşov

Gălaţi

Reni

Râmnicu Vâlcea

Buzău

Târgovişte

Tulcea

Drobeta-Turnu Severin

Piteşti

Ploieşti

Brăila

SERBIA

Craiova

Olt

BUCHAREST

Danube

Constanţa

Eforie Sud

Corabia

Giurgui

Mangalia

BULGARIA

30°

35°

RUSSIAN

FEDERATION

40°

1

Shostka

Chernihiv

Chornobyl'

Kyyivs'ke Vdskh.

KIEV

Sumy

◆ A monument in central Kiev stands as testament to the 7–12 million Ukrainian peasants who died during the Great Famine of 1932–33.

Kanins'ke Vdskh.

Bila Tserkva

Lubny

Kharkiv

50°

2

A I N E

Cherkasy

Poltava

Kremenchuts'ke Vdskh.

Kremenchuk

Donets

Syeverodonets'k

Oleksandriya

Slov''yans'k

Luhans'k

Kirovohrad

Pavlohrad

Horlivka

Kostyantynivka

Dnipropetrovs'k

Makiyivka

Yenakiyeve

Kryvyy Rih

Nikopol'

Donets'k

Krasnyy Luch

3

Pivdennyy Buh

Zaporizhzhya

Mariupol'

Kakhovs'ka Vdskh.

Mykolayiv

Melitopol'

Berdyans'k

Kherson

Kakhovka

◆ In 1872 an ironworks was founded at Donets'k by British industrialist John Hughes (from whom the town's pre-Revolutionary name Yuzovka was derived) to produce rails for the growing Russian transportation network.

Odesa

Dnieper

Sea

of

Azov

Karkinits'ka Zatoka

Kryms'kyy Pivostriv

Kerch

RUSSIAN

45°

4

Yevpatoriya

Simferopol'

B l a c k

FEDERATION

Sevastopol'

Yalta

S e a

0 km   100

0 miles   100

5

◆ Odesa was one of the major flashpoints in the Russian Revolution of 1905, and was the scene of the mutiny on the warship Potemkin, when sailors protesting against the serving of rotten meat eventually threw the officers overboard.

40°

E   F   35°   G   H

European Russia

A | B | C | D | E

ARCTIC OCEAN

Norwegian Sea

Arctic Circle

0 km 400
0 miles 400

NORWAY

SWEDEN

Gulf of Bothnia

Baltic Sea

FINLAND

ESTONIA

LATVIA

LITHUANIA

Novaya Zemlya

Karskoye More

Ostrov Vaygach

Barents Sea

Ostrov Kolguyev

Murmansk

Kol'skiy Poluostrov

Beloye More

Arkhangel'sk

Mezen'

Pinega

Severnaya Dvina

Onezhskoye Ozero

Petrozavodsk

Ladozhskoye Ozero

Sankt Petersburg

Pskov

Onega

Velikiy Novgorod

Velikiye Luki

Cherepovets

Rybinskoye Vdkhr.

Smolensk

Tver'

BELARUS

Dnepr

R U S S I A N   F E D E R A T I O N

(Ural Mountains)

Arctic Circle

Usa

Vorkuta

Pechora

Ukhta

Syktyvkar

Kama

Kotlas

Vologda

Yaroslavl'

Kirov

MOSCOW

◆ The port of Murmansk remains ice free throughout the winter thanks to the Gulf Stream, whereas St. Petersburg 600 miles (965 km) to the south on the Baltic Sea is ice-bound between December and May.

1 | 2 | 3

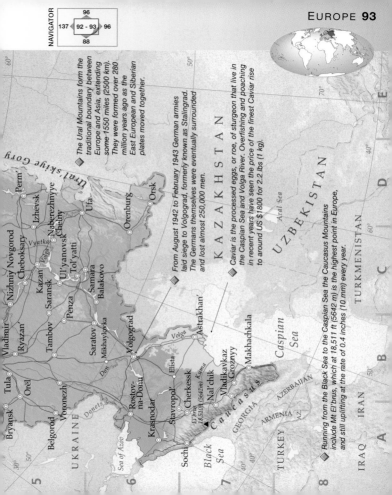

The Ural Mountains form the traditional boundary between Europe and Asia, extending some 1550 miles (2500 km). They were formed over 280 million years ago as the East European and Siberian plates moved together.

From August 1942 to February 1943 German armies laid siege to Volgograd, formerly known as Stalingrad. The Germans themselves were eventually surrounded and lost almost 250,000 men.

Caviar is the processed eggs, or roe, of sturgeon that live in the Caspian Sea and Volga River. Overfishing and poaching in recent years have seen the price of the finest Caviar rise to around US $1800 for 2.2 lbs (1 kg).

Running from the Black Sea to the Caspian Sea the Caucasus Mountains include Mt El'brus, which at 18,511 ft (5642 m) is the highest point in Europe, and still uplifting at the rate of 0.4 inches (10 mm) every year.

KAZAKHSTAN

UZBEKISTAN

TURKMENISTAN

Ural'skiye Gory

Perm'

Izhevsk

Naberezhnyye Chelny

Ufa

Orsk

Orenburg

Nizhniy Novgorod

Cheboksary

Vyatka

Kazan'

Saransk

Ul'yanovsk

Samara

Tol'yatti

Balakovo

Vladimir

Ryazan'

Tambov

Penza

Saratov

Tula

Orël

Mikhaylovka

Volgograd

Astrakhan'

Bryansk

Belgorod

Voronezh

Rostov-na-Donu

Elista

Volga

Don

Kama

Caspian Sea

Aral Sea

Donets

UKRAINE

Stavropol'

Cherkessk

Nal'chik

Vladikavkaz

Grozny

Makhachkala

El'brus 18,511ft (5642m)

Caucasus

Krasnodar

Sochi

Sea of Azov

Black Sea

GEORGIA

AZERBAIJAN

ARMENIA

TURKEY

IRAN

IRAQ

North & West Asia

ARCTIC

1 80°

Franz Josef Land

Severnaya Zemlya

Svalbard (Norway)

Novaya Zemlya

Kara Sea

Nort

Khe

Norwegian Sea

North Cape

Barents Sea

2 Arctic Circle

60°

Gulf of Bothnia

Lake Onega

Northern Dvina

R U S S I A N

Centra

Ob'

West Siberian Plain

Irtysh

Ob'

Ishim

Yenisey

Chulym

Ang

S

Lake Ladoga

Baltic Sea

North Sea

Volga

3

KALININGRAD (Russ. Fed.)

Central Russian Upland

Volga

Don

Ural

KAZAKHSTAN

Aral Sea

Lake Balkhash

Ili

Ozero Zaysan

A

S

Tien Shan

E U R O P E

Danube

Black Sea

Caucasus

Caspian Sea

UZBEKISTAN

Amu Darya

KYRGYZSTAN

4 40°

GEORGIA
ARMENIA AZERB.

TURKEY

Lake Van

TURKMEN.

TAJIKISTAN

SYRIA

Mediterranean Sea

LEBANON

IRAQ

Tigris

IRAN

AFGHANISTAN

Tibetan Plateau

Himalayas

ISRAEL JORDAN

Euphrates

KUWAIT

The Gulf

Ganges

Tropic of Cancer

20°

BAHRAIN
QATAR

Nile

SAUDI ARABIA

Red Sea

U.A.E.

OMAN

5

A F R I C A

YEMEN

Gulf of Aden

Socotra (Yemen)

Arabian Sea

Bay of Bengal

A   B   C   D

20°   40°   60°   80°

O C E A N

140° 160° 180° 80° 1

Ozero Taymyr

Laptev Sea

New Siberian Islands

East Siberian Sea

Siberian Lowland

Wrangel Island

Long Strait

Chukchi Sea

Kotuy *Anabar* *Olenëk* *Lena* *Yana* *Indigirka* *Kolyma*

Arctic Circle

Bering Strait

Siberian Plateau

F E D E R A T I O N

Velikaya

2

b *e* *r* *i* *a*

Chona *Lena* *Amga*

Bering Sea

60°

Vitim

Lake Baikal

Sea of Okhotsk

Kamchatka

I *Amur* *Zeya* **A**

Aleutian Islands

3

Argun *Sakhalin*

Kurile Islands

Gobi

Sea of Japan (East Sea)

(administered by Russian Federation, claimed by Japan.)

40°

Yellow River

P A C I F I C

4

Yangtze

East China Sea

O C E A N

Tropic of Cancer

20°

Mekong

South China Sea

0 km   800
0 miles   800

5

E 120° F 140° G 160° H 180°

Russia & Kazakhstan

NORWAY
GERMANY
DENMARK
SWEDEN
FINLAND
ARCTIC
Barents Sea
Murmansk
Zemlya
Frantsa
Iosifa
Novaya Zemlya
Karskoye More
POLAND
KALININGRAD
(part of Russian Federation)
LAT. EST.
LITH.
BELARUS
Pskov
Sankt-Peterburg
Velikiy
Novgorod
Arkhangel'sk
Vorkuta
Salekhard
Nori'lsk
UKRAINE
MOLDOVA
Cherepovets
MOSCOW
Vologda
Bryansk
Yaroslavl'
Tula
Ryazan'
Nizhniy
Novgorod
Kirov
Syktyvkar
*Zapadno-
Sibirskaya*
Ravnina
RUS
Voronezh
Kazan'
Izhevsk
Perm'
Serov
Yekaterinburg
Nizhnevartovsk
FEDE
Rostov-
na-Donu
Samara
Ufa
Chelyabinsk
Volgograd
GEORGIA
Sochi
Stavropol'
Nal'chik
Ural'sk
Orenburg
Rudnyy
Kostanay
Petropavlovsk
Omsk
Krasnoyars
Tomsk
Novosibirsk
ARM.
Groznyy
Makhachkala
Astrakhan'
Orsk
Kokshetau
ASTANA
Pavlodar
Kemerovo
AZ.
Aktau
Caspian Sea
KAZAKHSTAN
Karaganda
Barnaul
Novokuznetsk
Semipalatinsk
Ust'-
Kamenogorsk
*Aral
Sea*
Zhezkazgan
Kyzylorda
Balkhash
*Ozero
Balkhash*
IRAN
TURKMENISTAN
UZBEKISTAN
Shymkent
Taraz
Taldykorgan
Almaty
CHINA
KYRGYZSTAN

OCEAN

80°

Ostrov
Vrangelya

70°

160°

Vostochno-
Sibirskoye
More

Pevek

Anadyr'

60°

180°

1

100°

Severnaya
Zemlya

140°

120°

Novosibirskiye
Ostrova

Ambarchik

Bering
Sea

170°

More
Laptevykh

Ossora

2

Poluostrov
Taymyr

Ozero Taymyr

Tiksi

Ust'-Kamchatsks

50°

160°

Olenëk

Verkhoyanskiy Khrebet

Magadan

Poluostrov
Kamchatka

Petropavlovsk
-Kamchatskiy

Okhotsk

3

Srednesibirskoye
Ploskogor'ye

Lena

S I A N

Yakutsk

Sea of
Okhotsk

Sibir
(Siberia)

Suntar

150°

R A T I O N

Lena

Sakhalin

Kuril'skiye Ostrova

Kansk

Bratsk

Skovorodno

Komsomol'sk-
na-Amure

4

Yuzhno-
Sakhalinsk

Ozero
Baykal

Blagoveshchensk

Khabarovsk

40°

Irkutsk

Chita

Amur

Ulan-Ude

C H I N A

JAPAN

130°

◆ The Trans-Siberian Railroad, completed in 1916, runs
5866 miles (9440 km) between Moscow and Vladivostok.
Crossing eight time zones, the journey takes eight days.

Vladivostok

0 km   500

0 miles   500

MONGOLIA

100°   110°   120°

E   F   G   H

Turkey & the Caucasus

ROMANIA

Black Sea

BULGARIA

◆ An average of 50,000 commercial ships pass through the Bosporus a year, along with thousands of ferries and smaller passenger boats. The strait is three times busier than the Suez Canal and four times as busy as the Panama Canal.

Edirne • Kırklareli

GREECE
Tekirdağ

Bosporus

Zonguldak • *Küre Dağları* • Sinop

Kastamonu • Samsun

Çanakkale Boğazı (Dardanelles)

Marmara Denizi

İstanbul

Karabük

Ördu

Çalık Dağları

Çanakkale

Bursa • İzmit • Adapazarı

Çankırı • *Kızıl Irmak*

Çorum

Ayvalık

Lésvos

Balıkesir

Eskişehir

ANKARA

Kırıkkale

Tokat

Sivas

Manisa • Uşak

Kütahya

T U R K

Chíos

İzmir

Afyon

Anatolia

Nevşehir • Kayseri

Sámos

Aydın

Denizli

Isparta

Tuz Gölü

Konya

Niğde

Kahraman-maraş

Muğla

Bodrum

Ereğli

Toros Dağları

Adana • Osmaniye

Dalaman

Antalya

Mersin • Tarsus

Gaziantep

Ródos

Megísti

Antalya Körfezi

İskenderun

Antakya

Kríti

Kárpathos

TURKISH REPUBLIC OF NORTHERN CYPRUS (recognized only by Turkey)

Girne (Kyrenia)

Gazimağusa (Famagusta)

NICOSIA

Mediterranean Sea

Paphos

Larnaca

Limassol

CYPRUS

LEBANON

RUSSIAN FEDERATION

◆ An earthquake struck Armenia in 1988,
killing 55,000 people and devastating
the country's infastructure.

*Caspian
Sea*

Gagra
Sokhumi
Och'amch'ire
P'ot'i
Bat'umi
Hopa
Trabzon   Rize
Doğu Karadeniz Dağları

Caucasus

Enguri

K'ut'aisi
GEORGIA
T'BILISI   Rust'avi

Quba

Kura

Vanadzor   Gänca
Gyumri   Mingäçevir
Kars   Sumqayıt
ARMENIA **AZERBAIJAN** **BAKU**

Sevana Lich
YEREVAN Nagorno-
Aras Karabakh
Xankändi

Erzincan   Erzurum
E Y

*Büyükağrı Dağı
(Mount Ararat)
16,853ft (5137m)* ▲

AZERBAIJAN

Naxçıvan

Aras

Länkäran

Elazig
Güney Doğu Toroslar
Malatya   Muş   *Van
Gölü*
Diyarbakır   Van
Adıyaman   Batman
Şanlıurfa   Mardin   *Kurdistan*

Tigris

Siirt

◆ Azerbaijan has substantial oil reserves located
in and around the Caspian Sea. They were
some of the earliest oilfields in the world
to be exploited.

I R A N

◆ The salty water of Lake Van inhibits all animal
life except the Darekh, a small fish that has
adapted to the harsh conditions.

◆ Atatürk Dam, one of the largest dams in the world, was completed in 1990.
The reservoir behind the dam covers an area of 315 sq miles (816 sq km)
and often requires interruptions in the flow of the Euphrates River
to maintain water levels.

S Y R I A   **I R A Q**

0 km   200

0 miles   200

The Near East

The Euphrates is 1700 miles (2470 km) long and drains an area of 171,000 sq mi (443,000 sq km). Although less than 30 percent of the river's drainage basin is in Turkey, about 95 percent of the river's water originates in the Turkish highlands.

Lebanon only has one permanent river, the Nahr el Litani, which runs for 110 miles (175 km).

Manufactured by a secret process, Damascus steel was much prized in the preindustrial era as an extremely hard metal used for high quality sword blades.

IRAQ

TURKEY

Tigris

Al Qamishli

Al Hasakah

Al Jazirah

Dayr az Zawr

Euphrates

Ar Raqqah

SYRIA

Buhayrat al-Asad

Tudmur

Syrian

Halab

A'zāz

Idlib

Hamāh

Hims

Orontes

Anti-Lebanon

DAMASCUS

Jabal Lubnan

Al Lādhiqiyah

Tartūs

LEBANON

Tripoli

Baalbek

Zahlé

Litani

BEIRUT

Saida

Sour

Mediterranean Sea

CYPRUS

0 km 100

0 miles 100

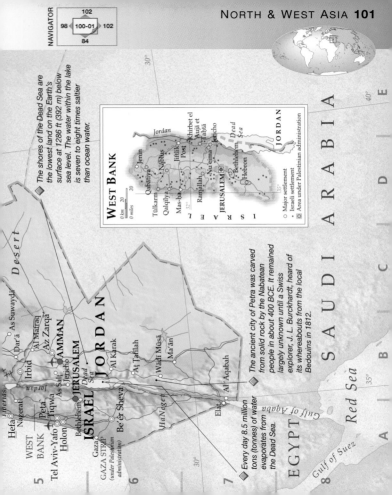

The Middle East

KAZAKHSTAN

UZBEKISTAN

TURKMENISTAN

AFGHANISTAN

PAKISTAN

RUSSIAN FEDERATION

UKRAINE

GEORGIA

AZERBAIJAN

ARMENIA

TURKEY

SYRIA

LEBANON

CYPRUS

ISRAEL

JORDAN

IRAQ

IRAN

KUWAIT

Syr Darya

Kyzyl Kum

Aral Sea

Ustyurt Plateau

Caspian Sea

Black Sea

Sea of Azov

Anatolia

Syrian Desert

Sinai

Dead Sea

An Nafūd

Al Jawf

Sakākah

Ḥāʾil

Tabūk

Jabal ash Shā...

Wādī al Ḥamḍ

Mashhad

Neyshābūr

Zāhedān

Khāsh

Kermān

Bandar-e...

Ḥāmūn-e...

Sabzevār

Gorgān

Sārī

Āmol

Rasht

Ardabīl

Tabrīz

Khvoy

Van Gölü

Marāgheh

Orūmīyeh

Kirkūk

Arbīl

Al Mawşil (Mosul)

Tigris

Euphrates

TEHRAN

Qom

Kāshān

Eşfahān

Yazd

Dasht-e Kavīr

Irānshahr

Plateau

Zagros Mountains

Kūhhā-ye Zāgros

Shīrāz

Bandar-e Būshehr

Ahvāz

Ābādān

Dezfūl

Arāk

Hamadān

Qazvīn

Zanjān

Sanandaj

Kermānshāh (Bākhtarān)

BAGHDAD

Buḥayrat ath Tharthār

Euphrates

An Najaf

Al Başrah (Basra)

KUWAIT CITY

The...

Wādī al Bāṭin

Caucasus

In the 10th century, the Grand Vizier of Persia took his entire library with him wherever he went. The 117,000 volume library was carried by camels trained to walk in alphabetical order.

Four thousand years ago Babylonian law laid down a minimum wage for every class of workers in the kingdom.

0 km   400
0 miles 400

Saudi Arabia contains the world's largest oil reserves. The region can produce around 10 million barrels of oil every day.

Ar Rub' al Khali, also known as the Empty Quarter, is the largest uninterrupted sand desert in the world, with sand dune ridges up to 25 miles (40 km) long.

Every Muslim must make at least one pilgrimage to Mecca during their lifetime. Muslims regard the small shrine called the Ka'bah, located near the center of the Great Mosque in Mecca, as the most sacred place on Earth.

The name "Red Sea" is derived from the extensive blooms of algae that occasionally occur. These change color when they die, turning the sea's normally intense blue-green waters a deep red.

Gulf of Oman
Tropic of Cancer
Sharjah
MUSCAT
Dubayy
Ar Rustāq Nazwa Ramlat Sur
Suhār
Jazīrat Maṣīrah
Al Wahtibah
Aṣ Ṣuwayra
Al Huffūf
QATAR Jūzur al Ḥalānīyāt
MANAMA
ABU DHABI **DOHA**
U.A.E.
Dawḥah
Jazīrat Maṣīrah
Duqm
Ḥaramīyāt
RIYADH
Layla
SAUDI ARABIA
Harad
Ṣawqirah
Ṣalālah
Arabian Sea
Arabian Peninsula
Sanāw
Sayhūt
OMAN
Suquṭrā (Socotra) (to Yemen)
Raas Xaafuun
As Sulayyil
Ar Rub' al Khāli (Empty Quarter)
Wuday'ah
Say'ūn
Ḥaḍramawt
Al Mukallā
Gulf of Aden
YEMEN
Najrān
Ramlat as Sab'atayn
INDIAN OCEAN
Makkah (Mecca)
Aṭ Ṭā'if
Abhā
Sa'dah
SANA
SOMALILAND
Ta'izz
Jīzān
Adan
SOMALIA
JIDDAH (JEDDA)
Al Madīnah
Jazā'ir Farasān
Al Ḥudaydah
DJIBOUTI
Red Sea
ETHIOPIA
ERITREA
SUDAN
GYPT

Central Asia

KAZAKHSTAN

Aral Sea

◆ Since 1960, the Aral Sea has shrunk by 40 percent, becoming extremely saline and consequently losing all but one of it's once-abundant fish species.

Ustyurt Plateau

Turan Lowland

Syr Darya

Köneürgench

Nukus

UZBEKISTAN

Caspian

Daşoguz

Urganch

To'rtko'l

Uchquduq

Zarafshon

Aydarko'l Ko'li

Türkmenbaşy

TURKMENISTAN

Hazar

Balkanabat

Bereket

Turan

Garagum

Buxoro

Seýdi

Navoiy

Samarqar

Qarshi

Sea

Serdar

Baharly

Gökdepe

Abadan

AŞGABAT

Türkmenabat

Anıu Darya

Kaka

Garagum Kanaly

Mary

Bayramaly

Saýat

Atamyrat

Tejen

◆ The desert of Kara Kum (Garagum) occupies over 70 percent of Turkmenistan, severely limiting human settlement across much of the country.

Murgap

Sheberghān

Āqcha

Mazār-e Shar

Meymaneh

Bālā Morghāb

Serhetabat

Darya-ye Morghāb

I R A N

Herāt

Harīrūd

AFGHANISTAN

◆ The Kara Kum (Garagum) Canal, the world's longest irrigation canal, stretches some 683 miles (1100 km) and is known as the "River of Life" as it irrigates large areas of arid land.

Farāh

Gereshk

Kalāt

Zaranj

Dasht-e Mārgow

Kandahār

Daryā-ye Helmand

0 km   200

0 miles   200

A   B   C   D

Ozero Balkhash

K A Z A K H S T A N

70°   80°

1

BISHKEK
Kara-Balta   Tokmak   Tyup
Talas   Karakol
Ozero
Issyk-Kul
KYRGYZSTAN   *Tien Shan*

SHKENT   Chirchiq
Namangan   Dzhalal-Abad   • Naryn
Olmaliq   Angren   Andijon
Qo'qon   Osh
roteppa   Khujand   Farg'ona   40°
Snlyukta   Khaydarkan
Zeravshan

◆ *Mount Communism was so named for being the highest point in the former Soviet Union, rising to 24,590 ft (7495 m).*

USHANBE   *Surkhob*
Norak   *Bartang*
Danghara   • Murghob
eppa   • Kulob   **C H I N A**
ırmez   • Farkhor   Khorugh
nölm   Feyzabad   *Pamir*
• Kondoz
• Baghlān
Pol-e   *Hindu Kush*
Khomri

◆ *Until recent years, people living in remote areas of Afghanistan were immunized against smallpox by having dried powdered scabs from victims of the disease blown up their noses. This treatment was invented by the Chinese in the 11th century, and is thought to be the oldest form of vaccination.*

Asadābād
ABUL   • Jalalābād

4

• Ghaznī
• Gardīz

◆ *Despite an area of 251,771 sq miles (652,090 sq km), Afghanistan has a limited road network and no railroads whatsoever, making access to much of the country extremely difficult.*

Indus

P A K I S T A N   **I N D I A**

70°   80°   30°

5

E   F   G   H

South & East Asia

Black Sea

Caspian Sea

Aral Sea

Syr Darya

Lake Balkhash

Irtysh

Yenisey

Uvs Nuur

Lake Baikal

Hovsgol Nuur

Altai Mountains

MONGOLIA

Tien Shan

Gobi

Yellow River

Iranian Plateau

Hindu Kush

Takla Makan Desert

Kunlun Mountains

Altun Shan

CHINA

The Gulf

Gulf of Oman

PAKISTAN

Indus

Sutlej

Thar Desert

Himalayas

Yamuna

Ganges

NEPAL

Plateau of Tibet

Brahmaputra

Salween

Mekong

▲ Mount Everest 29, 035ft (8850m)

BHUTAN

Yan

Rann of Kachchh

Gulf of Khambhat

INDIA

Deccan

Western Ghats

Eastern Ghats

BANGLADESH

MYANMAR (BURMA)

Irrawaddy

Red River

Xi Ji

VIETNAM

LAOS

Ha

Arabian Sea

Laccadive Islands (to India)

Bay of Bengal

Andaman Islands (to India)

Mekong

THAILAND

CAMBODIA

Tônle Sap

MALDIVES

Gulf of Mannar

SRI LANKA

Andaman Sea

Nicobar Islands (to India)

Gulf of Thailand

Equator

INDIAN

MALA

Sumatra

SINGA

Ja

OCEAN

0 km 1000

0 miles 1000

40°

60°

80°

100°

40°

20°

20°

140°

160°

40°

Amur

Ugun

Khingan Range

Manchuria
Plain

Lake Khanka

Sakhalin

Hokkaido

1

Liao He

Yalu

JAPAN

Sea of
Japan
(East Sea)

20°

NORTH
KOREA

Great Plain of China

SOUTH
KOREA

Yellow
Sea

Korea Strait

Honshu

Shikoku

PACIFIC

2

East China
Sea

Kyushu

Ryukyu Islands

Taiwan Strait

TAIWAN

Philippine

Sea

Northern
Marianas Is.
(to US)

OCEAN

3

Luzon Strait

racel Islands
puted)

Luzon

Guam
(to US)

outh China
Sea

PHILIPPINES

M i c r o n e s i a

pratly
slands
isputed)

Palawan

Sulu
Sea

Mindanao

Equator

4

UNEI

*Celebes
Sea*

Halmahera

M e l a n e s i a

Bismarck Archipelago

Solomon
Islands

A

orneo

Moluccas

Seram

Pegunungan Maoke

Solomon
Sea

NDONESIA

Celebes

New Guinea

5

Flores
Sea

Banda Sea

Lesser Sunda Islands

Arafura
Sea

Timor

EAST TIMOR

Coral
Sea

140°

160°

E

F

G

H

Western China & Mongolia

◇ The Altai Mountains provide one of the last refuges for the endangered snow leopard. There are thought to be only 600 animals left in the wild.

◇ The Turpan Depression is the lowest and hottest place in China. Temperatures can exceed 117°F (47°C) around the lake of Aydingkol Hu, which lies 505 ft (154 m) below sea level.

◇ Although forming around 20 percent of China's landmass, Tibet is sparsely populated, supporting only 1 percent of China's 1.3 billion population.

RUSSIAN FED

KAZAKHSTAN

Zapadnyy Sayan

Yenisey

Ulaangom
Uvs Nuur
Ölgiy
Hyargas Nuur
Har Us Nuur
Altay
Hovd
Hovsgol Nuur
Mörö
Tsetser
Altay
Bayanhongor
Hangayn Nuru

MONG

Altai Mountains

Ulungur Hu
Gurbantünggüt Shamo
Karamay
Kuytun
Shihezi
ÜRÜMQI
Qitai
Yining
Turpan
Hami
Bosten Hu
Xingxingxia
Dalain
G

KYRGYZSTAN
Ozero Issyk-Kul'
Tien Shan
Korla
Lop Nur
GANSU
Qilian Sha

Kashi
Yengisar
Shache
Tarim He
XINJIANG UYGUR ZIZHIQU
Ruoqiang
Altun Shan
Tarim Basin
TAJIKISTAN
AFGH.
Yecheng
Moyu
Qira
Taklimakan Shamo
Qaidam Pendi
Qinghai H
Golmud
Dulan

Karakoram Range
Kunlun Shan
AKSAI CHIN (administered by China, claimed by India)
Qingzang Gaoyuan (Plateau of Tibet)
QINGHAI
Bayan Har Sh
Tongtian He
Yushu
PAKISTAN
Kashmir
Indus
JAMMU AND KASHMIR
Rutög
Mekong
DEMCHOK/DÊMQOG (administered by China, claimed by India)
Gar
XIZANG ZIZHIQU (Tibet)
Nyima
Tanggula Shan
Amdo
Nagqu
Qamdo
Zanda
Tangra Yumco
Siling Co
Salween
INDIA
Brahmaputra
Nam Co
Damxung
Nyainqêntanglha Shan
ARUNACHAL PRADESH (claimed by China)
Himalayas
NEPAL
Lhazê
LHASA
Gyangzê
△ Mount Everest 29,035ft (8850m)
BHUTAN
INDIA

0 km   400
0 miles   400

50° 70° 80° 90° 100°
1
40°
2
70°
3
30°
4
5
A   B   C   D

80°

R A T I O N

Ozero Baykal

110°

120°

130°

Amur

Genhe

Jagdaqi

Argun (Ergun He)

Onon

Hailar

Selenga

Manzhouli

Hulun Nur

Sühbaatar

Darhan

HEILONGJIANG

Erdenet

ulgan

ULAN BATOR

Ondörhaan

Kerulen

Menengiyn Tal

Lake Khanka

Baruun-Urt

Saynshand

JILIN

40°

Da Hingan Ling

Xilinhot

Tongliao

Sea of Japan (East Sea)

alandzadgad

ayn Nu

Erenhot

Liao He

Chifeng

LIAONING

NORTH KOREA

Jining

BEIJING

Korea Bay

SOUTH KOREA

HOHHOT

TIANJIN

Bo Hai

JAPAN

Huang He

Baotou

Wuhai

Mu Us Shadi

NINGXIA HUIZU ZIZHIQU

Great Wall of China

SHANXI

Yellow Sea

East China Sea

NING

N

A

GANSU

Huang He (Yellow River)

SHAANXI

Han Shui

JIANGSU

30°

Chang Jiang (Yangtze)

HUBEI

ZHEJIANG

SICHUAN

CHONGQING

HUNAN

JIANGXI

FUJIAN

YUNNAN

GUIZHOU

110°

120°

TAIWAN

Tropic of Cancer

5

♦ The name Gobi Desert is derived from Mongolian meaning "waterless place." Bare rock rather than sand dunes typify the cold desert landscape that stretches for some 500,000 sq miles (1,295,000 sq km).

♦ Begun in the 7th century BCE, work on the 3700 mile (6000 km) long Great Wall of China continued for hundreds of years. A major renovation begun in 1386 took 200 years to complete.

♦ The Huang He (Yellow River) has flooded more than 1500 times in the last 1800 years. In 1931 catastrophic flooding was responsible for the deaths of 3.7 million people. The river has also changed its course at least nine times.

♦ Despite a population of 1.3 billion, China has only about 200 family names.

Eastern China & Korea

◆ Whereas European languages such as English or French use an alphabet of 26 letters, the Chinese language uses a system of over 50,000 characters or symbols.

◆ The "Yongle dadian," an encyclopedia of the Chinese Ming dynasty, had 22,937 chapters in 10,000 volumes. More than 2000 Chinese scholars worked on the book for 5 years before it was finished.

◆ Tangshan, China, suffered the deadliest earthquake of the 20th century on July 28, 1976. One quarter of the population was killed or seriously injured, with an estimated death toll of 242,000 people.

◆ Tiananmen Square in Beijing is the largest public square in the world covering an area of 100 acres (40.5 hectares).

RUSSIAN FEDERATION

MONGOLIA

NEI MONGOL (Inner Mongolia)

HEILONGJIANG

JILIN

LIAONING

NORTH KOREA

SOUTH KOREA

HEBEI

SHANXI

SHANDONG

NINGXIA

SHAANXI

QINGHAI

XINJIANG UYGUR ZIZHIQU

Amur (Heilong Jiang)

Xiao Hinggan Ling

Argun (Ergun He)

Shilka

Onon

Selenga

Ozero Baykal

Orhon

Qilian Shan

Qaidam Pendi

Qinghai Hu

Da Hinggan Ling (Greater Khingan Range)

Great Wall

Huang He (Yellow River)

Lake Khanka

Sea of Japan (East Sea)

Korea Bay

Bo Hai

LIAODONG BANDAO

SHANDONG BANDAO

Qiqihar

HARBIN

Mudanjiang

Jilin

CHANGCHUN

Fushun

Hunjiang

Ch'ŏngjin

Hamhŭng

PYONGYANG

Namp'o

Heicheng

Dandong

Dalian

Tangshan

TIANJIN

BEIJING

Datong

Shijiazhuang

TAIYUAN

Handan

Zibo

Qingdao

SHENYANG

Fuxin

Jinzhou

SEOUL

Taejŏn

Taegu

Pusan

YINCHUAN

LANZHOU

JAPAN

Cheju-do

East China
Sea

Yellow Sea

SHANGHAI

Nanjing

Hangzhou

Ningbo

Jiaxing

Wenzhou

Jinhua

ZHEJIANG

Shangrao

Okinawa (under Japan)

Tropic of Cancer

North Taiwan (China and Taiwan claim all of each other's territory)

TAIPEI

Taichung

Tainan

TAIWAN

Kaohsiung

Luzon Strait

PACIFIC

OCEAN

PHILIPPINES

◆ Li is the family name for over 87 million people in China.

Bengbu

Huainan

ANHUI

HUBEI

Jingdezhen

Fuzhou

FUJIAN

Xiamen

Shantou

Dongguan

HONG KONG (Xianggang)

Macao (Aomen)

GUANGZHOU

◆ By far the biggest tidal bore in the World is the Ch'ien-t'ang kiah (Hang-chou-fe) in China. At spring tides the wave attains a height of up to 25 ft (7.5 m) and a speed of 13-15 knots (24-27 km/h).

HENAN

Hanzhong

Mianyang

Nanchang

NANCHANG

Changsha

CHANGSHA

Yueyang

HUNAN

Hengyang

GUANGDONG

JIANGXI

Liuzhou

GUANGXI ZHUANGZU

NANNING

Hainan Dao

HAINAN

Paracel Islands (disputed by China, Taiwan and Vietnam)

South China Sea

Spratly Islands (disputed by China, Malaysia, Philippines, Taiwan and Vietnam)

SICHUAN Pendi

CHENGDU

Leshan

Zigong

CHONGQING

GUIZHOU

Guiyang

YUNNAN

KUNMING

Yalong Jiang

Jinsha Jiang

Wuliang Shan

Hengduan Shan

Salween

XIZANG ZIZHIQU (Tibet)

C H I N A

SHAANXI

HEBEI

Lichuan

WUHAN

HUBEI

Gulf of Tongkin

Red River

VIETNAM

LAOS

Mekong

THAILAND

CAMBODIA

M Y A N M A R

◆ The Giant Bamboo is the fastest growing plant in the world, able to grow at the rate of 3 ft (90 cm) a day.

0 km   400
0 miles 400

30°

20°

Tropic of Cancer

20°

10°

100°

110°

120°

E

D

C

B

A

5

6

7

8

Japan

At 33.4 miles (53.8 km), 14.3 miles (23.3 km) of which lie under the Tsugaru Strait, the Seikan Tunnel is the longest tunnel in the world. Construction began in 1964 and took 24 years to complete.

The Toyota Motor Corporation was first established in 1937 as a spin-off from Toyota Automatic Loom Works. The company now produces 8.5 million cars a year equivalent to one every three seconds.

CHINA

RUSSIAN FEDERATION

NORTH KOREA

Sea of Japan

(East Sea)

Liancourt Rocks
claimed by Japan

Ostrov Sakhalin

Kurile Islands
(administered by the
Russian Federation,
claimed by Japan)

Kurile Islands

Ostrov Iturup

Ostrov Shikotan

Ostrov Kunashir

Sea of Okhotsk

Nemuro

Abashiri

Kitami

Kushiro

Hokkaidō

Asahikawa

Obihiro

Tomakomai

La Pérouse Strait

Wakkanai

Rebun-tō

Rishiri-tō

Sapporo

Otaru

Hakodate

Okushiri-tō

Aomori

Hachinohe

Morioka

Honshū

Akita

Sendai

Niigata

Fukushima

Kōriyama

Iwaki

Hitachi

Sado

Shinano-gawa

Toyama

JAPAN

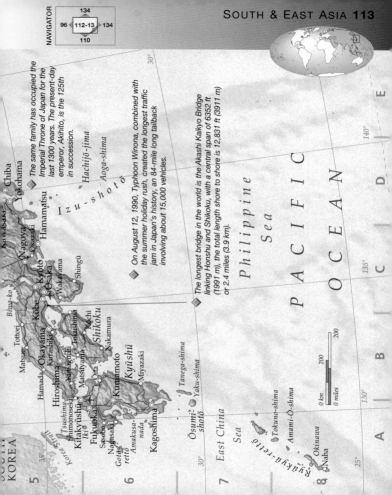

◆ The same family has occupied the Imperial Throne of Japan for the last 1300 years. The present-day emperor, Akihito, is the 125th in succession.

◆ On August 12, 1990, Typhoon Winona, combined with the summer holiday rush, created the longest traffic jam in Japan's history, an 84-mile long tailback involving about 15,000 vehicles.

◆ The longest bridge in the world is the Akashi Kaikyo Bridge linking Honshu and Shikoku, with a central span of 6352 ft (1991 m), the total length shore to shore is 12,831 ft (3911 m) or 2.4 miles (3.9 km).

KOREA

Korea Strait

Tsushima

Matsue

Tottori

Hamada

Hiroshima

Shimonoseki

Iki

Kitakyūshū

Fukuoka

Sasebo

Nagasaki

Gotō-rettō

Kumamoto

Amakusa-nada

Kagoshima

Ōsumi-shotō

Yaku-shima

Tanega-shima

Okayama

Kurashiki

Kōbe

Ōsaka

Kyōto

Shingu

Wakayama

Kōchi

Nakamura

Shikoku

Tokushima

Takamatsu

Matsuyama

Yamaguchi

Ōita

Miyazaki

Kyūshū

Biwa-ko

Ōtsu

Nagoya

Okazaki

Hamamatsu

Niigata

Chiba

Yokohama

Hachijō-jima

Aoga-shima

Izu-shotō

PHILIPPINE SEA

PACIFIC OCEAN

East China Sea

Tokuno-shima

Amami-O-shima

Ryūkyū-rettō

Okinawa

Naha

0 km   200

0 miles   200

38°

30°

30°

25°

130°

135°

140°

A   B   C   D   E

5

6

7

8

Southern India & Sri Lanka

A r a b i a n

S e a

Amīndīvi Is.

Lakshadweep
(part of India)

Kavaratti I.

Kalpeni I.

Minicoy I.

MALDIVES

◆ The Mumbai (Bombay) movie industry, known as
Bollywood, makes around 900 films each year,
compared to America's 100, making it the most
prolific film-producing country in the world.

◆ The word ghats, literally "stairs that
descend to a river," refers to the
stair-like appearance of the slopes
of the Western Ghats mountain
range, as they descend to
the coastal plain.

◆ There are over 1300 islands in the Maldives
but only about 200 are inhabited. All the
islands are low lying, none rising more
than 6 ft (1.8m) above sea level.

Mumbai
(Bombay)

Kalyān Nānded

Nizāmābād

Pune

D e c c a

Solāpur

Krishna

Hyderābād

I N D I

Karnātaka

Belgaum

Hubli

Kurnool

Pānāji

Dāvangere

Anantapur

Bangalore

Vello

Mangalore

Mysore

Tam

Salem

Na

Calicut

Coimbatore

Tiruch

rāppa

Ernākulam

Kerala

Cochin
(Kochi)

Madurai

Trivandrum

*Gul
of
Man*

Nāgercoil

*Ihavandippolhu
Atoll*

✈
● MALE'

Kolhumadulu Atoll

0 km   300

0 miles   300

Huvadhu Atoll

I N D I A N

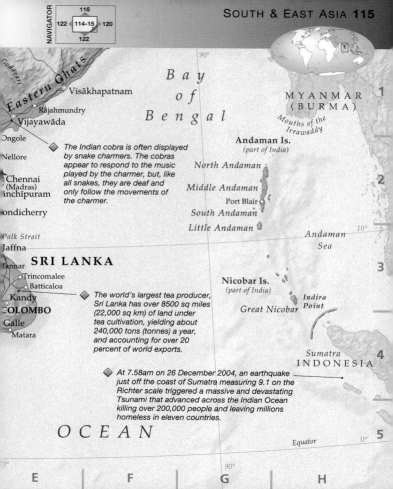

Godavari

Eastern Ghats

• Visākhapatnam

• Rājahmundry
◉ Vijayawāda

Ongole

Nellore

Chennai
(Madras)
īnchīpuram

ondicherry

Palk Strait
Jaffna

Iannar

• Trincomalee
• Batticaloa
Kandy
ⓒOLOMBO
Galle
• Matara

SRI LANKA

B a y
o f
B e n g a l

MYANMAR
(BURMA)

Mouths of the
Irrawaddy

Andaman Is.
(part of India)

North Andaman

Middle Andaman
Port Blair ◉
South Andaman
Little Andaman

Andaman
Sea

Nicobar Is.
(part of India)

Indira
Point
Great Nicobar

Sumatra
INDONESIA

O C E A N

Equator

10°

90°

0°

The Indian cobra is often displayed by snake charmers. The cobras appear to respond to the music played by the charmer, but, like all snakes, they are deaf and only follow the movements of the charmer.

The world's largest tea producer, Sri Lanka has over 8500 sq miles (22,000 sq km) of land under tea cultivation, yielding about 240,000 tons (tonnes) a year, and accounting for over 20 percent of world exports.

At 7.58am on 26 December 2004, an earthquake just off the coast of Sumatra measuring 9.1 on the Richter scale triggered a massive and devastating Tsunami that advanced across the Indian Ocean killing over 200,000 people and leaving millions homeless in eleven countries.

E   F   G   H

North India, Pakistan & Bangladesh

(claimed by India)

◆ The Karakoram Highway was finally completed in 1978 after 24,000 workers had toiled for almost 20 years. The road climbs to 16,000 ft (4890 m) at the Khunjerab Pass.

Hindu Kush

Indus

Karakoram Range

K2 28,251ft (8611m) ▲

(A "line of control" was agreed between India and Pakistan in 1972)

Mardān

Peshāwar
ISLĀMĀBĀD
Rāwalpindi

Jamu & Kashmir

AFGHANISTAN

Jhelum
Gujrāt

Pu n j a b

Chenab

Sargodha
Gujrānwāla

Lahore
Amritsar
Jalandhar

Toba Kākar Range

Faisalābād
Ludhiāna
Chandīgarh

IRAN

30°

Quetta

Dera Ghāzi Khān

Okāra

Multān

Meeru

Chāgai Hills

PAKISTAN

Bahāwalpur

Delhi

NEW DELHI

Shikārpur

Rahīmyār Khān
Bīkāner

Indus

Lārkāna

Thar Desert

Sukkur

Rajasthān

Jaipur
Āgra

Central Makrān Range

Nawābshāh

Jodhpur
Ajmer

Gwalior

Hyderābād

Kota

Karāchī

Indus

I N D

Mouths of the Indus

Rann of Kachchh

Tropic of Cancer

0 km   200
0 miles   200

Gulf of Kachchh

Gāndhīdhām

Gujarāt

Ahmadābād
Indore
Bhop

Arabian

Jāmnagar
Rājkot
Vadodara

Madhy

Sea

Porbandar
Bhāvnagar

Narmada

Sūrat

Nāgp

20°

Gulf of Khambhāt

Dāman

Maharashtra

◆ On January 26, 2001 a massive earthquake devastated the Gujarat region of India, costing some 25,000 lives.

Nāshik
Nānded

Mumbai (Bombay)
Kalyān

D e

✕ ✕ ✕ *Ceasefire Line*

Pune
Nizāmābād

Solāpur

60°   70°   70°

A   B   C   D

80°   90°

XINJIANGUYGUR
ZIZHIQU

AKSAI CHIN
(administered by China,
claimed by India)

C H I N A   QINGHAI

◆ The northern ranges of the Himalayas contain the highest
mountains in the world, with average heights of more than
23,000 ft (7000 m) and many peaks higher
than 26,000 ft (8000m).

DEMCHOK/DÊMOQG
(administered by China,
claimed by India)

◆ Cerrapunji, 4232 ft (1290 m) above sea level, has an average annual
rainfall of 503 inches (1279 cm), although this is monsoon rain and
the winter is a virtual drought. The highest ever seasonal rainfall
was 901 inches (2290 cm).

XIZANG ZIZHIQU
(Tibet)   30°

◆ In the kingdom of Bhutan, all   ARUNACHAL PRADESH
citizens officially become a   (claimed by China)
year older on New Year's Day.

H i m a l a y a s

Bareilly   Mount Everest
29,035ft (8850m)▲   THIMPHU

N E P A L   KATHMANDU   ●BHUTAN
Uttar   Gangtok   ●   Guwāhāti
Pradesh   Birātnagar   Dispur   Kohima
Lucknow   Saidpur
Kānpur   Vārānasi   Patna   Sylhet   Imphāl
Yamuna   Ganges   Jamālpur   Brahmaputra
Allahābād   Bihār   Rājshāhi   BANGLADESH
Gaya   DHAKA   Tropic of Cancer
I A   Dhanbād   West   Comilla   MYANMAR
Jabalpur   Rānchi   Bengal   Khulna   (BURMA)
Kolkata
(Calcutta)   Chittagong
Pradesh   Mouths of the Ganges
Raipur

a n   Orissa   Mahanadi   Cuttack   B a y   ◆ The heaviest hailstones
of   on record, weighing about
Eastern Ghats   2.25 lbs (1 kg), are
B e n g a l   reported to have killed 92
Godavari   people in the Gopalganj
Warangal   Visākhapatnam   area of Bangladesh on
April 14, 1986.

20°

Mainland Southeast Asia

Around 70 percent of the world's teak grows in the hills of northern Myanmar. However overexploitation means that supplies may soon be exhausted.

MYANMAR'S TWO CAPITALS

Rangoon - Capital
Pyinmana - Administrative capital

The *Anopheles* mosquito, which carries the malaria parsite *Plasmodium*, is estimated to have been responsible for half of all human deaths not caused by war.

CHINA

INDIA

MYANMAR (BURMA)

THAILAND

LAOS

VIETNAM

Tropic of Cancer

Mekong

Kumon Range

Shan Plateau

Irrawaddy

Chindwin

Salween

Sittang

Mae Nam Ping

Red River

Black River

Ou

Gulf of Tongking

Bay of Bengal

Mouths of the Irr.

Da Nang
Huế
Vinh
Nam Dinh
Hai Phong
Hông Gai
Lang Son
HANOI
Phongsali
Xam Nua
Pakse
Louangphabang
Kaignabouri
VIENTIANE
Sirikit Res.
Udon Thani
Khanthabouli
Thakhek
Nakthani
Khon Kaen
Chiang Mai
Bhamo
Katha
Mandalay
Taunggyi
Monywa
Pakokku
Chauk
Prome
Henzada
Bassein
Insein
RANGOON
Pegu
Thaton
Oba-an
Moulmein
Toungoo
PYINMANA
Sittwe
Ramree Island

Tropic of Cancer

Brahmaputra

Following years of conflict it is estimated that around 3 million landmines remain buried in the soils of Cambodia.

Bangkok has some of the worst traffic jams in the world. In July 1992, after a monsoon storm, it took 11 hours for one jam to clear.

The world's smallest mammal is the bumblebee bat of Thailand, weighing less than 0.09 oz (2.5g).

N A M
Qui Nhon
Nha Trang
Da Lat
Tonlé Kong
Tonlé San
Srêng
Tonlé Srêpok
Stiêng Trêng
Mekong
Kâmpông Cham
Hô Chi Minh
Ratchathani
Muang
Tônlé Sab
Svay Riêng
Can Tho
Phumi Sâmraông
Bâtdâmbâng
Mékong
Mouths of the Mekong
Nakhon
Ratchasima
Kâmpông
Chhnang
C A M B O D I A
PHNOM PENH
Ayutthaya
Chon Buri
BANGKOK
Pattaya
Kâmpông Saôm
Kâmpôt
Rach Gia
Srinagarind
Res.
Ratchaburi
Gulf
of
Thailand
Ko Chang
Ko Phangan
Ko Samui
Chumphon
Nakhon Si
Thammarat
Tavoy
Mergui
Surat Thani
Songkhla
Pattani
Yala
Mergui
Archipelago
Ko Phuket
Phuket
Trang
Hat Yai
Isthmus of
Kra
South
China
Sea
Malay
Peninsula
M A L A Y S I A
Strait of Malacca
I N D O N E S I A
Sumatra
Andaman
Sea
Nicobar Islands
(part of India)
I N D I A N
O C E A N

0 km   200
0 miles   200

Maritime Southeast Asia

MALAYSIA'S TWO CAPITALS

Kuala Lumpur - Capital
Putrajaya - Administrative capital

◆ The Rafflesia plant has the largest flower in the world. The bloom, 3 ft (90 cm) in diameter attracts insects by imitating the foul smell of rotting flesh.

◆ In August 1883 a devastating volcanic eruption destroyed most of the island of Krakatau and triggered a tsunami that claimed around 33,000 lives.

MYANMAR
(BURMA)

THAILAND

LAOS

VIETNAM

Gulf of
Tongking

Hainan Dao
(to China)

Paracel Islands
(disputed by China, Taiwan
and Vietnam)

South China
Sea

CAMBODIA

Spratly Islands
(disputed by China,
Malaysia, Philippines,
Taiwan and Vietnam)

Andaman
Sea

Gulf of
Thailand

Nicobar Islands
(to India)

Isthmus of Kra

Bandaaceh

George
Town

Kota Bharu

Kota Kinabalu

BANDAR SERI
BEGAWAN

BRUNEI

Kuala Terengganu

Taiping Ipoh

Kuantan

Medan

Strait of Malacca

Klang

KUALA LUMPUR

Pematangsiantar

Danau
Toba

PUTRAJAYA

MALAYSIA

Sibu

Sarawak

Pegunungan
Muller

Sibolga

Pulau Simeulue

Johor Bahru

Kuching

SINGAPORE

Pontianak

Kapuas

Borneo

Pulau Nias

Pekanbaru

Equator

Sumatera
(Sumatra)

Padang

Pulau Siberut

Jambi

Kalimantan

Samarind

Balikpapan

Barisan

Bangka

Selat Karimata

Pegunungan

Kepulauan
Mentawai

Palembang

Banjarmasin

I N D

Bengkulu

Pulau
Belitung

Java

Sea

Pulau
Laut

I N D I A N

Bandar Lampung

Cirebon

Tegal

Pekalongan

Makassa

O C E A N

Selat Sunda

JAKARTA

Semarang

Surabaya

Bogor

Kudus

Mataram

Sukabumi

Bandung

Cilacap

Magelang

Jawa
(Java)

Yogyakarta

Surakarta

Kediri

Madiun

Malang

Denpasar

Bali

Jember

Lomb

Pula

120°

Luzon Strait

Babuiyan Channel

P h i l i p p i n e

130°

Luzon

Tuguergarao
Ilagan

Baguio

Dagupan

Ilagan

S e a

Angeles

Cabanatuan

MANILA

Lucena

Batangas

Mindoro

Naga

Mindoro Strait

Legazpi City

PHILIPPINES

Roxas City

Calbayog

Tacloban

Iloilo
Cadiz

Cebu

Bacolod
City

Butuan

Puerto
Princesa

Iligan

Cagayan de Oro

Palawan

Bohol

Mindanao

Strait

Sulu Sea

Zamboanga

Davao

Davao Gulf

Tawau

General
Santos

Sulu Archipelago

Kepulauan Talaud

Celebes Sea

Kepulauan Sangir

Manado

Gorontalo

Molucca Sea

Palu

Gulf of Tomini

Sulawesi (Celebes)

Kepulauan Banggai

Kendari

Kepulauan Sula

Ambon

Wahai

Ceram Sea

Pulau Seram

Parepare

Pulau Buton

Pulau Buru

Makassar

Banda Sea

Flores Sea

N u s a

T e n g g a r a

Pulau Alor

Pulau Wetar

Kepulauan Kai

Kepulauan Aru

Pulau Tanimbar

Pulau Yamdena

Pulau Sumba

Flores

DILI

EAST TIMOR

Kepulauan Leti

Timor

Savu Sea

120°

Kupang

Timor Sea

130°

Arafura Sea

A U S T R A L I A

140°

◆ The Philippines take their name from Philip II of Spain, who was king when the islands were colonized during the 16th century.

Northern
Mariana
Islands
(to US)

1

Guam *(to US)*

P A C I F I C

Yap

10°

MICRONESIA

P A L A U

Babeldaob

O C E A N

◆ Indonesia is the world's largest archipelago with almost 14,000 islands stretching 3100 miles (5000 km) between the Indian and Pacific oceans.

3

Pulau Morotai

Pulau Halmahera

Sorong

Jazirah Doberai

Pulau Biak

Jayapura

Equator

Halmahera Sea

Teluk (Moluccas)

Sungai Mamberamo

Pegunungan Maoke

PAPUA

Papua
(Irian Jaya)

Sungai Digul

**New
Guinea**

**PAPUA
NEW
GUINEA**

10°

Torres Strait

The Indian Ocean

With no part of the Maldives over 8 ft (2.4 m) above sea level, they are under great threat by global warming. There are over 2000 islands yet the total land area is only 115 sq miles.

ASIA

Lake Baikal

Lake Balkhash

Yenisey

Ob'

Aral Sea

Caspian Sea

Volga

Black Sea

Caucasus

Iranian Plateau

Arabian Peninsula

Tigris

Euphrates

Red Sea

Kuwait

Karachi

Indus

Indus Fan

Dubai

Mina Qabus

The Gulf

Gulf of Oman

Aden

Gulf of Aden

Socotra (to Yemen)

Ethiopian Highlands

Horn of Africa

AFRICA

Mombasa

Tropic of Cancer

Equator

Somali Basin

SEYCHELLES

Aldabra Group

Mascarene

Yellow River

Yangtze

Mekong

Hong Kong (Xianggang)

Tropic of Cancer

South China Sea

Borneo

Singapore

Equator

Sumatra

Java Sea

Java

East Indies

Andaman Sea

Gulf of Thailand

Irrawaddy

Himalayas

Brahmaputra

Ganges

Ganges Fan

Kolkata (Calcutta)

Bay of Bengal

Andaman Islands (to India)

Nicobar Islands (to India)

Kepulauan Mentawai

Cocos Basin

Investigat

Mid-Indian Ridge

Sri Lanka

Colombo

Ceylon Plain

British Indian Ocean Territory

Chagos Trench

Chagos-Laccadive Plateau

Mumbai (Bombay)

Arabian Sea

Arabian Basin

Murray Ridge

Owen Fracture Zone

MALDIVES

Laccadive Islands (to India)

Carlsberg Ridge

Mid-I

Australasia & Oceania

Hawaiian Islands
(to US)

Johnston Atoll
(to US)

Central
Pacific
Basin

Clarion Fracture Zone

P A C I F I C   O C E A N

Kingman Reef
(to US)

Palmyra Atoll
(to US)

Christmas Ridge

Clipperton Fracture Zone

Baker & Howland
Islands
(to US)

Teraina

Tabuaeran

Kiritimati

Jarvis Island
(to US)

Equator

Galapagos Fracture Zone

KIRIBATI

Phoenix Islands

Malden Island

Starbuck Island

KIRIBATI

Line Islands

Tokelau
(to NZ)

Northern Cook Islands

Penrhyn

Millennium
Island
Flint Island

Marquesas Islands

Marquesas Fracture Zone

Wallis &
Futuna
to France

Manihiki

SAMOA

TONGA

American
Samoa
(to US)

Cook Islands
(to NZ)

Society Islands

Tuamotu Islands

Tuamotu Fracture Zone

Vava'u
Group

Niue
(to NZ)

Tahiti

Southern Cook Islands

Tongatapu
Group

Rarotonga

Îles Australes

French Polynesia
(to France)

Austral Fracture Zone

Kermadec Islands
(to New Zealand)

Marotiri

Pitcairn
Islands
(to UK)

Tropic of Capricorn

Pitcairn Island

Kermadec Trench

Louisville Ridge

P O L Y N E S I A

Southwest

Pacific Basin

0 km   1000

0 miles   1000

Chatham Islands
(to New Zealand)

The Southwest Pacific

MARSHALL ISLANDS

30° 140° 150° 160° 170°

1

10° Guam
(US unincorporated
territory) HAGÅTÑA

Yap Marianas Trench Micronesia Ratak Chain

Caroline Islands Ralik Chain Majuro

KOROR Chuuk Is. Pohnpei
PALIKIR

PALAU **MICRONESIA** Kosrae **BAIRIK**
Tarawa

2 Banaba

◇ The Pitohui bird has a poison on its feathers and skin
similar to the poison arrow tree frog, making it the
only known example of a poisonous bird. **NAURU**

0° Equator

PAPUA NEW GUINEA

I N D O N E S I A Bismarck Archipelago New Ireland

Mt Wilhelm Madang Bougainville I. Melanesia
14,793ft (4509m) ▲

3 New Guinea Lae New Britain New
Georgia
Islands

PORT MORESBY Solomon
Sea

10° A r a f u r a HONIARA Santa Cruz Is.

S e a Torres Strait **SOLOMON
ISLANDS**

Arnhem Gulf C o r a l   S e a Banks Is.
Land of
Carpentaria **VANUATU**

4 ◇ Found only in the rain forest of New Guinea,
Queen Alexandra's Birdwing, with a wingspan
of 11 inches (280 mm), is the **PORT VILA**
largest butterfly in the world.

Coral Sea Islands
(Australian external
territory) New Caledonia
(French overseas
territory)

20° **A U S T R A L I A** Great Barrier Reef

NOUMÉA Îles
Loyauté

5

A 140° B 150° C 160° D 170°

180°
*International
Date Line*
170°
160°
150°

P A C I F I C O C E A N

10°

1

◇ *In 1994 the International Date Line was repositioned around Kiribati territory
bringing Millennium Island 14 hours ahead of GMT, making it the first
landfall for sunrise at the dawn of the new millennium.*

Kingman Reef
(administered by US)
Palmyra Atoll
(administered by US)

*Teraina
Tabuaeran
Kiritimati*

Baker & Howland Is.
(administered by US)

Jarvis I.
(administered by US)

Line Islands

Equator 0°

2

*Tungaru
(Gilbert Islands)*

K I R I B A T I *Phoenix Islands* **KIRIBATI**

TUVALU

◇ *Samoa is home to the world's smallest spider,
the Patu marplesi, which spans a mere 0.017
inches (0.4mm).*

3

●**FONGAFALE**

Tokelau
(NZ dependent territory)

Vostok I.

Flint I.

Millennium I.

10°

P o l y n e s i a

**American
Samoa**
*(US unincorporated
territory)*

*Northern
Cook Is.*

French Polynesia
*(French overseas
territory)*

**Wallis
& Futuna**
*(French overseas
territory)*

SAMOA
●**ĀPIA**
○**PAGO**
●**PAGO**

Îles de la Société

4

FIJI

*Vanua
Levu*

*Vava'u
Group*

Cook Islands
*(in free assoc.
with NZ)*

PAPEETE

Tahiti

*Viti
Levu*
●SUVA

Niue
*(in free assoc.
with NZ)*
○**ALOFI**

*Southern
Cook Is.*

*Ha'apai
Group*

TONGA

AVARUA

0 km   500

0 miles   500

●**NUKU'ALOFA**

*International
Date Line*

Rarotonga

Tropic of Capricorn

20°

5

180°
170°

E | F | G | H

Western Australia

On Christmas Day, 1974, Cyclone Tracy devastated Darwin with winds of up to 175 mph (280km/h) resulting in 66 deaths, thousands of injuries and 95 percent of the city destroyed.

One of the largest states in the world, with an area of more than 975,000 sq miles (2.5 million sq km), Western Australia covers a third of the Australian continent.

A R C A D I E

Arafura Sea

Croker Island

Melville Island

Van Diemen Gulf

Arnhem Land

Bathurst Island

DARWIN

Daly Waters

Katherine

Pine Creek

Victoria River

Top Springs

Kununurra

Tanami Desert

Tennant Creek

NORTHERN TERRITORY

Macdonnell Ranges

Alice Springs

Timor Sea

Cape Londonderry

Joseph Bonaparte Gulf

Wyndham

Halls Creek

Fitzroy Crossing

Kimberley Plateau

Lake Mackay

I N D O N E S I A

Bali

Java

Pulau Lombok

Bonaparte Archipelago

Heywood Islands

King Sound

Fitzroy River

Percival Lakes

Lake Disappointment

Great Sandy Desert

Broome

Eighty Mile Beach

Marble Bar

Newman

W E S T E R N

I N D I A N   O C E A N

Port Hedland

Dampier

Onslow

Fortescue River

Hamersley Range

Ashburton River

Gascoyne R.

Exmouth Gulf

Exmouth

Tropic of Capricorn

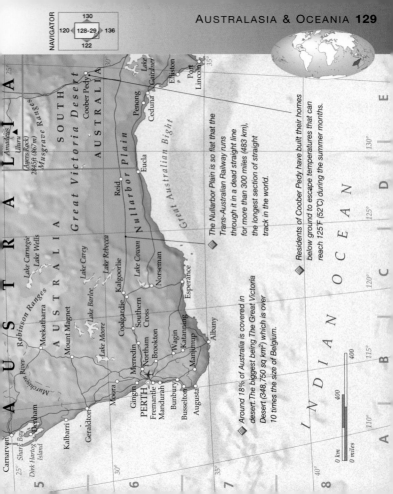

A U S T R A L A S I A
SOUTH
AUSTRALIA
AUSTRALIA

Amadeus
Uluru
(Ayers Rock)
2845ft (867m)
Musgrave Range

Great Victoria Desert

Coober Pedy
Penong
Ceduna
Eucla
Reid
Nullarbor Plain
Great Australian Bight

Lake Gairdner
Elliston
Port Lincoln

Lake Carnegie
Lake Wells
Robinson Ranges
Meekatharra
Mount Magnet
Lake Carey
Lake Barlee
Lake Moore
Lake Rebecca
Lake Cowan
Kalgoorlie
Coolgardie
Southern Cross
Norseman
Esperance

Murchison River
Cue
Kalbarri
Geraldton

Moora
Gingin
Merredin
Northam
Brookton
PERTH
Fremantle
Mandurah
Bunbury
Busselton
Augusta
Wagin
Katanning
Manjimup
Albany

I N D I A N   O C E A N

Carnarvon
Shark Bay
Dirk Hartog Island

◆ The Nullarbor Plain is so flat that the
Trans-Australian Railway runs
through it in a dead straight line
for more than 300 miles (483 km),
the longest section of straight
track in the world.

◆ Residents of Coober Pedy have built their homes
below ground to escape temperatures that can
reach 125°F (52°C) during the summer months.

◆ Around 18% of Australia is covered in
desert, the biggest being The Great Victoria
Desert (348,750 sq km²) which is over
10 times the size of Belgium.

0 km   400
0 miles   400

25°
30°
35°
110°   115°   120°   125°   130°

Eastern Australia

◊ The venom of the Sea Wasp, Marine Stinger, or Box Jellyfish can kill a person in between 30 seconds and four minutes.

◊ Australia's Great Barrier Reef is the world's largest area of coral islands and reefs, running for about 1,240 miles (2,000 km) along the coast of Queensland.

◊ Koalas feed only on nutrient-poor eucalypt leaves and consequently have evolved a low energy lifestyle based around sleeping for 20 hours each day.

PAPUA NEW GUINEA

INDONESIA

Arafura Sea

Torres Strait

Cape York

Cape York Peninsula

Princess Charlotte Bay

Cooktown

Port Douglas

Cairns

Tully

Hinchinbrook Island

Townsville

Bowen

Whitsunday Group

Mackay

Rockhampton

Bundaberg

Coral Sea

Coral Sea Islands (to Australia)

Great Barrier Reef

Great Dividing Range

Charters Towers

Hughenden

Winton

Emerald

Clermont

Barcaldine

Longreach

Biloela

Wessel Islands

Groote Eylandt

Gulf of Carpentaria

Wellesley Islands

Burketown

Normanton

Mitchell River

Gilbert River

Flinders River

Gregory Range

Selwyn Range

Cloncurry

Mount Isa

QUEENSLAND

Windorah

Simpson

Barkly Tableland

NORTHERN TERRITORY

Tennant Creek

Tanami Desert

Daly Waters

Top Springs Roadhouse

Pine Creek

Katherine

DARWIN

Arnhem Land

Alice Springs

Macdonnell Ranges

Uluru (Ayers Rock)

AUSTRALIA

Tropic of Capricorn

Maryborough

BRISBANE
Balby Gold
Surfer's Paradise
Coast
Murwillumbah

Roma
Miles
Toowoomba
Grafton
Coffs Harbour
Port Macquarie

St.
George
Goondiwindi
Moree

Charleville
Cunnamulla
Walgett
Armidale
Tamworth
Newcastle
Gosford
SYDNEY
Wollongong

Bourke
Nyngan
Dubbo
Parramatta
CANBERRA
AUSTRALIAN
CAPITAL TERRITORY

Great Dividing Range

N E W S O U T H W A L E S

Grey Range

Wilcannia
Ivanhoe
Cootamundra
Cooma

Barwon River

Darling River

Wagga Wagga
Mount
Kosciuszko
7310 ft (2228m) ▲

Barrier Range
Broken
Hill
Mildura
Murray River
Murrumbidgee River

Tumbarumba
Traralgon
South East Point

V I C T O R I A
MELBOURNE

Ouyen
Murray River
Bendigo
Ballarat
Geelong

Lake
Callabonna

S O U T H A U S T R A L I A

Lake
Blanche

Lake
Frome

Marree

Crystal Brook
Peterborough
Horsham
Warrnambool
Portland

Lake Eyre
North
76m

Lake Eyre South

Lake
Torrens

Lake
Gairdner

Flinders Ranges

Port
Augusta
Gawler
ADELAIDE

Mount Gambier

Great
Victoria
Desert

Penong
Ceduno

Whyalla
Port
Lincoln

Eyre
Peninsula

Spencer Gulf

Kangaroo Island

Cooper
Pedy

Musgrave Ranges

Tarcoola

T a s m a n

S e a

Flinders Island

◆ The Platypus lives in an aquatic
environment, suckles its young
like a mammal, lays eggs, and
has webbed feet and a bill
resembling that of a duck.

B a s s   S t r a i t

Banks Strait

Launceston

HOBART

Marrawah
Burnie
Devonport

King Island

TASMANIA

◆ Huge truck rigs known as
Road Trains, which can reach
up to 175 ft (53.5 m) in length,
carry freight across the vast
distances of the Australian interior.
They often have as many as three
trailers, weighing more than
100 tons (tonnes) in total.

0 km   400
0 miles   400

30°

40°

160°

150°

140°

30°

40°

A   B   C   D   E

5

6

7

8

New Zealand

◇ The lizardlike tuatara is found on some of the islands and rocky stacks off New Zealand. It is the sole remaining representative of the reptilian order Rhynchocephalia, which first evolved before the dinosaurs. It has a third 'eye' on the top of its head which is sensitive to light.

◆ Ninety Mile Beach is in fact only about 60 miles long. Nevertheless, this still makes it one of the longest sandy beaches in the world.

◆ Around AD 130 something in the order of 33 billion tons (tonnes) of pumice was ejected in a massive volcanic eruption that left a 20,000 sq mile (51,800 sq km) debris field and created an enormous caldera that subsequently became Lake Taupo.

◇ More than 46 million sheep thrive in New Zealand's mild climate, outnumbering the human population by 12 to 1.

Tasman Sea

North Island

NEW ZEALAND

Three Kings Islands
Te Kao
Kaitaia
North Cape
Great Exhibition Bay
Kaikohe
Paihia
Whangarei
Ruawai
Warkworth
Takapuna
Auckland
Manurewa
Manukau
Waiuku
Hamilton
Cambridge
Te Kuiti
Kawhia
Taumarunui
Stratford
New Plymouth
Hawera
Taihape
Wanganui
Palmerston North
Levin
North Taranaki Bight
South Taranaki Bight
Cape Farewell
North Cape
Cape Reinga
Great Barrier Island
Hauraki Gulf
Whitianga
Whangamata
Paeroa
Tauranga
Te Puke
Rotorua
Lake Rotorua
Lake Taupo
Taupo
Bay of Plenty
Whakatane
Ruatoria
East Cape
Gisborne
Wairoa
Hawke Bay
Napier
Hastings
Waipawa
Waipukurau
Woodville
Cape Turnagain

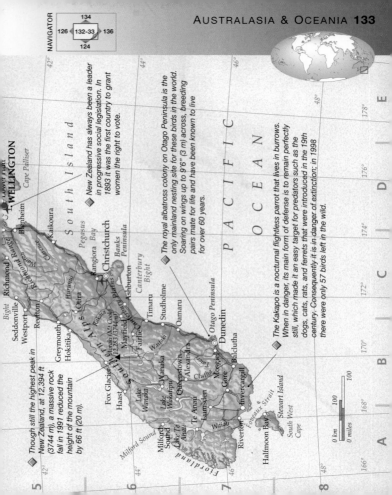

New Zealand has always been a leader in progressive social legislation. In 1893 it was the first country to grant women the right to vote.

The royal albatross colony on Otago Peninsula is the only mainland nesting site for these birds in the world. Soaring on wings up to 9'6" (3 m) across, breeding pairs mate for life and have been known to live for over 60 years.

The Kakapo is a nocturnal flightless parrot that lives in burrows. When in danger, its main form of defense is to remain perfectly still, which made it an easy target for predators such as the dogs, cats, rats, and ferrets that were introduced in the 19th century. Consequently it is in danger of extinction; in 1998 there were only 57 birds left in the wild.

Though still the highest peak in New Zealand, at 12,394 ft (3744 m), a massive rock fall in 1991 reduced the height of the mountain by 66 ft (20 m).

The Pacific Ocean

◆ Challenger Deep in the Mariana Trench is 35,838 ft (10,923 m), or almost 7 miles (11 km), below the surface of the Pacific. At this depth water pressures is around 16,000 lbs/sq inch (1,127 kg/cm sq).

Arctic Circle

Bering Strait

Ob'
Yenisey
Lena

Bering Sea

Aleutian Islands
Aleutian Basin
Aleutian Trench

Sea of Okhotsk

Chinook Trough

Gobi

Vladivostok

ASIA

Yellow River

Kurile Islands

Kurile Trench

Northwest Pacific Basin

Mendocino F

Yellow Sea

Shanghai
Osaka
Tokyo
Nagoya

Sea of Japan (East Sea)

Midway Islands (to US)

Yangtze

Hawaiian Ridge

East China Sea

Hong Kong (Xianggang)

Japan

Northern Mariana Islands (to US)

Wake Island (to US)

Johnston Atoll (to US)

Tropic of Cancer

Ryukyu Is.

Taiwan

Mekong

Philippine Sea

Shikoku Basin

Pacific Mountains

PAC

Manila

Philippine Trench

Guam (to US)

Marianas Trench

MARSHALL ISLANDS

Central Pacific Basin

Kingman Reef (to US)

Philippines

36,201ft (11,034m)
Challenger Deep

MICRONESIA

Baker & Howland Is. (to US)

Singapore

South China Sea

Celebes Sea

PALAU

Caroline Islands

Melanesian Basin

Jarvis (to US)

Equator

Sumatra

Borneo

Celebes

East Indies

Ontong Java

NAURU

KIRIBATI

Jakarta

Java

Java Sea

Banda Sea

New Guinea

Melanesia

TUVALU

Tokelau (to NZ)

Timor

Timor Sea

Arafura Sea

SOLOMON ISLANDS

Wallis & Futuna (to France)

SAMOA

America Samoa (to US)

INDIAN

Coral Sea

VANUATU

Polynesia

Coo
Islan
(to N

Tropic of Capricorn

OCEAN

AUSTRALIA

Great Dividing Range

Great Barrier Reef

Coral Sea Is. (to Australia)

New Caledonia (to France)

FIJI

TONGA

Niue (to NZ)

Kermadec Islands (to NZ)

P
o

Great Australian Bight

Murray

Sydney

Norfolk Island (to Australia)

Lord Howe Rise

South Australian Basin

Tasman Sea

North Island

| 0 km | 2000 |
| 0 miles | |

Tasmania

Hobart

New Zealand

Chatham Islands (to NZ)

South Island

Campbell Plateau

International Dateline

◆ Manua Loa on the Big Island of Hawaii rises 33,132 ft (10,098 m) from the ocean floor to it's peak 13,677 ft (4169 m) above the surface of the Pacific Ocean, and contains around 9,700 cubic miles (39,731 cu km) of rock.

Pacific Antarc

Antarctic Circle

ANTARCTICA

A   B   C   D

Anchorage

Gulf of
Alaska

Hudson
Bay

Arctic Circle

Labrador
Sea

Rocky Mountains

NORTH
AMERICA

Vancouver

Cascadia
Basin

Zone

San Francisco

◇ Pacific giant kelp can grow up to 18 inches (45 cm)
a day, and may eventually reach up to 197 ft (60 m)
or 34 times the height of the average man.

Long Beach

ATLANTIC

Murray Fracture Zone

Molokai Fracture Zone

Gulf of
Mexico

OCEAN

Tropic of Cancer

Hawaiian Islands
(to US)

Clarion Fracture Zone

Greater Antilles

Lesser Antilles

IC OCEAN

Caribbean Sea

myra
oll (to US)

Clipperton Fracture Zone

Clipperton Island
(to France)

Guatemala
Basin

Middle America Trench

Panama City

◇ The Pacific Equatorial
Counter Current flows
eastward toward South
America, carrying up
to 40 million tons
(tonnes) of warm water
with it every second.

ritimati
hristmas Island)

Galapagos Fracture Zone

Galapagos Islands
(to Ecuador)

RIBATI

Marquesas
Islands

Gallego Rise

Bauer
Basin

Galapagos
Rise

Callao

thiti
asin

Marquesas
Fracture Zone

East Pacific Rise

Tahiti

French
Polynesia
(to France)

Austral
Fracture Zone

French
Basin

Mendaña Fracture Zone

SOUTH

les
Australes

Îles Gambier

Pitcairn Islands
(to UK)

Sala y Gomez
(to Chile)

Isla San Ambrosio
(to Chile)

AMERICA

Tropic of Capricorn

Easter Fracture Zone

Isla San Félix
(to Chile)

Valparaiso

Peru-Chile Trench

Easter Island
(to Chile)

Islas Juan Fernández
(to Chile)

outhwest
acific
asin

Agassiz Fracture Zone

Chile Basin

Andes

Chile Rise

Eltanin Fracture Zone

Mornington
Abyssal
Plain

Cape Horn

Limit of winter pack ice

ige

Southeast
Pacific Basin

Bellingshausen Plain

Drake Passage

Amundsen Plain

Peter I Island
(to Norway)

Limit of summer pack ice

Antarctic Circle

ATLANTIC OCEAN

20°

INDIAN OCEAN

40°

South Georgia (to UK)

South Sandwich Islands (to Uk)

Scotia Sea

Weddell Plain

Atlantic-Indian Basin

Antarctic Circle

Lazarev Sea

Enderby Plain

South Orkney Islands

Dronning Maud Land

South Shetland Islands

Limit of summer pack ice

60°

Weddell Sea

Coats Land

Enderby Land

◆ Ground visibility in the Antarctic during the summer months can be as much as 150 miles (250 km).

Antarctic Peninsula

Palmer Land

Ronne Ice Shelf

ANTARCTICA

Mackenzie Bay

Alexander Island

85°

Princess Elizabeth Land

Davis Sea

Bellingshausen Sea

+ South Pole

Greater Antarctica

Peter I Island (to Norway)

Ellsworth Land

Lesser Antarctica

Transantarctic Mountains

+ South Geomagnetic Pole

Shackleton Ice Shelf

Amundsen Sea

Marie Byrd Land

Ross Ice Shelf

Wilkes Land

PACIFIC OCEAN

Amundsen Plain

Ross Sea

Victoria Land

Terre Adélie

◆ The largest iceberg of recent times broke off from the Ross Ice Shelf in the spring of 2000. It was about 186 miles (300 km) from end to end and 25 miles (40 km) wide.

George V Land

◆ The world's windiest place is reputed to be Commonwealth Bay, George V Land, where wind speeds of 200 mph (320 km/h) have been recorded.

Pacific-Antarctic Ridge

0 km 1000
0 miles 1000

A   B   C   D

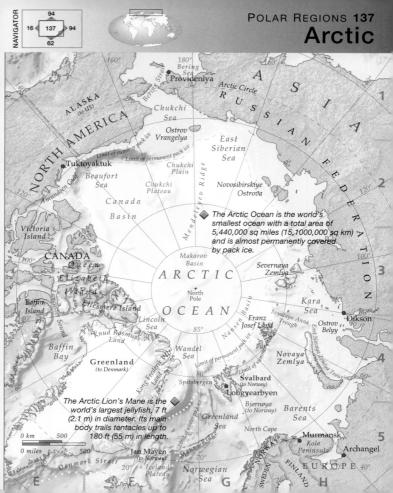

The Arctic Ocean is the world's smallest ocean with a total area of 5,440,000 sq miles (15,1000,000 sq km) and is almost permanently covered by pack ice.

The Arctic Lion's Mane is the world's largest jellyfish, 7 ft (2.1 m) in diameter. Its main body trails tentacles up to 180 ft (55 m) in length.

NORTH AMERICA
ALASKA (to US)
Tuktoyaktuk
Beaufort Sea
Amundsen Gulf
Canada Basin
Victoria Island
CANADA
Queen Elizabeth Islands
Baffin Island
Ellesmere Island
M'Clintock Channel
Nares Sound
Baffin Bay
Lincoln Sea
Knud Rasmus Land
Kong Frederik Land
Greenland (to Denmark)
Denmark Strait
Jan Mayen (to Norway)
Iceland Plateau
Norwegian Sea

A S I A
Providentya
Bering Sea
Bering Strait
Arctic Circle
Chukchi Sea
Ostrov Vrangelya
Limit of summer pack ice
Limit of permanent pack ice
Chukchi Plain
East Siberian Sea
Chukchi Plateau
Novosibirskiye Ostrova
RUSSIAN FEDERATION
Mendeleyev Ridge
Makarov Basin
ARCTIC
North Pole
OCEAN
Severnaya Zemlya
Kara Sea
Ostrov Belyy
Franz Josef Land
Nansen Basin
Severnaya Anna Trough
East Novaya Zemlya Trough
Dikson
85°
80°
Wandel Sea
Spitsbergen
Svalbard (to Norway)
Longyearbyen
Bjørnøya (to Norway)
Greenland Sea
Novaya Zemlya
Barents Sea
North Cape
Murmansk
Kola Peninsula
Archangel
NORWAY
SWEDEN
FINLAND
EUROPE
40°

0 km   500
0 miles   500

The
Country
Factfiles

Franz Josef Land
(to Russia)

Svalbard
(to Norway)

Jan Mayen
(to Norway)

Greenland
(Denmark)

NUUK

St Pierre &

Labrador

Laurentian Mountains

Gulf of St Lawrence

Lawrence

Baffin Bay

Baffin Island

A R C T I C   OCEAN

North Pole

Queen Elizabeth Islands

Hudson Bay

Lake Superior

C   A   N   A   D   A

A S I A

Reindeer Lake

Lake Winnipeg

Great Bear Lake

Great Slave Lake

Lake Athabasca

Mackenzie

Arctic Circle

UNITED STATES

R o c k y   M o u n

ALASKA

Yukon

Snake

PACIFIC

OCEAN

ATLANTIC OCEAN

Sargasso Sea

Bermuda (UK)

Virgin Islands (US)

British Virgin Islands (UK)

Anguilla (UK)

ST KITTS & NEVIS

ANTIGUA & BARBUDA

Guadeloupe (France)

DOMINICA

Martinique (France)

ST LUCIA

BARBADOS

ST VINCENT & THE GRENADINES

GRENADA

Netherlands Antilles (Neth.)

TRINIDAD & TOBAGO

Turks & Caicos Islands (UK)

DOMINICAN REPUBLIC

Puerto Rico (US)

SANTO DOMINGO

Montserrat (UK)

Lake Ontario

WASHINGTON, DC

Lake Erie

Lake Michigan

Appalachian Mountains

Ohio

Missouri

Mississippi

Arkansas

OF AMERICA

Gulf of Mexico

NASSAU

BAHAMAS

HAVANA

Cayman Islands (UK)

CUBA

PORT-AU-PRINCE

HAITI

KINGSTON

JAMAICA

Aruba (Neth.)

Colorado

Rio Grande

MEXICO

Sierra Madre Occidental

MEXICO CITY

BELMOPAN

BELIZE

GUATEMALA CITY

GUATEMALA

SAN SALVADOR

EL SALVADOR

TEGUCIGALPA

HONDURAS

MANAGUA

NICARAGUA

SAN JOSÉ

COSTA RICA

PANAMA CITY

PANAMA

Andes

SOUTH AMERICA

Clipperton Island (French Polynesia)

Tropic of Cancer

Equator

0 km 1000

0 miles 1000

POLITICAL FACTFILE

TOTAL AREA:
9,400,000 sq miles
(24,346,000 sq km)

TOTAL NUMBER OF COUNTRIES:
23

TOTAL POPULATION:
511.3 million

LARGEST CITY WITH POPULATION:
Mexico City, Mexico 22.8 million

COUNTRY WITH HIGHEST POPULATION DENSITY:
Barbados 1627 people per sq mile
(628 people per sq km)

LARGEST COUNTRY:
Canada 3,855,171 sq miles
(9,984,670 sq km)

SMALLEST COUNTRY:
St Kitts & Nevis 101 sq miles
(261 sq km)

ATLANTIC

OCEAN

South Georgia
(UK)

0 km   500

0 miles   500

Isla San Ambrosio   (Chile)

Islas Juan Fernández
(Chile)

Lagoa dos Patos

MONTEVIDEO

URUGUAY

BUENOS AIRES

Paraná

Uruguay

Paraguay

A R G E N T I N A

C H I L E

SANTIAGO

Colorado

Río Negro

Patagonia

Strait of Magellan

Tierra del Fuego

Cape Horn

Falkland Islands
(UK)

Isla de Chiloé

PACIFIC

OCEAN

POLITICAL FACTFILE

TOTAL AREA:
6,880,000 sq miles
(17,819,000 sq km)

TOTAL NUMBER OF COUNTRIES:
12

TOTAL POPULATION:
375.1 million

LARGEST CITY WITH POPULATION:
São Paulo, Brazil 20.2 million

**COUNTRY WITH HIGHEST
POPULATION DENSITY:**
Ecuador 123 people per sq mile
(48 people per sq km)

LARGEST COUNTRY:
Brazil 3,286,470 sq miles
(8,511,965 sq km)

SMALLEST COUNTRY:
Suriname 63,039 sq miles
(163,270 sq km)

ATLANTIC
OCEAN

E U R O P E

Black Sea

A S I A

The Gulf

Tropic of Cancer

Arabian Peninsula

Syrian Desert

Red Sea

Mediterranean Sea

Atlas Mountains

CAIRO

Nile

TUNIS
•TRIPOLI

TUNISIA

ALGIERS•

MOROCCO

Ceuta (Spain) Melilla (Spain)

RABAT•

Libyan Desert

LIBYA

EGYPT

KHARTOUM•

Blue Nile

White Nile

S U D A N

ERITREA

ASMARA

DJIBOUTI
DJIBOUTI
ADDIS
ABABA

SOMALILAND
(not internationally recognized)

SOMALIA

E T H I O P I A

Sobat

Lake T

Tibesti

CHAD

CENTRAL AFRICAN
REPUBLIC

NDJAMENA•

FANGUI

Ubangi

CAMEROON

NIGER

NIAMEY•

MALI

S   a   h   a   r   a

ALGERIA

LAAYOUNE•

WESTERN
SAHARA
(disputed)

Tropic of Cancer

MAURITANIA

NOUAKCHOTT•

Senegal

DAKAR•

SENEGAL

GAMBIA
BANJUL
GUINEA-
BISSAU
BISSAU

BAMAKO•

GUINEA

CONAKRY•

SIERRA LEONE

FREETOWN•

MONROVIA•

LIBERIA

CÔTE
D'IVOIRE
(IVORY COAST)

YAMOUSSOUKRO•

Niger

BURKINA

OUAGADOUGOU•

GHANA

ACCRA

TOGO

BENIN

PORTO-NOVO

LOMÉ

NIGERIA

ABUJA•

Niger

MALABO

Madeira (Portugal)

Islas Canarias (Spain)

POLITICAL FACTFILE

TOTAL AREA:
11,677,250 sq miles
(30,244,050 sq km)

TOTAL NUMBER OF COUNTRIES:
53

TOTAL POPULATION:
904.5 million

LARGEST CITY WITH POPULATION:
Cairo, Egypt 15.6 million

COUNTRY WITH HIGHEST POPULATION DENSITY:
Mauritius 1671 people per sq mile
(645 people per sq km)

LARGEST COUNTRY:
Sudan 967,493 sq miles
(2,505,810 sq km)

SMALLEST COUNTRY:
Seychelles 176 sq miles
(455 sq km)

POLITICAL FACTFILE

TOTAL AREA:
4,809,200 sq miles
(12,456,000 sq km)

TOTAL NUMBER OF COUNTRIES:
45

TOTAL POPULATION:
710.8 million

LARGEST CITY WITH POPULATION:
Moscow, European Russia 13.8 million

COUNTRY WITH HIGHEST POPULATION DENSITY:
Monaco 43,212 people per sq mile
(16,620 people per sq km)

LARGEST COUNTRY:
European Russia 1,527,341 sq miles
(3,955,818 sq km)

SMALLEST COUNTRY:
Vatican City, Italy 0.17 sq miles
(0.44 sq km)

REYKJAVÍK

ICELAND

Arctic Circle

Norwegian
Sea

Faeroe Islands
(Denmark)

NOR

Shetland Islands

OSLO

Outer
Hebrides

Orkney Islands

British
Isles

North
Sea

DENMARK

IRELAND

COPENHAGEN

DUBLIN

UNITED
KINGDOM

AMSTERDAM

Elbe

BERLIN

Channel Is.
(UK)

LONDON

THE
HAGUE
NETH.

GERMANY

BELGIUM
BRUSSELS

PRAGU

LUXEMBOURG

LUXEMBOURG

CZECH REPUBL

PARIS

Loire

Rhine

LIECH.

BRATISLA

VIENNA

ATLANTIC

Bay of Biscay

FRANCE

BERN

AUSTRI

OCEAN

Garonne

SWITZERLAND

SLOVENI

LJUBLJANA

PORTUGAL

Duero

ZAGRE

Tagus

Ebro

MONACO

ANDORRA

SAN MARINO

CROATIA

MADRID

Corsica

SARAJE
BOSN
& HER

LISBON

Madeira
(Portugal)

SPAIN

VATICAN CITY

ROME

ITALY

Guadalquivir

Gibraltar
(UK)

Balearic Islands

Sardinia

Canary Islands
(Spain)

Ceuta
(Spain)

Melilla
(Spain)

Mediterra

Atlas
Mountains

Sicily

AFRICA

VALLETTA

ea

MALTA

20°   40°   80°   80°

NORWAY

Ural Mountains

Ob

Irtysh   80°

Northern Dvina

Lake Onega   50°

FINLAND

Lake Ladoga   R U S S I A N

HELSINKI

STOCKHOLM   *Baltic Sea*   TALLINN   F E D E R A T I O N
ESTONIA
LATVIA   MOSCOW
RIGA   *Volga*   *Ural*
LITHUANIA   VILNIUS
KALININGRAD   MINSK   *Aral Sea*
(Russ.Fed.)   BELARUS
WARSAW   *Don*
POLAND   KIEV   *Dnieper*   40°

UKRAINE   *Caspian Sea*

SLOVAKIA
BUDAPEST   MOLDOVA   *Caucasus*
HUNGARY   CHISINĂU
ROMANIA   *Black Sea*   A S I A
BELGRADE   BUCHAREST
SERBIA   *Danube*   60°
ODGORICA   SOFIA   BULGARIA
ON.   SKOPJE   TURKEY
MACED.   TIRANA
ALBANIA
GREECE

ATHENS   0 km   1000
                   0 miles   1000
Sea   *Crete*   *Cyprus*
20°   40°   30°

ARCTIC OCEAN

Franz Josef Land

Severnaya Zemlya

Laptev Sea

Kara Sea

EUROPE

RUSSIAN FEDERATION

Ob'

Irtysh

Yenisey

Lena

Lake Baikal

Black Sea

ASTANA

ULAN BATOR

ANKARA

GEORGIA

TBILISI

KAZAKHSTAN

MONGOLIA

TURKEY

CYPRUS

NICOSIA

ARMENIA

YEREVAN

AZERBAIJAN

BAKU

Aral Sea

Lake Balkhash

UZBEKISTAN

BISHKEK

BEIRUT

SYRIA

DAMASCUS

TURKMENISTAN

KYRGYZSTAN

LEBANON

JERUSALEM

AMMAN

ASGABAT

TASHKENT

ISRAEL

JORDAN

Tehran

DUSHANBE

TAJIKISTAN

C H I N A

BAGHDAD

IRAQ

I R A N

KABUL

ISLAMABAD

KUWAIT

KUWAIT

AFGHANISTAN

Tropic of Cancer

AFRICA

BAHRAIN

MANAMA

JEDDA

QATAR

RIYADH

DOHA

PAKISTAN

NEW DELHI

NEPAL

THIMPHU

Yangt

ABU DHABI

BHUTAN

SAUDI ARABIA

U.A.E.

MUSCAT

Indus

KATHMANDU

Ganges

BANGLADESH

DHAKA

VIETNAM

HANOI

Red Sea

SANA

OMAN

I N D I A

MYANMAR (BURMA)

LAOS

YEMEN

Arabian Sea

PYINMANA

VIENTIAN

Socotra (Yemen)

Bay of Bengal

RANGOON

BANGKOK

THAILAND

Equator

Laccadive Islands (India)

Andaman & Nicobar Islands (India)

CAMBODI

PHNO PEN

MALE

COLOMBO

SRI LANKA

MAL

MALDIVES

KUALA LUMPUR

PUTRAJAYA

SINGAPORE

I N

JAKART

INDIAN OCEAN

POLITICAL FACTFILE

TOTAL AREA:
16,838,365 sq miles
(43,608,000 sq km)

TOTAL NUMBER OF COUNTRIES:
49

TOTAL POPULATION:
3933.7 million

LARGEST CITY WITH POPULATION:
Tokyo, Japan 34.2 million

COUNTRY WITH HIGHEST POPULATION DENSITY:
Singapore 18,220 people per sq mile
(7049 people per sq km)

LARGEST COUNTRY:
Asiatic Russia 5,065,394 sq miles
(13,119,382 sq km)

SMALLEST COUNTRY:
Maldives 116 sq miles
(300 sq km)

Australasia & Oceania

Philippine Sea

120°

140°

160°

Wake Island
(to US)

Northern
Mariana
Islands
(US)

20°

HAGÁTÑA
Guam
(US)

**MARSHALL
ISLANDS**

Micronesia

MAJURO

PALIKIR

Caroline Islands

KOROR
Babeldaob

MICRONESIA

BAIRIK

PALAU

Melanesia

NAURU

NAURU

KIRIBAT

Equator

A S I A

**PAPUA NEW
GUINEA**

TUVALU
FONGAFA

PORT MORESBY

**SOLOMON
ISLANDS**

HONIARA

VANUATU

SUV

Coral Sea
Islands
(Australia)

PORT VILA

FIJ

Ashmore &
Cartier Islands
(Australia)

New Caledonia
(France)

NOUMÉA

**INDIAN

OCEAN**

Great Dividing Range

AUSTRALIA

Norfolk Island
(Australia)

20°

Lake Eyre North

Lake Torrens

Lake Gairdner

Darling

Lord Howe
Island
(Australia)

**NEW
ZEALAND**

Tropic of Capricorn

Murray

CANBERRA

WELLINGTON

100°

120°

40°

140°

Tasmania

Tasman
Sea

160°

Auckland Islands
(New Zealand)

POLITICAL FACTFILE

TOTAL AREA:
3,376,700 sq miles (8,745,750 sq km)

TOTAL NUMBER OF COUNTRIES:
14

TOTAL POPULATION:
32.2 million

LARGEST CITY WITH POPULATION:
Sydney, Australia 4.4 million

COUNTRY WITH HIGHEST POPULATION DENSITY:
Nauru 1611 people per sq mile
(621 people per sq km)

LARGEST COUNTRY:
Australia 2,967,893 sq miles
(7,686,860 sq km)

SMALLEST COUNTRY:
Nauru 8.1 sq miles (21 sq km)

Johnston Atoll
(US)

Baker & Howland
Islands
(US)

Jarvis Island
(US)

PACIFIC

OCEAN

Equator

KIRIBATI

Phoenix Islands

KIRIBATI

Tokelau
(NZ)

Marquesas Islands

Wallis &
Futuna
(Fr.)

SAMOA

American
Samoa
(US)

Cook Islands
(NZ)

ATA'UTU

APIA

PAGO PAGO

TONGA

Niue
(NZ)

PAPEETE

Society Islands

NUKU'ALOFA

AVARUA

French Polynesia
(France)

Iles Australes

Kermadec Islands
(New Zealand)

Pitcairn
Islands
(UK)

Tropic of Capricorn

International Dateline

P

Chatham Islands
(New Zealand)

0 km   1000

0 miles   1000

Key to factfile maps

FOREWORD

THIS FACTFILE is intended as a guide to a world that is continually changing as political fashions and personalities come and go. Nevertheless, all the material in these factfiles has been researched from the most up-to-date and authoritative sources to give an incisive portrait of the geographical, social, and economic characteristics that make each country unique.

KEY TO MAP SYMBOLS

ELEVATION

4000m / 13,124ft
3000m / 9843ft
2000m / 6562ft
1000m / 3281ft
500m / 1640ft
200m / 656ft
0
Below sea level

BORDERS

———————— Full international

---------- Disputed *de facto*

.... Territorial claim

✱✱✱✱✱✱✱ Cease-fire line

———————— State / Province

DRAINAGE FEATURES

———————— River

———————— Seasonal river

.... Canal

⬭ Lake

⬮ Seasonal lake

SYMBOLS

● Capital city

○ Major town

✈ International airport

▲ Mountain

The asterisk in the Factfile denotes the country's official language(s)

Date of formation denotes the date of political origin or independence; the second date (if any) identifies when its current borders were established

The area figure denotes total land area

Afghanistan

Landlocked in southwestern Asia, about 75% of Afghanistan is inaccessible. The strict Islamist regime imposed by the *taliban* was swept aside with the help of the US in 2001.

GEOGRAPHY

Predominantly mountainous. Highest range is the Hindu Kush. Mountains are bordered by fertile plains. Desert plateau in the south.

CLIMATE

Harsh continental. Hot, dry summers. Cold winters with heavy snow, especially in the Hindu Kush.

PEOPLE & SOCIETY

Mujahideen factions fought first against Soviet invaders (from 1979), and then against each other (after 1989), before the *taliban* won control in 1996. Under their strict Islamist regime women were denied all rights and ethnic tensions were exacerbated. The US assisted anti-*taliban* forces in 2001 as part of its "war on terrorism." A new democratic government struggles to maintain control over the war-ravaged country.

THE ECONOMY

Economy has collapsed: infrastructure destroyed. Illicit opium trade is the main earner. Hopes from oil pipelines crossing Afghan territory.

◆ **INSIGHT:** *The UN estimates that it could take 100 years to remove the ten million landmines laid in the country*

3000m/9843ft
2000m/6562ft
1000m/3281ft
500m/1640ft
200m/656ft

0   100 km
0   100 miles

FACTFILE

OFFICIAL NAME: Islamic State of Afghanistan
DATE OF FORMATION: 1919
CAPITAL: Kabul
POPULATION: 29.9 million
TOTAL AREA: 250,000 sq. miles (647,500 sq. km)

DENSITY: 119 people per sq. mile
LANGUAGES: Pashtu*, Dari*, Tajik, other
RELIGIONS: Sunni Muslim 84%, Shi'a Muslim 15%, other 1%
ETHNIC MIX: Pashtun 38%, Tajik 25%, Hazara 19%, Uzbek, Turkmen, other 18%
GOVERNMENT: Presidential system
CURRENCY: New afghani = 100 puls

Albania

Lying at the southeastern end of the Adriatic Sea, Albania was the last east European country to liberalize its economy. The regional wars of the 1990s have left a difficult legacy.

 GEOGRAPHY
Narrow coastal plain. Interior is mostly hills and mountains. Forest and scrub cover over 40% of the land.

 CLIMATE
Mediterranean coastal climate, with warm summers and cool winters. Mountains receive heavy rains or snows in winter.

PEOPLE & SOCIETY
The pace of economic reform remains a major issue, particularly as the country steers toward European integration. Mosques and churches have reopened in what was once the world's only officially atheist state. Greek minority in the south suffers much discrimination.

INSIGHT: *The Albanians' name for their country, Shqipërisë, means "Land of the Eagles"*

THE ECONOMY
Oil and gas reserves plus steady growth have potential to offset rudimentary infrastructure and lack of foreign investment.

MONTENEGRO
Lake Scutari
42° Shkodër • Kukës
Adriatic Sea
MACEDONIA
Durrës • **TIRANA**
Elbasan
41° Lushnjë Lake Ohrid
Fier • Berat Lake Prespa
Vlorë • Korçë
40° Delvinë
Ionian Sea GREECE
20°

2000m/6562ft
1000m/3281ft
500m/1640ft
200m/656ft
Sea Level

0   50 km
0   50 miles

FACTFILE

OFFICIAL NAME: Republic of Albania
DATE OF FORMATION: 1912
CAPITAL: Tirana
POPULATION: 3.1 million
TOTAL AREA: 11,100 sq. miles (28,748 sq. km)
DENSITY: 293 people per sq. mile

LANGUAGES: Albanian*, Greek
RELIGIONS: Sunni Muslim 70%, Orthodox Christian 20%, Roman Catholic 10%
ETHNIC MIX: Albanian 93%, Greek 5%, other 2%
GOVERNMENT: Parliamentary system
CURRENCY: Lek = 100 qindarka (qintars)

Algeria

 Africa's second-largest country, Algeria won independence from France in 1962. Today, national reconciliation is key to recovery from a bloody conflict launched by Islamic extremists in 1992.

 ## GEOGRAPHY
85% of the country lies within the Sahara Desert. Fertile coastal region with plains and hills rises from the southeast to the Atlas Mountains.

 ## CLIMATE
Coastal areas are warm and temperate, with most rainfall during the mild winters. The south is very hot, with negligible rainfall.

 ## PEOPLE & SOCIETY
Algerians are predominantly Arab, under 30 years of age, and urban. Most indigenous Berbers consider the mountainous Kabylia region in the northeast to be their homeland. They have been granted greater ethnic rights in recent years. The Sahara sustains just 500,000 people, mainly oil workers and Tuareg nomads with goat and camel herds, who move between the irrigated oases.

THE ECONOMY
Oil and gas exports. Political turmoil has led to exodus of skilled foreign labor. Limited agriculture.

◆ **INSIGHT**: *The world's highest dunes are located in the deserts of east central Algeria*

 ## FACTFILE
OFFICIAL NAME: People's Democratic Republic of Algeria
DATE OF FORMATION: 1962
CAPITAL: Algiers
POPULATION: 32.9 million
TOTAL AREA: 919,590 sq. miles (2,381,740 sq. km)

DENSITY: 36 people per sq. mile
LANGUAGES: Arabic*, Tamazight, French
RELIGIONS: Sunni Muslim 99%, Christian and Jewish 1%
ETHNIC MIX: Arab 75%, Berber 24%, European and Jewish 1%
GOVERNMENT: Presidential system
CURRENCY: Algerian dinar = 100 centimes

Andorra

A tiny landlocked principality, Andorra lies high in the eastern Pyrenees between France and Spain. It held its first full elections in 1993. Tourism is the main source of income.

 GEOGRAPHY
High mountains, with six deep, glaciated valleys that drain into the Valira River as it flows into Spain.

 CLIMATE
Cool, wet springs followed by dry, warm summers. Mountain snows linger until March.

 PEOPLE & SOCIETY
Immigration is strictly monitored and restricted by quota to French and Spanish nationals seeking employment in Andorra. Low taxes attract wealthy expatriates. A referendum in 1993 ended 715 years of semifeudal status, but Andorran society remains conservative.

◆ **INSIGHT:** *Andorra's coprincipality status dates from the 13th century. The "princes" are the president of France and the bishop of Urgel in Spain.*

THE ECONOMY
Tourism and duty-free sales dominate the economy. Strict banking secrecy laws and low consumer taxes promote investment and commerce. France and Spain effectively decide economic policy. Dependence on imported food and raw materials.

 FACTFILE

OFFICIAL NAME: Principality of Andorra
DATE OF FORMATION: 1278
CAPITAL: Andorra la Vella
POPULATION: 70,549
TOTAL AREA: 181 sq. miles (468 sq. km)
DENSITY: 392 people per sq. mile

LANGUAGES: Spanish, Catalan*, French, Portuguese
RELIGIONS: Roman Catholic 94%, other 6%
ETHNIC MIX: Spanish 46%, Andorran 28%, other 18%, French 8%
GOVERNMENT: Parliamentary system
CURRENCY: Euro = 100 cents

Angola

Located in southwest Africa, Angola suffered almost constant civil war following independence from Portugal in 1975. A 2002 peace deal ended the conflict, but elections are yet to be held.

 GEOGRAPHY
Most of the land is hilly and grass-covered. Desert in the south. Mountains in the center and north.

 CLIMATE
Varies from temperate to tropical. Rainfall decreases north to south. Coast is cooler and dry.

 PEOPLE & SOCIETY
Civil war was fought between UNITA, representing the Ovimbundu, and the ruling Kimbundu-dominated MPLA. Free and fair elections in 1991–1992, after the MPLA had abandoned Marxism, failed to stall the war for long. Hundreds of thousands of people died. A peace deal in 2002 saw UNITA join the government.

◆ **INSIGHT:** *Angola has the greatest number of amputees (caused by landmines) in the world*

 THE ECONOMY
Potentially one of Africa's richest countries, but civil war has hampered economic development. Oil and diamonds are exported.

 FACTFILE

OFFICIAL NAME: Republic of Angola
DATE OF FORMATION: 1975
CAPITAL: Luanda
POPULATION: 15.9 million
TOTAL AREA: 481,351 sq. miles (1,246,700 sq. km)
DENSITY: 33 people per sq. mile

LANGUAGES: Portuguese*, Umbundu, Kimbundu, Kikongo
RELIGIONS: Roman Catholic 50%, other 30%, Protestant 20%
ETHNIC MIX: Ovimbundu 37%, other 25%, Kimbundu 25%, Bakongo 13%
GOVERNMENT: Presidential system
CURRENCY: Readjusted kwanza = 100 lwei

Antarctica

The circumpolar continent of Antarctica is almost entirely covered by ice, some up to 1.2 miles (2 km) thick. It also contains 90% of the Earth's freshwater reserves.

GEOGRAPHY

The bulk of Antarctica's ice is contained in the Greater Antarctic Ice Sheet – a huge dome that rises steeply from the coast and flattens to a plateau in the interior.

CLIMATE

Powerful winds create a storm belt around the continent, which brings cloud, fog, and blizzards. Winter temperatures can fall to −112°F (−80°C).

PEOPLE & SOCIETY

No indigenous population. Scientists and logistical staff work at the 40 permanent, and as many as 100 temporary, research stations. A few Chilean settler families live on King George Island. Tourism is mostly by cruise ship to the Antarctic Peninsula. Annual tourist numbers had reached 27,000 by 2005.

Territorial Claims:
- Chilean claim
- Argentinian claim
- Brazilian zone of interest
- British claim
- Norwegian undefined limit
- Australian claim
- French claim
- New Zealand claim

The Antarctic Treaty of 1959 holds all territorial claims in abeyance in the interest of international cooperation

FACTFILE

DATE OF FORMATION: 1961
TOTAL AREA: 5,405,000 sq. miles (14,000,000 sq. km)

◆ **INSIGHT:** *If the ice sheets of Antarctica were to melt, the world's oceans would rise by as much as 200–210 ft (60–65 m)*

Antigua & Barbuda

A former colony of Spain, France, and the UK, Antigua and Barbuda lies at the outer edge of the Leeward Islands group in the Caribbean, and includes the uninhabited islet of Redonda.

GEOGRAPHY

Mainly low-lying limestone and coral islands with some higher volcanic areas. Antigua's coast is indented with bays and harbors.

CLIMATE
Tropical, moderated by trade winds and sea breezes. Humidity and rainfall are low for the region.

PEOPLE & SOCIETY
Population almost entirely of African origin, with small communities of Europeans and South Asians. Women's status has risen as a result of greater access to education. Wealth disparities are small. The Bird family dominated politics from 1960, but lost power to the UPP at the 2004 election.

◆ **INSIGHT:** *In 1865, Redonda was "claimed" by an eccentric Englishman as a kingdom for his son*

THE ECONOMY
Tourism is the main source of revenue and the biggest provider of jobs. Financial services and Internet gambling are expanding. High debt.

FACTFILE

OFFICIAL NAME: Antigua and Barbuda
DATE OF FORMATION: 1981
CAPITAL: St. John's
POPULATION: 68,722
TOTAL AREA: 170 sq. miles (442 sq. km)
DENSITY: 404 people per sq. mile

LANGUAGES: English*, English patois
RELIGIONS: Anglican 45%, other Protestant 42%, Roman Catholic 10%, other 2%, Rastafarian 1%
ETHNIC MIX: Black African 95%, other 5%
GOVERNMENT: Parliamentary system
CURRENCY: E. Caribbean $ = 100 cents

Argentina

Argentina occupies most of the southern portion of South America. After 30 years of intermittent military rule, multiparty democracy returned in 1983. The economy collapsed in 2001.

GEOGRAPHY
The Andes form a natural border with Chile in the west. East are the heavily wooded plains (Gran Chaco) and treeless but fertile Pampas plains. Bleak and arid Patagonia in the south.

CLIMATE
The Andes are semiarid in the north and snowy in the south. Pampas have a mild climate with summer rains.

PEOPLE & SOCIETY
People are largely of European descent; over one-third are of Italian origin. Indigenous peoples are now in a minority, living mainly in Andean regions or in the Gran Chaco. The middle classes were worst hit by the economic meltdown of 2001–2002.

◆ **INSIGHT:** *The Tango originated in the poorer quarters of Buenos Aires at the end of the 19th century*

THE ECONOMY
The 2001 crisis saw the world's largest default on debt. Agricultural exports have led to a rapid revival.

FACTFILE
OFFICIAL NAME: Republic of Argentina
DATE OF FORMATION: 1816
CAPITAL: Buenos Aires
POPULATION: 38.7 million
TOTAL AREA: 1,068,296 sq. miles (2,766,890 sq. km)
DENSITY: 37 people per sq. mile

LANGUAGES: Spanish*, Italian, Amerindian languages
RELIGIONS: Roman Catholic 90%, other 6%, Protestant 2%, Jewish 2%
ETHNIC MIX: Indo-European 83%, Mestizo 14%, Jewish 2%, Amerindian 1%
GOVERNMENT: Presidential system
CURRENCY: Argentine peso = 100 centavos

Armenia

The smallest of the former USSR's republics, Armenia lies landlocked in the Lesser Caucasus Mountains. Since 1988, the confrontation with Azerbaijan has dominated national life.

GEOGRAPHY
Rugged and mountainous, with expanses of semidesert and a large lake in the east: Sevana Lich.

CLIMATE
Continental climate, with little rainfall in the lowlands. The winters are often bitterly cold.

PEOPLE & SOCIETY
Christianity is the dominant religion, but minority groups are well integrated. War with Azerbaijan over the enclave of Nagorno Karabakh forced 350,000 Armenians living in Azerbaijan to return home, many to live in poverty. There are close and important ties to the five-million-strong Armenian diaspora.

◆ **INSIGHT:** *In the 4th century, Armenia became the first country to adopt Christianity as its state religion*

THE ECONOMY
Few natural resources. Agriculture accounts for over 25% of GDP. Main products are wine, tobacco, potatoes, and fruit. Well-developed machine-building and manufacturing – includes textiles and bottling of mineral water.

FACTFILE
OFFICIAL NAME: Republic of Armenia
DATE OF FORMATION: 1991
CAPITAL: Yerevan
POPULATION: 3 million
TOTAL AREA: 11,506 sq. miles (29,800 sq. km)
DENSITY: 261 people per sq. mile

LANGUAGES: Armenian*, Azeri, Russian
RELIGIONS: Armenian Apostolic Church (Orthodox) 88%, Armenian Catholic Church 6%, other 6%
ETHNIC MIX: Armenian 98%, Yezidi 1%, other 1%
GOVERNMENT: Presidential system
CURRENCY: Dram = 100 luma

Australia

An island continent in its own right, Australia is the world's sixth-largest country. European settlement began over 200 years ago. Most Australians now live in cities along the coast.

GEOGRAPHY

Located between the Indian and Pacific Oceans, Australia has a variety of landscapes including tropical rainforests, the arid plateaus, ridges, and vast deserts of the "red center," the lowlands and river systems draining into Lake Eyre, rolling tracts of pastoral land, and magnificent beaches around much of the coastline. In the far east are the mountains of the Great Dividing Range. Famous natural features include Uluru (Ayers Rock) and the Great Barrier Reef.

CLIMATE

The west and south are semi-arid with hot summers. The arid interior can reach 120°F (50°C) in the central desert areas. The north is hot throughout the year, and humid during the summer monsoon. East, southeast, and southwest coastal areas are temperate.

PEOPLE & SOCIETY

The first settlers arrived in Australia at least 100,000 years ago. Today, the Aborigines make up around 2% of the population. European colonization began in 1788, and was dominated by British and Irish immigrants, some of whom were convicts. White-only immigration drives brought many Europeans to Australia, but since the 1960s multiculturalism has been encouraged and most new settlers are Asian; Cantonese is now the third most widely spoken language after English and Italian. Wealth disparities are small, but Aborigines, the exception in an otherwise integrated society, are marginalized: their average life expectancy is around 17 years less than other Australians. Politics is increasingly right-wing and illegal immigration is a major concern. Obesity is a growing problem among adults.

FACTFILE

OFFICIAL NAME: Commonwealth of Australia
DATE OF FORMATION: 1901
CAPITAL: Canberra
POPULATION: 20.2 million
TOTAL AREA: 2,967,893 sq. miles (7,686,850 sq. km)

DENSITY: 7 people per sq. mile
LANGUAGES: English*, Italian, other
RELIGIONS: Various Protestant 38%, other 36%, Roman Catholic 26%
ETHNIC MIX: European 92%, Asian 5%, Aboriginal 2%, other 1%
GOVERNMENT: Parliamentary system
CURRENCY: Australian dollar = 100 cents

$ THE ECONOMY

Efficient mining and agricultural industries: particular success in viticulture. Large resource base. Tourism growing. Concentration on Asian markets; hit hard by the 1997 financial crisis which tipped the region into recession. Regional competition is intense. Protectionism abandoned to open up Australian markets. Japan remains the most important trading partner, though China's expanding market for minerals has spurred strong economic growth.

◆ **INSIGHT:** *Sydney has the world's largest suburban area, a conurbation so vast that the city is twice as large as Beijing and six times the size of Rome*

Austria

Bordering eight countries in the heart of Europe, Austria was created in 1918 after the collapse of the Habsburg Empire. It joined the EU in 1995 and adopted the euro fully in 2002.

GEOGRAPHY

Mainly mountainous. Alps and foothills cover the west and south. Lowlands in the east are part of the Danube River basin.

CLIMATE

Temperate continental climate. The western Alpine regions have colder winters and more rainfall.

PEOPLE & SOCIETY

Austrian society is homogeneous. Though Austrians speak German, they like to stress their distinctive identity in relation to Germany. Minorities are few; there are some ethnic Croats, Slovenes, and Hungarians, plus refugees from conflict in former Yugoslavia. Though strongly Roman Catholic, Austrian society is less conservative than some southern German *Länder*. Class divisions remain strong.

THE ECONOMY

Large manufacturing base, despite lack of energy resources. The skilled labor force is key to the production of high-tech exports. Euro has boosted investment.

INSIGHT: *Many of the world's great composers were Austrian, including Mozart, Haydn, Schubert, and Strauss*

FACTFILE

OFFICIAL NAME: Republic of Austria
DATE OF FORMATION: 1918
CAPITAL: Vienna
POPULATION: 8.2 million
TOTAL AREA: 32,378 sq. miles (83,858 sq. km)
DENSITY: 257 people per sq. mile

LANGUAGES: German*, Croatian, Slovenian, Hungarian
RELIGIONS: Roman Catholic 78%, nonreligious 9%, other 8%, Protestant 5%
ETHNIC MIX: Austrian 93%, Croat, Slovene, and Hungarian 6%, other 1%
GOVERNMENT: Parliamentary system
CURRENCY: Euro = 100 cents

Azerbaijan

Situated on the western coast of the Caspian Sea, Azerbaijan was the first Soviet republic to declare independence in 1991. Territorial disputes with Armenia have dominated politics since.

GEOGRAPHY
Caucasus Mountains in west, including Naxçivan exclave south of Armenia. Flat, low-lying terrain on the coast of the Caspian Sea.

CLIMATE
Low rainfall. Continental, with bitter winters, inland. Subtropical in coastal regions.

PEOPLE & SOCIETY
Azeris, a Muslim people with ethnic links to Turks, form a large majority. Thousands of Armenians, Russians, and Jews have left since independence. Influx of half a million Azeri refugees fleeing war with Armenia over the disputed enclave of Nagorno Karabakh. Armenians there operate de facto independence. The status of women deteriorated after the fall of communism but they are slowly regaining their position.

THE ECONOMY
Extensive oil and gas reserves have come on stream. Legacy of war still drains state resources. Industry antiquated; infrastructure poor.

◆ **INSIGHT:** *The fire-worshipping Zoroastrian faith originated in Azerbaijan in the 6th century BCE*

FACTFILE
OFFICIAL NAME: Republic of Azerbaijan
DATE OF FORMATION: 1991
CAPITAL: Baku
POPULATION: 8.4 million
TOTAL AREA: 33,436 sq. miles (86,600 sq. km)
DENSITY: 251 people per sq. mile

LANGUAGES: Azeri*, Russian
RELIGIONS: Shi'a Muslim 68%, Sunni Muslim 26%, Russian Orthodox 3%, Armenian Orthodox 2%, other 1%
ETHNIC MIX: Azeri 91%, other 3%, Lazs 2%, Russian 2%, Armenian 2%
GOVERNMENT: Presidential system
CURRENCY: Manat = 100 gopik

Bahamas

Located off the Florida coast in the western Atlantic, the Bahamas comprises an archipelago of some 700 islands and 2400 cays, only around 30 of which are inhabited.

GEOGRAPHY
Long, mainly flat coral formations with a few low hills. Some islands have pine forests, lagoons, and mangrove swamps.

CLIMATE
Subtropical. Hot summers and mild winters. Heavy rainfall, especially in summer. Hurricanes can strike in July–December.

PEOPLE & SOCIETY
Over 60% of the population live on New Providence. Tourism employs over 30% of the labor force. The remainder are engaged in traditional fishing and agriculture, or in administration. Haitian and Cuban immigrants form the poorest group in society. More women are now entering the professions. Government priorities are tackling narcotics trafficking and money laundering.

THE ECONOMY
Major tourist destination, especially for US visitors. Financial services: banking and insurance.

◆ **INSIGHT:** *Only a tiny fraction of the country's extensive merchant fleet is owned by Bahamians*

FACTFILE

OFFICIAL NAME: Commonwealth of the Bahamas
DATE OF FORMATION: 1973
CAPITAL: Nassau
POPULATION: 323,000
TOTAL AREA: 5382 sq. miles (13,940 sq. km)

DENSITY: 84 people per sq. mile
LANGUAGES: English*, English Creole, French Creole
RELIGIONS: Baptist 32%, other 29%, Anglican 20%, Roman Catholic 19%
ETHNIC MIX: Black African 85%, other 15%
GOVERNMENT: Parliamentary system
CURRENCY: Bahamian dollar = 100 cents

Bahrain

Bahrain is an archipelago of 49 islands between the Qatar peninsula and the Saudi Arabian mainland. Only three of the islands are inhabited. It was the first Gulf emirate to export oil.

 GEOGRAPHY

All islands are low-lying. The largest, Bahrain Island, is mainly sandy plains and salt marshes.

 CLIMATE

Summers are hot and humid. Winters are mild. Low rainfall.

PEOPLE & SOCIETY

The key social division is between the Shi'a majority and Sunni minority. Sunnis hold the best jobs in bureaucracy and business while Shi'as tend to do menial work. The al-Khalifa family has ruled since 1783, and only transformed Bahrain into a constitutional monarchy, with limited democracy, in 2002. Bahrain is socially liberal.

◆ **INSIGHT:** *The 16 Hawar Islands were awarded to Bahrain in 2001 after a lengthy dispute with Qatar*

$ THE ECONOMY

Main exports are refined petroleum and aluminum products. As oil reserves run out, gas is of increasing importance. Regional offshore banking center. Government debts are high.

FACTFILE

OFFICIAL NAME: Kingdom of Bahrain
DATE OF FORMATION: 1971
CAPITAL: Manama
POPULATION: 727,000
TOTAL AREA: 239 sq. miles (620 sq. km)
DENSITY: 2663 people per sq. mile

LANGUAGES: Arabic
RELIGIONS: Muslim (mainly Shi'a) 99%, other 1%
ETHNIC MIX: Bahraini 70%, Iranian, Indian, and Pakistani 24%, other Arab 4%, European 2%
GOVERNMENT: Monarchy
CURRENCY: Bahraini dinar = 1000 fils

Bangladesh

Bangladesh lies at the north end of the Bay of Bengal. It seceded from Pakistan in 1971 and, after much political instability, returned to democracy in 1991.

GEOGRAPHY

Mostly flat alluvial plains and deltas of the Brahmaputra and Ganges Rivers. Southeast coasts are fringed with mangrove forests.

CLIMATE

Hot and humid. During the monsoon, water levels can rise 20 ft (6 m) above sea level.

PEOPLE & SOCIETY

Bangladesh often suffers devastating floods, cyclones, and famine. Democracy was restored in 1991 after a period of military rule. Half of the population live in poverty, but living standards are improving. Women are prominent in politics, but their rights are neglected.

◆ **INSIGHT:** *Torrential monsoon rains flood two-thirds of the country every year*

THE ECONOMY

Agriculture is vulnerable to unpredictable climate. Bangladesh accounts for 90% of world jute fiber exports. Poor infrastructure deters investment. Growing textile industry.

FACTFILE

OFFICIAL NAME: People's Republic of Bangladesh
DATE OF FORMATION: 1971
CAPITAL: Dhaka
POPULATION: 142 million
TOTAL AREA: 55,598 sq. miles (144,000 sq. km)

DENSITY: 2743 people per sq. mile
LANGUAGES: Bengali*, Urdu, Chakma, Marma, Garo, Khasi, Santhali, Tripuri, Mro
RELIGIONS: Muslim (mainly Sunni) 87%, Hindu 12%, other 1%
ETHNIC MIX: Bengali 98%, other 2%
GOVERNMENT: Parliamentary system
CURRENCY: Taka = 100 poisha

Barbados

Barbados is the most easterly of the Caribbean islands.
Once solely inhabited by the native Arawak, Barbados
was first colonized by British settlers in the 1620s.

GEOGRAPHY
Encircled by coral reefs.
Fertile and predominantly flat,
with a few gentle hills to the north.

CLIMATE
Moderate tropical climate.
Sunnier and drier than its more
mountainous neighbors.

PEOPLE & SOCIETY
Some latent tension between
white community, which controls
politics and much of the economy,
and majority black population, but
violence is rare. Increasing social
mobility has enabled black
Barbadians to enter the professions.
Despite political stability, and good
welfare and education services,
pockets of abject poverty remain.

INSIGHT: *Barbados retains a strong
British influence and is referred to
by its neighbors as "Little England"*

THE ECONOMY
Well-developed tourist industry
based on climate and accessibility.
Financial services and information
processing are important new growth
sectors. Sugar industry, once the main
cash crop, now ailing.

FACTFILE
OFFICIAL NAME: Barbados
DATE OF FORMATION: 1966
CAPITAL: Bridgetown
POPULATION: 270,000
TOTAL AREA: 166 sq. miles
(430 sq. km)
DENSITY: 1627 people per sq. mile

LANGUAGES: Bajan (Barbadian English),
English*
RELIGIONS: Anglican 40%, other 24%,
nonreligious 17%, Pentecostal 8%,
Methodist 7%, Roman Catholic 4%
ETHNIC MIX: Black African 92%, other 8%
GOVERNMENT: Parliamentary system
CURRENCY: Barbados dollar = 100 cents

Belarus

 Literally "White Russia," Belarus lies landlocked in eastern Europe. It reluctantly became independent of the USSR in 1991. There are few resources other than agriculture.

 GEOGRAPHY
Mainly plains and low hills. The Dnieper and Dvina Rivers drain the eastern lowlands. Vast Pripet Marshes in the southwest.

 CLIMATE
Extreme continental climate. Winters are long, sub-freezing, but mainly dry; summers are hot.

PEOPLE & SOCIETY
Only 2% of people are non-Slav, so ethnic tension is minimal. Russian culture dominates. Belarus was the slowest ex-Soviet state to implement political reform; President Lukashenka has been labeled as Europe's last dictator. Enthusiasm for a merger with Russia has waned. Wealth is held by a small ex-communist elite. Fallout from 1986 Chernobyl nuclear disaster in Ukraine still seriously affects health and the environment.

 THE ECONOMY
Low unemployment but high inflation. Outmoded industry; dependence on Russia for energy and raw materials. Privatization stalled.

INSIGHT: *The number of cancer and leukemia cases has soared since the 1986 Chernobyl disaster*

FACTFILE

OFFICIAL NAME: Republic of Belarus
DATE OF FORMATION: 1991
CAPITAL: Minsk
POPULATION: 9.8 million
TOTAL AREA: 80,154 sq. miles (207,600 sq. km)
DENSITY: 122 people per sq. mile

LANGUAGES: Belarussian*, Russian*
RELIGIONS: Orthodox Christian 60%, other (including Muslim, Jewish, and Protestant) 32%, Roman Catholic 8%
ETHNIC MIX: Belarussian 81%, Russian 11%, Polish 4%, Ukrainian 2%, other 2%
GOVERNMENT: Presidential system
CURRENCY: Belarussian rouble = 100 kopeks

Belgium

Belgium lies in northwestern Europe. Its history has been marked by tensions between the majority Dutch-speaking (Flemish) and minority French-speaking (Walloon) communities.

GEOGRAPHY

Low-lying coastal plain covers two-thirds of the country. Land becomes hilly and forested in the southeast (Ardennes) region.

CLIMATE

Maritime climate with Gulf Stream influences. Temperatures are mild, with heavy cloud cover and rain. More rainfall and weather fluctuations at the coast.

PEOPLE & SOCIETY

Since 1970, Flemish regions have become more prosperous than those of the minority Walloons, overturning traditional roles and increasing friction. In order to contain tensions, Belgium began to move toward federalism in 1980. Both groups now have their own governments and have control over most of their own affairs.

THE ECONOMY

Variety of industrial exports, including steel, glassware, cut diamonds, and textiles. Very high levels of public debt. Bureaucracy larger than European average.

INSIGHT: *The Ardennes region, in the southeast of the country, is famous for its forests, cuisine, and lakes*

FACTFILE

OFFICIAL NAME: Kingdom of Belgium
DATE OF FORMATION: 1830
CAPITAL: Brussels
POPULATION: 10.4 million
TOTAL AREA: 11,780 sq. miles (30,510 sq. km)
DENSITY: 821 people per sq. mile

LANGUAGES: Dutch*, French*, German*
RELIGIONS: Roman Catholic 88%, other 10%, Muslim 2%
ETHNIC MIX: Fleming 58%, Walloon 33%, other 6%, Italian 2%, Moroccan 1%
GOVERNMENT: Parliamentary system
CURRENCY: Euro = 100 cents

Belize

Belize lies on the eastern shore of the Yucatan Peninsula. Formerly called British Honduras, Belize was the last Central American country to gain its independence, in 1981.

GEOGRAPHY

Almost half the land area is forested. Low mountains in southeast. Flat swampy coastal plains.

CLIMATE

Tropical. Very hot and humid, with May–December rainy season.

PEOPLE & SOCIETY

English-speaking black Creoles are outnumbered by Spanish speakers, including native *mestizos* and immigrants from neighboring states. The Creoles have traditionally dominated society, but high levels of emigration to the US have weakened their influence. Newcomers provide manpower for agriculture. The Afro-Carib *garifuna* have their own language.

◆ **INSIGHT:** *Belize's barrier reef is the second-largest in the world*

THE ECONOMY

Tourism, agriculture and offshore banking. Oil extraction began in 2005. Sugar, textiles, lobsters, and shrimp are exported. Serious hurricane damage is a recurring problem.

FACTFILE

OFFICIAL NAME: Belize
DATE OF FORMATION: 1981
CAPITAL: Belmopan
POPULATION: 270,000
TOTAL AREA: 8867 sq. miles (22,966 sq. km)
DENSITY: 31 people per sq. mile

LANGUAGES: English Creole, Spanish, English*, Mayan, Garifuna (Carib)
RELIGIONS: Roman Catholic 62%, other 20%, Anglican 12%, Methodist 6%
ETHNIC MIX: Mestizo 49%, Creole 25%, Maya 11%, other 9%, Garifuna 6%
GOVERNMENT: Parliamentary system
CURRENCY: Belizean dollar = 100 cents

Benin

Benin stretches north from the west African coast. In 1990, it became one of the pioneers of African democratization, ending 17 years of one-party Marxist-Leninist rule.

GEOGRAPHY
Sandy coastal region. Numerous lagoons lie just behind the shoreline. Forested plateaus inland. Mountains in the northwest.

CLIMATE
Hot and humid in the south. Two rainy seasons. Hot, dusty *harmattan* winds blow during the December–February dry season.

PEOPLE & SOCIETY
There are 42 different ethnic groups. The southern Fon have tended to dominate politics. Other major groups are the Adja and Yoruba. The northern Fulani follow a nomadic lifestyle. North–south tension is mainly due to the south being more developed. French culture is highly prized in urban areas. Substantial differences in wealth reflect a strongly hierarchical society.

THE ECONOMY
Strong agricultural sector: cash crops include cotton, oil palm, and cashew nuts. Large-scale smuggling is a serious problem. France is the main aid donor.

INSIGHT:
Voodoo is thought to have originated in Benin, and was taken to Haiti by slaves

FACTFILE

OFFICIAL NAME: Republic of Benin
DATE OF FORMATION: 1960
CAPITAL: Porto-Novo
POPULATION: 8.4 million
TOTAL AREA: 43,483 sq. miles (112,620 sq. km)
DENSITY: 197 people per sq. mile

LANGUAGES: Fon, Bariba, Yoruba, Adja, Houeda, Somba, French*
RELIGIONS: Voodoo 50%, Muslim 30%, Christian 20%
ETHNIC MIX: Fon 41%, other 21%, Adja 16%, Yoruba 12%, Bariba 10%
GOVERNMENT: Presidential system
CURRENCY: CFA franc = 100 centimes

Bhutan

Perched in the eastern Himalayas between India and China lies the landlocked Kingdom of Bhutan. It is largely closed to the outside world to protect its culture; TV was banned until 1999.

GEOGRAPHY

Low, tropical southern strip rising through fertile central valleys to high Himalayas in the north. Around 70% of the land is forested.

CLIMATE
South is tropical, north is alpine, cold, and harsh. Central valleys warmer in east than west.

PEOPLE & SOCIETY

The king was absolute monarch until 1998, and legislative elections are to be held in 2008. Most people are devoutly Buddhist and originate from Tibet. A quarter are Hindu Nepalese, who settled in the south. Bhutan has 20 languages. In 1988, Dzongkha (a Tibetan dialect native to just 16% of the people) was made the official language. The Nepalese community regard this as "cultural imperialism," causing considerable ethnic tensions.

THE ECONOMY
Reliant on India for trade. Most people farm their own plots of land and herd cattle and yaks. Steep land unsuited for cultivation. Development of cash crops for Asian markets.

◆ **INSIGHT:** *In 2004 Bhutan became the first country in the world to ban smoking and the sale of tobacco*

FACTFILE

OFFICIAL NAME: Kingdom of Bhutan
DATE OF FORMATION: 1656
CAPITAL: Thimphu
POPULATION: 2.2 million
TOTAL AREA: 18,147 sq. miles (47,000 sq. km)
DENSITY: 121 people per sq. mile

LANGUAGES: Dzongkha*, Nepali, Assamese
RELIGIONS: Mahayana Buddhist 70%, Hindu 24%, other 6%
ETHNIC MIX: Bhute 50%, other 25%, Nepalese 25%
GOVERNMENT: Monarchy
CURRENCY: Ngultrum = 100 chetrum

Bolivia

Landlocked high in central South America, Bolivia is one of the region's poorest countries. La Paz is the world's highest capital city: 13,385 feet (3631 m) above sea level.

GEOGRAPHY

A high windswept plateau, the *altiplano*, lies between two Andean mountain ranges. Semiarid grasslands to the east; dense tropical forests to the north.

CLIMATE

Altiplano has extreme tropical climate, with night-frost in winter. North and east are hot and humid.

PEOPLE & SOCIETY

The indigenous majority faces widespread discrimination. Wealthy Spanish-descended families have traditionally controlled the economy. Amerindian Evo Morales, president from 2005, has pledged to cut poverty, legalize coca, and redistribute land.

◆ INSIGHT: *Between 1825 and 1982 Bolivia averaged more than one armed coup a year*

THE ECONOMY

Gold, silver, zinc, tin, oil and natural gas are extracted. Social issues and nationalization of gas industry have deterred overseas investors. Lack of manufacturing: primary products vulnerable to world price fluctuations.

3000m/9843ft
2000m/6562ft
1000m/3281ft
500m/1640ft
200m/656ft
Sea Level

FACTFILE

OFFICIAL NAME: Republic of Bolivia
DATE OF FORMATION: 1825
CAPITALS: La Paz (administrative); Sucre (judicial)
POPULATION: 9.2 million
TOTAL AREA: 424,162 sq. miles (1,098,580 sq. km)

DENSITY: 22 people per sq. mile
LANGUAGES: Aymara*, Quechua*, Spanish*
RELIGIONS: Roman Catholic 93%, other 7%
ETHNIC MIX: Quechua 37%, Aymara 32%, mixed 13%, European 10%, other 8%
GOVERNMENT: Presidential system
CURRENCY: Boliviano = 100 centavos

Bosnia & Herzegovina

Perched in the highlands of southeast Europe, Bosnia and Herzegovina was the focus of the bitter ethnic conflict which accompanied the dissolution of the former Yugoslav state.

GEOGRAPHY
Hills and mountains, with narrow river valleys. Lowlands in the north. Mainly deciduous forest covers about half of the total area.

CLIMATE
Continental. Hot summers and cold, often snowy winters.

PEOPLE & SOCIETY
Despite sharing the same origin and spoken language, Bosnians have been divided by history between Orthodox Serbs, Roman Catholic Croats, and Muslim Bosniaks. Ethnic cleansing was practiced by all sides in the civil war displacing around 60% of the population. Refugees are still returning.

◆ **INSIGHT:** *The murder of Archduke Ferdinand of Austria in Sarajevo in 1914 triggered the First World War*

THE ECONOMY
Bosnia has the potential to recover its status as a thriving market economy with a strong manufacturing base, but still struggles with the legacy of war. Little investment.

FACTFILE
OFFICIAL NAME: Bosnia and Herzegovina
DATE OF FORMATION: 1992
CAPITAL: Sarajevo
POPULATION: 3.9 million
TOTAL AREA: 19,741 sq. miles (51,129 sq. km)

DENSITY: 198 people per sq. mile
LANGUAGES: Serbo-Croat
RELIGIONS: Muslim 40%, Orthodox Christian 31%, Catholic 15%, other 14%
ETHNIC MIX: Bosniak 44%, Serb 31%, Croat 17%, other 8%
GOVERNMENT: Parliamentary system
CURRENCY: Marka = 100 pfeninga

Botswana

Landlocked in the heart of southern Africa, Botswana boasts the world's largest inland river delta. Diamonds provide potential wealth, but the country is crippled by HIV/AIDS.

GEOGRAPHY
Lies on vast plateau, high above sea level. Hills in the east. Kalahari Desert in center and southwest. Swamps and salt pans elsewhere and in Okavango Basin.

CLIMATE
Dry and prone to drought. Summer wet season, April–October. Winters are warm, with cold nights.

PEOPLE & SOCIETY
Tswana make up 98% of the population. The San bushmen, the first inhabitants, are marginalized. They were ordered in 2002 to abandon their nomadic lifestyle. Botswana had the highest rate of HIV-positive adults in the world (38.8%) in 2001–2002.

◆ **INSIGHT:** *Water, Botswana's most precious resource, is honored in the name of the currency – pula*

THE ECONOMY
Diamonds are the leading export. Deposits of other minerals. Beef is exported to Europe. Tourism aimed at wealthy wildlife enthusiasts. AIDS is devastating the population.

FACTFILE

OFFICIAL NAME: Republic of Botswana
DATE OF FORMATION: 1966
CAPITAL: Gaborone
POPULATION: 1.8 million
TOTAL AREA: 231,803 sq. miles (600,370 sq. km)
DENSITY: 8 people per sq. mile

LANGUAGES: Setswana, English*, Shona, San, Khoikhoi, isiNdebele
RELIGIONS: Traditional beliefs 50%, Christian (mainly Protestant) 30%, other (including Muslim) 20%
ETHNIC MIX: Tswana 98%, other 2%
GOVERNMENT: Presidential system
CURRENCY: Pula = 100 thebe

Brazil

Covering almost half of South America, Brazil is the site of the world's largest and ecologically most important rainforest. The country has immense natural and economic resources.

GEOGRAPHY

Rainforest grows around the massive Amazon River and its delta, covering almost half of Brazil's total land area. Apart from the basin of the River Plate to the south, the rest of the country consists of highlands. The mountainous east is part-forested and part-desert. The coastal plain in the southeast has swampy areas. The Atlantic coastline is 1240 miles (2000 km) long.

CLIMATE

Brazil's share of the Amazon Basin, occupying half the country, has a model tropical equatorial climate. Temperatures are high with almost no seasonal variation. The Brazilian plateau has far greater ranges of temperature and rainfall. The east is very dry and suffers from frequent droughts. The south has hot summers and cool winters.

PEOPLE & SOCIETY

Diverse population includes Amerindians, blacks, European immigrants, and people of mixed race. Amerindians suffer prejudice from most other peoples in Brazil. Shanty towns in the cities attract poor migrants from the northeast. Urban crime, violent land disputes, and unchecked development in Amazonia tarnish Brazil's image as a modern nation. Catholicism and the family unit remain strong.

THE ECONOMY

Dominant regional economy. Huge potential for growth based on abundant natural resources. Brazil is a leading exporter of coffee, sugar, and orange juice. Social tension threatens stability. Debts are high.

Equator

COLOMBIA

PERU

FACTFILE

OFFICIAL NAME: Federative Rep. of Brazil
DATE OF FORMATION: 1822
CAPITAL: Brasília
POPULATION: 186 million
TOTAL AREA: 3,286,470 sq. miles (8,511,965 sq. km)
DENSITY: 57 people per sq. mile

LANGUAGES: Portuguese*, German, Italian, Spanish, Polish, Japanese, other
RELIGIONS: Roman Catholic 74%, Protestant 15%, atheist 7%, other 4%
ETHNIC MIX: White 54%, mixed race 38%, Black 6 %, other 2%
GOVERNMENT: Presidential system
CURRENCY: Real = 100 centavos

INSIGHT: *Since 1900, a third of Brazil's indigenous Amerindian groups have become extinct due to disease, starvation, or the forceful taking of land by miners, loggers, and settlers*

VENEZUELA

French Guiana *(France)*

SURINAME

GUYANA

Boa Vista

Guiana Highlands

Macapá

Japurá

Rio Negro

Branco

Amazon

Ilha de Marajó

Belém

Equator

ATLANTIC

OCEAN

A m a z o n

Manaus

Santarém

São Luís

B a s i n

Juruá

Purus

Madeira

Tapajós

Iriri

Xingu

Tocantins

Parnaíba

Teresina

Imperatriz

Fortaleza

San Fernando de Noronha

Porto Velho

Rio Branco

Chapada dos Parecis

Guaporé

Juruena

São Manuel

Planalto de Mato Grosso

Araguaia

Juazeiro do Norte

Represa de Sobradinho

Campina Grande

Natal

João Pessoa

Olinda

Recife

Maceió

Aracaju

BOLIVIA

Cuiabá

Taguatinga

São Francisco

Feira de Santana

Salvador

Pantanal

Paraguay

BRASÍLIA

Goiânia

Brazilian Highlands

Montes Claros

Itabuna

Vitória da Conquista

Uberlândia

Uberaba

Governador Valadares

Belo Horizonte

Campo Grande

Ribeirão Preto

Vitória

Bauru

Campinas

Nova Iguaçu

Campos

Londrina

Paraná

São Paulo

Duque de Caxias

Rio de Janeiro

Santos

PARAGUAY

Curitiba

Joinville

Florianópolis

0   500 km

0   500 miles

ARGENTINA

Caxias do Sul

Porto Alegre

ATLANTIC

Lagoa dos Patos

OCEAN

Pelotas

Rio Grande

URUGUAY

Mirim Lagoon

2000m/6562ft
1000m/3281ft
500m/1640ft
200m/656ft
Sea Level

60°

60°

10°

20°

30°

40°

50°

Brunei

Lying on the northern coast of the island of Borneo, Brunei is surrounded and divided in two by the Malaysian state of Sarawak. It has been independent since 1984.

GEOGRAPHY

Mostly dense lowland rainforest and mangrove swamps, with some mountains in the southeast.

CLIMATE

Tropical. Six-month rainy season with very high humidity.

PEOPLE & SOCIETY

Malays benefit from positive discrimination. Many in the Chinese community are stateless. Since a failed rebellion in 1962, Brunei has been ruled by decree of the sultan. In 1990, "Malay Muslim Monarchy" was introduced, promoting Islamic values as state ideology. Women, less restricted than in some Muslim states, are obliged to wear headscarves but not the veil.

◆ **INSIGHT:** *The sultan spent US$450 million building the world's largest palace at Bandar Seri Begawan*

THE ECONOMY

Oil and natural gas reserves have brought one of the world's highest standards of living. Massive overseas investments. Major consumer of high-tech hi-fi, video equipment, and Western designer clothes.

FACTFILE

OFFICIAL NAME: Sultanate of Brunei
DATE OF FORMATION: 1984
CAPITAL: Bandar Seri Begawan
POPULATION: 374,000
TOTAL AREA: 2228 sq. miles (5770 sq. km)
DENSITY: 184 people per sq. mile

LANGUAGES: Malay*, English, Chinese
RELIGIONS: Muslim (mainly Sunni) 66%, Buddhist 14%, other 10%, Christian 10%
ETHNIC MIX: Malay 67%, Chinese 16%, other 11%, indigenous 6%
GOVERNMENT: Monarchy
CURRENCY: Brunei dollar = 100 cents

Bulgaria

Located in southeastern Europe, Bulgaria was under communist rule from 1947 to 1989. Since then, the country has made gradual progress with political and economic reform.

GEOGRAPHY

Mountains run east–west across center and along southern border. Danube plain in north, Thracian plain in southeast. Black Sea to the east.

CLIMATE

Warm summers and snowy winters, especially in mountains. East winds bring seasonal extremes.

PEOPLE & SOCIETY

The communists tried forcibly to suppress cultural identities, leading to a large exodus of Bulgarian Turks in 1989. Recent privatization programs have left many Turks landless and prompted further emigration. Roma suffer discrimination at all levels of society. Women have equal rights in theory, but society remains patriarchal. Organized crime, human trafficking, and corruption needed curbing as a precondition of EU accession in 2007.

THE ECONOMY

Good agricultural production, including grapes, for well-developed wine industry, and tobacco. Expertise in software development. Industry and infrastructure are outdated.

INSIGHT: *Archaeologists have found evidence of wine-making in Bulgaria dating back over 5000 years*

FACTFILE

OFFICIAL NAME: Republic of Bulgaria
DATE OF FORMATION: 1908
CAPITAL: Sofia
POPULATION: 7.7 million
TOTAL AREA: 42,822 sq. miles (110,910 sq. km)
DENSITY: 180 people per sq. mile

LANGUAGES: Bulgarian*, Turkish, Romani
RELIGIONS: Orthodox Christian 83%, Muslim 12%, other 4%, Catholic 1%
ETHNIC MIX: Bulgarian 84%, Turkish 9%, Roma 5%, other 2%
GOVERNMENT: Parliamentary system
CURRENCY: Lev = 100 stotinki

Burkina

Known as Upper Volta until 1984, the west African state of Burkina has been ruled by military dictators for most of its postindependence history. It is now a multiparty state.

GEOGRAPHY

The Sahara covers the north of the country. The south is largely savanna. The three main rivers are the Black, White, and Red Voltas.

CLIMATE

Tropical. Dry, cool weather November–February. Erratic rain March–April, mostly in southeast.

PEOPLE & SOCIETY

No single ethnic group is dominant, but the Mossi, from around Ouagadougou, have always played an important part in government. The people from the west are much more ethnically mixed. Extreme poverty has led to a strong sense of egalitarianism. Most women are still denied access to education, though their absence from public life belies their real power and social influence.

THE ECONOMY

Cotton is the major cash crop, but the soil quality is poor and worsening as the Sahara Desert encroaches.

INSIGHT: *Droughts and poor soils mean that many Burkinabes seek work southward in Ghana and Côte d'Ivoire*

FACTFILE

OFFICIAL NAME: Burkina Faso
DATE OF FORMATION: 1960
CAPITAL: Ouagadougou
POPULATION: 13.2 million
TOTAL AREA: 105,869 sq. miles (274,200 sq. km)
DENSITY: 125 people per sq. mile

LANGUAGES: Mossi, Fulani, French*, Tuareg, Dyula, Songhai
RELIGIONS: Muslim 55%, Traditional beliefs 35%, Roman Catholic 9%, other Christian 1%
ETHNIC MIX: Other 52%, Mossi 48%
GOVERNMENT: Presidential system
CURRENCY: CFA franc = 100 centimes

Burundi

 Small, densely populated and landlocked, Burundi lies just south of the equator, on the Nile–Congo watershed in central Africa. Ethnic tensions are the main factor in politics.

 GEOGRAPHY
Hilly with high plateaus in center and savanna in the east. Great Rift Valley on western side.

CLIMATE
Temperate, with high humidity. Heavy and frequent rainfall, mostly October–May. Highlands have frost.

 PEOPLE & SOCIETY
Most people are subsistence farmers. Burundi has been riven by ethnic conflict between majority Hutu and the Tutsi, who controlled the army – with repeated large-scale massacres. Hundreds of thousands of people have been killed since 1993. A power-sharing deal is now in place. Twa pygmies were not involved in the conflict.

◆ **INSIGHT:** *Burundi's fertility rate is one of the highest in Africa. On average, women have seven children*

THE ECONOMY
Overwhelmingly agricultural economy. Small quantities of gold and tungsten. Potential of oil in Lake Tanganyika. Little prospect of lasting stability.

FACTFILE

OFFICIAL NAME: Republic of Burundi
DATE OF FORMATION: 1962
CAPITAL: Bujumbura
POPULATION: 7.5 million
TOTAL AREA: 10,745 sq. miles (27,830 sq. km)
DENSITY: 757 people per sq. mile

LANGUAGES: Kirundi*, French*, Kiswahili
RELIGIONS: Christian (mainly Roman Catholic) 60%, traditional beliefs 39%, Muslim 1%
ETHNIC MIX: Hutu 85%, Tutsi 14%, Twa 1%
GOVERNMENT: Presidential system
CURRENCY: Burundi franc = 100 centimes

Cambodia

Located on the Indochinese peninsula in southeast Asia, Cambodia has emerged from two decades of civil war and invasion from Vietnam. Rice is the principal crop.

GEOGRAPHY
Mostly low-lying basin. Tônlé Sap (Great Lake) drains into the Mekong River. Forested mountains and plateau east of the Mekong.

CLIMATE
Tropical. High temperatures throughout the year. Heavy rainfall during May–October monsoon.

PEOPLE & SOCIETY
Under Pol Pot's Marxist Khmer Rouge regime, between 1975 and 1979, over one million Cambodians died. Effects of revolution and civil war are still felt and are reflected in the high rates of orphans, widows, and land-mine victims. A fragile stability has lasted since elections in 1993. The Khmer Rouge discontinued its armed struggle after the death of Pol Pot in 1998. King Norodom Sihanouk, a key figure in politics, abdicated in 2004.

THE ECONOMY
Economy is still recovering from civil war. Modest trade in rubber and timber, and self-sufficiency in rice. Reliant on imports and aid. Small tax base limits the scope of reforms.

INSIGHT: *Cambodia has many impressive temples, dating from when the country was the center of the Khmer empire*

FACTFILE

OFFICIAL NAME: Kingdom of Cambodia
DATE OF FORMATION: 1953
CAPITAL: Phnom Penh
POPULATION: 14.1 million
TOTAL AREA: 69,900 sq. miles
(181,040 sq. km)
DENSITY: 207 people per sq. mile

LANGUAGES: Khmer*, French, Chinese, Vietnamese, Cham
RELIGIONS: Buddhist 93%, Muslim 6%, Christian 1%
ETHNIC MIX: Khmer 90%, other 5%, Vietnamese 4%, Chinese 1%
GOVERNMENT: Parliamentary system
CURRENCY: Riel = 100 sen

Cameroon

Situated in the corner of the Gulf of Guinea, Cameroon was effectively a one-party state for 30 years. Multiparty elections were held in 1992, returning the former ruling party to power.

GEOGRAPHY
Over half the land is forested: equatorial rainforest in north, evergreen forest and wooded savanna in south. Mountains in the west.

CLIMATE
South is equatorial, with plentiful rainfall, declining inland. Far north is beset by drought.

PEOPLE & SOCIETY
Around 230 ethnic groups; no single group is dominant. The Bamileke is the largest, though it has never held political power. North–south tensions are diminished by the ethnic diversity. There is more rivalry between majority French- and minority English-speakers.

◆ INSIGHT: *Cameroon's name derives from the Portuguese word* camarões – *after the shrimp fished by the early European explorers*

THE ECONOMY
Oil reserves. Very diversified agricultural economy – timber, cocoa, bananas, coffee. Fuel smuggling from Nigeria undermines refinery profits. Corruption is widespread.

FACTFILE

OFFICIAL NAME: Republic of Cameroon
DATE OF FORMATION: 1960
CAPITAL: Yaoundé
POPULATION: 16.3 million
TOTAL AREA: 183,567 sq. miles (475,400 sq. km)
DENSITY: 91 people per sq. mile

LANGUAGES: Bamileke, Fang, Fulani, French*, English*
RELIGIONS: Catholic 35%, traditional beliefs 25%, Muslim 22%, Protestant 18%
ETHNIC MIX: Highlanders 31%, other 39%, equatorial Bantu 19%, Kirdi 11%
GOVERNMENT: Presidential system
CURRENCY: CFA franc = 100 centimes

Canada

Canada extends from its long border with the US to the Arctic Ocean. The relationship of French-speaking Québec with the rest of the country has become a less contentious issue.

GEOGRAPHY

The world's second-largest country, stretching north to Cape Colombia on Ellesmere Island, south to Lake Erie, and across five time zones from the Pacific seaboard to Newfoundland. Arctic tundra and islands in the far north give way southward to forests, interspersed with lakes and rivers, and then the vast Canadian Shield, which covers over half the area of Canada. Rocky Mountains in west, beyond which are the Coast Mountains, islands, and fjords. Fertile lowlands in the east.

CLIMATE

Ranges from polar and subpolar in the north, to continental in the south. Winters in the interior are colder and longer than on the coast, with temperatures well below freezing and deep snow; summers are hotter. Pacific coast has the mildest winters.

PEOPLE & SOCIETY

Two-thirds of the population live in the Great Lakes–St. Lawrence lowlands, fostering some shared cultural values with the neighboring US. Important differences, however, include wider welfare provision and Commonwealth membership. The Québécois wish to preserve their culture and language from further Anglicization, and demand to be recognized as a "distinct society." The government welcomes ethnic diversity among immigrants, promoting a policy which encourages each group to maintain its own culture. Land claims made by the indigenous peoples are being redressed. Nunavut, an Inuit-governed territory which covers nearly a quarter of Canada's land area, was created from a portion of the Northwest Territories in 1999. Women are well represented at most levels of business and government.

FACTFILE

OFFICIAL NAME: Canada
DATE OF FORMATION: 1867
CAPITAL: Ottawa
POPULATION: 32.3 million
TOTAL AREA: 3,851,788 sq. miles (9,976,140 sq. km)
DENSITY: 9 people per sq. mile

LANGUAGES: English*, French*, other
RELIGIONS: Roman Catholic 44%, Protestant 29%, other 27%
ETHNIC ORIGIN: British, French and other European 27m, Asian 3m, Amerindian, Métis, and Inuit 1.3m
GOVERNMENT: Parliamentary system
CURRENCY: Canadian dollar = 100 cents

Canada

$ THE ECONOMY

Wide-ranging resources, providing exports, cheap energy, and raw materials for manufacturing, underpin a high standard of living, with smaller wealth disparities than in the US. Prices for primary exports fluctuate, but the high oil price has enabled the development of Alberta's vast oil fields. Manufactured exports have flourished under growing global competition, especially since Canada joined NAFTA. Unemployment has fallen steadily over the last decade from a high of around 10%. Economic growth quickly rebounded from the effect of the 2001 slowdown in the US.

◆ **INSIGHT:** The magnetic north pole, where the dipping needle of a compass stands still, migrates across northern Canada

Cape Verde

Off the west coast of Africa, in the Atlantic Ocean, lies the group of islands that make up Cape Verde, a Portuguese colony until it gained independence in 1975.

GEOGRAPHY
Ten main islands and eight smaller islets, all of volcanic origin. Mostly mountainous, with steep cliffs and rocky headlands.

CLIMATE
Warm, and very dry. Subject to droughts that can sometimes last for years at a time.

PEOPLE & SOCIETY
Most people are of mixed Portuguese–African origin; the rest are largely African, descended from slaves or more recent immigrants. Creolization of the culture negates ethnic tensions. Half of the population live on Santiago. Over 600,000 Cape Verdeans now live abroad.

 INSIGHT: *Poor soils and lack of surface water mean that Cape Verde is dependent on food aid*

THE ECONOMY
Most people are subsistence farmers. Clothing is the main export. Only minerals produced are salt, and volcanic rock for cement.

	2000m/6562ft
	1000m/3281ft
	500m/1640ft
	200m/656ft
	Sea Level

Santo Antão
17°
Mindelo
Santa Luzia
São Vicente
Sal
São Nicolau
Ilhas de Barlavento
Sal Rei
Boa Vista
25°
16°
ATLANTIC
OCEAN
Ilhas de Sotavento
Maio
15°
Tarrafil
Brava
São Filipe
Santiago
(São Tiago)
+PRAIA
23°
Fogo
24°

0   50 km
0   50 miles

FACTFILE

OFFICIAL NAME: Republic of Cape Verde
DATE OF FORMATION: 1975
CAPITAL: Praia
POPULATION: 507,000
TOTAL AREA: 1557 sq. miles (4033 sq. km)
DENSITY: 326 people per sq. mile

LANGUAGES: Creole, Portuguese*
RELIGIONS: Roman Catholic 97%, other 2%, Protestant 1%
ETHNIC MIX: Mestiço 60%, African 30%, other 10%
GOVERNMENT: Mixed presidential–parliamentary system
CURRENCY: C.V. escudo = 100 centavos

Central African Republic

The Central African Republic (CAR) is a landlocked country lying between the basins of the Chad and Congo Rivers. The country is prone to coups; the last was in 2003.

GEOGRAPHY

Comprises a low plateau, covered by scrub or savanna. Equatorial rainforests in the south. The Ubangi River forms the border with the Democratic Republic of the Congo.

CLIMATE

The south is equatorial; the north is hot and dry. Rain occurs all year round, with heaviest falls between July and October.

PEOPLE & SOCIETY

The Baya and Banda are the largest ethnic groups, but the lingua franca is Sango, a trading creole spoken by the minorities in the south who have traditionally provided most political leaders. Women have considerable power. Ethnic diversity helps limit disputes. Less than 2% of the population live in the arid north.

THE ECONOMY

Dominated by subsistence farming. Exports include gold, diamonds, cotton, and timber. Self-sufficient in food. Instability and poor infrastructure hinder progress.

INSIGHT: *"Emperor" Bokassa's eccentric rule from 1965 to 1979 was followed by military dictatorship until democracy was restored in 1993*

1000m/3281ft
500m/1640ft
200m/656ft
Sea Level

0   200 km
0   200 miles

FACTFILE

OFFICIAL NAME: Central African Republic
DATE OF FORMATION: 1960
CAPITAL: Bangui
POPULATION: 4 million
TOTAL AREA: 240,534 sq. miles (622,984 sq. km)
DENSITY: 17 people per sq. mile

LANGUAGES: Sango, Banda, Gbaya, French*
RELIGIONS: Traditional beliefs 60%, Christian 35%, Muslim 5%
ETHNIC MIX: Baya 34%, Banda 27%, Mandjia 21%, Sara 10%, other 8%
GOVERNMENT: Presidential system
CURRENCY: CFA franc = 100 centimes

Chad

Landlocked in north central Africa, Chad has had a turbulent history since independence from France in 1960. Intermittent periods of civil war followed a military coup in 1975.

 GEOGRAPHY

Mostly plateaus sloping westward to Lake Chad. Northern third is Sahara. Tibesti Mountains in north rise to 10,826 ft (3300 m).

 CLIMATE

Three distinct zones: desert in north, semiarid region in center, and tropics in south.

 PEOPLE & SOCIETY

Half the population live in the southern fifth of Chad. Northern third has only 100,000 people, mainly Muslim Toubou nomads. Democracy was restored in 1996 by ex-coup leader Idriss Déby. Four years of political strife between northern Muslims and southern Christians ended in 2003, but rebellion has since erupted in the east.

◆ **INSIGHT:** *Lake Chad is slowly drying up – it is now estimated to be just 10% of the size it was in 1970*

$ THE ECONOMY

The discovery of oil, and the opening of a pipeline to the coast via Cameroon, are transforming Chad's economy, though the new wealth is unlikely to reach most people.

3000m/9843ft	
2000m/6562ft	
1000m/3281ft	
500m/1640ft	
200m/656ft	
Sea Level	

LIBYA

Tibesti

Sahara

NIGER

Lake Chad
Bol Abéché
NIGERIA Mongo SUDAN
NDJAMENA
Bongor
Fianga Bénoy Sarh
CAMEROON Moundou Doba CENTRAL AFRICAN REPUBLIC

0   200 km
0   200 miles

📖 FACTFILE

OFFICIAL NAME: Republic of Chad
DATE OF FORMATION: 1960
CAPITAL: N'Djamena
POPULATION: 9.7 million
TOTAL AREA: 495,752 sq. miles (1,284,000 sq. km)
DENSITY: 20 people per sq. mile

LANGUAGES: French*, Sara, Arabic*, Maba
RELIGIONS: Muslim 55%, traditional beliefs 35%, Christian 10%
ETHNIC MIX: Other 30%, Sara 28%, Mayo-Kebbi 12%, Arab 12%, Ouaddai 9%, Kanem-Bornou 9%
GOVERNMENT: Presidential system
CURRENCY: CFA franc = 100 centimes

Chile

Chile extends in a ribbon down the west coast of South America. It returned to elected civilian rule in 1989 after a referendum had rejected military dictator General Pinochet.

GEOGRAPHY
Fertile valleys in the center between the coast and the Andes. Atacama Desert in north. Deep sea channels, lakes, and fjords in south.

CLIMATE
Arid in the north. Hot, dry summers and mild winters in the center. Higher Andean peaks have glaciers and year-round snow. Very wet and stormy in the south.

PEOPLE & SOCIETY
Most people are of mixed Spanish–Amerindian descent, and are highly urbanized; a third of the population live in Santiago, many in large slums. There are three main indigenous groups, including the Rapa Nui of Easter Island. General Pinochet's dictatorship was brutally repressive, but the business and middle classes prospered.

THE ECONOMY
World's biggest copper producer. Growth in foreign investment due to political stability. Exports include wine, fishmeal, fruits, and salmon.

4000m/13124ft	
3000m/9843ft	
2000m/6562ft	
1000m/3281ft	
Sea Level	

PERU 72° **BOLIVIA**
Arica 68°
Iquique 20°
Antofagasta 24°
28°
PACIFIC OCEAN
Viña del Mar 32° **SANTIAGO**
Valparaíso
Rancagua
Talcahuano Talca
Concepción Chillán
Temuco
Valdivia 40°
Puerto Montt 76°
Isla de Chiloé 44°
ARGENTINA 48°
68°
Punta Arenas 52°
Strait of Magellan 56°
Cape Horn

0 300 km
0 300 miles

Atacama Desert

◆ **INSIGHT:** *Chile's Atacama Desert is the driest place on Earth*

FACTFILE

OFFICIAL NAME: Republic of Chile
DATE OF FORMATION: 1818
CAPITAL: Santiago
POPULATION: 16.3 million
TOTAL AREA: 292,258 sq. miles (756,950 sq. km)
DENSITY: 56 people per sq. mile

LANGUAGES: Spanish*, Amerindian languages
RELIGIONS: Roman Catholic 80%, other and nonreligious 20%
ETHNIC MIX: Mixed and European 90%, other Amerindian 9%, Mapuche 1%
GOVERNMENT: Presidential system
CURRENCY: Chilean peso = 100 centavos

China

Covering a vast area of eastern Asia, China is bordered by 14 countries. From the founding of Communist China in 1949, until his death in 1976, Mao Zedong dominated the country.

GEOGRAPHY

A land of huge physical diversity, China has a long Pacific coastline to the east. Two-thirds of the country is uplands. The southwestern mountains include Tibet, the world's highest plateau; in the northwest, the Tien Shan Mountains separate the arid Tarim and Dzungarian basins. The rolling hills and plains of the low-lying east are home to two-thirds of the population.

CLIMATE

China is divided into two main climatic regions. The north and west are semiarid or arid, with extreme temperature variations. The south and east are warmer and more humid, with year-round rainfall. Winter temperatures vary with latitude, but are warmest on the subtropical southeast coast. Summer temperatures are more uniform, rising above 70°F (21°C).

PEOPLE & SOCIETY

Most people are Han Chinese. The rest of the population belong to one of 55 minority nationalities, or recognized ethnic groups. Many of these groups have a disproportionate political significance as they live in strategic border areas. A policy of resettling Han Chinese in remote regions is deeply resented and has led to uprisings in Xinjiang and Tibet. The government has relaxed the one-child family policy for minorities after some small groups were brought close to extinction; Han Chinese still face controls. Chinese society is patriarchal in practice, and generations tend to live together. However, economic change is breaking down the social controls of the Mao era. Divorce and unemployment are rising; materialism has replaced the puritanism of the past. A resurgence of religious belief has occurred in recent years.

FACTFILE

OFFICIAL NAME: People's Rep. of China
DATE OF FORMATION: 960
CAPITAL: Beijing
POPULATION: 1.32 billion
TOTAL AREA: 3,705,386 sq. miles
(9,596,960 sq. km)
DENSITY: 365 people per sq. mile

LANGUAGES: Mandarin*, other
RELIGIONS: Nonreligious 59%, traditional beliefs 20%, other 13%, Buddhist 6%, Muslim 2%
ETHNIC MIX: Han 92%, other 4%, Hui 1%, Miao 1%, Manchu 1%, Zhuang 1%
GOVERNMENT: One-party state
CURRENCY: Yuan = 10 jiao = 100 fen

China

THE ECONOMY

China has shifted from a centrally planned to a market-oriented economy; liberalization has gone furthest in the south where the emerging business class is based. The Tenth Five-Year Plan (2001–2005) emphasized rapid development, while the Eleventh Plan aims to address widening wealth disparities. The government now runs a record deficit of almost $40 billion. A substantial growth in imports followed a deal with the EU and the normalization of US trade relations, while a boost in exports has aided GDP growth of over 9% since 2003, placing China among the world's top five economies.

INSIGHT: *China has the world's oldest continuous civilization. Its recorded history began 4000 years ago, with the Shang dynasty*

RUSSIAN FEDERATION

Amur

Heihe — 50°

Manzhouli

Qiqihar

Harbin

Jixi

KAZAKHSTAN

Altay

Karamay

Yining

Ürümqi

Hami

MONGOLIA

Gobi

Xilinhot

Fuxin

Changchun

Jilin

Shenyang

Fushun

Anshan

NORTH KOREA

KYRGYZSTAN

Tien Shan

Korla

Lop Nur

INNER MONGOLIA

Jinzhou

Tangshan

Dandong

40°

TAJIKISTAN

Kashi

Taklimakan Shamo

Yumen

BEIJING

Tianjin

Dalian

130°

AFGHANISTAN

Altun Shan

Golmud

Qinghai Hu

Shijiazhuang

Bo Hai

PAKISTAN

Aksai Chin-administered by China, claimed by India

Kunlun Shan

Xining

Lanzhou

Luoyang

Zhengzhou

Jinan

Zibo

Qingdao

Demchok/Dêmqog-administered by China, claimed by India

Plateau of Tibet

XIZANG ZIZHIQU

(TIBET)

Huang He

Baoji

Xi'an

Nanyang

Huainan

Xuzhou

Nanjing

Yellow Sea

Lhasa

Saluven

Guangyuan

Chengdu

Wuhan

Shanghai

Hangzhou

30°

NEPAL

Himalayas

Mekong

Shashi

Chongqing

Yangtze

Poyang Hu

Zigong

Changsha

Nanchang

East China Sea

80°

BHUTAN

90°

Guiyang

Hengyang

Fuzhou

INDIA

Kunming

Liuzhou

Wuzhou

Shantou

4000m/13124ft
3000m/9843ft
2000m/6562ft
1000m/3281ft
500m/1640ft
200m/656ft
Sea Level

MYANMAR (BURMA)

Nanning

Guangzhou

Macao (Aomen)

Hong Kong (Xianggang)

120°

VIETNAM

LAOS

Gulf of Tongking

Hainan Dao

20°

South China Sea

100°

110°

0   400 km

0   400 miles

Colombia

Lying in northwest South America, Colombia has coastlines on both the Caribbean and the Pacific. It is primarily noted for its coffee, emeralds, gold, and narcotics trafficking.

GEOGRAPHY
The densely forested and almost uninhabited east is separated from the western coastal plains by the Andes, which divide into three ranges (*cordilleras*) with intervening valleys.

CLIMATE
Coastal plains are hot and wet. The highlands are much cooler. The equatorial east has two wet seasons.

PEOPLE & SOCIETY
Most Colombians are of mixed blood. Blacks and Amerindians have the least political representation. The four-decade-long civil conflict has displaced millions of people, and left over 50,000 dead. The war is now entwined with the narcotics trade. Violent crime is common.

 INSIGHT: Over 50% of the world's cocaine is produced in Colombia

THE ECONOMY
Healthy and diversified export sector – includes coffee and coal. Considerable growth potential, but drugs-related violence and corruption deter foreign investors.

3000m/9843ft
2000m/6562ft
1000m/3281ft
500m/1640ft
Sea Level

0   200 km
0   200 miles

FACTFILE
OFFICIAL NAME: Republic of Colombia
DATE OF FORMATION: 1819
CAPITAL: Bogotá
POPULATION: 45.6 million
TOTAL AREA: 439,733 sq. miles (1,138,910 sq. km)
DENSITY: 114 people per sq. mile

LANGUAGES: Spanish*, Amerindian languages, English Creole
RELIGIONS: Catholic 95%, other 5%
ETHNIC MIX: Mestizo 58%, White 20%, European–African 14%, Black African 4%, Black Amerindian 3%, other 1%
GOVERNMENT: Presidential system
CURRENCY: Peso = 100 centavos

Comoros

Off the east African coast, between Mozambique and Madagascar, lies the archipelago republic of the Comoros, comprising three main islands and a number of smaller islets.

 GEOGRAPHY
Main islands are of volcanic origin and are heavily forested. The remainder are coral atolls.

 CLIMATE
Hot and humid all year round, especially on the coasts. November to May is hottest and wettest period.

 PEOPLE & SOCIETY
The Comoros has absorbed a diversity of people over the years, including Africans, Arabs, Polynesians, and Persians. There have also been Portuguese, Dutch, French, and Indian immigrants. Ethnic discord is rare, but regional tensions between islands are marked. The country is politically unstable and there have been frequent coups over the last decade. A fragile new federal system has been in place since 2002. Wealth is concentrated among a political and business elite.

THE ECONOMY
One of the world's poorest countries. Subsistence-level farming. Vanilla and cloves are main cash crops. Lack of basic infrastructure.

◆ **INSIGHT:** *The Comoros is the world's largest producer of ylang-ylang – an extract from tree blossom used in manufacturing perfumes*

FACTFILE

OFFICIAL NAME: Union of the Comoros
DATE OF FORMATION: 1975
CAPITAL: Moroni
POPULATION: 798,000
TOTAL AREA: 838 sq. miles (2170 sq. km)
DENSITY: 927 people per sq. mile

LANGUAGES: Arabic*, Comoran*, French*
RELIGIONS: Muslim (mainly Sunni) 98%, other 1%, Roman Catholic 1%
ETHNIC MIX: Comoran 97%, other 3%
GOVERNMENT: Presidential system
CURRENCY: Comoros franc = 100 centimes

Congo

Astride the equator in west central Africa, this former French colony emerged from 20 years of Marxist-Leninist rule in 1990. Democracy was soon overshadowed by years of violence.

GEOGRAPHY
Mostly forest- or savanna-covered plateaus, drained by the Ubangi and Congo River systems. Narrow coastal plain is lined with sand dunes and lagoons.

CLIMATE
Hot, tropical. Temperatures rarely fall below 86°F (30°C). Two wet and two dry seasons. Rainfall is heaviest south of the equator.

PEOPLE & SOCIETY
One of the most tribally conscious and heavily urbanized countries in Africa, with most people living in the Brazzaville–Pointe-Noire region. Main tensions are between the Bakongo in the north and the Mbochi in the south. Relative peace was secured in 1999, and "ninja" rebels in the Pool region, around Brazzaville, signed a peace deal in 2003.

THE ECONOMY
Oil provides over 80% of export revenue. Timber supplies. Substantial industrial base around Brazzaville and Pointe-Noire. Large foreign debt.

INSIGHT: *In 1970, Congo became the first African country to declare itself a communist state*

FACTFILE
OFFICIAL NAME: Republic of the Congo
DATE OF FORMATION: 1960
CAPITAL: Brazzaville
POPULATION: 4 million
TOTAL AREA: 132,046 sq. miles (342,000 sq. km)
DENSITY: 30 people per sq. mile

LANGUAGES: Kongo, Teke, Lingala, French*
RELIGIONS: Traditional 50%, Catholic 25%, Protestant 23%, Muslim 2%
ETHNIC MIX: Bakongo 51%, Teke 17%, other 16%, Mbochi 11%, Mbédé 5%
GOVERNMENT: Presidential system
CURRENCY: CFA franc = 100 centimes

Congo, (DRC)

Lying in east-central Africa, the Democratic Republic of the Congo (DRC) is one of Africa's largest countries, and the scene of one of its worst regional wars.

 GEOGRAPHY
Rainforested basin of Congo River occupies 60% of the land area. High mountain ranges and lakes stretch down the eastern border.

 CLIMATE
Tropical and humid. Distinct wet and dry seasons south of the equator. The north is mainly wet.

 PEOPLE & SOCIETY
There are over 12 main ethnic groups and around 190 smaller ones. The indigenous forest pygmies are now a marginalized group, victimized during the war. Civil war from 1996 drew neighboring countries into a long and bloody conflict. Peace was achieved in 2003 but tensions remain.

♦ **INSIGHT:** *The DRC's rainforests comprise 6% of the world's, and 50% of Africa's, remaining woodlands*

THE ECONOMY
Rich resource base: diamonds provide half of export earnings. 80% of debt was canceled in 2003. War, corruption, and mismanagement have seen economy collapse. Food aid is needed to ease humanitarian crisis.

2000m/6562ft	
1000m/3281ft	
500m/1640ft	
200m/656ft	
Sea Level	

0   200 km
0   200 miles

 FACTFILE

OFFICIAL NAME: Democratic Republic of the Congo
DATE OF FORMATION: 1960
CAPITAL: Kinshasa
POPULATION: 57.5 million
TOTAL AREA: 905,563 sq. miles (2,345,410 sq. km)

DENSITY: 66 people per sq. mile
LANGUAGES: Kiswahili, Tshiluba, French*
RELIGIONS: Christian 70%, Kimbanguist 10%, traditional beliefs 10%, Muslim 10%,
ETHNIC MIX: Other 55%, Bantu and Hamitic 45%
GOVERNMENT: Transitional regime
CURRENCY: Congolese franc = 100 centimes

Costa Rica

Costa Rica is the most stable country in Central America. Its neutrality in foreign affairs is long-standing, but it has strong ties with the US. The national army was abolished in 1949.

GEOGRAPHY
Coastal plains of swamp and savanna rise to a fertile central plateau, which leads to a mountain range with active volcanic peaks.

CLIMATE
Hot and humid in coastal regions. Temperate central uplands. High annual rainfall.

PEOPLE & SOCIETY
Most people are *mestizo*, of partly Spanish origin. There is a black, English-speaking minority and around 35,000 indigenous Amerindians. Plantation-owners are the wealthiest group, while a fifth of people live in poverty. Nonetheless, living standards are high for the region.

◆ **INSIGHT:** *Costa Rica's constitution is the only one in the world to forbid a national army*

THE ECONOMY
Bananas, beef, and coffee are the leading exports but are all vulnerable to fluctuating world prices. Tourism is booming and also fuels construction industry. The country's stability has attracted multinationals. History of high inflation.

0   50 km
0   50 miles

NICARAGUA

Liberia
Cañas
San Ramón
Puntarenas
Quesada
Heredia
SAN JOSÉ
Turrialba Limón
Cartago
San Isidro

San Juan

Caribbean Sea

PACIFIC OCEAN

Cordillera de Talamanca

Península de Osa

PANAMA

3000m/9843ft
2000m/6562ft
1000m/3281ft
500m/1640ft
200m/656ft
Sea Level

FACTFILE

OFFICIAL NAME: Republic of Costa Rica
DATE OF FORMATION: 1838
CAPITAL: San José
POPULATION: 4.3 million
TOTAL AREA: 19,730 sq. miles (51,100 sq. km)
DENSITY: 218 people per sq. mile

LANGUAGES: Spanish*, English Creole, Bribri, Cabecar
RELIGIONS: Roman Catholic 76%, other (including Protestant) 24%
ETHNIC MIX: Mestizo and European 96%, Black 2%, Chinese 1%, Amerindian 1%
GOVERNMENT: Presidential system
CURRENCY: Colón = 100 céntimos

Côte d'Ivoire (Ivory Coast)

One of the larger nations along the coast of west Africa, Côte d'Ivoire is the world's biggest cocoa producer. An image of stability was rocked by civil war in 2002–2005.

 GEOGRAPHY
Sandy coastal strip backed by a largely rainforested interior, and a savanna plateau in the north.

 CLIMATE
High temperatures all year round. South has two wet seasons; north has one, with lower rainfall.

 PEOPLE & SOCIETY
There are more than 60 tribes, the key ones being the two main Akan groups: Baoulé in the center and Agni in the east, Senufo in the north, and Dan-Yacouba in the west. Christians in the south harbor resentment against non-Ivorian Muslims in the north. Conflict from 2002 forced hundreds of thousands of migrant workers to flee.

 INSIGHT: *The Basilica of Our Lady of the Peace in Yamoussoukro is the largest church in the world*

THE ECONOMY
Main crops are cocoa and coffee. Expanding oil and gas industries. Instability threatens investment. Lack of professional training.

Scale: 1000m/3281ft / 500m/1640ft / 200m/656ft / Sea Level
0 — 100 km
0 — 100 miles

FACTFILE

OFFICIAL NAME: Republic of Côte d'Ivoire
DATE OF FORMATION: 1960
CAPITAL: Yamoussoukro
POPULATION: 18.2 million
TOTAL AREA: 124,502 sq. miles (322,460 sq. km)

DENSITY: 148 people per sq. mile
LANGUAGES: Akan, French*, Kru, Voltaic
RELIGIONS: Muslim 38%, Christian 31%, traditional beliefs 25%, other 6%
ETHNIC MIX: Akan 42%, Voltaïque 18%, Mandé du Nord 17%, Krou 11%, other 12%
GOVERNMENT: Presidential system
CURRENCY: CFA franc = 100 centimes

Croatia

Though it was controlled by Hungary from medieval times and was a part of the Yugoslav state for much of the 20th century, Croatia has a very strong national identity.

GEOGRAPHY

Rocky, mountainous Adriatic coastline is dotted with islands. Interior is a mixture of wooded mountains and broad valleys.

CLIMATE

The interior has a temperate continental climate. Mediterranean climate along the Adriatic coast.

PEOPLE & SOCIETY

Croats are ethnically similar to Bosniaks and Serbs. They are distinguished by their Roman Catholic faith and their use of the Latin alphabet. War greatly altered Croatia's ethnic makeup. Serbs now constitute just 5% of the population. Minority rights are a key issue in the quest for EU membership.

◆ **INSIGHT:** *Croatia only regained control of Serb-occupied Eastern Slavonia, around Vukovar, in 1998*

THE ECONOMY

The war cost the economy an estimated $50 billion. There has been steady growth since, and tourism is thriving on the Dalmatian coast, but unemployment is persistently high.

🗺 FACTFILE

OFFICIAL NAME: Republic of Croatia
DATE OF FORMATION: 1991
CAPITAL: Zagreb
POPULATION: 4.6 million
TOTAL AREA: 21,831 sq. miles (56,542 sq. km)
DENSITY: 211 people per sq. mile

LANGUAGES: Croatian
RELIGIONS: Roman Catholic 88%, other 7%, Orthodox Christian 4%, Muslim 1%
ETHNIC MIX: Croat 90%, other 5%, Serb 5%
GOVERNMENT: Parliamentary system
CURRENCY: Kuna = 100 lipa

Cuba

A former Spanish colony, Cuba is the largest island in the Caribbean and the only communist country in the Americas. It has been led by Fidel Castro since 1959.

GEOGRAPHY

Mostly fertile plains and basins. Three mountainous areas. Forests of pine and mahogany cover one-quarter of the country.

CLIMATE

Subtropical. Hot all year round, and very hot in summer. Heaviest rainfall in the mountains. Hurricanes can strike in the fall.

PEOPLE & SOCIETY

Castro's regime has reduced formerly extreme wealth disparities, given education a high priority, and established an efficient health service. Political dissent, however, is not tolerated. A dramatic fall in living standards since the late 1980s has led thousands of Cubans to flee to the US, to seek asylum. About 70% of Cubans are of Spanish descent, and ethnic tension is minimal.

THE ECONOMY

The 30-year-old US trade embargo continues. The sugar industry has collapsed and has been replaced as Cuba's main industry by tourism. The free use of the US dollar, legal tender from 1993 to 2004, boosted investment and created a "dollarized" elite.

INSIGHT: *Most modern cars in Cuba are imported, along with computers, in exchange for sugar in a special trading deal with Japan*

FACTFILE

OFFICIAL NAME: Republic of Cuba
DATE OF FORMATION: 1902
CAPITAL: Havana
POPULATION: 11.3 million
TOTAL AREA: 42,803 sq. miles (110,860 sq. km)
DENSITY: 264 people per sq. mile

LANGUAGES: Spanish
RELIGIONS: Nonreligious 49%, Roman Catholic 40%, atheist 6%, other 4%, Protestant 1%
ETHNIC MIX: White 66%, European–African 22%, Black 12%
GOVERNMENT: One-party state
CURRENCY: Cuban peso = 100 centavos

Cyprus

Cyprus lies south of Turkey in the eastern Mediterranean. Since 1974, it has been partitioned between the Turkish-occupied north and the Greek-Cypriot south.

 GEOGRAPHY
Mountains in the center-west give way to a fertile plain in the east, flanked by hills to the northeast.

 CLIMATE
Mediterranean. Summers are hot and dry. Winters are mild, with snow in the mountains.

 PEOPLE & SOCIETY
The Greek majority practice Orthodox Christianity. Since the 16th century, a minority community of Turkish Muslims has lived in the north of the island. In 1974 Turkish troops occupied the north, which was proclaimed the Turkish Republic of Northern Cyprus, but is recognized only by Turkey. Over 100,000 mainland Turks have settled there since. UN-led mediation failed to reunite the island ahead of EU accession in 2004, so the south alone became a member.

 THE ECONOMY
Tourism is booming in the south where wages are more than double levels in the north. Shipping and light manufacturing. The north's isolation has hindered foreign investment.

◆ **INSIGHT:** *The Green Line, which separates north from south, was opened for the first time in 2003*

 FACTFILE

OFFICIAL NAME: Republic of Cyprus
DATE OF FORMATION: 1960
CAPITAL: Nicosia
POPULATION: 835,000
TOTAL AREA: 3571 sq. miles (9250 sq. km)
DENSITY: 234 people per sq. mile

LANGUAGES: Greek*, Turkish*
RELIGIONS: Orthodox Christian 78%, Muslim 18%, other 4%
ETHNIC MIX: Greek 81%, Turkish 11%, other 8%
GOVERNMENT: Presidential systems
CURRENCY: Cyprus pound = 100 cents (Turkish lira in TRNC = 100 kurus)

Czech Republic

Once part of Czechoslovakia in central Europe, the Czech Republic became independent in 1993, after peacefully dissolving its federal union with Slovakia.

GEOGRAPHY

Landlocked in central Europe. Bohemia, the western territory, is a plateau surrounded by mountains. Moravia, in the east, is characterized by hills and lowlands.

CLIMATE

Cool, sometimes cold winters and warm summer months, which bring most of the annual rainfall.

PEOPLE & SOCIETY

Secular and urban society, with high divorce rates. Czechs make up the vast majority of the population, while the next largest group are Moravians. The 300,000 Slovaks left after partition are now permitted dual citizenship. Ethnic tensions are few, but there is widespread hostility toward the Roma minority. A new commercial elite is emerging alongside postcommunist entrepreneurs.

THE ECONOMY

Traditional heavy industries (machinery, iron, car-making) have been successfully privatized. Large tourism revenues. Skilled labor force. Plans to join euro in 2010.

INSIGHT: *Charles University in Prague was founded in the 13th century.*

FACTFILE

OFFICIAL NAME: Czech Republic
DATE OF FORMATION: 1993
CAPITAL: Prague
POPULATION: 10.2 million
TOTAL AREA: 30,450 sq. miles
 (78,866 sq. km)
DENSITY: 335 people per sq. mile

LANGUAGES: Czech*, Slovak, Hungarian
RELIGIONS: Roman Catholic 39%, atheist 38%, other 18%, Protestant 3%, Hussite 2%
ETHNIC MIX: Czech 90%, other 4%, Moravian 4%, Slovak 2%
GOVERNMENT: Parliamentary system
CURRENCY: Czech koruna = 100 haleru

Denmark

Denmark occupies the Jutland peninsula and over 400 islands in southern Scandinavia. Greenland and the Faeroe Islands are self-governing associated territories.

GEOGRAPHY
Fertile farmland covers two-thirds of the terrain, which is among the flattest in the world. About 100 islands are inhabited.

CLIMATE
Damp, temperate climate with mild summers and cold, wet winters. Rainfall is moderate.

PEOPLE & SOCIETY
Society is homogeneous. There are growing ethnic tensions with the small immigrant population. Almost all women now work and Denmark is a world leader in childcare provision. Marriage is becoming less common and most babies are born to cohabiting parents. Income distribution is the most even in the West.

◆ **INSIGHT:** *Denmark is Europe's oldest kingdom – the monarchy dates back to the 10th century*

THE ECONOMY
Gas and oil reserves. Skilled workforce key to high-tech industrial success. Pigmeat and dairy products are exported. Opted not to join the euro, though its currency is pegged.

FACTFILE
OFFICIAL NAME: Kingdom of Denmark
DATE OF FORMATION: 950
CAPITAL: Copenhagen
POPULATION: 5.4 million
TOTAL AREA: 16,639 sq. miles
(43,094 sq. km)
DENSITY: 330 people per sq. mile

LANGUAGES: Danish
RELIGIONS: Evangelical Lutheran 89%, other 10%, Roman Catholic 1%
ETHNIC MIX: Danish 96%, other (including Scandinavian and Turkish) 3%, Faeroese and Inuit 1%
GOVERNMENT: Parliamentary system
CURRENCY: Danish krone = 100 øre

Djibouti

A city-state with a desert hinterland, Djibouti lies in northeast Africa at the entrance to the Red Sea. Once known as the French Territory of the Afars and Issas, independence came in 1977.

GEOGRAPHY

Mainly low-lying desert and semidesert, with a volcanic mountain range in the north.

CLIMATE

Almost no rain, though the monsoon is very humid. The 109°F (45°C) heat of summer is unbearable.

PEOPLE & SOCIETY

The main ethnic groups are the Issas in the south, and the nomadic Afars in the north. Tensions between them developed into a guerrilla war in 1991–1994. Smaller tribal groups make up the rest of the population, and the rural peoples are mostly nomadic. Wealth is concentrated in Djibouti city. France exerts considerable influence in Djibouti, supporting it financially and maintaining a naval base and a military garrison.

THE ECONOMY

Djibouti's major assets are its ports in a key Red Sea location.

INSIGHT: *Chewing the leaves of the mildly narcotic qat shrub is an age-old social ritual in Djibouti*

FACTFILE

OFFICIAL NAME: Republic of Djibouti
DATE OF FORMATION: 1977
CAPITAL: Djibouti
POPULATION: 793,000
TOTAL AREA: 8494 sq. miles (22,000 sq. km)
DENSITY: 89 people per sq. mile

LANGUAGES: Somali, Afar, French*, Arabic*
RELIGIONS: Muslim (mainly Sunni) 94%, Christian 6%
ETHNIC MIX: Issa 60%, Afar 35%, other 5%
GOVERNMENT: Presidential system
CURRENCY: Djibouti franc = 100 centimes

Dominica

Dominica is renowned as the Caribbean island that resisted European colonization until the 18th century. It achieved independence from the UK in 1978.

GEOGRAPHY
Mountainous and densely forested. Volcanic activity has given the land very fertile soils, hot springs, geysers, and black sand beaches.

CLIMATE
Tropical, cooled by constant trade winds. Heavy annual rainfall. Tropical depressions and hurricanes are likely June–November.

PEOPLE & SOCIETY
The majority of Dominicans are descendants of African slaves brought over to work on banana plantations. The Carib Territory on the northeast of the island is home to the only surviving indigenous community in the Caribbean. Wealth disparities are not as marked as elsewhere in the region, but the alleviation of poverty has become a major plank of government policy.

THE ECONOMY
Bananas and tourism are the economic mainstays, though preferential access for Dominican bananas to the EU has now gone.

◆ **INSIGHT:** *Dominica is known as "Nature Island" due to its spectacular flora and fauna*

■	2000m/6562ft
■	1000m/3281ft
■	500m/1640ft
■	200m/656ft
	Sea Level

61°30′ Dominica Passage
61°20′
Prince Rupert Bay Portsmouth
15°30′ Marigot
Northern Forest Reserve
Caribbean Sea Mahaut ATLANTIC OCEAN
15°20′ Canefield Airport
ROSEAU
Martinique Passage

0   10 km
0   10 miles

FACTFILE
OFFICIAL NAME: Commonwealth of Dominica
DATE OF FORMATION: 1978
CAPITAL: Roseau
POPULATION: 69,029
TOTAL AREA: 291 sq. miles (754 sq. km)

DENSITY: 238 people per sq. mile
LANGUAGES: French Creole, English*
RELIGIONS: Roman Catholic 77%, Protestant 15%, other 8%
ETHNIC MIX: Black 87%, mixed 9%, Carib 3%, other 1%
GOVERNMENT: Parliamentary system
CURRENCY: East Caribbean $ = 100 cents

Dominican Republic

The Dominican Republic occupies the eastern two-thirds of the island of Hispaniola in the Caribbean. Spanish-speaking, it seeks closer ties to the anglophone West Indies.

GEOGRAPHY

Highlands and rainforested mountains – including highest peak in Caribbean, Pico Duarte – interspersed with fertile valleys. Extensive coastal plain in the east.

CLIMATE

Hot and humid close to sea level, cooler at altitude. Heavy rainfall, especially in the northeast.

PEOPLE & SOCIETY

White landowners – especially those descended from the original Spanish settlers – form the wealthy elite. Mixed-race (mulatto) majority control commerce and form the bulk of the professional middle classes. White and mixed-race women are entering the professions. Great disparities of wealth exist; the black and Haitian-immigrant population occupy the bottom of the social ladder.

THE ECONOMY

Mining – mainly of nickel and gold – and sugar are major sectors. Hidden economy based on trans-shipment of narcotics to the US. Recent growth in tourism.

◆ **INSIGHT:** *Santo Domingo is the oldest city in the Americas. It was founded in 1496 by the brother of Christopher Columbus*

	2000m/6562ft
	1000m/3281ft
	500m/1640ft
	200m/656ft
	Sea Level

0   50 km
0   50 miles

FACTFILE

OFFICIAL NAME: Dominican Republic

DATE OF FORMATION: 1865

CAPITAL: Santo Domingo

POPULATION: 8.9 million

TOTAL AREA: 18,679 sq. miles (48,380 sq. km)

DENSITY: 476 people per sq. mile

LANGUAGES: Spanish*, French Creole

RELIGIONS: Roman Catholic 92%, other and nonreligious 8%

ETHNIC MIX: Mixed 75%, White 15%, Black 10%

GOVERNMENT: Presidential system

CURRENCY: Dominican Republic peso = 100 centavos

East Timor

East Timor occupies the once Portuguese-owned eastern half of the island of Timor. Invaded by Indonesia in 1975, it became independent in 2002 following a long struggle.

GEOGRAPHY

A narrow coastal plain gives way to forested highlands. Timor's mountain backbone rises to 9715 ft (2963 m).

CLIMATE

Tropical. Heavy rain in wet season (December–March), then dry and hot, particularly in the north.

PEOPLE & SOCIETY

The population is almost entirely Roman Catholic. The Timorese are a mix of Malay and Papuan peoples, and many indigenous Papuan tribes survive. There is an urban Chinese minority, and ethnic Indonesian settlers became numerous after annexation in 1975. Preindependence violence in 1999 was politically rather than ethnically motivated. Women do not have access to the professions and levels of domestic violence are notably high. Living standards are low.

THE ECONOMY

Agreement with Australia on the division of oil revenue from the Timor Sea. Coffee is the key export. Violence in 1999 damaged infrastructure. Riots in 2006 undermined stability, further deterring foreign investment.

INSIGHT: *Once dependent on sandalwood, the economy could be transformed by oil under the Timor Sea*

FACTFILE

OFFICIAL NAME: Democratic Republic of Timor Leste

DATE OF FORMATION: 2002

CAPITAL: Dili

POPULATION: 947,000

TOTAL AREA: 5756 sq. miles (14,874 sq. km)

DENSITY: 168 people per sq. mile

LANGUAGES: Tetum*, Bahasa Indonesia, Portuguese*

RELIGIONS: Catholic 95%, other 5%

ETHNIC MIX: Malay/Papuan groups c.85%, Indonesian c.13%, Chinese 2%

GOVERNMENT: Parliamentary system

CURRENCY: US dollar = 100 cents

Ecuador

Once part of the Inca heartland, Ecuador sits high on South America's western coast. Its territory includes the fascinating Galápagos Islands, 610 miles (970 km) to the west.

GEOGRAPHY
Broad coastal plain, inter-Andean central highlands, dense jungle in upper Amazon basin.

CLIMATE
The climate is hot and moist on the coast, cool in the Andes, and hot equatorial in the Amazon basin.

PEOPLE & SOCIETY
Over half of the population is of Amerindian–Spanish extraction (*mestizo*). Black communities exist on the coast. The strong and largely unified Amerindian movement is at the forefront of social protests. One-fifth of the population lives in extreme poverty, unable to afford basic levels of food.

◆ **INSIGHT:** *Darwin's study on the Galápagos Islands in 1856 played a major part in his theory of evolution*

THE ECONOMY
The world's biggest banana exporter, and a net oil exporter. Fishing industry. US dollar offers stability, but less control. Poor infrastructure and land productivity.

FACTFILE

OFFICIAL NAME: Republic of Ecuador
DATE OF FORMATION: 1830
CAPITAL: Quito
POPULATION: 13.2 million
TOTAL AREA: 109,483 sq. miles (283,560 sq. km)
DENSITY: 123 people per sq. mile

LANGUAGES: Spanish*, Quechua, other Amerindian languages
RELIGIONS: Roman Catholic 93%, Protestant, Jewish, and other 7%
ETHNIC MIX: Mestizo 55%, Amerindian 25%, White 10%, Black 10%
GOVERNMENT: Presidential system
CURRENCY: US dollar = 100 cents

Egypt

Occupying the northeast corner of Africa, Egypt is divided by the highly fertile Nile Valley. Its essentially pro-Western, military-backed regime is being challenged by Islamic fundamentalists.

GEOGRAPHY
Fertile Nile Valley separates arid Libyan Desert from smaller semiarid eastern desert. Sinai peninsula has mountains in south.

CLIMATE
Summers are very hot, but winters are cooler. Rainfall is negligible, except on the coast.

PEOPLE & SOCIETY
There is a long tradition of ethnic and religious tolerance, though the rise of Islamism has sparked clashes between Muslims and Copts (Coptic Christianity is one of the Church's earliest branches). Women play a full part in education and the economy, though this is threatened by Islamism. The rapidly growing population is a serious problem. Poverty is rife around Cairo, Africa's largest city.

THE ECONOMY
Oil and gas are main sources of revenue. Tolls from the Suez Canal. Successful tourist industry. High birthrate and rural poverty main problems.

◆ **INSIGHT:** *Egypt has been a major tourist destination since the 1880s*

- 2000m/6562ft
- 1000m/3281ft
- 500m/1640ft
- 200m/656ft
- Sea Level
- Below Sea Level

0   200 km
0   200 miles

FACTFILE

OFFICIAL NAME: Arab Republic of Egypt
DATE OF FORMATION: 1936
CAPITAL: Cairo
POPULATION: 74 million
TOTAL AREA: 386,660 sq. miles (1,001,450 sq. km)
DENSITY: 193 people per sq. mile

LANGUAGES: Arabic*, French, English, Berber
RELIGIONS: Muslim (mainly Sunni) 94%, Coptic Christian and other 6%
ETHNIC MIX: Egyptian 99%, other (Nubian, Armenian, Greek, Berber) 1%
GOVERNMENT: Presidential system
CURRENCY: Egyptian pound = 100 piastres

El Salvador

El Salvador is Central America's smallest and most densely populated country. Already struggling to recover from a civil war in the 1980s, it was badly struck by earthquakes in 2001.

GEOGRAPHY
El Salvador is a narrow coastal belt backed by two mountain ranges. There is a central plateau. Located within a seismic zone, there are more than 20 volcanic peaks.

CLIMATE
Tropical coastal belt is very hot, with seasonal rains. Cooler, temperate climate in highlands.

PEOPLE & SOCIETY
Population is largely *mestizo*; ethnic tensions are few. The 1981–1991 civil war was fought between the US-backed right-wing government and left-wing FMLN guerrillas, over gross economic disparities, which still exist despite some reform. During the war 75,000 people died, many of whom were unarmed civilians, and human rights abuses were widespread. The FMLN is now a major political party.

THE ECONOMY
Overdependence on coffee, main export crop. Series of powerful earthquakes in early 2001 devastated infrastructure and deepened the country's reliance on aid. There are no significant resources.

◆ **INSIGHT:** *Independent since 1841, El Salvador is named after Jesus Christ, "the savior" of Christians*

FACTFILE

OFFICIAL NAME: Republic of El Salvador
DATE OF FORMATION: 1841
CAPITAL: San Salvador
POPULATION: 6.9 million
TOTAL AREA: 8124 sq. miles
(21,040 sq. km)
DENSITY: 862 people per sq. mile

LANGUAGES: Spanish
RELIGIONS: Roman Catholic 80%, Evangelical 18%, other 2%
ETHNIC MIX: Mestizo 94%, Amerindian 5%, White 1%
GOVERNMENT: Presidential system
CURRENCIES: Salvadorean colón = 100 centavos; US dollar = 100 cents

Equatorial Guinea

Comprising the mainland territory of Río Muni and five islands on the west coast of central Africa, Equatorial Guinea lies, as its name suggests, just north of the equator.

GEOGRAPHY

The islands are mountainous and volcanic. The mainland is lower, with mangrove swamps along the coast.

CLIMATE

Bioko is extremely wet and humid. The mainland is only marginally drier and cooler.

PEOPLE & SOCIETY

Equatorial Guinea is the only Spanish-speaking country in Africa. Río Muni is sparsely populated and most people there are Fang, an ethnic group also found in Cameroon and northern Gabon. Bioko is populated mostly by Bubi and a minority of Creoles known as Fernandinos. Tensions between the two territories have been reignited by the discovery of oil off Bioko. Wealth is concentrated in the ruling clan, oil revenue has made little impact on most people as yet.

THE ECONOMY

Oil and gas reserves have come on stream; the government has promised to reinvest the new funds in development. Timber and coffee.

◆ INSIGHT: *In 2003, state radio declared President Obiang Nguema to be "like God in Heaven"*

2000m/6562ft
1000m/3281ft
500m/1640ft
200m/656ft
Sea Level

MALABO

3°30'N — Isla de Bioco
Bight of Biafra 9°

ATLANTIC OCEAN
CAMEROON
Gulf of Guinea
Micomeseng — 2°
Bata — Niefang
Mbini — Mongomo
Río — Uolo
Muni
Cabo San Juan — Etembue — Cogo — Nsoc
Isla de Corisco
GABON
10°

0 40 km
0 40 miles

📓 FACTFILE

OFFICIAL NAME: Republic of Equatorial Guinea
DATE OF FORMATION: 1968
CAPITAL: Malabo
POPULATION: 504,000
TOTAL AREA: 10,830 sq. miles (28,051 sq. km)

DENSITY: 47 people per sq. mile
LANGUAGES: Spanish*, Fang, Bubi, French*
RELIGIONS: Roman Catholic 90%, other 10%
ETHNIC MIX: Fang 85%, other 11%, Bubi 4%
GOVERNMENT: Presidential system
CURRENCY: CFA franc = 100 centimes

Eritrea

Lying along the southwest shore of the Red Sea, Eritrea won a long war for independence from Ethiopia in 1993. The two neighbors fought a bitter border war in 1998–2000.

GEOGRAPHY
Mostly consists of rugged mountains, bush, and the Danakil Desert, which falls below sea level.

CLIMATE
Warm in the mountains; desert areas are hot. Droughts from July onward are common.

PEOPLE & SOCIETY
Tigrinya-speakers, mainly Orthodox Christians, are the most numerous of nine main ethnic groups. A strong sense of nationhood has been forged by war. Women played a vital role in combat. Over 80% of people are subsistence farmers. Multiparty elections, expected since 1997, have been persistently postponed.

◆ **INSIGHT:** *Eritrea is the only country to secede successfully in postcolonial Africa*

THE ECONOMY
Legacy of disruption and destruction from wars. Susceptible to drought and famine. Most of the population live at subsistence level. Potential for mining of gold, copper, silver, and zinc. Possible foreign earnings from oil exports.

	2000m/6562ft
	1000m/3281ft
	500m/1640ft
	200m/656ft
	Sea Level
	Below Sea Level

FACTFILE
OFFICIAL NAME: State of Eritrea
DATE OF FORMATION: 1993
CAPITAL: Asmara
POPULATION: 4.4 million
TOTAL AREA: 46,842 sq. miles (121,320 sq. km)
DENSITY: 97 people per sq. mile

LANGUAGES: Tigrinya*, English*, Tigre, Afar, Arabic*, Bilen, Kunama, other
RELIGIONS: Christian 45%, Muslim 45%, other 10%
ETHNIC MIX: Tigray 50%, Tigray and Kunama 40%, Afar 4%, other 6%
GOVERNMENT: Transitional regime
CURRENCY: Nakfa = 100 cents

Estonia

Traditionally the most Western-oriented of the Baltic states, Estonia is the smallest and most developed of the three. However, the standard of living is well below the EU average.

GEOGRAPHY

Estonia's terrain is flat, boggy, and partly forested, with over 1500 islands. Lake Peipus forms much of the eastern border with Russia.

CLIMATE

Maritime, with some continental extremes. Harsh winters, with cool summers and damp springs.

PEOPLE & SOCIETY

Estonians are related ethnically and linguistically to the Finns. Friction between ethnic Estonians and the large Russian minority led to a reassertion of Estonian culture and language. Outright discrimination against the Russian language was only ended in 2000. Estonians are predominantly Lutheran. Families are small and divorce rates are high. Market reforms have increased prosperity; a few people have become very rich.

THE ECONOMY

Stable currency pegged to the euro. Good productivity. Timber and oil shale are the most important of few natural resources. Estonia is dependent on imported energy.

◆ **INSIGHT:** *Estonia is a popular tourist destination for Finns, who come for the water and winter sports, architectural heritage, and nature tours*

FACTFILE

OFFICIAL NAME: Republic of Estonia
DATE OF FORMATION: 1991
CAPITAL: Tallinn
POPULATION: 1.3 million
TOTAL AREA: 17,462 sq. miles
(45,226 sq. km)
DENSITY: 75 people per sq. mile

LANGUAGES: Estonian*, Russian
RELIGIONS: Evangelical Lutheran 56%, Russian Orthodox 25%, other 19%
ETHNIC MIX: Estonian 68%, Russian 26%, other 4%, Ukrainian 2%
GOVERNMENT: Parliamentary system
CURRENCY: Kroon = 100 senti

Ethiopia

Located in northeast Africa, the former empire of Ethiopia was a Marxist regime in 1974–1991. Now a free-market democracy, it has suffered a series of economic, civil, and natural crises.

GEOGRAPHY

Great Rift Valley divides mountainous northwest region from desert lowlands in northeast and southeast. Ethiopian Plateau is drained mainly by the Blue Nile.

CLIMATE

Moderate with summer rains. Highlands are warm, with night frost and snowfalls on the mountains.

PEOPLE & SOCIETY

76 Ethiopian nationalities speak 286 languages. Oromo (or Gallas) are the largest group. Ethnic representation is a major political issue. Orthodox Christianity has a very ancient history in Ethiopia. Former emperor Haile Selassie inspired Rastafarianism.

◆ **INSIGHT:** *King Solomon and the Queen of Sheba are said to have founded the Kingdom of Abyssinia (Ethiopia) c.1000 BCE*

THE ECONOMY

Ethiopia is overwhelmingly dependent on agriculture. War-damaged infrastructure and periodic serious droughts and famines undermine growth. There is a heavy reliance on food aid.

4000m/13124ft	
3000m/9843ft	
2000m/6562ft	
1000m/3281ft	
500m/1640ft	
200m/656ft	
Sea Level	
Below Sea Level	

FACTFILE

OFFICIAL NAME: Federal Democratic Republic of Ethiopia
DATE OF FORMATION: 1896
CAPITAL: Addis Ababa
POPULATION: 77.4 million
TOTAL AREA: 435,184 sq. miles (1,127,127 sq. km)

DENSITY: 181 people per sq. mile
LANGUAGES: Amharic*, Tigrinya, other
RELIGIONS: Orthodox Christian 40%, Muslim 40%, traditional 15%, other 5%
ETHNIC MIX: Oromo 32%, Amhara 30%, other 26%, Tigraway 6%, Somali 6%
GOVERNMENT: Parliamentary system
CURRENCY: Ethiopian birr = 100 cents

Fiji

A volcanic archipelago in the southern Pacific Ocean, comprising two large islands and 880 islets. Severe tensions exist between native Fijians and the substantial Indian minority.

GEOGRAPHY
Main islands are mountainous, fringed by coral reefs. Remainder are limestone and coral formations.

CLIMATE
Tropical. High temperatures all year round. Cyclones are a hazard.

PEOPLE & SOCIETY
The British introduced workers from India in the late 19th century, and by 1946 their descendants outnumbered the indigenous Fijian population. Ethnic-Fijian nationalism is strong and the first ethnic Indian-dominated government was overthrown in 2000; serious tensions persist. Many Indo-Fijians have left the country. Women are lobbying for more rights.

◆ **INSIGHT:** *Both Fijians and Indians practice fire-walking; Indians walk on hot embers, Fijians on heated stones*

THE ECONOMY
Well-diversified economy based on sugar production, gold mining, timber, and commercial fishing. Tourists are returning after a drop in numbers prompted by instability.

FACTFILE

OFFICIAL NAME: Republic of the Fiji Islands
DATE OF FORMATION: 1970
CAPITAL: Suva
POPULATION: 848,000
TOTAL AREA: 7054 sq. miles (18,270 sq. km)
DENSITY: 120 people per sq. mile

LANGUAGES: Fijian, English*, Hindi, Urdu, Tamil, Telugu
RELIGIONS: Hindu 38%, Methodist 37%, Catholic 9%, Muslim 8%, other 8%
ETHNIC MIX: Melanesian (Fijian) 51%, Indian 44%, other 5%
GOVERNMENT: Parliamentary system
CURRENCY: Fiji dollar = 100 cents

Finland

Finland's language and national identity have been influenced by both its Scandinavian and Russian neighbors. Once closely associated with the USSR, Finland is now a member of the EU.

GEOGRAPHY

South and center are flat, with low hills and many lakes. Uplands and low mountains in the north. 60% of the land area is forested.

CLIMATE

Long, harsh winters with frequent snowfalls. Short, warmer summers. Rainfall is low, and decreases northward.

PEOPLE & SOCIETY

One in four of the population live in the Greater Helsinki region. The Swedish minority live mainly in the Åland Islands in the southwest. The Sami (Lapps) lead a seminomadic existence inside the Arctic Circle. Women make up 48% of the labor force, continuing a long tradition of equality between the sexes. Families tend to be close-knit, though marriage is becoming less common.

THE ECONOMY

Strong engineering and electronics sectors. World leader in pulp and paper production.

◆ **INSIGHT:** *Finland has Europe's largest inland waterway system*

FACTFILE

OFFICIAL NAME: Republic of Finland
DATE OF FORMATION: 1917
CAPITAL: Helsinki
POPULATION: 5.2 million
TOTAL AREA: 130,127 sq. miles
(337,030 sq. km)
DENSITY: 44 people per sq. mile

LANGUAGES: Finnish*, Swedish*, Sami
RELIGIONS: Evangelical Lutheran 89%, other 9%, Orthodox Christian 1%, Roman Catholic 1%
ETHNIC MIX: Finnish 93%, other (including Sami) 7%
GOVERNMENT: Parliamentary system
CURRENCY: Euro = 100 cents

France

Stretching across western Europe, from the English Channel (la Manche) to the Mediterranean Sea, France was Europe's first modern republic, and is still a leading industrial power.

GEOGRAPHY

Broad plain covers northern half of the country. Tall mountain ranges in the east and southwest, with a mountainous plateau in the center.

CLIMATE

Three main climates: temperate and damp northwest; continental east; and Mediterranean south.

PEOPLE & SOCIETY

Strong French national identity coexists with pronounced regional differences, including local languages. Immigration laws have been tightened since the 1970s, but ethnic minorities growing up in city suburbs feel increasingly alienated. New rules aim to bring more women into politics.

◆ **INSIGHT:** *France is the most popular tourist destination in the world, with over 76 million visitors a year*

THE ECONOMY

Chemicals, electronics, heavy engineering, and aircraft typify a strong and diversified export sector. World leader in cosmetics, perfumes, and quality wines.

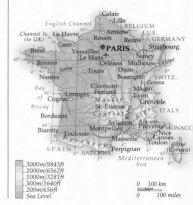

3000m/9843ft
2000m/6562ft
1000m/3281ft
500m/1640ft
200m/656ft
Sea Level

0   100 km
0   100 miles

FACTFILE

OFFICIAL NAME: French Republic
DATE OF FORMATION: 987
CAPITAL: Paris
POPULATION: 60.5 million
TOTAL AREA: 211,208 sq. miles (547,030 sq. km)
DENSITY: 285 people per sq. mile

LANGUAGES: French*, Provençal, other
RELIGIONS: Catholic 88%, Muslim 8%, Protestant 2%, Jewish 1%, Buddhist 1%
ETHNIC MIX: French 90%, North African 6%, German 2%, Breton 1%, other 1%
GOVERNMENT: Mixed presidential–parliamentary system
CURRENCY: Euro = 100 cents

Gabon

Gabon is a former French colony straddling the equator on Africa's west coast. Independent since 1960, it returned to multiparty politics in 1990, after 22 years of one-party rule.

GEOGRAPHY

Low plateaus and mountains lie beyond the coastal strip. Two-thirds of the land is covered by rainforest.

CLIMATE

Hot and tropical, with little distinction between seasons. Cold Benguela current cools the coast.

PEOPLE & SOCIETY

Some 40 different languages are spoken. The Fang, who live mainly in the north, are the largest ethnic group, but have yet to gain control of the government. Oil wealth has led to the growth of an affluent middle class. Menial jobs are done by immigrant workers. Education follows the French system. With over 80% of people living in towns, Gabon is one of Africa's most urbanized countries. The government is encouraging population growth.

THE ECONOMY

Oil is the main source of revenue. Tropical hardwoods are being exploited. Cocoa beans, coffee, and rice are grown for export.

◆ **INSIGHT:** *Libreville was founded as a settlement for freed French slaves in 1849*

FACTFILE

OFFICIAL NAME: Gabonese Republic
DATE OF FORMATION: 1960
CAPITAL: Libreville
POPULATION: 1.4 million
TOTAL AREA: 103,346 sq. miles (267,667 sq. km)
DENSITY: 14 people per sq. mile

LANGUAGES: Fang, French*, Punu, other
RELIGIONS: Christian (predominantly Roman Catholic) 55%, traditional beliefs 40%, other 4%, Muslim 1%
ETHNIC MIX: Fang 26%, Shira-punu 24%, other 24%, foreign 15%, Nzabi-duma 11%
GOVERNMENT: Presidential system
CURRENCY: CFA franc = 100 centimes

Gambia

Gambia is a narrow state on the west coast of Africa, almost entirely surrounded by Senegal. It was renowned for its stability until its government was overthrown in a coup in 1994.

GEOGRAPHY

Located on the narrow strip of land bordering the Gambia River. Long, sandy beaches are backed by mangrove swamps along the river. Savanna and tropical forests higher up.

CLIMATE

Subtropical, with wet, humid months July–October, and warm, dry season November–May.

PEOPLE & SOCIETY

Little tension between various ethnic groups. The largest group, the Mandinka, has traditionally held power. Islam is a strong social influence, though there is no official state religion. A small expatriate community from the UK lives on the coast. Each year seasonal migrants come from neighboring states to farm groundnuts. Women are very active as traders.

THE ECONOMY

Around 80% of the labor force is involved in agriculture. Groundnuts are the principal crop. Fish stocks are declining. "Eco-tourism" is promoted, though most visitors come for the beaches. Smuggling problems. Banjul is one of west Africa's finest deepwater ports.

◆ **INSIGHT:** *Overfishing in the waters off the Gambia and Senegal, mainly by foreign vessels, is a growing problem*

FACTFILE

OFFICIAL NAME: Republic of the Gambia
DATE OF FORMATION: 1965
CAPITAL: Banjul
POPULATION: 1.5 million
TOTAL AREA: 4363 sq. miles (11,300 sq. km)
DENSITY: 389 people per sq. mile

LANGUAGES: Mandinka, Fulani, Wolof, Jola, Soninke, English*
RELIGIONS: Sunni Muslim 90%, Christian 9%, traditional beliefs 1%
ETHNIC MIX: Mandinka 40%, Fulani 19%, Wolof 15%, Jola 11%, Serahuli 9%, other 6%
GOVERNMENT: Presidential system
CURRENCY: Dalasi = 100 butut

Georgia

Located on the eastern shore of the Black Sea, Georgia has been torn by civil war and ethnic disputes since achieving independence from the Soviet Union in 1991.

GEOGRAPHY
Kura Valley lies between Caucasus Mountains in the north and Lesser Caucasus range in south. Lowlands along the Black Sea coast.

CLIMATE
Subtropical along the coast, changing to continental extremes at high altitudes. Rainfall is moderate.

PEOPLE & SOCIETY
Paternalistic society, with strong family, cultural, and literary traditions. Georgia was converted to Christianity in 326 CE. Civil conflict and wars against Abkhaz and Osset separatists in the early 1990s displaced over 300,000 people. Abkhazia and South Ossetia now effectively operate as separate states. A small, wealthy elite is found in Tbilisi while the ethnic Armenians of the south are among the poorest people in society.

THE ECONOMY
Georgia is a gateway to the West for Azeri oil. It has a long-established and booming wine industry, exporting mostly to Russia. Political instability deters investment.

◆ **INSIGHT:** *Western Georgia was the land of the legendary Golden Fleece of Greek mythology*

■ 3000m/9843ft	
■ 2000m/6562ft	
■ 1000m/3281ft	
■ 500m/1640ft	
■ 200m/656ft	
■ Sea Level	

0   100 km
0   100 miles

FACTFILE

OFFICIAL NAME: Georgia
DATE OF FORMATION: 1991
CAPITAL: Tbilisi
POPULATION: 4.5 million
TOTAL AREA: 26,911 sq. miles
(69,700 sq. km)
DENSITY: 167 people per sq. mile

LANGUAGES: Georgian*, Russian, other
RELIGIONS: Georgian Orthodox 65%, Muslim 11%, Russian Orthodox 10%, Armenian Orthodox 8%, other 6%
ETHNIC MIX: Georgian 84%, Armenian 6%, Azeri 6%, Russian 2%, other 2%
GOVERNMENT: Presidential system
CURRENCY: Lari = 100 tetri

Germany

 Europe's strongest industrial power and its most populous nation, Germany was divided after military defeat in 1945 into a democratic west and a communist east, but reunified in 1990.

 GEOGRAPHY
Central European coastal plains in the north, rising to rolling hills of central region and Alps in far south.

CLIMATE
Damp, temperate in northern and central regions. Continental extremes in mountainous south.

 PEOPLE & SOCIETY
Regionalism is strong. The north is mainly Protestant while the south is staunchly Roman Catholic. Social and economic differences still exist between east and west. Turks are the largest single ethnic minority; many came as guest workers in the 1950s–1970s. Immigration rules now favor skilled workers. Feminism is strong.

 INSIGHT: *Germany's rivers and canals carry as much freight as its busy highways*

THE ECONOMY
Massive exports of electronics, heavy engineering, chemicals, and cars. Growth restored after 2001 global slowdown, but unemployment high.

2000m/6562ft
1000m/3281ft
500m/1640ft
200m/656ft
Sea Level

0   100 km
0   100 miles

FACTFILE

OFFICIAL NAME: Federal Republic of Germany
DATE OF FORMATION: 1871
CAPITAL: Berlin
POPULATION: 82.7 million
TOTAL AREA: 137,846 sq. miles (357,021 sq. km)

DENSITY: 613 people per sq. mile
LANGUAGES: German*, Turkish
RELIGIONS: Protestant 34%, Roman Catholic 33%, other 30%, Muslim 3%
ETHNIC MIX: German 92%, other 3%, other European 3%, Turkish 2%
GOVERNMENT: Parliamentary system
CURRENCY: Euro = 100 cents

Ghana

The heartland of the ancient Ashanti kingdom, Ghana in west Africa was once known as the Gold Coast. It has experienced intermittent periods of military rule since independence in 1957.

GEOGRAPHY
Mostly low-lying. The west is covered by rainforest. One of the world's largest artificial lakes – Lake Volta – was created by damming the White Volta River.

CLIMATE
Tropical. There are two wet seasons in the south, but the north is drier, and has just one.

PEOPLE & SOCIETY
Around 75 cultural-linguistic groups. The largest is the Akan, who include the Ashanti and Fanti peoples. Over 100 languages and dialects are spoken. Southern peoples are richer and more urban than those of the north. There are few tribal tensions. Family ties are strong. The election of John Kufuor in 2000 marked Ghana's first peaceful handover of power since independence.

THE ECONOMY
Produces 17% of the world's cocoa. Gold-mining is also important. Hardwood trees such as maple and sapele. Hydropower is exported.

INSIGHT: *Ghana was the first colony in west Africa to gain independence*

FACTFILE

OFFICIAL NAME: Republic of Ghana
DATE OF FORMATION: 1957
CAPITAL: Accra
POPULATION: 22.1 million
TOTAL AREA: 92,100 sq. miles (238,540 sq. km)
DENSITY: 249 people per sq. mile

LANGUAGES: Twi, Fanti, Ewe, Ga, Adangbe, Gurma, Dagomba, English*
RELIGIONS: Christian 69%, Muslim 16%, traditional beliefs 9%, other 6%
ETHNIC MIX: Akan 49%, Mole-Dagbani 17%, Ewe 13%, other 13%, Ga 8%
GOVERNMENT: Presidential system
CURRENCY: Cedi = 100 pesewas

Greece

The Balkan state of Greece is bounded on three sides by the Mediterranean, Aegean, and Ionian Seas. It has a strong seafaring tradition, with some of the world's richest shipowners.

 GEOGRAPHY
Mountainous peninsula and over 2000 islands. Large plain along the mainland's Aegean coast.

 CLIMATE
Mainly Mediterranean with dry, hot summers. Alpine climate in northern mountain areas.

PEOPLE & SOCIETY
Postwar industrial development altered the dominance of agriculture and seafaring. The rural exodus to industrial cities has been stemmed but a third of the population now live in Athens. Age-old culture and Greek Orthodox Church balance social mobility. Civil marriage and divorce only became legal in 1982.

◆ **INSIGHT:** *Classical sights have made tourism one of the most important industries in Greece*

$ THE ECONOMY
One of Europe's leading tourist destinations. The world's largest beneficially owned shipping fleets. Large black economy. Public debt and unemployment remain high.

■	2000m/6562ft
■	1000m/3281ft
■	500m/1640ft
■	200m/656ft
	Sea Level

0   100 km
0   100 miles

 FACTFILE

OFFICIAL NAME: Hellenic Republic
DATE OF FORMATION: 1829
CAPITAL: Athens
POPULATION: 11.1 million
TOTAL AREA: 50,942 sq. miles
(131,940 sq. km)
DENSITY: 220 people per sq. mile

LANGUAGES: Greek*, Turkish, Macedonian, Albanian
RELIGIONS: Orthodox Christian 98%, Muslim 1%, other 1%
ETHNIC MIX: Greek 98%, other 2%
GOVERNMENT: Parliamentary system
CURRENCY: Euro = 100 cents

Grenada

The southernmost of the Windward Islands, Grenada became a focus of world attention in 1983 when the US and Caribbean allies mounted an invasion to sever links with Castro's Cuba.

GEOGRAPHY
Volcanic in origin, with densely forested central mountains. Its territory also includes the islands of Carriacou and Petite Martinique.

CLIMATE
Tropical, tempered by trade winds. Hurricanes are a hazard in the July–November wet season.

PEOPLE & SOCIETY
Grenadians are mainly of African origin; their traditions remain strong, especially on Carriacou. Inter-ethnic marriage has reduced tensions between the groups. Extended families, often headed by women, are the norm. Wealth disparities are not marked, but levels of poverty are growing.

◆ **INSIGHT:** *Known as "the spice island of the Caribbean," it is the world's second-largest nutmeg producer*

THE ECONOMY
Severe damage from Hurricane Ivan in 2004; nutmeg production still to recover. Mace, cocoa, saffron, and cloves are also exported. Smuggling is a serious problem.

FACTFILE

OFFICIAL NAME: Grenada
DATE OF FORMATION: 1974
CAPITAL: St. George's
POPULATION: 89,502
TOTAL AREA: 131 sq. miles (340 sq. km)
DENSITY: 683 people per sq. mile

LANGUAGES: English*, English Creole
RELIGIONS: Roman Catholic 68%, Anglican 17%, other 15%
ETHNIC MIX: Black African 82%, Mulatto 13%, East Indian 3%, other 2%
GOVERNMENT: Parliamentary system
CURRENCY: East Caribbean $ = 100 cents

Guatemala

The largest and most populous nation on the Central American isthmus, Guatemala returned to civilian rule in 1986 after 32 years of violent and repressive military rule.

GEOGRAPHY

Narrow Pacific coastal plain. Central highlands with volcanoes. Short coast on the Caribbean Sea. Tropical rainforests in the north.

CLIMATE

Tropical: hot and humid in coastal regions and north. More temperate in central highlands.

PEOPLE & SOCIETY

Amerindians, concentrated in the highlands, form a majority. Power, wealth, and land are controlled by a *ladino* elite. Roman Catholicism is predominant, mixed with traditional Amerindian spiritual beliefs. Over 30% of the population live below the UN's poverty line of $2 a day.

◆ **INSIGHT:** *Guatemala, which means "land of trees," was the center of the ancient Mayan civilization*

THE ECONOMY

Agriculture is the key sector. Coffee, sugar, bananas, and shrimp are top exports. Wealth inequalities inhibit domestic market.

FACTFILE

OFFICIAL NAME: Republic of Guatemala
DATE OF FORMATION: 1838
CAPITAL: Guatemala City
POPULATION: 12.6 million
TOTAL AREA: 42,042 sq. miles (108,890 sq. km)
DENSITY: 301 people per sq. mile

LANGUAGES: Quiché, Mam, Cakchiquel, Kekchí, Spanish*
RELIGIONS: Roman Catholic 65%, Protestant 33%, other 2%
ETHNIC MIX: Amerindian 60%, Mestizo 30%, other 10%
GOVERNMENT: Presidential system
CURRENCY: Quetzal = 100 centavos

Guinea

Facing the Atlantic Ocean, on the west coast of Africa, Guinea became the first French colony in Africa to gain independence, in 1958. The country was under military rule from 1984 to 1995.

GEOGRAPHY

Coastal plains and mangrove swamps in west rise to forested or savanna highlands in the south. Semidesert in the north.

CLIMATE

Tropical, with a wet season April–October. Conakry is especially rainy. Hot, dry *harmattan* wind blows from Sahara during dry season.

PEOPLE & SOCIETY

Peul and Malinke make up most of the population, but rivalries between them have allowed coastal peoples such as the Soussou to come to dominate politics. Daily life revolves around the extended family. Women acquired influence under Marxist party rule between 1958 and 1984, but the Muslim revival since then has reversed the trend. Private enterprise has created a business class.

THE ECONOMY

Over 80% of people are farmers. Cash crops include bananas and palm oil. Substantial gold, diamond, and especially bauxite reserves.

INSIGHT: *The colors of Guinea's flag represent the three words of the country's motto: work (red), justice (yellow), and solidarity (green)*

1000m/3281ft	
500m/1640ft	
200m/656ft	
Sea Level	

0 100 km
0 100 miles

FACTFILE

OFFICIAL NAME: Republic of Guinea
DATE OF FORMATION: 1958
CAPITAL: Conakry
POPULATION: 9.4 million
TOTAL AREA: 94,925 sq. miles (245,857 sq. km)
DENSITY: 99 people per sq. mile

LANGUAGES: Pulaar, Malinke, Soussou, French*
RELIGIONS: Muslim 65%, traditional beliefs 33%, Christian 2%
ETHNIC MIX: Peul 39%, Malinke 23%, other 21%, Soussou 11%, Kissi 6%
GOVERNMENT: Presidential system
CURRENCY: Guinea franc = 100 centimes

Guinea-Bissau

Known as Portuguese Guinea while a colony, Guinea-Bissau is situated on Africa's west coast. Since 1994, multiparty democracy has been interrupted by coups and rebellions.

GEOGRAPHY

Low-lying, apart from savanna highlands in northeast. Rainforests and swamps are found along coastal areas.

CLIMATE

Tropical, with wet season May–November and dry season December–April. Hot, dry *harmattan* desert wind blows during dry season.

PEOPLE & SOCIETY

The largest ethnic group is the Balante, who live in the south. Though only around 1% of the population, the mixed Portuguese–African *mestiços* dominate the top ranks of government and bureaucracy. Most people live and work on small family farms, grouped in self-contained villages. The bulk of the urban population live in the capital, Bissau, where they face economic hardship and increasing political instability.

THE ECONOMY
Mostly subsistence farming – maize, sweet potatoes, cassava. Lack of sufficiency in rice staple. Main cash crops are cashew nuts and cotton. Offshore oil as yet untapped. Fisheries and timber potential.

◆ **INSIGHT:** *In 1974, Guinea-Bissau became the first Portuguese colony to gain independence*

FACTFILE

OFFICIAL NAME: Rep. of Guinea-Bissau
DATE OF FORMATION: 1974
CAPITAL: Bissau
POPULATION: 1.6 million
TOTAL AREA: 13,946 sq. miles (36,120 sq. km)
DENSITY: 147 people per sq. mile

LANGUAGES: Portuguese Creole, Balante, Fulani, Malinke, Portuguese*
RELIGIONS: Indigenous beliefs 52%, Muslim 40%, Christian 8%
ETHNIC MIX: Balante 30%, other 24%, Fulani 20%, Mandyako 14%, Mandinka 12%
GOVERNMENT: Presidential system
CURRENCY: CFA franc = 100 centimes

Guyana

On the northeast coast of the continent, Guyana is South America's only English-speaking country. Independent since 1966, it has close ties with the anglophone Caribbean.

GEOGRAPHY

Mainly artificial coast, reclaimed by dikes and dams from swamps and tidal marshes. Forests cover 85% of the interior, rising to savanna uplands and mountains.

CLIMATE

Tropical. Coast cooled by sea breezes. Lowlands are hot, wet, and humid. Highlands are a little cooler.

PEOPLE & SOCIETY

Guyana is a complex multiracial society. Tension exists between the Afro-Guyanese, descended from slaves, and the Indo-Guyanese, descendants of laborers brought over after slavery was abolished. Politics is highly polarized around this split and often spills over into violence on the streets. Amerindian subsistence farmers are the poorest people in society and have little representation.

THE ECONOMY

Diverse exports: bauxite, gold, timber, sugar, rice, and diamonds. High unemployment and rising crime.

INSIGHT: *Guyana means "land of many waters," reflecting its dense network of rivers*

FACTFILE

OFFICIAL NAME: Cooperative Republic of Guyana

DATE OF FORMATION: 1966

CAPITAL: Georgetown

POPULATION: 751,000

TOTAL AREA: 83,000 sq. miles (214,970 sq. km)

DENSITY: 10 people per sq. mile

LANGUAGES: Creole, Hindi, English*

RELIGIONS: Christian 57%, Hindu 33%, Muslim 9%, other 1%

ETHNIC MIX: East Indian 43%, Black African 30%, other 18%, Amerindian 9%

GOVERNMENT: Presidential system

CURRENCY: Guyanese dollar = 100 cents

Haiti

Formerly a French colony, Haiti shares the Caribbean island of Hispaniola with the Dominican Republic. At independence in 1804, it became the world's first black republic.

 GEOGRAPHY
Predominantly mountainous, with forests and fertile plains.

CLIMATE
Tropical, with rain throughout the year. Humid in coastal areas, much cooler in the mountains.

PEOPLE & SOCIETY
Most Haitians are of African descent. A few have European roots, primarily French. The rigid class structure maintains vast disparities of wealth. The majority of the population live in extreme poverty; Haiti is one of the poorest countries in the Americas. A combination of political oppression and a collapsing economy has led thousands to seek asylum in the US or the Dominican Republic. As well as being Christians, many Haitians practice Voodoo, which was recognized as an official religion in 2003.

THE ECONOMY
Few natural resources. Transshipment of narcotics to the US provides a large source of income to smugglers. 70% unemployment.

INSIGHT: *A slave rebellion headed by Toussaint Louverture in 1791 led to Haiti's independence*

FACTFILE

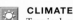

OFFICIAL NAME: Republic of Haiti
DATE OF FORMATION: 1804
CAPITAL: Port-au-Prince
POPULATION: 8.5 million
TOTAL AREA: 10,714 sq. miles (27,750 sq. km)
DENSITY: 799 people per sq. mile

LANGUAGES: French Creole*, French*
RELIGIONS: Roman Catholic 80%, Protestant 16%, other 3%, nonreligious 1%; Voodoo is widely practiced
ETHNIC MIX: Black African 95%, Mulatto and European 5%
GOVERNMENT: Presidential system
CURRENCY: Gourde = 100 centimes

Honduras

Straddling the Central American isthmus, Honduras returned to democratic civilian rule in 1984, after a period of military government. Hurricane Mitch devastated the country in 1998.

GEOGRAPHY

Narrow plains along both coasts, with a mountainous interior, cut by river valleys. Tropical forests, swamps, and lagoons in the east.

CLIMATE

Tropical coastal lowlands are hot and humid, with May–October rains. Interior is cooler and drier.

PEOPLE & SOCIETY

The majority of the population is *mestizo* (mixed race). An English-speaking *garifuna* (black) community and Miskito Amerindians struggle to preserve their rights to land along the remote Caribbean coast. Women's status remains low. Hurricane Mitch killed 5600 people in 1998 and impoverished 85% of the population. Wealth inequalities are large and poverty is at the root of social tension. Violent crime is a major issue.

THE ECONOMY

Coffee, bananas, and shellfish are the main exports; low world prices have hit revenues. Honduras qualified for debt relief from 2005. Corruption and high underemployment.

◆ **INSIGHT:** *The Honduran currency is named after a Lenca Indian chief who was the main leader of resistance to the Spanish conquest in the 16th century*

FACTFILE

OFFICIAL NAME: Republic of Honduras
DATE OF FORMATION: 1838
CAPITAL: Tegucigalpa
POPULATION: 7.2 million
TOTAL AREA: 43,278 sq. miles
(112,090 sq. km)
DENSITY: 167 people per sq. mile

LANGUAGES: Spanish*, Garífuna, English Creole
RELIGIONS: Roman Catholic 97%, Protestant 3%
ETHNIC MIX: Mestizo 90%, Black African 5%, Amerindian 4%, White 1%
GOVERNMENT: Presidential system
CURRENCY: Lempira = 100 centavos

Hungary

Landlocked in central Europe, Hungary was once the heart of the powerful Habsburg Empire. It lost two-thirds of its historical territory for supporting Germany in World War I.

GEOGRAPHY

Landlocked. Fertile plains in east and northwest; west and north are hilly. The Danube River cuts through the country and the capital.

CLIMATE

Continental, with wet springs, late but very hot summers, and cold, cloudy winters. The transition between seasons tends to be sudden.

PEOPLE & SOCIETY

Hungary's population shrank in the 1990s. Mostly ethnic Hungarian (Magyar), there are small minorities of Germans, Jews, and neighboring peoples. Roma face particular discrimination. The government is greatly concerned about the fate of ethnic Hungarians in Romania, Serbia, and Slovakia. Living standards are high, though working hours are longer than in Western Europe.

THE ECONOMY

High industrial production. Open access for foreign investors. Return of export-led growth, notably high-tech goods and wine. Budget deficit must be cut to join eurozone.

INSIGHT: *The Hungarian language is Asian in origin and is most closely related to Finnish*

FACTFILE

OFFICIAL NAME: Republic of Hungary
DATE OF FORMATION: 1918
CAPITAL: Budapest
POPULATION: 10.1 million
TOTAL AREA: 35,919 sq. miles (93,030 sq. km)
DENSITY: 283 people per sq. mile

LANGUAGES: Hungarian*
RELIGIONS: Catholic 52%, Calvinist 16%, other 15%, nonreligious 14%, Lutheran 3%
ETHNIC MIX: Magyar 94%, other 5%, Roma 1%
GOVERNMENT: Parliamentary system
CURRENCY: Forint = 100 fillér

Iceland

Europe's westernmost country, Iceland has a strategic location in the north Atlantic, straddling the Mid-Atlantic Ridge. Its spectacular landscape is largely uninhabited.

GEOGRAPHY
Grassy coastal lowlands, with fjords in the north. Central plateau of cold lava desert, geothermal springs, and glaciers. Around 200 volcanoes, with numerous geysers and solfataras.

CLIMATE
Its location in the middle of the Gulf Stream moderates the climate. Mild winters and brief, cool summers.

PEOPLE & SOCIETY
Prosperous and homogeneous, Icelandic society includes only a few thousand foreign residents. There is high social mobility, free health care, and low-cost heating (geothermal and hydropower). Longevity rates are among the highest in the world. Strong emphasis on education and literacy. The Icelandic language has changed little in 700 years, in part due to the country's isolation.

THE ECONOMY
The high-tech fishing industry dominates export earnings. Tourism is growing. Geothermal and hydro-electric energy are abundant.

INSIGHT: *The word geyser is taken from Geysir (the "gusher") in southwest Iceland*

Denmark Strait
Arctic Circle
Norwegian Sea
24°
Akureyri
Húsavík
Keflavík
Akranes
66°
REYKJAVÍK
Hafnarfjördhur
Kópavogur
Selfoss
Egilsstadhir
22°
Vestmannaeyjar
Vatnajökull
20°
18°
16°
64°
14°
ATLANTIC OCEAN

1000m/3281ft
500m/1640ft
200m/656ft
Sea Level
Ice Cap

0   50 km
0   50 miles

FACTFILE
OFFICIAL NAME: Republic of Iceland
DATE OF FORMATION: 1944
CAPITAL: Reykjavík
POPULATION: 295,000
TOTAL AREA: 39,768 sq. miles (103,000 sq. km)
DENSITY: 8 people per sq. mile

LANGUAGES: Icelandic*
RELIGIONS: Evangelical Lutheran 93%, nonreligious 6%, other (mostly Christian) 1%
ETHNIC MIX: Icelandic 94%, other 5%, Danish 1%
GOVERNMENT: Parliamentary system
CURRENCY: Icelandic króna = 100 aurar

India

India is the world's second most populous country. The birth-rate has recently been falling, but even at its current level India's population will probably overtake China's by 2030.

GEOGRAPHY

Separated from northern Asia by the Himalaya mountain range, India forms a subcontinent. As well as the Himalayas, there are two other main geographical regions, the Indo-Gangetic plain, which lies between the foothills of the Himalayas and the Vindhya Mountains, and the central-southern Deccan plateau. The Ghats are smaller mountain ranges located on the east and west coasts.

CLIMATE

Varies greatly according to latitude, altitude, and season. Most of India has three seasons: hot, wet, and cool. In summer, temperatures in the north can reach 104°F (40°C). The monsoon breaks in June and peters out in September to October. In the cool season, the weather is mainly dry. The climate in the warmer south is less variable than in the north.

PEOPLE & SOCIETY

Cultural and religious pressures encourage large families. Nationwide awareness campaigns aim to promote the idea of smaller families. India's planners consider the rise in the population the most significant brake on development. Despite a major birth control program, the decrease in population growth has been marginal. Rural deprivation encourages urban growth. Almost 80% of people survive on less than $2 a day. The majority of Indians are Hindu. Various attempts to reform the Hindu caste system, which determines social standing and even marriage, have met with violent opposition. Severe tensions exist between Hindus and the Muslim minority, especially in Kashmir and Gujarat. Smaller ethnic groups exist in the northeast, and many struggle for greater autonomy. Over five million people are living with HIV / AIDS.

FACTFILE

OFFICIAL NAME: Republic of India
DATE OF FORMATION: 1947
CAPITAL: New Delhi
POPULATION: 1.1 billion
TOTAL AREA: 1,269,338 sq. miles (3,287,590 sq. km)
DENSITY: 961 people per sq. mile

LANGUAGES: Hindi*, English*, Urdu, Bengali, Marathi, Telugu, Tamil, other
RELIGIONS: Hindu 83%, Muslim 11%, Christian 2%, Sikh 2%, other 2%
ETHNIC MIX: Indo-Aryan 72%, Dravidian 25%, Mongoloid and other 3%
GOVERNMENT: Parliamentary system
CURRENCY: Indian rupee = 100 paise

THE ECONOMY

India has the fastest-growing economy in Asia after China. Protectionism has given way to free-market economics. The success of "Bollywood" films and high-tech industries contrast with massive levels of poverty.

◆ **INSIGHT:** *India's national animal, the tiger, was worshipped as early as 4000 years ago by the Mohenjo-Daro civilization*

5000m/16405ft
4000m/13124ft
3000m/9843ft
2000m/6562ft
1000m/3281ft
500m/1640ft
200m/656ft
Sea Level

A 'line of control' was agreed between India and Pakistan in 1972

Aksai Chin - administered by China, claimed by India

Demchok/Dêmqog - administered by China, claimed by India

Much of Arunāchal Pradesh is claimed by China

Srīnagar
Jammu & Kashmir
Amritsar
Jalandhar
Ludhiāna
Chandīgarh

CHINA

Thar Desert
Meerut
Delhi
NEW DELHI
Bareilly
NEPAL
Shiliguri
BHUTAN
Brahmaputra
Assam
MYANMAR (BURMA)

PAKISTAN
Jodhpur
Jaipur
Agra
Lucknow
Kānpur
Ganges
Patna
BANGLADESH
Imphāl
Gwalior
Kota
Vārānasi
Dhanbād
Bhōpāl
Jabalpur
Rānchī
Kolkata (Calcutta)
Haora
Jamshedpur
Mouths of the Ganges

Rann of Kachchh
Ahmadābād
Indore
Narmada
Nāgpur
Cuttack
Gulf of Kachchh
Jāmnagar
Rajkot
Vadodara
Sūrat
Mahānadi

Gulf of Khambhāt
Kalyān
Nānded
Goday
Visākhapatnam
Mumbai (Bombay)
Pune
Deccan
Solāpur
Hyderābād
Krishna
Bay of Bengal

Arabian Sea

Western Ghats
Hubli
Pānāji

Andaman Islands
North Andaman
Middle Andaman
South Andaman
Port Blair
Little Andaman

Chennai (Madras)
Bangalore
Mysore
Salem
INDIAN OCEAN
Cochin (Kochi)
Coimbatore
Madurai
Lakshadweep (Laccadive Is.)

Nicobar Islands

Indira Point
Great Nicobar

0   200 km
0   200 miles

Indonesia

Formerly known as the Dutch East Indies, Indonesia is the world's largest archipelago. Its 18,108 islands stretch 3000 miles (5000 km) eastward from the Indian Ocean to the Pacific.

GEOGRAPHY

Indonesia is highly mountainous with numerous tropical swamps. The land is covered with dense rainforest, especially on New Guinea, where it remains largely unexplored. There are more than 200 volcanoes in the region, many of which are still active. The land masses of Java, Bali, Sumatra, Lombok, and Borneo were once joined together by dry land, which has since been submerged by rising sea levels. Some of the islands are large enough to have formed coastal lowlands.

CLIMATE

The climate of Indonesia is predominantly tropical monsoon. Variations relate mainly to differences in latitude and altitude; hilly areas are cooler overall. Rain falls throughout the year, often in thunderstorms, but there is a relatively dry season from June to September.

THE ECONOMY

Varied resources, especially energy. Cheap and plentiful labor pool. Bureaucracy and corruption damages investor confidence. Large foreign debt has been rescheduled. Piracy is a serious problem.

Bandaaceh, Strait of Malacca, 100°
Langsa, Aceh, Medan, Pematangsiantar
Kepulauan Natuna, 110°
Pulau Nias, Pakanbaru, Singkawang, Pontianak
Padang, Sumatra
Pegunungan Mentawai, Jambi, Bangka, Pangkalpinang, Ketapang
Pegunungan Barisan, Palembang, Pulau Belitung
Bengkulu, Bandar Lampung
JAKARTA
INDIAN OCEAN
Bogor, Semarang
Bandung, Java, Yogyakarta, Surakarta

4000m/13124ft
3000m/9843ft
2000m/6562ft
1000m/3281ft
500m/1640ft
Sea Level

FACTFILE

OFFICIAL NAME: Republic of Indonesia

DATE OF FORMATION: 1949

CAPITAL: Jakarta

POPULATION: 223 million

TOTAL AREA: 741,096 sq. miles (1,919,440 sq. km)

DENSITY: 321 people per sq. mile

LANGUAGES: Javanese, Sundanese, Madurese, Bahasa Indonesia*, Dutch

RELIGIONS: Sunni Muslim 87%, Christian 9%, Hindu 2%, other 2%

ETHNIC MIX: Javanese 42%, other 31%, Sundanese 15%, coastal Malays 12%

GOVERNMENT: Presidential system

CURRENCY: Rupiah = 100 sen

Indonesia

PEOPLE & SOCIETY

The basic Melanesian–Malay ethnic division disguises a diverse society. Bahasa Indonesia, the national language, coexists with at least 250 other spoken languages or dialects. Attempts by the Javanese political elite to suppress local cultures have been vigorously opposed, especially by the Aceh of northern Sumatra, and the Papuans. Religious and interethnic hostility is increasing. There have been clashes between Christians and Muslims in many areas, and discrimination against ethnic Chinese has encouraged vicious attacks on their businesses. Gender equality is enshrined in law, and women are active in public life. The *tsunami* (tidal wave) in 2004 devastated northern Sumatra; around 128,000 people were killed with 37,000 more missing.

◆ **INSIGHT:** *Indonesia has a very youthful population; almost 30% of its people are under 15 years of age*

Iran

Since the 1979 Islamic fundamentalist revolution led by Ayatollah Khomeini, the Middle Eastern country of Iran has become the world's largest theocracy.

GEOGRAPHY
High desert plateau with large salt pans in the east. West and north are mountainous. Coastal land bordering Caspian Sea is rainy and forested.

CLIMATE
Desert climate. Hot summers, and bitterly cold winters. Area around the Caspian Sea is more temperate.

PEOPLE & SOCIETY
Many ethnic groups, including Persians, Azaris (ethnically related to Azeris), and Kurds. Militant Shi'a Islamism has dominated since the 1979 revolution. The mullahs' belief that adherence to religious values is more important than economic welfare has resulted in declining living standards. Female emancipation has also been reversed. Liberal attitudes, particularly prevalent among students, have led to clashes.

THE ECONOMY
One of the world's biggest oil producers. Government restricts contact with the West, blocking acquisition of vital technology. High unemployment and inflation.

◆ **INSIGHT:** *More than a hundred offenses carry the death penalty*

3000m/9843ft
2000m/6562ft
1000m/3281ft
500m/1640ft
200m/656ft
Sea Level

0   200 km
0   200 miles

FACTFILE
OFFICIAL NAME: Islamic Republic of Iran
DATE OF FORMATION: 1502
CAPITAL: Tehrān
POPULATION: 69.5 million
TOTAL AREA: 636,293 sq. miles
(1,648,000 sq. km)
DENSITY: 110 people per sq. mile

LANGUAGES: Farsi*, Azeri, Luri, Gilaki, Mazanderani, Kurdish, Turkmen, Arabic
RELIGIONS: Shi'a Muslim 93%, Sunni Muslim 6%, other 1%
ETHNIC MIX: Persian 50%, Azari 24%, other 10%, Kurd 8%, Lur and Bakhtiari 8%
GOVERNMENT: Islamic theocracy
CURRENCY: Iranian rial = 100 dinars

Oil-rich Iraq is situated in the central Middle East. The last 50 years have been dominated by periods of war and civil conflict. A US-led Coalition ousted Saddam Hussein in April 2003.

GEOGRAPHY

Mainly desert. The Tigris and Euphrates Rivers water fertile regions and create the southern marshland. Mountains along northeast border.

CLIMATE

Southern deserts have hot, dry summers and mild winters. North has dry summers, but winters can be harsh in the mountains. Rainfall is low.

PEOPLE & SOCIETY

Carved out of remnants of the Ottoman Empire, Iraq is home to three distinct ethnic groups, as well as smaller minorities. The Arab Muslims are divided between Shi'a and Sunni. The northern Kurds were persecuted by the regime of Saddam Hussein. Since his removal, religious tensions have fuelled an insurgency bordering on all-out civil war. After years of war and sanctions, poverty is widespread.

THE ECONOMY

The country's infrastructure has been destroyed. If stability can be achieved, hopes of recovery rest on massive oil reserves and aid.

INSIGHT: *As Mesopotamia, Iraq was the site where the Sumerians established the world's first civilization*

FACTFILE

OFFICIAL NAME: Republic of Iraq
DATE OF FORMATION: 1932
CAPITAL: Baghdad
POPULATION: 28.8 million
TOTAL AREA: 168,753 sq. miles (437,072 sq. km)
DENSITY: 171 people per sq. mile

LANGUAGES: Arabic*, Kurdish, Turkic languages, Armenian, Assyrian
RELIGIONS: Shi'a Muslim 60%, Sunni Muslim 35%, other 5%
ETHNIC MIX: Arab 80%, Kurdish 15%, Turkmen 3%, other 2%
GOVERNMENT: Parliamentary system
CURRENCY: New Iraqi dinar = 1000 fils

Ireland

Lying in the Atlantic Ocean, off the west coast of Britain, the Irish republic occupies about 85% of the island of Ireland, with the remainder (Northern Ireland) being part of the UK.

GEOGRAPHY

Low mountain ranges along an irregular coastline surround an inland plain punctuated by lakes, undulating hills, and peat bogs.

CLIMATE

The Gulf Stream accounts for the mild and wet climate. Snow is rare, except in the mountains.

PEOPLE & SOCIETY

Though homogeneous in ethnicity and Roman Catholic religion, the population show signs of change. The younger Irish question teachings on birth control, divorce, and abortion. Traditionally an emigrant nation, there is now net immigration. Living standards have improved greatly. The Good Friday peace agreement over Northern Ireland was reached in 1998, though a definitive peace remains elusive.

THE ECONOMY

Historically high, unemployment in Ireland is now one of the lowest rates in Europe. The workforce is highly educated. Efficient agriculture and food-processing industries.

◆ **INSIGHT:** *About 40% of Irish people speak Irish Gaelic*

1000m/3281ft
500m/1640ft
200m/656ft
Sea Level

Donegal
Donegal
Bay
Sligo
Westport
Galway
Athlone
ATLANTIC
OCEAN
Shannon
Lough
Derg
Shannon
Airport
Limerick
Tralee
Tipperary
Clonmel
Killarney
Cork

UNITED
KINGDOM
(Northern Ireland)
Dundalk
Irish
Sea
Mullingar
DUBLIN
Dún Laoghaire
Wicklow
Mts.
Kilkenny
Wexford
Waterford
Celtic
Sea

54°
52°
10°
8°

0   50 km
0   50 miles

FACTFILE

OFFICIAL NAME: Ireland

DATE OF FORMATION: 1922

CAPITAL: Dublin

POPULATION: 4.1 million

TOTAL AREA: 27,135 sq. miles (70,280 sq. km)

DENSITY: 154 people per sq. mile

LANGUAGES: English*, Irish Gaelic*

RELIGIONS: Roman Catholic 88%, other and nonreligious 9%, Anglican 3%

ETHNIC MIX: Irish 99%, other 1%

GOVERNMENT: Parliamentary system

CURRENCY: Euro = 100 cents

Israel

Created as a new state in 1948, Israel lies in the eastern Mediterranean. The Palestinian population launched the latest *intifada* (armed struggle) against Israeli occupation in 2000.

GEOGRAPHY
Coastal plain. Desert in the south. In the east lie the Great Rift Valley and the Dead Sea – the lowest point on the Earth's land surface.

CLIMATE
Summers are hot and dry. Wet season, March–November, is mild.

PEOPLE & SOCIETY
Large numbers of Jews settled in Palestine before Israel was founded in 1948. After World War II, there was a massive increase in immigration. Sephardi Jews from the Middle East and Mediterranean are now in the majority, but Ashkenazi Jews from central Europe still dominate business and politics. Palestinians in Gaza and Jericho gained limited autonomy in 1994 but their desire, backed by most of the world, for a separate state has led to years of fierce violence.

THE ECONOMY
The benefits of a modern infrastructure and educated labor force are overshadowed by conflict.

◆ **INSIGHT:** *All Jews worldwide have the right to Israeli citizenship*

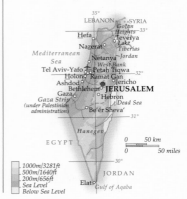

1000m/3281ft
500m/1640ft
200m/656ft
Sea Level
Below Sea Level

0   50 km
0   50 miles

📖 FACTFILE

OFFICIAL NAME: State of Israel
DATE OF FORMATION: 1948
CAPITAL: Jerusalem (unrecognized by UN)
POPULATION: 6.7 million
TOTAL AREA: 8019 sq. miles (20,770 sq. km)
DENSITY: 854 people per sq. mile

LANGUAGES: Hebrew*, Arabic*, Yiddish, German, Russian, Polish, other
RELIGIONS: Jewish 76%, Muslim (mainly Sunni) 16%, other 6%, Christian 2%
ETHNIC MIX: Jewish 76%, other (mostly Arab) 24%
GOVERNMENT: Parliamentary system
CURRENCY: Shekel = 100 agorot

Italy

The Italian peninsula was home to the Roman Empire, one of the greatest ancient civilizations. The south has two famous volcanoes, Vesuvius and Etna.

GEOGRAPHY

The Appennino form the backbone of a rugged peninsula, extending from the Alps into the Mediterranean Sea. Alluvial plain in the north.

CLIMATE

Mediterranean in the south. Seasonal extremes in the mountains and on the northern alluvial plain.

PEOPLE & SOCIETY

Ethnically homogeneous, but with a gulf between the prosperous, industrial north and the poorer, agricultural south. Strong regional identities persist, especially on the islands of Sicily and Sardinia. Allegiance to the family survives the lessened influence of the Church.

◆ **INSIGHT:** *Italy was a collection of dukedoms, monarchies, and city-states before unification in the 1860s*

THE ECONOMY

World leader in industrial and product design, as well as textiles. Strong tourism and agriculture sectors. Large public sector debt.

FACTFILE

OFFICIAL NAME: Italian Republic
DATE OF FORMATION: 1861
CAPITAL: Rome
POPULATION: 58.1 million
TOTAL AREA: 116,305 sq. miles (301,230 sq. km)
DENSITY: 512 people per sq. mile

LANGUAGES: Italian*, German, French, Rhaeto-Romanic, Sardinian
RELIGIONS: Roman Catholic 85%, other and nonreligious 13%, Muslim 2%
ETHNIC MIX: Italian 94%, other 4%, Sardinian 2%
GOVERNMENT: Parliamentary system
CURRENCY: Euro = 100 cents

Jamaica

First colonized by the Spanish and then by the English, the Caribbean island of Jamaica achieved independence in 1962. It remains an influential force in Caribbean politics.

GEOGRAPHY

Mainly mountainous, with lush tropical vegetation. Inaccessible limestone area in the northwest. Low, irregular coastal plains are broken by hills and plateaus.

CLIMATE

Tropical. Hot and humid at sea level, with temperate mountain areas. Hurricanes are likely June–November.

PEOPLE & SOCIETY

Social tensions result from vast disparities in wealth, rather than race. Economic and political life is dominated by a few wealthy, long-established families. Many women hold senior positions in public life. Armed crime, much of it narcotics-related, is a problem. Large areas of Kingston, which have their own *patois*, are ruled by violent gangs. Jamaican music styles are influential worldwide.

THE ECONOMY

Major producer of bauxite (aluminum ore). Tourism well developed. Light industry and data processing for US companies. Sugar, bananas, coffee, and rum are exported.

◆ **INSIGHT:** *Jamaica's Rastafarians look to the late emperor of Ethiopia, Haile Selassie, as their spiritual leader, and Africa as their spiritual home*

FACTFILE

OFFICIAL NAME: Jamaica
DATE OF FORMATION: 1962
CAPITAL: Kingston
POPULATION: 2.7 million
TOTAL AREA: 4243 sq. miles (10,990 sq. km)
DENSITY: 646 people per sq. mile

LANGUAGES: English Creole, English*
RELIGIONS: Protestant 55%, other and nonreligious 45%
ETHNIC MIX: Black African 92%, Mulatto 6%, European and Chinese 1%, East Indian 1%
GOVERNMENT: Parliamentary system
CURRENCY: Jamaican dollar = 100 cents

Japan

Japan is located off the east Asian coast and comprises four principal islands and over 3000 smaller ones. A powerful economy, it has an emperor as ceremonial head of state.

GEOGRAPHY

The terrain is predominantly mountainous, with fertile coastal plains; over two-thirds is woodland. There is no single continuous mountain range; the mountains divide into many small land blocks separated by lowlands and dissected by numerous river valleys. The islands lie on the Pacific "Ring of Fire," and earthquakes and volcanic eruptions are frequent. The Pacific coast is vulnerable to *tsunamis* – tidal waves triggered by submarine earthquakes.

CLIMATE

Generally temperate–oceanic. Spring is warm and sunny, while summer is hot and humid, with high rainfall. In western Hokkaido and northwest Honshu, winters are very cold, with heavy snowfall. Freak storms and damaging floods in recent years have raised concern over global climate changes.

PEOPLE & SOCIETY

One of the most racially homogeneous societies in the world. Its sense of order is reflected in the phenomenon of the lifetime employer. People define themselves by the company they work for, not the job they do. Employers organize social activities and even encourage and approve marriages. Women traditionally run the home; though, some are beginning to take up long-term careers. Social form remains very important. Respect for elders and social and business superiors is strongly ingrained. There is little tradition of generation rebellion, but the youth market is powerful and current fashions focus on teenagers. The education system is highly pressurized. Nongraduates have difficulty reaching management-level jobs, so competition for university places is intense.

FACTFILE

OFFICIAL NAME: Japan
DATE OF FORMATION: 1590
CAPITAL: Tokyo
POPULATION: 128 million
TOTAL AREA: 145,882 sq. miles
(377,835 sq. km)
DENSITY: 881 people per sq. mile

LANGUAGES: Japanese*, Korean, Chinese
RELIGIONS: Shinto and Buddhist 76%, Buddhist 16%, other (including Christian) 8%
ETHNIC MIX: Japanese 99%, other (mainly Korean) 1%
GOVERNMENT: Parliamentary system
CURRENCY: Yen = 100 sen

Japan

$ THE ECONOMY

The world's most competitive producer of high-tech electronic goods and cars. Talent for developing ideas from abroad. Once-revolutionary management and production methods. Global spread of business, especially to EU and US. Commitment to long-term research and development. Trade surplus is a source of international tension. Period of zero inflation ended in 2006. Desperately needed reform of financial sector has been slow, obstructed by traditional economic power brokers.

◆ **INSIGHT:** *The Japanese are among the world's most avid newspaper readers, with daily sales exceeding 70 million copies*

Jordan

The Kingdom of Jordan lies east of Israel, and borders the Palestinian West Bank. Its relations with its Arab neighbors are troubled by its relatively close ties to the US.

GEOGRAPHY

Mostly desert plateaus, with occasional salt pans. Lowest parts lie along the eastern shores of the Dead Sea and the Jordan River.

CLIMATE

Hot, dry summers. Cool, wet winters. Areas below sea level very hot in summer, and warm in winter.

PEOPLE & SOCIETY

A predominantly Muslim country with a strong national identity, Jordan's population has Bedouin roots. There is a Christian minority while half of the population are Palestinians who emigrated from Israeli-occupied territory. Jordan ceded its claim to the West Bank to the aspiring Palestinian state in 1988. The monarchy's power base lies among the rural tribes, which also provide the backbone of the military.

THE ECONOMY

Main exports are phosphates, chemicals, and fertilizers. Tourism hit by regional instability and terrorism.

INSIGHT: *The Nabataean ruins of the ancient city of Petra attract thousands of tourists every year*

FACTFILE

OFFICIAL NAME: Hashemite Kingdom of Jordan
DATE OF FORMATION: 1946
CAPITAL: Amman
POPULATION: 5.6 million
TOTAL AREA: 35,637 sq. miles (92,300 sq. km)

DENSITY: 163 people per sq. mile
LANGUAGES: Arabic
RELIGIONS: Muslim (mainly Sunni) 92%, other (mostly Christian) 8%
ETHNIC MIX: Arab 98%, Circassian 1%, Armenian 1%
GOVERNMENT: Monarchy
CURRENCY: Jordanian dinar = 1000 fils

Kazakhstan

Mineral-rich Kazakhstan was the last of the former Soviet republics to declare independence. Foreign investment in the oil and gas sector are strengthening its regional power.

GEOGRAPHY
Mainly steppe. Volga delta and Caspian Sea in the west. Central plateau. Inhospitable Altai Mountains in the east. Semidesert in the south.

CLIMATE
Dry continental. Temperature variations between desert south and northern steppes are large. Winters are mildest near the Caspian Sea.

PEOPLE & SOCIETY
Kazakhstan's ethnic diversity arose mainly from forced settlements there during Soviet times. The proportion of ethnic Russians has dropped considerably since independence. Many emigrated, while ethnic Kazakhs arrived from neighboring states. Very few Kazakhs maintain a nomadic lifestyle, but Islam and loyalty to traditional clans remain strong.

THE ECONOMY
Vast mineral resources: gas, oil, bismuth, and cadmium. Increasing foreign investment. The sale of farm land has only been allowed since 2003. Large disparities of wealth.

INSIGHT: The Soviet-built Baykonyr space center is still an important launch site for international missions

FACTFILE

OFFICIAL NAME: Republic of Kazakhstan
DATE OF FORMATION: 1991
CAPITAL: Astana
POPULATION: 14.8 million
TOTAL AREA: 1,049,150 sq. miles (2,717,300 sq. km)
DENSITY: 14 people per sq. mile

LANGUAGES: Kazakh*, Russian, Ukrainian, Tatar, Uzbek, Uighur, other
RELIGIONS: Muslim (mainly Sunni) 47%, Orthodox Christian 44%, other 9%
ETHNIC MIX: Kazakh 57%, Russian 27%, other 10%, Ukrainian 3%, Uzbek 3%
GOVERNMENT: Presidential system
CURRENCY: Tenge = 100 tiyn

Kenya

Kenya straddles the equator on Africa's east coast. After nearly 40 years in power the KANU party was soundly defeated in elections in 2002. Corruption is a serious issue.

GEOGRAPHY

A central plateau is divided by the Great Rift Valley. North of the equator is mainly semidesert. To the east lies a fertile coastal belt.

CLIMATE

The coast and the Great Rift Valley are hot and humid. The plateau interior is temperate. The northeastern desert is hot and dry. Rain usually falls April–May and October–November.

PEOPLE & SOCIETY

70 ethnic groups share about 40 languages. Strong clan and family links in rural areas are being weakened by urban migration. Poverty, severe drought, and years of high population growth exacerbate ethnic tensions.

◆ **INSIGHT:** *Kenya has more than 50 game reserves, national parks, and marine reservations*

THE ECONOMY

Tourism is the leading foreign exchange earner. Tea and coffee are grown as cash crops. There is a large and diversified manufacturing sector.

SUDAN • Elem° 36° ETHIOPIA 40°
Triangle
Lake • 4°
Turkana
Chalbi
Desert
UGANDA • Marsabit

Eldoret SOMALIA
Kisumu Nakuru • Meru • Equator
Lake Kericho • Nyeri
Victoria NAIROBI • Thika
• Machakos
TANZANIA

Ungama
Malindi Bay

Mombasa • 4°
INDIAN
OCEAN

5000m/16405ft
4000m/13124ft
3000m/9843ft
2000m/6562ft 0 100 km
1000m/3281ft
500m/1640ft 0 100 miles
200m/656ft
Sea Level

FACTFILE

OFFICIAL NAME: Republic of Kenya
DATE OF FORMATION: 1963
CAPITAL: Nairobi
POPULATION: 34.3 million
TOTAL AREA: 224,961 sq. miles (582,650 sq. km)
DENSITY: 157 people per sq. mile

LANGUAGES: Kiswahili*, English*, Kikuyu, Luo, Kalenjin, Kamba
RELIGIONS: Christian 60%, traditional beliefs 25%, other 9%, Muslim 6%
ETHNIC MIX: Other 41%, Kikuyu 21%, Luhya 14%, Luo 13%, Kalenjin 11%
GOVERNMENT: Presidential system
CURRENCY: Kenya shilling = 100 cents

Kiribati

Part of the British colony of the Gilbert and Ellice Islands in the mid-Pacific, the Gilberts adopted the name Kiribati (pronounced "Keer-ee-bus") at independence in 1979.

GEOGRAPHY

Kiribati consists of three groups of tiny, very low-lying coral atolls scattered across 1,930,000 sq. miles (5 million sq. km) of ocean. Most of the 33 atolls have central lagoons.

CLIMATE

Central islands have a maritime equatorial climate. Those to north and south are tropical, with constant high temperatures. There is little rainfall.

PEOPLE & SOCIETY

Officially I-Kiribati, many local people still refer to themselves as Gilbertese. Almost all are Micronesian, apart from the inhabitants of the island of Banaba, who employed anthropologists to establish their racial distinction. Most people are poor subsistence farmers and many travel abroad to work. The islands are effectively ruled by traditional chiefs.

THE ECONOMY

Since Banaba's phosphate deposits were exhausted in 1980, coconuts, copra, and fish have become the main exports. Foreign aid is vital to compensate for the country's isolation and the lack of resources.

◆ **INSIGHT:** *In 1981, the UK paid A$10 million to Banabans for the destruction of their island by mining*

All land under 200m/656ft

PACIFIC OCEAN

Tungaru
Tarawa
Banaba
Equator
Kiritimati
Phoenix Islands
Line Islands
Millennium Island

Tarawa 173°
1°30'N
Betio
Bonriki
BAIRIKI

0   600 km
0   600 miles

FACTFILE

OFFICIAL NAME: Republic of Kiribati
DATE OF FORMATION: 1979
CAPITAL: Bairiki (Tarawa Atoll)
POPULATION: 103,092
TOTAL AREA: 277 sq. miles (717 sq. km)
DENSITY: 376 people per sq. mile

LANGUAGES: English*, Kiribati
RELIGIONS: Roman Catholic 53%, Kiribati Protestant Church 39%, other 8%
ETHNIC MIX: Micronesian 99%, other 1%
GOVERNMENT: Nonparty system
CURRENCY: Australian dollar = 100 cents

North Korea

 Separated from the democratic South by the world's most heavily defended border, the Stalinist North Korean state has been isolated from the outside world since its creation in 1948.

 GEOGRAPHY
Mostly mountainous, with fertile plains in the southwest.

 CLIMATE
Continental. Warm summers and cold winters, especially in the north, where snow is common.

PEOPLE & SOCIETY
Life is heavily regulated; divorce is nonexistent, extramarital sex is highly frowned upon, and religion, including Korea's own Chondogyo, is strictly regulated. Women are expected to work and to run the home. Children are looked after in state-run crèches. The Korean Worker's Party is the sole political party. The political elite leads a privileged lifestyle. Its grip on power relies on its international isolation.

◆ **INSIGHT:** *Only the political elite are allowed phones and private cars*

THE ECONOMY
Other than minerals, there are few economic strengths. Vital aid streams were lost with the global collapse of communism after 1989. Decades of economic mismanagement have caused chronic food shortages.

2000m/6562ft
1000m/3281ft
500m/1640ft
200m/656ft
Sea Level

RUSS. FED.

CHINA

Ch'ŏngjin

Kanggye

Kimch'aek

Hŭich'on

Sinŭiju

Iwŏn

Hamhŭng

Korea Bay

Hŭngnam

Wŏnsan

East Sea

● PYONGYANG

Namp'o

Haeju

SOUTH KOREA

Kaesŏng

Yellow Sea

0   50 km
0   50 miles

 FACTFILE

OFFICIAL NAME: Democratic People's Republic of Korea
DATE OF FORMATION: 1948
CAPITAL: Pyongyang
POPULATION: 22.5 million
TOTAL AREA: 46,540 sq. miles (120,540 sq. km)

DENSITY: 484 people per sq. mile
LANGUAGES: Korean*, Chinese
RELIGIONS: Government-controlled religions include Chondogyo, Buddhism, and Christianity
ETHNIC MIX: Korean 100%
GOVERNMENT: One-party state
CURRENCY: N. Korean won = 100 chon

South Korea

South Korea occupies the southern half of the Korean peninsula Under US sponsorship, it was separated from the communist North in 1948, and is now a successful capitalist economy.

GEOGRAPHY
Over 80% is mountainous and two-thirds is forested. The flattest and most populous parts lie along the west coast and in the extreme south.

CLIMATE
There are four distinct seasons. Winters are dry, and bitterly cold. Summers are hot and humid.

PEOPLE & SOCIETY
Inhabited for the last 2000 years by a single ethnic group. The nuclear family is replacing traditional extended households. Since the 1953 armistice, North and South Korea have remained technically at war. Reunification is still the ultimate goal. Talks spurred new links in 2000, but progress has since stalled amid mutual suspicion.

◆ **INSIGHT:** *Half of all Koreans are named Kim, Lee, Park, or Choi*

THE ECONOMY
World's biggest shipbuilder. High demand in China for Korean goods, especially cars. There is very strong competition from Japan.

1000m/3281ft
500m/1640ft
200m/656ft
Sea Level

NORTH KOREA

East Sea

SEOUL
Inch'ŏn
Suwŏn
Sŏngnam
Kangnŭng
Tonghae

Yellow Sea
Kunsan
Taejŏn
Taegu
Ulsan

Kwangju
Masan
Pusan

Mokp'o
Yŏsu

Korea Strait

Cheju Strait
Cheju
Cheju-do

0   50 km
0   50 miles

FACTFILE

OFFICIAL NAME: Republic of Korea
DATE OF FORMATION: 1948
CAPITAL: Seoul
POPULATION: 47.8 million
TOTAL AREA: 38,023 sq. miles
(98,480 sq. km)
DENSITY: 1254 people per sq. mile

LANGUAGES: Korean*, Chinese
RELIGIONS: Mahayana Buddhist 47%, Protestant 38%, Roman Catholic 11%, Confucianist 3%, other 1%
ETHNIC MIX: Korean 100%
GOVERNMENT: Presidential system
CURRENCY: South Korean won = 100 chon

Kuwait

Kuwait lies at the northwest extreme of the Gulf, dwarfed by its neighbors Iraq, Iran, and Saudi Arabia. It was a British protectorate until 1961, when full independence was granted.

GEOGRAPHY

Terrain is low-lying desert. The lowest land is in the north. Cultivation is only possible along the coast.

CLIMATE

Summers are very hot and dry. Winters are cooler, with some rain and occasional frost at night.

PEOPLE & SOCIETY

An oil-rich monarchy, ruled by the al-Sabah family. Oil wealth has attracted workers from India, Pakistan, and other Arab states, and immigrants outnumber native Kuwaitis. Though it is a very conservative Sunni Muslim society, women are relatively free. Nonetheless, a decree to give women the vote was blocked for six years by Islamic traditionalists in parliament. Kuwait was invaded by Iraq in 1990 and was used as the launchpad for the 2003 invasion of its northern neighbor.

THE ECONOMY

Oil and gas production dominates the economy. Skilled labor, raw materials, and food are imported. Strategic vulnerability has deterred significant foreign investment.

◆ **INSIGHT:** *During the 1991 Gulf War, 800 of Kuwait's 950 oil wells were deliberately set on fire*

FACTFILE

OFFICIAL NAME: State of Kuwait
DATE OF FORMATION: 1961
CAPITAL: Kuwait City
POPULATION: 2.7 million
TOTAL AREA: 6880 sq. miles
(17,820 sq. km)
DENSITY: 392 people per sq. mile

LANGUAGES: Arabic*, English
RELIGIONS: Sunni Muslim 45%, Shi'a Muslim 40%, Christian, Hindu, and other 15%
ETHNIC MIX: Kuwaiti 45%, other Arab 35%, South Asian 9%, other 11%
GOVERNMENT: Monarchy
CURRENCY: Kuwaiti dinar = 1000 fils

Kyrgyzstan

A small and very mountainous landlocked state in central Asia, Kyrgyzstan is one of the least urbanized of the ex-Soviet republics, and was slow to develop its own cultural nationalism.

GEOGRAPHY

The mountainous spurs of the Tien Shan range contain glaciers, alpine meadows, forests, and narrow valleys. Semidesert in the west.

CLIMATE

Varies from permanent snow and cold deserts at high altitudes, to hot deserts in low regions.

PEOPLE & SOCIETY

Ethnic Kyrgyz have only been in the majority since the late 1980s – due to a high birthrate and the emigration of ethnic Russians. Wary of losing skills vital to the economy, the government has attempted to deter Russians from leaving; concessions include making Russian an official language. There are tensions between Kyrgyz and Uzbeks. The trend in politics is toward greater Islamization, and the rural population is growing.

THE ECONOMY

The economy remains under state control. Agriculture employs half of the labor force. Mining of gold, other metals, and small quantities of coal, oil, and gas. There is great potential for hydroelectric power.

◆ **INSIGHT:** *Kyrgyz folklore is based around the 1000-year-old poem,* Manas, *which takes a week to recite*

FACTFILE

OFFICIAL NAME: Kyrgyz Republic
DATE OF FORMATION: 1991
CAPITAL: Bishkek
POPULATION: 5.3 million
TOTAL AREA: 76,641 sq. miles
(198,500 sq. km)
DENSITY: 69 people per sq. mile

LANGUAGES: Kyrgyz*, Russian*, other
RELIGIONS: Muslim (mainly Sunni) 70%, Orthodox Christian 30%
ETHNIC MIX: Kyrgyz 65%, Uzbek 14%, Russian 13%, other 6%, Dungan 1%, Ukrainian 1%
GOVERNMENT: Presidential system
CURRENCY: Som = 100 tyiyn

Laos

A former French colony, independent in 1953, Laos lies landlocked in southeast Asia. Heavily bombed during the Vietnam War, it has been under communist rule since 1975.

GEOGRAPHY

Largely forested mountains, broadening in the north to a plateau. Lowlands along the Mekong valley.

CLIMATE

Monsoon rains September–May. The rest of the year is hot and dry.

PEOPLE & SOCIETY

There are over 60 ethnic groups. Lowland Laotians (Lao Loum) live along the Mekong River and are rice farmers. Upland and highland Laotians (Lao Theung and Lao Soung) traditionally employ environmentally damaging slash-and-burn farming, and grow illegal cash crops (notably opium). Government efforts to reform these practices are resisted.

◆ **INSIGHT:** *Three small Laotian kingdoms were unified under French control in 1899*

THE ECONOMY

Laos is one of the world's least developed nations. Coffee, timber, and garments are the main exports. Levels of foreign investment are rising, especially in expanding mining sector.

FACTFILE

OFFICIAL NAME: Lao People's Democratic Republic
DATE OF FORMATION: 1953
CAPITAL: Vientiane
POPULATION: 5.9 million
TOTAL AREA: 91,428 sq. miles (236,800 sq. km)

DENSITY: 66 people per sq. mile
LANGUAGES: Lao*, Mon-Khmer, other
RELIGIONS: Buddhist 85%, other (including animist) 15%
ETHNIC MIX: Lao Loum 66%, Lao Theung 30%, Lao Soung 2%, other 2%
GOVERNMENT: One-party state
CURRENCY: New kip = 100 at

Latvia

Latvia lies on the east coast of the Baltic Sea, between Estonia and Lithuania. Like its Baltic neighbors, it became independent from Moscow in 1991. It retains a large Russian population.

GEOGRAPHY
A flat coastal plain which is deeply indented by the Gulf of Riga. Poor drainage creates many bogs and swamps in the forested interior.

CLIMATE
Temperate, with warm summers and cold winters. There is steady rainfall throughout the year.

PEOPLE & SOCIETY
Latvians make up just over half of the population and are mostly Lutheran. They have been officially favored by the state since 1991 over the largely Orthodox Christian Russian minority. Latvian was declared the only official language in 2000 and has been used exclusively in schools since 2004. This discrimination has strained relations with neighboring Russia. Women enjoy full equality. The divorce rate is high.

THE ECONOMY
The thriving services sector now accounts for over 70% of GDP: tourism is growing. Manufacturing industry remains buoyant. Germany has replaced Russia as the main trading partner as Latvia turns increasingly to the West.

INSIGHT: *Ethnic Latvians form a minority of the population in Riga*

FACTFILE

OFFICIAL NAME: Republic of Latvia
DATE OF FORMATION: 1991
CAPITAL: Riga
POPULATION: 2.3 million
TOTAL AREA: 24,938 sq. miles (64,589 sq. km)
DENSITY: 92 people per sq. mile

LANGUAGES: Latvian*, Russian
RELIGIONS: Lutheran 55%, Catholic 24%, other 12%, Orthodox Christian 9%
ETHNIC MIX: Latvian 59%, Russian 29%, Belarussian 4%, Ukrainian 3%, Polish 3%, other 2%
GOVERNMENT: Parliamentary system
CURRENCY: Lats = 100 santimi

Lebanon

Once a vibrant cultural hotspot, Lebanon suffered badly from years of civil war and occupation until a 1989 peace deal. Reconstruction was reversed by Israeli bombardment in 2006.

GEOGRAPHY

Behind a narrow Mediterranean coastal plain, two parallel mountain ranges run the length of the country, separated by the fertile Beqaa Valley.

CLIMATE

Winters are mild and summers are hot, with high coastal humidity. Snow falls on high ground in winter.

PEOPLE & SOCIETY

Politics has long been dominated by divisions between Sunni and Shi'a Muslims and the traditional ruling group of Maronite Christians. A power-sharing deal ended 14 years of civil war in 1989, but left Syria as the main power broker until it was forced to withdraw in 2005. Israel attacked from the south in 2006 in a bid to crush Iranian-backed Hezbollah militants. A huge economic gulf exists between the poor and a small, immensely rich elite.

THE ECONOMY

Much infrastructure destroyed in 2006. Instability undermines Beirut's role as regional financial center. Wine and fruit production.

◆ **INSIGHT:** *The Cedar of Lebanon has been the nation's symbol for more than 2000 years*

FACTFILE

OFFICIAL NAME: Republic of Lebanon
DATE OF FORMATION: 1941
CAPITAL: Beirut
POPULATION: 3.6 million
TOTAL AREA: 4015 sq. miles (10,400 sq. km)
DENSITY: 911 people per sq. mile

LANGUAGES: Arabic*, French, Armenian, Assyrian
RELIGIONS: Muslim 70%, Christian 30%
ETHNIC MIX: Arab 94%, Armenian 4%, other 2%
GOVERNMENT: Parliamentary system
CURRENCY: Lebanese pound = 100 piastres

Lesotho

The landlocked Kingdom of Lesotho is entirely surrounded by – and economically dependent on – South Africa, which even sent in troops to restore calm after rioting in 1998.

GEOGRAPHY
A high mountainous plateau, cut by valleys and ravines. The Maluti range runs through the center. The Drakensberg range lies to the east.

CLIMATE
Temperate. Summers are hot with torrential rain storms. Snow is frequent in the mountains in winter.

PEOPLE & SOCIETY
The overwhelming majority of people are Sotho, though there are some South Asians, Europeans, and Chinese. A strong sense of national identity has tended to minimize ethnic tensions. Many men work as migrant laborers in South Africa, leaving women to run households.

◆ **INSIGHT:** *Lesotho has one of the highest literacy rates in Africa – and one of the highest rates of HIV/AIDS*

THE ECONOMY
Few natural resources; dependent on South Africa. Subsistence farming is the main activity. Water and energy are being exported from the new Highlands Water Scheme.

▨ 3000m/9843ft	
▨ 2000m/6562ft	0 50 km
▨ 1000m/3281ft	0 50 miles

FACTFILE

OFFICIAL NAME: Kingdom of Lesotho
DATE OF FORMATION: 1966
CAPITAL: Maseru
POPULATION: 1.8 million
TOTAL AREA: 11,720 sq. miles (30,355 sq. km)
DENSITY: 154 people per sq. mile

LANGUAGES: English*, Sesotho*, isiZulu
RELIGIONS: Christian 90%, traditional beliefs 10%
ETHNIC MIX: Sotho 97%, European and Asian 3%
GOVERNMENT: Parliamentary system
CURRENCY: Loti = 100 lisente

Liberia

Liberia, Africa's oldest republic, faces the Atlantic Ocean. A tentative peace deal in 2003 ended more than a decade of brutal civil war, but gang violence and looting are widespread.

GEOGRAPHY

A coastline of beaches and mangrove swamps rises to forested plateaus and highlands inland.

CLIMATE

High temperatures. There is only one wet season, from May to October, except in the extreme southeast.

PEOPLE & SOCIETY

The key social distinction used to be between Americo-Liberians – descendants of freed slaves – and the indigenous tribal peoples. However, political assimilation and intermarriage have eased tensions. Intertribal tension is now a much more serious problem, fueling the civil war which ravaged the country from 1990 to 2003.

INSIGHT: *Liberia is named after the people liberated from slavery who arrived from the US in the 1800s*

THE ECONOMY

Civil war caused the collapse of the economy – there is very little commercial activity. Only 1% of the land is suitable for cultivation. There are an estimated one billion tonnes of iron ore reserves at Mount Nimba.

FACTFILE

OFFICIAL NAME: Republic of Liberia
DATE OF FORMATION: 1847
CAPITAL: Monrovia
POPULATION: 3.3 million
TOTAL AREA: 43,000 sq. miles (111,370 sq. km)
DENSITY: 89 people per sq. mile

LANGUAGES: Kpelle, Vai, Bassa, Kru, Grebo, Kissi, Gola, Loma, English*
RELIGIONS: Christian 68%, traditional beliefs 18%, Muslim 14%
ETHNIC MIX: Indigenous tribes (16 main groups) 95%, Americo-Liberians 5%
GOVERNMENT: Presidential system
CURRENCY: Liberian dollar = 100 cents

Libya

Situated on the Mediterranean coast of north Africa, Libya is a military dictatorship. Years of political marginalization by the West for its terrorist links have now ended.

GEOGRAPHY

Apart from the coastal strip and a mountain range in the south, Libya is desert or semidesert. Natural oases provide the agricultural land.

CLIMATE

Hot and arid. The coastal area has a temperate climate, with mild, wet winters and hot, dry summers.

PEOPLE & SOCIETY

Most Libyans are of Arab and Berber origin. A revolution in 1969 brought Colonel Gaddafi to power. He represents independence, Islamic faith, belief in communal lifestyle, and hatred of the urban rich. Revolution wiped out private enterprise and the middle classes. Jews and European settlers were banished. Since then, Libya has changed from being largely a nation of nomads and livestock herders to almost 90% city dwellers.

THE ECONOMY

Oil is key export. Dates, olives, peaches, and grapes grown in oases. Sanctions ended after Libya offered compensation for terrorist bombings.

◆ **INSIGHT:** *90% of Libya is still desert, despite grand irrigation schemes*

FACTFILE

OFFICIAL NAME: Great Socialist People's Libyan Arab Jamahariyah
DATE OF FORMATION: 1951
CAPITAL: Tripoli
POPULATION: 5.9 million
TOTAL AREA: 679,358 sq. miles (1,759,540 sq. km)

DENSITY: 9 people per sq. mile
LANGUAGES: Arabic*, Tuareg
RELIGIONS: Muslim (mainly Sunni) 97%, other 3%
ETHNIC MIX: Arab and Berber 95%, other 5%
GOVERNMENT: One-party state
CURRENCY: Libyan dinar = 1000 dirhams

Liechtenstein

Perched in the Alps between Switzerland and Austria, the small state of Liechtenstein became an independent principality of the Holy Roman Empire in 1719. It has close links with Switzerland.

GEOGRAPHY

The upper Rhine Valley covers the western third of the country. The mountains and narrow valleys of the eastern Alps make up the remainder.

CLIMATE

Warm, dry summers. Winters are cold, with heavy snow in the mountains from December to March.

PEOPLE & SOCIETY

The country's role as a financial center accounts for its many foreign residents (a third of the population), of whom almost a third are Swiss. A high standard of living results in few social or ethnic tensions. There is a close alliance with Switzerland, which handles its foreign relations and defense policies.

◆ **INSIGHT:** *Women in Liechtenstein only received the vote in 1984*

THE ECONOMY

Banking secrecy and low taxes help to attract foreign investment. A well-diversified export market includes dental products, furniture, chemicals, and precision instruments.

FACTFILE

OFFICIAL NAME: Principality of Liechtenstein
DATE OF FORMATION: 1719
CAPITAL: Vaduz
POPULATION: 33,717
TOTAL AREA: 62 sq. miles (160 sq. km)

DENSITY: 544 people per sq. mile
LANGUAGES: German*, Alemannish dialect, Italian
RELIGIONS: Catholic 81%, other 19%
ETHNIC MIX: Liechtensteiner 66%, other 18%, Swiss 10%, Austrian 6%
GOVERNMENT: Parliamentary system
CURRENCY: Swiss franc = 100 centimes

Lithuania

Lying on the eastern coast of the Baltic Sea, Lithuania is the largest and most powerful of the Baltic states. It was the first Soviet republic to declare independence from Moscow in 1991.

GEOGRAPHY

Mostly flat with moors, bogs, and an intensively farmed central lowland. Numerous lakes and forested sandy ridges in the east.

CLIMATE

Coastal location moderates continental extremes. Cold winters, cool summers, and steady rainfall.

PEOPLE & SOCIETY

Homogeneous population, with Lithuanians forming a large majority. Strong Roman Catholic tradition and historic links with Poland. There are better relations among ethnic groups than in other Baltic states and inter-ethnic marriages are fairly common. However, ethnic Russians and Poles see a threat from "Lithuanianization." Only 4000 Jews, known as Litvaks, remain in Lithuania. A large income gap has grown since independence.

THE ECONOMY

A wide range of high-tech and heavy industries includes textiles, engineering, shipbuilding, and food processing. Litas pegged to the euro.

INSIGHT: *The "amber coasts" of the Baltic states, particularly Lithuania, produce most of the world's amber – fossilized resin*

FACTFILE

OFFICIAL NAME: Republic of Lithuania
DATE OF FORMATION: 1991
CAPITAL: Vilnius
POPULATION: 3.4 million
TOTAL AREA: 25,174 sq. miles (65,200 sq. km)
DENSITY: 135 people per sq. mile

LANGUAGES: Lithuanian*, Russian
RELIGIONS: Roman Catholic 83%, other 12%, Protestant 5%
ETHNIC MIX: Lithuanian 83%, Polish 7%, Russian 6%, other 3%, Belarussian 1%
GOVERNMENT: Parliamentary system
CURRENCY: Litas = 100 centu

Luxembourg

Making up part of the plateau of the Ardennes in western Europe, Luxembourg is one of Europe's richest states. A tax haven and banking center, it is also home to key EU institutions.

GEOGRAPHY
Dense Ardennes forests in the north, with a low, open plateau to the south. Undulating terrain throughout.

CLIMATE
The climate is moist, with warm summers and mild winters. Snow is common only in the Ardennes.

PEOPLE & SOCIETY
Ethnic tensions are rare, despite a large proportion of foreigners (over a third of residents). Integration has been straightforward; most are fellow western Europeans and Catholics, mainly from Italy and Portugal. Low unemployment and high salaries promote stability. Divorce is rising and marriage is becoming less common.

INSIGHT: Luxembourg's capital is home to around 2000 investment funds and over 160 banks

THE ECONOMY
Traditional industries such as steelmaking have given way in recent years to a thriving banking and service sector. Its banking and secrecy laws attract foreign companies.

500m/1640ft
200m/656ft
Sea Level

Clervaux

GERMANY

Ettelbrück

Echternach

Mersch

BELGIUM

●LUXEMBOURG

Pétange

Differdange
Esch-sur-Alzette

Dudelange

FRANCE

0   10 km
0   10 miles

FACTFILE

OFFICIAL NAME: Grand Duchy of Luxembourg
DATE OF FORMATION: 1867
CAPITAL: Luxembourg-Ville
POPULATION: 465,000
TOTAL AREA: 998 sq. miles (2586 sq. km)
DENSITY: 466 people per sq. mile

LANGUAGES: Luxembourgish*, German*, French*
RELIGIONS: Roman Catholic 97%, Jewish, Greek Orthodox, and Protestant 3%
ETHNIC MIX: Luxembourger 62%, foreign residents 38%
GOVERNMENT: Parliamentary system
CURRENCY: Euro = 100 cents

Macedonia

Landlocked in the southern Balkans, Macedonia was troubled by the sanctions placed on its northern trading partners in the mid-1990s, and by violent conflict with ethnic Albanians in 2001.

 GEOGRAPHY

Mainly mountainous or hilly, with deep river basins in the center. Plains in the northeast and southwest.

 CLIMATE

Continental climate with wet springs and dry autumns. Heavy snowfalls in northern mountains.

 PEOPLE & SOCIETY

Slav Macedonians comprise two-thirds of the population; they are mostly Orthodox Christians, with some Muslims. Officially 25% of the population are Muslim Albanians, though they claim to account for a third. Albanian militants fought a bitter war against the government in 2001. A peace deal promised greater equality. The Greek government is still wary that Macedonia may try to absorb historic "Macedonian" lands in northern Greece.

 THE ECONOMY

Regional instability deterred foreign investment, but the country has now been granted EU candidate status. High levels of unemployment and large gray economy.

 INSIGHT: *Ohrid is the deepest lake in Europe at 964 ft (294 m)*

 FACTFILE

OFFICIAL NAME: Republic of Macedonia
DATE OF FORMATION: 1991
CAPITAL: Skopje
POPULATION: 2 million
TOTAL AREA: 9781 sq. miles (25,333 sq. km)
DENSITY: 201 people per sq. mile

LANGUAGES: Macedonian*, Albanian*
RELIGIONS: Orthodox Christian 59%, Muslim 26%, other 11%, Catholic 4%
ETHNIC MIX: Macedonian 64%, Albanian 25%, other 5%, Turkish 4%, Serb 2%
GOVERNMENT: Mixed presidential–parliamentary system
CURRENCY: Macedonian denar = 100 deni

Madagascar

Lying off the east African coast in the Indian Ocean, the former French colony of Madagascar is the world's fourth-largest island. An electoral dispute spilled over into civil conflict in 2002.

GEOGRAPHY
More than two-thirds of the country forms a savanna-covered plateau, which drops sharply to a narrow coastal belt in the east.

CLIMATE
Tropical and often hit by cyclones. Monsoons affect the east coast. The southwest is much drier.

PEOPLE & SOCIETY
People are Malay-Indonesian in origin, intermixed with later migrants from the African mainland. The main ethnic division is between the Merina of the central plateau and the poorer *côtier* (coastal) peoples. The Merina were the country's historic rulers, and remain the social elite.

◆ **INSIGHT:** *80% of Madagascar's plants and many of its animal species are found nowhere else*

THE ECONOMY
The majority of people are farmers. Vanilla, cloves, and coffee are the most important cash crops. Prawns are a valuable export.

FACTFILE

OFFICIAL NAME: Republic of Madagascar
DATE OF FORMATION: 1960
CAPITAL: Antananarivo
POPULATION: 18.6 million
TOTAL AREA: 226,656 sq. miles (587,040 sq. km)
DENSITY: 83 people per sq. mile

LANGUAGES: Malagasy*, French*
RELIGIONS: Traditional beliefs 52%, Christian 41%, Muslim 7%
ETHNIC MIX: Other Malay 46%, Merina 26%, Betsimisaraka 15%, Betsileo 12%, other 1%
GOVERNMENT: Presidential system
CURRENCY: Ariary = 5 iraimbilanja

Malawi

A former colony of the UK, Malawi lies landlocked in southeast Africa, following the Great Rift Valley. Its name means "the land where the sun is reflected in the water like fire."

GEOGRAPHY
Lake Nyasa takes up one-fifth of the landscape. Highlands lie west of the lake. Much of the land is covered by forests and savanna.

CLIMATE
Mainly subtropical. The south is hot and humid. Highlands are cooler.

PEOPLE & SOCIETY
Ethnicity has not been exploited for political ends in Malawi as has been the case in neighboring states. Most Malawians share a common Bantu origin. The election in 1994 of a member of the Muslim minority as president signaled the failure of previous attempts to enforce Protestant dominance.

◆ **INSIGHT:** *Lake Nyasa is 353 miles (568 km) in length and contains at least 500 species of fish*

THE ECONOMY
Tobacco accounts for just under half of export earnings. Tea and sugar production. Drought is a serious problem.

2000m/6562ft	
1000m/3281ft	
500m/1640ft	
200m/656ft	
Sea Level	

FACTFILE
OFFICIAL NAME: Republic of Malawi
DATE OF FORMATION: 1964
CAPITAL: Lilongwe
POPULATION: 12.9 million
TOTAL AREA: 45,745 sq. miles (118,480 sq. km)
DENSITY: 355 people per sq. mile

LANGUAGES: Chewa, Lomwe, Yao, Ngoni, English*
RELIGIONS: Protestant 55%, Muslim 20%, Catholic 20%, traditional beliefs 5%
ETHNIC MIX: Bantu 99%, other 1%
GOVERNMENT: Presidential system
CURRENCY: Malawi kwacha = 100 tambala

Malaysia

Comprising the three territories of Peninsular Malaysia, Sarawak, and Sabah, Malaysia stretches 1240 miles (2000 km) from the Malay peninsula to eastern Borneo.

GEOGRAPHY

Almost three-quarters of the land is tropical rainforest or swamp forest. A central mountain chain, the Banjaran Titiwangsa, divides Peninsular Malaysia, separating a narrow eastern coastal belt from fertile western plains and sheltered beaches and bays. The territories of Sarawak and Sabah share the island of Borneo with Indonesia, and surround Brunei. They are characterized by swampy coastal plains rising to mountains along the southern border.

CLIMATE

Warm equatorial. Rainfall is heavy throughout the year, but with distinct rainy seasons from March to May and from September to November. Coastal areas are subject to the alternating southwest and northeast monsoon winds.

INSIGHT: *Malaysia is southeast Asia's major tourist destination, with over 15 million visitors a year. Most come for the beaches and highlands of Malaya, or the ancient rainforests of Borneo*

FACTFILE

OFFICIAL NAME: Federation of Malaysia
DATE OF FORMATION: 1963
CAPITALS: Kuala Lumpur and Putrajaya
POPULATION: 25.3 million
TOTAL AREA: 127,316 sq. miles (329,750 sq. km)
DENSITY: 199 people per sq. mile

LANGUAGES: Bahasa Malaysia*, Malay, Chinese, Tamil, English
RELIGIONS: Muslim 53%, Buddhist 19%, Chinese faiths 12%, other 9%, Christian 7%
ETHNIC MIX: Malay 50%, Chinese 25%, indigenous tribes 11%, other 14%
GOVERNMENT: Parliamentary system
CURRENCY: Ringgit = 100 sen

PEOPLE & SOCIETY

The key distinction in Malaysian society is between the indigenous Malays, termed the "Bumiputras" (literally, sons of the soil), and the Chinese. The Malays form the larger group, accounting for half of the population. However, the smaller Chinese population has traditionally controlled most economic activity. Malays have been favored in the education system and job market since the 1970s, in order to address this imbalance. There are estimated to be more than one million Indonesian and Filipino immigrants, attracted by labor shortages; a recent amnesty saw 300,000 illegal immigrants return home. Gender discrimination was only outlawed in 2001. In an attempt to promote Islamic tradition, Muslim women are encouraged to wear veils.

THE ECONOMY

Rapid growth since late 1980s, largely state-directed and under-pinned by a push for foreign investment and privatization of state assets. Asian financial crisis of 1997–1998 forced Malaysia to adopt economic austerity measures, and revise plans for industrialization. Successful car and electronics industries – the *Proton* car is regarded as a national success, while the new capital Putrajaya is being promoted as a high-tech center. Tourism is a major earner. Heavy industries such as steel. Leading producer of palm oil, pepper, tin, and tropical hardwoods. High level of debt. Shortage of skilled labor.

Maldives

The Maldives is an archipelago of 1190 small coral islands, or atolls, set in the Indian Ocean, southwest of Sri Lanka. The word atoll comes from the Dhivehi word "atolu."

GEOGRAPHY
Consists of low-lying islands and coral atolls. The larger ones are covered in lush, tropical vegetation.

CLIMATE
Tropical. Rain falls throughout the year, but is heaviest June–November, during the monsoon. Violent storms occasionally hit the northern islands.

PEOPLE & SOCIETY
Maldivians, who are all Sunni Muslim, are descended from Sinhalese, Dravidian, Arab, and black ancestors. About 25% of the population live on Male'. Tourism has grown on separate resort islands away from residents. Politics has been controlled by a small group of influential families, with Maumoon Abdul Gayoom as president since 1978. However, a new, young elite has pushed for political reform: political parties were legalized in 2005.

THE ECONOMY
Too dependent on the fluctuating tourist industry, which is the economic mainstay. Fish, especially tuna, are the leading exports.

INSIGHT:
The islands, which all lie below 4 ft (1.2 m), are threatened by rising sea levels, brought about by global warming and climatic changes

Ihavandippolhu Atoll

Faadhippolhu Atoll

Horsburgh Atoll

Male' Atoll

Ari Atoll

●MALE'

Felidhu Atoll

Mulaku Atoll

Kolhumadulu Atoll

Hadhdhunmathi Atoll

One and Half Degree Channel

INDIAN OCEAN

North Huvadhu Atoll

South Huvadhu Atoll

0   100 km
0   100 miles

Equator

Addu Atoll

Gan

□ Sea Level

6°

73°

FACTFILE
OFFICIAL NAME: Republic of Maldives
DATE OF FORMATION: 1965
CAPITAL: Male'
POPULATION: 329,000
TOTAL AREA: 116 sq. miles (300 sq. km)

DENSITY: 2836 people per sq. mile
LANGUAGES: Dhivehi* (Maldivian), Sinhala, Tamil, Arabic
RELIGIONS: Sunni Muslim 100%
ETHNIC MIX: All Maldivians are of Arab–Sinhalese–Malay descent
GOVERNMENT: Nonparty system
CURRENCY: Rufiyaa = 100 laari

A former French colony, Mali is landlocked in the heart of west Africa. The 1991 coup ended the 23-year dictatorship of Moussa Traoré and ushered in multiparty elections from 1992.

GEOGRAPHY
The northern half of the country lies in the Sahara. The inland delta of the Niger River flows through a grassy savanna region in the south.

CLIMATE
In the south, intensely hot, dry weather precedes the westerly rains. The north is almost rainless.

PEOPLE & SOCIETY
Most people live in southern savanna region. The Bambara tribe are culturally and politically dominant. A few nomadic Fulani and Tuareg herders travel the northern plains. There is tension between the peoples of the south and Tuareg in the north. Malian women have little status.

◆ **INSIGHT:** *Tombouctou (Timbuktu) was the center of the 14th-century Malinke trading empire*

THE ECONOMY
Less than 2% of land can be cultivated. Most people are farmers, herders, or river fishermen. Cotton is major crop. Vulnerable to drought. Gold deposits are now being mined.

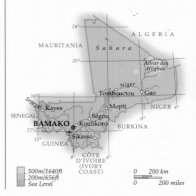

500m/1640ft
200m/656ft
Sea Level

0   200 km
0   200 miles

FACTFILE
OFFICIAL NAME: Republic of Mali
DATE OF FORMATION: 1960
CAPITAL: Bamako
POPULATION: 13.5 million
TOTAL AREA: 478,764 sq. miles (1,240,000 sq. km)
DENSITY: 29 people per sq. mile

LANGUAGES: Bambara, Fulani, Senufo, Soninke, French*
RELIGIONS: Muslim 80%, traditional beliefs 18%, Christian 1%, other 1%
ETHNIC MIX: Bambara 32%, other 33%, Fulani 14%, Senufu 12%, Soninka 9%
GOVERNMENT: Presidential system
CURRENCY: CFA franc = 100 centimes

Malta

The Maltese archipelago lies midway between Europe and Africa. Controlled throughout its history by successive colonial powers, it gained independence from the UK in 1964.

GEOGRAPHY
The main island of Malta has low hills and a ragged coastline with numerous harbors, bays, sandy beaches, and rocky coves. The island of Gozo is more densely vegetated.

CLIMATE
Mediterranean climate. There are many hours of sunshine all year round, with very little rainfall.

PEOPLE & SOCIETY
Over the centuries, the Maltese have been subject to Arab, Sicilian, Spanish, French, and British influences. Today, the population is socially conservative and devoutly Roman Catholic – on a percentage basis more so than virtually any other nation. Only 30% of the female labor force have jobs. Divorce is illegal. Since joining the EU, Malta has become a target for illegal migration from Africa.

THE ECONOMY
Tourism is the chief source of income. Developing offshore banking and foreign high-tech industry. Hopes to join eurozone in 2008. Almost all requirements have to be imported.

◆ **INSIGHT:** *The Maltese language has Phoenician origins but features Arabic etymology and intonation*

FACTFILE

OFFICIAL NAME: Republic of Malta
DATE OF FORMATION: 1964
CAPITAL: Valletta
POPULATION: 402,000
TOTAL AREA: 122 sq. miles (316 sq. km)
DENSITY: 3242 people per sq. mile

LANGUAGES: Maltese*, English*
RELIGIONS: Roman Catholic 98%, other and nonreligious 2%
ETHNIC MIX: Maltese 96%, other 4%
GOVERNMENT: Parliamentary system
CURRENCY: Maltese lira = 100 cents

Marshall Islands

Under US rule as part of the UN Trust Territory of the Pacific Islands until independence in 1986, the Marshall Islands comprises a group of 34 widely scattered atolls.

GEOGRAPHY

Narrow coral rings with sandy beaches enclosing lagoons. Those in the south have thicker vegetation. Kwajalein is the world's largest atoll.

CLIMATE

Tropical oceanic, cooled year round by northeast trade winds.

PEOPLE & SOCIETY

Majuro, the capital city and commercial center, is home to almost half the population. Tensions are high due to poor living conditions. Life on the outlying islands is still traditional, based around subsistence agriculture and fishing. Marshallese society is matrilineal: titles are chiefly handed down from the mother's side.

◆ **INSIGHT:** *In 1954, Bikini Atoll was the site for the testing of the largest US H-bomb – the 18–22 megaton Bravo*

THE ECONOMY

Almost totally dependent on US aid and the rent paid by the US for its missile base on Kwajalein Atoll. Revenue from Japan for the use of Marshallese waters for tuna fishing. Copra and coconut oil are the only significant agricultural exports.

FACTFILE

OFFICIAL NAME: Republic of the Marshall Islands

DATE OF FORMATION: 1986

CAPITAL: Majuro

POPULATION: 59,071

TOTAL AREA: 70 sq. miles (181 sq. km)

DENSITY: 844 people per sq. mile

LANGUAGES: Marshallese*, English*, Japanese, German

RELIGIONS: Protestant 90%, Roman Catholic 8%, other 2%

ETHNIC MIX: Micronesian 97%, other 3%

GOVERNMENT: Presidential system

CURRENCY: US dollar = 100 cents

Mauritania

Two-thirds of Mauritania's territory is desert – the only productive land is that drained by the Senegal River. The country has taken a strongly Arab direction since 1964.

GEOGRAPHY

The Sahara, barren except for some scattered oases, covers the north. Savanna lands lie to the south.

CLIMATE

The climate is generally hot and dry, aggravated by the dusty *harmattan* wind. Summer rain in the south, virtually none in the north.

PEOPLE & SOCIETY

The majority Maures control political life. There is a sizable black minority. Ethnic tension centers on the oppression of blacks by Maures. Tens of thousands of blacks are estimated to be in illegal slavery. Family solidarity among nomadic peoples is particularly strong.

◆ **INSIGHT:** *Slavery officially became illegal in Mauritania in 1980, but de facto slavery still persists*

THE ECONOMY

Agriculture and herding. Iron and copper mining. World's largest gypsum deposits. Some of the best fishing grounds in west Africa.

FACTFILE

OFFICIAL NAME: Islamic Republic of Mauritania
DATE OF FORMATION: 1960
CAPITAL: Nouakchott
POPULATION: 3.1 million
TOTAL AREA: 397,953 sq. miles (1,030,700 sq. km)

DENSITY: 8 people per sq. mile
LANGUAGES: Hassaniyah Arabic*, Wolof, French
RELIGIONS: Sunni Muslim 100%
ETHNIC MIX: Maure 81%, Wolof 7%, Tukolor 5%, other 4%, Soninka 3%
GOVERNMENT: Transitional regime
CURRENCY: Ouguiya = 5 khoums

Mauritius

The islands that make up Mauritius lie in the Indian Ocean east of Madagascar. They have enjoyed considerable economic success following recent industrial diversification and expansion.

GEOGRAPHY

The volcanic main island of Mauritius is ringed by coral reefs, and rises from the coast to a fertile central plateau. The outer islands – Rodriguez, the Agalega Islands, and the Cargados Carajos Shoals – lie some 300 miles (500 km) to the north.

CLIMATE

Warm and humid. Tropical storms are frequent December–March, the hottest and wettest months.

PEOPLE & SOCIETY

Most people are descendants of laborers brought over from India in the 19th century. A small minority of French descent form the wealthiest group. The Creole community complains of discrimination. Criminal offenses are usually traffic-related; the outer islands are virtually free from crime altogether.

THE ECONOMY

Clothing manufacture, tourism, and sugar are main sources of income. Loss of preferential trade terms for sugar exports. Offshore financial center. Most food has to be imported.

INSIGHT: *The islands lie on the Mascarene Archipelago – once a land bridge between Asia and Africa*

FACTFILE

OFFICIAL NAME: Republic of Mauritius
DATE OF FORMATION: 1968
CAPITAL: Port Louis
POPULATION: 1.2 million
TOTAL AREA: 718 sq. miles (1860 sq. km)
DENSITY: 1671 people per sq. mile

LANGUAGES: French Creole, Hindi, Urdu, Tamil, Chinese, English*, French
RELIGIONS: Hindu 52%, Catholic 26%, Muslim 17%, other 3%, Protestant 2%
ETHNIC MIX: Indo-Mauritian 68%, Creole 27%, other 5%
GOVERNMENT: Parliamentary system
CURRENCY: Mauritian rupee = 100 cents

Mexico

Mexico stretches from the US border southward into the ancient Aztec and Mayan heartlands. Independence from Spain came in 1836. One in four Mexicans lives in the sprawling capital.

GEOGRAPHY

Coastal plains along the Pacific and Atlantic seaboards rise to a high arid central plateau. To the east and west are the Sierra Madre mountain ranges. Limestone lowlands form the projecting Yucatan peninsula.

CLIMATE

The plateau and high mountains are warm for much of the year. Pacific coast is tropical: storms occur mostly March–December. Northwest is dry.

PEOPLE & SOCIETY

Most Mexicans are *mestizos* of mixed Spanish and Amerindian descent. Rural Amerindians are largely segregated from Hispanic society and most live in poverty, though their culture is promoted by the state. Zapatista movement backs indigenous rights. Few women in male-dominated politics and business.

THE ECONOMY

One of the world's largest oil producers. Remittances from abroad are second foreign exchange earner. Exotic fruits and vegetables are cash crops. The North American Free Trade Agreement (1994) boosted exports, but exposes farmers to subsidized US competition. Huge wealth disparities.

◆ **INSIGHT:** *More people cross the US Mexican border each year – illegally o legally – than any other border in the worl*

FACTFILE

OFFICIAL NAME: United Mexican States
DATE OF FORMATION: 1836
CAPITAL: Mexico City
POPULATION: 107 million
TOTAL AREA: 761,602 sq. miles (1,972,550 sq. km)
DENSITY: 145 people per sq. mile

LANGUAGES: Spanish*, Nahuatl, Mayan, Zapotec, Mixtec, Otomi, Totonac, other
RELIGIONS: Roman Catholic 88%, other 7%, Protestant 5%
ETHNIC MIX: Mestizo 60%, Amerindian 30%, European 9%, other 1%
GOVERNMENT: Presidential system
CURRENCY: Mexican peso = 100 centavos

Micronesia

The Federated States of Micronesia (FSM), situated in the western Pacific, comprise 607 islands and atolls grouped into four main island states: Pohnpei, Kosrae, Chuuk, and Yap.

GEOGRAPHY
Mixture of high volcanic islands with forested interiors, and low-lying coral atolls. Some of the islands have coastal mangrove swamps.

CLIMATE
Tropical, with high humidity. There is very heavy rainfall outside the January–March dry season.

◆ **INSIGHT:** *Chuuk's lagoon contains the sunken wrecks of over 100 Japanese ships and 270 planes from World War II*

PEOPLE & SOCIETY
Micronesians are physically, culturally, and linguistically diverse. Melanesians live on Yap and Polynesians in Pohnpei. Most islanders live without electricity or running water. Society is traditionally matrilineal.

THE ECONOMY
Dependent on US aid. Tourism, fishing, betel nuts, and copra are economic mainstays. Fishing licenses are a key source of foreign revenue.

FACTFILE

OFFICIAL NAME: Federated States of Micronesia

DATE OF FORMATION: 1986

CAPITAL: Palikir (Pohnpei Island)

POPULATION: 108,105

TOTAL AREA: 271 sq. miles (702 sq. km)

DENSITY: 399 people per sq. mile

LANGUAGES: Trukese, Pohnpeian, Mortlockese, Kosraean, English*

RELIGIONS: Roman Catholic 50%, Protestant 48%, other 2%

ETHNIC MIX: Chuukese 49%, Pohnpeian 24%, other 19%, Kosraean 6%, Asian 2%

GOVERNMENT: Nonparty system

CURRENCY: US dollar = 100 cents

Moldova

The smallest and most densely populated of the former Soviet republics, Moldova has strong ethnic, linguistic, and cultural links with Romania to the west.

GEOGRAPHY
The steppes and hilly plains are drained by Dniester and Prut Rivers.

CLIMATE
Warm summers and relatively mild winters. Moderate rainfall is evenly spread throughout the year.

PEOPLE & SOCIETY
A shared heritage with Romania defines national identity, though in 1994 Moldovans voted against possible reunification with Romania. Most of the population is engaged in intensive agriculture. Transdniestria is a breakaway state along the east bank of the Dniester, home to a largely ethnic Slav population. The Gagauz, in the south, have accepted autonomy.

◆ **INSIGHT:** *Vast underground wine vaults contain entire "streets" of bottles built into rock quarries*

THE ECONOMY
Poorest country in Europe. Well-developed agricultural sector: wine, tobacco, cotton, food processing. Light manufacturing. Chronic instability deters investors.

FACTFILE
OFFICIAL NAME: Republic of Moldova
DATE OF FORMATION: 1991
CAPITAL: Chisinau
POPULATION: 4.2 million
TOTAL AREA: 13,067 sq. miles (33,843 sq. km)
DENSITY: 323 people per sq. mile

LANGUAGES: Moldovan*, Ukrainian, Russian
RELIGIONS: Orthodox Christian 98%, Jewish 2%
ETHNIC MIX: Moldovan 64%, Ukrainian 14%, Russian 13%, Gagauz 4%, other 5%
GOVERNMENT: Parliamentary system
CURRENCY: Moldovan leu = 100 bani

Monaco

Monaco is a tiny enclave on the Côte d'Azur. Its destiny changed radically when the casino was opened in 1863. Today, it promotes its image as an upmarket, glamorous destination.

GEOGRAPHY

A rocky promontory overlooking a narrow coastal strip that has been enlarged through land reclamation.

CLIMATE

Mediterranean. Summers are hot and dry; days with 12 hours of sunshine are not uncommon. Winters are mild and sunny.

PEOPLE & SOCIETY

Less than 20% of residents are Monégasques. Around a third are French, the rest Italian, American, British, Belgian, and many others. Nationals enjoy considerable privileges, including housing subsidies to protect them from Monaco's high property prices, and the right of first refusal before a job can be offered to a foreigner. Women have equal status but only acquired the vote in 1962.

THE ECONOMY

Tourism and gambling are the mainstays. Banking secrecy laws and tax-haven conditions are attractive to foreign investment. Monaco is almost totally dependent on imports due to its lack of natural resources.

INSIGHT: *High-profile social and sporting events attract large crowds each spring, including the Rose Ball, Tennis Open, and Grand Prix*

FACTFILE

OFFICIAL NAME: Principality of Monaco

DATE OF FORMATION: 1861

CAPITAL: Monaco-Ville

POPULATION: 32,409

TOTAL AREA: 0.75 sq. miles (1.95 sq. km)

DENSITY: 43,212 people per sq. mile

LANGUAGES: French*, Italian, Monégasque, English

RELIGIONS: Roman Catholic 89%, Protestant 6%, other 5%

ETHNIC MIX: French 32%, other 29%, Italian 20%, Monégasque 19%

GOVERNMENT: Monarchy

CURRENCY: Euro = 100 cents

Mongolia

Landlocked between Russia and China, Mongolia is a vast and isolated country with a large nomadic population. Over two-thirds of the country is part of the vast Gobi Desert.

GEOGRAPHY

A mountainous steppe plateau in the north, with lakes in the north and west. The desert region of the Gobi dominates the south.

CLIMATE

Continental. Mild summers and long, dry, very cold winters, with heavy snowfall. Temperatures can drop as low as –22°F (–30°C).

PEOPLE & SOCIETY

Mongolia was unified by Genghis Khan in 1206 and was later absorbed into Manchu China. A majority of ethnic Mongolians live over the border in Inner Mongolia. Tibetan Buddhism dominates. The traditional, nomadic way of life has been eroded as urban migration continues, spurred by recent ferocious winters, known as *zud*, which have devastated the rural economy.

THE ECONOMY

Rich deposits of oil, coal, copper, uranium, and other minerals remain largely untapped. Democracy, from 1990, has brought a shift toward a market economy, but also rising poverty. State involvement in mining is an issue. Agriculture employs 40% of the workforce, mainly animal herding.

◆ **INSIGHT:** *Horseracing, wrestling, and archery are the national sports*

FACTFILE

OFFICIAL NAME: Mongolia
DATE OF FORMATION: 1924
CAPITAL: Ulan Bator
POPULATION: 2.6 million
TOTAL AREA: 604,247 sq. miles (1,565,000 sq. km)
DENSITY: 4 people per sq. mile

LANGUAGES: Khalkha Mongolian*, other
RELIGIONS: Tibetan Buddhist 96%, Muslim 4%
ETHNIC MIX: Khalkh 82%, other 9%, Kazakh 4%, Dorvod 3%, Bayad 2%
GOVERNMENT: Mixed presidential–parliamentary system
CURRENCY: Tugrik (tögrög) = 100 möngö

Montenegro

Perched on the Adriatic coast, the tiny republic of Montenegro became a separate state in 2006, after 88 years of federation with its neighbors in various forms of the state of Yugoslavia.

GEOGRAPHY

A narrow coastal strip on the Adriatic. Fertile lowland plains around Lake Skadar. Mountainous interior with deep canyons.

CLIMATE

The lowlands have hot, dry summers and mild winters. Heavy snow in winter in the mountains.

PEOPLE & SOCIETY

Most Montenegrins are Orthodox Christians. They speak a language closely related to Serbian, using the same Cyrillic script. Muslim Albanians, who make up 80% of the population of the southern Ulcinj region, supported independence and are now asking for autonomy.

INSIGHT: *Dark forests once cloaked Montenegro's mountains; its name means "Black Mountain"*

THE ECONOMY

Sanctions aimed at Serbia also hurt Montenegro before it seceded. Economy dominated by black market; cigarette smuggling is rife. Tourism now expanding along Adriatic. Return of international aid and investment. Hopes for eventual EU accession.

FACTFILE

OFFICIAL NAME: Republic of Montenegro
DATE OF FORMATION: 2006
CAPITAL: Podgorica
POPULATION: 620,145
TOTAL AREA: 5332 sq. miles (13,812 sq. km)
DENSITY: 116 people per sq. mile

LANGUAGES: Montenegrin*, Serbian, Albanian
RELIGIONS: Orthodox Christian 74%, Muslim 18%, Catholic 4%, other 4%
ETHNIC MIX: Montenegrin 43%, Serb 32%, other 12%, Bosniak 8%, Albanian 5%
GOVERNMENT: Parliamentary system
CURRENCY: Euro = 100 cents

Morocco

 Morocco is a former French colony in northwest Africa. Since 1975 it has occupied the territory of Western Sahara, the future of which is yet to be determined by UN-supervised referendum.

GEOGRAPHY

Fertile coastal plain is interrupted in the east by the Rif Mountains. Atlas Mountain ranges to the south. Beyond lies the outer fringe of the Sahara.

CLIMATE

Ranges from temperate and warm in the north, to semiarid in the south. Cooler in the mountains.

PEOPLE & SOCIETY

Around 30% of the population are descendants of original Berber inhabitants of north Africa, and live mainly in mountain villages. The Arab majority inhabits the lowlands. Morocco is unusual among Arab states in granting Jews religious freedom and civil rights. The government is pressured by Islamic traditionalists who fear the loss of Arab identity. The king is spiritual leader and head of state.

THE ECONOMY

A leading world exporter of phosphates. Tourism and agriculture have great potential. Production of cannabis complicates closer EU links.

INSIGHT: *Karueein University in Fès, founded in 859 CE, is the world's oldest existing educational institution*

Map:
Mediterranean Sea
ATLANTIC OCEAN
Tanger, Ceuta (to Spain), Melilla (to Spain)
Tétouan
RABAT Kénitra
Mohammedia, Salé, Fès, Oujda
Casablanca, Meknès
Safi, Khouribga
Beni Mellal
Marrakech
Essaouira
Agadir, Ouarzazate
ALGERIA
Haut Atlas
Atlas Mountains
Anti-Atlas
WESTERN SAHARA (Occupied by Morocco)

3000m/9843ft
2000m/6562ft
1000m/3281ft
500m/1640ft
200m/656ft
Sea Level

0 100 km
0 100 miles

FACTFILE

OFFICIAL NAME: Kingdom of Morocco
DATE OF FORMATION: 1956
CAPITAL: Rabat
POPULATION: 31.5 million
TOTAL AREA: 172,316 sq. miles (446,300 sq. km)
DENSITY: 183 people per sq. mile

LANGUAGES: Arabic*, Tamazight (Berber), French, Spanish
RELIGIONS: Muslim (mainly Sunni) 99%, other (mostly Christian) 1%
ETHNIC MIX: Arab 70%, Berber 29%, European 1%
GOVERNMENT: Monarchy
CURRENCY: Dirham = 100 centimes

Mozambique

Mozambique lies on the southeast African coast. It was torn apart by a savage and devastating civil war between the Marxist government and a rebel faction between 1977 and 1992.

GEOGRAPHY
Largely a savanna-covered plateau. The coast is fringed by coral reefs and lagoons. The Zambezi River bisects the country.

CLIMATE
Tropical. Temperatures are hottest on the coast. Extremes of rainfall: drought and flood.

PEOPLE & SOCIETY
Tensions exist between north and south, rather than ethnic groups. Life is centered on the extended family. Polygamy is fairly common. The country is struggling with the legacy of a war which killed over one million people, and the effects of terrible flooding in 2000 and 2001. Half of the population live in abject poverty.

◆ **INSIGHT:** *Maputo's busy port serves Zimbabwe and South Africa*

THE ECONOMY
Mozambique is almost entirely dependent on foreign aid. Mineral resources have yet to be fully exploited.

2000m/6562ft
1000m/3281ft
500m/1640ft
200m/656ft
Sea Level

TANZANIA
Rovuma
Lake Nyasa
MALAWI · Lichinga
Pemba
Lúrio
ZAMBIA
Nacala
Lake
Cahora Bassa
Lumbo
Nampula
Tete
Quelimane
ZIMBABWE
Zambezi
Mozambique Channel
Beira
INDIAN
OCEAN
Limpopo
Funhalouro
Inhambane
SOUTH
AFRICA
Xai-Xai
MAPUTO
SWAZILAND
SOUTH
AFRICA

0   200 km
0   200 miles

FACTFILE

OFFICIAL NAME: Rep. of Mozambique
DATE OF FORMATION: 1975
CAPITAL: Maputo
POPULATION: 19.8 million
TOTAL AREA: 309,494 sq. miles (801,590 sq. km)
DENSITY: 65 people per sq. mile

LANGUAGES: Makua, Xitsonga, Sena, Lomwe, Portuguese*
RELIGIONS: Traditional beliefs 56%, Christian 30%, Muslim 14%
ETHNIC MIX: Makua Lomwe 47%, Tsonga 23%, Malawi 12%, Shona 11% other 7%
GOVERNMENT: Presidential system
CURRENCY: Metical = 100 centavos

Myanmar (Burma)

Forming the eastern shores of the Bay of Bengal and the Andaman Sea in southeast Asia, Myanmar suffers from extensive political repression and ethnic conflict.

 GEOGRAPHY
The fertile Irrawaddy basin lies at the center. Mountains to the west, Shan plateau to the east. Tropical rainforest covers much of the land.

 CLIMATE
Tropical. Hot summers, with high humidity, and warm winters.

 PEOPLE & SOCIETY
The military, in power since 1962, rules Myanmar with little regard to human rights. Opposition is not tolerated. The National League for Democracy won elections in 1990, but was kept from power. Its leader, Aung San Suu Kyi, is frequently detained. Minority groups maintain low-level guerrilla activity against the state.

◆ **INSIGHT:** *Myanmar is the one of the world's biggest teak exporters, though reserves are diminishing rapidly*

THE ECONOMY
Aid suspensions and sanctions. The ruling junta has encouraged foreign investment. Prices are soaring on the black market. Illicit opium production. Teak, rice, and gems exported.

FACTFILE

OFFICIAL NAME: Union of Myanmar
DATE OF FORMATION: 1948
CAPITAL: Rangoon (Yangon)/Pyinmana
POPULATION: 50.5 million
TOTAL AREA: 261,969 sq. miles (678,500 sq. km)
DENSITY: 199 people per sq. mile

LANGUAGES: Burmese*, Shan, Karen, Rakhine, Chin, Yangbye, Kachin, Mon
RELIGIONS: Buddhist 87%, Christian 6%, Muslim 4%, other 2%, Hindu 1%
ETHNIC MIX: Burman 68%, other 13%, Shan 9%, Karen 6%, Rakhine 4%
GOVERNMENT: Military-based regime
CURRENCY: Kyat = 100 pyas

Namibia

Located in southwestern Africa, Namibia gained independence from South Africa in 1990, after 24 years of armed struggle. It regained the territory of Walvis Bay in 1994.

GEOGRAPHY

The Namib Desert stretches along the coastal strip. Inland, a ridge of mountains rises to 8000 ft (2500 m). The Kalahari Desert lies in the east.

CLIMATE

Almost rainless. The coast is usually shrouded in thick fog, unless the hot, dry *berg* wind is blowing.

PEOPLE & SOCIETY

The largest ethnic group, the Ovambo, live mainly in the north. Whites, including a large German community, are centered around Windhoek. Whites still control the economy. The minority San and Khoi bushmen are among the oldest human communities in the world. Toleration of homosexuality is slowly increasing.

◆ **INSIGHT:** *The Namib is the Earth's oldest, and one of its driest, deserts*

THE ECONOMY

Varied mineral resources, including uranium and diamonds. Rich offshore fishing grounds. High unemployment, and a growing AIDS epidemic.

FACTFILE

OFFICIAL NAME: Republic of Namibia
DATE OF FORMATION: 1990
CAPITAL: Windhoek
POPULATION: 2 million
TOTAL AREA: 318,694 sq. miles (825,418 sq. km)
DENSITY: 6 people per sq. mile

LANGUAGES: Ovambo, Kavango, English*, Bergdama, German, Afrikaans
RELIGIONS: Christian 90%, traditional beliefs 10%
ETHNIC MIX: Ovambo 50%, other tribes 25%, Kavango 9%, Damara 8%, Herero 8%
GOVERNMENT: Presidential system
CURRENCY: Namibian dollar = 100 cents

Nauru

Nauru lies in the Pacific, northeast of Australia. Phosphate deposits made its citizens among the wealthiest in the world, but economic mismanagement has left it facing ruin.

GEOGRAPHY
A single low-lying coral atoll, with a fertile coastal belt. Coral cliffs encircle an elevated interior plateau.

CLIMATE
Equatorial, moderated by sea breezes. Occasional long droughts.

PEOPLE & SOCIETY
Native Nauruans are of mixed Micronesian and Polynesian origin. Most live in simple, traditional houses and spend their money on luxury cars and consumer goods. Welfare and education are free. A diet of imported processed foods has caused widespread obesity and diabetes. Mining was left to an imported labor force, mainly from Kiribati, who live in enclaves of male-only barracks and have few rights. Many of the young attend boarding schools in Australia and New Zealand.

THE ECONOMY
Phosphate revenues all but dried up by 2003. No other resources. State trust fund invested badly overseas. Offshore banking facilities were closed after international pressure.

◆ **INSIGHT:** *Phosphate mining has left 80% of the island uninhabitable*

FACTFILE
OFFICIAL NAME: Republic of Nauru
DATE OF FORMATION: 1968
CAPITAL: None
POPULATION: 13,048
TOTAL AREA: 8.1 sq. miles (21 sq. km)
DENSITY: 1611 people per sq. mile

LANGUAGES: Nauruan*, Kiribati, Chinese, Tuvaluan, English
RELIGIONS: Nauruan Congregational Church 60%, Catholic 35%, other 5%
ETHNIC MIX: Nauruan 62%, other Pacific islanders 27%, Asian 8%, European 3%
GOVERNMENT: Parliamentary system
CURRENCY: Australian $ = 100 cents

Nepal

Nepal, lying between India and China on the southern shoulder of the Himalayas, is one of the world's poorest countries. Its agricultural economy is heavily dependent on the monsoon.

GEOGRAPHY
Mainly mountainous. The area includes some of the highest mountains in the world, such as Everest. Flat, fertile river plains form the south.

CLIMATE
Warm monsoon season from July to October. The rest of the year is dry, sunny, and mild. Winter temperatures in the Himalayas average 14°F (−10°C).

PEOPLE & SOCIETY
There are few tensions between the diverse ethnic groups. Sherpa women, like other Buddhists, face fewer social restrictions than Hindus. A Maoist insurgency, seeking a socialist republic, began in 1999 and threw the country into a state of virtual civil war. In 2002, the king sacked the government; opposition protests forced the return of democracy in 2006, with the king reduced to a figurehead.

THE ECONOMY
Agriculture employs over 90% of people. Crops include rice, maize, and millet. Tourism has been affected by instability and Maoist insurgency. There is potential for hydropower.

◆ **INSIGHT:** *Southern Nepal was the birthplace of Buddha (Prince Siddhartha Gautama) in 563 BCE*

FACTFILE
OFFICIAL NAME: Kingdom of Nepal
DATE OF FORMATION: 1769
CAPITAL: Kathmandu
POPULATION: 27.1 million
TOTAL AREA: 54,363 sq. miles (140,800 sq. km)
DENSITY: 513 people per sq. mile

LANGUAGES: Nepali*, Maithili, Bhojpuri
RELIGIONS: Hindu 90%, Buddhist 5%, Muslim 3%, other 2%
ETHNIC MIX: Other 52%, Chhetri 16%, Hill Brahman 13%, Tharu 7%, Magar 7%, Tamang 5%
GOVERNMENT: Parliamentary system
CURRENCY: Nepalese rupee = 100 paisa

Netherlands

Astride the delta of five major rivers in northwest Europe, the Netherlands was one of the world's first confederative republics. The main port, Rotterdam, is also the world's largest.

GEOGRAPHY

Mainly flat, with 27% of the land below sea level and protected by dunes, dikes, and canals. There are a few low hills in the south and east.

CLIMATE

Mild, rainy winters and cool summers. Gales from the North Sea are common in fall and winter.

PEOPLE & SOCIETY

The Dutch have a long history of welcoming immigrants from former colonies and refugees seeking asylum. However, lack of integration is now raising fears about the failing asylum system, immigrant crime, and militant Islam. Population density is high and mostly urban. The state does not try to impose a particular morality on its citizens. Laws concerning sexuality, narcotics-taking, and euthanasia, are among the world's most liberal.

THE ECONOMY

Diverse industrial sector exports metals, machinery, electronics, and chemicals. High-profile multinationals. The social welfare system is costly.

◆ **INSIGHT:** *In 2002 the Netherlands became the first country in the world to legalize euthanasia*

Sea Level
Below Sea Level

North Sea

Waddeneilanden
Wadden

Groningen — 53°

AMSTERDAM
Haarlem
Apeldoorn Enschede
'S-GRAVENHAGE
(THE HAGUE) Leiden Utrecht
Delft Neder Rijn Arnhem — 52°
Rotterdam Nijmegen
Maas
Breda Tilburg GERMANY
Eindhoven
BELGIUM
Maastricht — 51°

0   40 km
0   40 miles

4°   6°

FACTFILE

OFFICIAL NAME: Kingdom of the Netherlands
DATE OF FORMATION: 1648
CAPITALS: Amsterdam and The Hague
POPULATION: 16.3 million
TOTAL AREA: 16,033 sq. miles (41,526 sq. km)

DENSITY: 1245 people per sq. mile
LANGUAGES: Dutch*, Frisian
RELIGIONS: Roman Catholic 36%, other 34%, Protestant 27%, Muslim 3%
ETHNIC MIX: Dutch 82%, other 12%, Surinamese, Turkish, and Moroccan 6%
GOVERNMENT: Parliamentary system
CURRENCY: Euro = 100 cents

AUSTRALASIA & OCEANIA **287**

New Zealand

Lying in the South Pacific, 990 miles (1600 km) southeast of Australia, New Zealand comprises North and South Island, separated by the Cook Strait, and many smaller islands.

GEOGRAPHY

North Island contains hot springs and geysers, and the bulk of the population. South Island is mostly mountainous, with eastern lowlands.

CLIMATE

Generally temperate and damp. The far north is almost subtropical, whereas southern winters are cold.

PEOPLE & SOCIETY

Maoris were the first settlers, 1200 years ago. Today's majority European population is descended mainly from British migrants who settled after 1840. Maoris' living and education standards are generally lower than average. The government is continuing to negotiate the settlement of Maori land claims.

◆ **INSIGHT:** *New Zealand women were the first to get the vote (1893)*

THE ECONOMY

Modern agricultural sector; one of the world's five biggest exporters of dairy products. Manufacturing and tourism industries growing. Very high debt.

2000m/6562ft
1000m/3281ft
500m/1640ft
200m/656ft
Sea Level

North Island

36°

Auckland
Manurewa
Hamilton   Tauranga
Rotorua
New   Taupo
Plymouth
Napier
Hastings
Palmerston
North
Tasman   Blenheim   Lower Hutt
Sea   **WELLINGTON**
176°
Cook Strait

40°

South Island

Christchurch

44°   Timaru
172°

Southern Alps

PACIFIC
OCEAN

Dunedin

Invercargill
Stewart Island
168°

0   200 km
0   200 miles

FACTFILE

OFFICIAL NAME: New Zealand
DATE OF FORMATION: 1947
CAPITAL: Wellington
POPULATION: 4 million
TOTAL AREA: 103,737 sq. miles (268,680 sq. km)
DENSITY: 39 people per sq. mile

LANGUAGES: English*, Maori*
RELIGIONS: Anglican 24%, other 22%, Presbyterian 18%, nonreligious 16%, Roman Catholic 15%, Methodist 5%
ETHNIC MIX: European 75%, Maori 15%, other 7%, Samoan 3%
GOVERNMENT: Parliamentary system
CURRENCY: New Zealand $ = 100 cents

Nicaragua

Nicaragua lies at the heart of Central America. The Sandinista revolution of 1978 led to 11 years of civil war between the left-wing Sandinistas and the right-wing US-backed, Contras.

GEOGRAPHY

Extensive forested plains in the east. Central mountain region with many active volcanoes. The Pacific coastlands are dominated by lakes.

CLIMATE

Tropical. The lowlands are hot all year round. The mountains are cooler. Prone to occasional hurricanes.

PEOPLE & SOCIETY

Most of the population is mixed race, and there is a large white elite. The Caribbean regions are home to communities of Miskito Amerindians and blacks, who gained autonomy in 1987. The revolution improved the status of women, but these gains have been undone by rampant poverty.

◆ **INSIGHT:** *Lake Nicaragua is the only freshwater lake in the world to contain ocean animals*

THE ECONOMY

Coffee, meat, and gold are the main exports; affected by world price fluctuations. Corruption. A heavy debt burden, though substantial debt relief has recently been approved.

1000m/3281ft
500m/1640ft
200m/656ft
Sea Level

HONDURAS

Coco

14°

Ocotal

Estelí   Jinotega
         Matagalpa
Chinandega   Telica   Matiguas
Corinto
   León
   Nagarote   **MANAGUA**
                        Juigalpa
San Rafael del Sur   Granada
         Diriamba   Nandaime
         Jinotepe   Rivas   Lago de
                           Nicaragua
                      (Lake Nicaragua)
86°   COSTA RICA

Caribbean
Sea

Mosquito Coast

Bluefields

San Juan

84°

0   100 km
0   100 miles

FACTFILE

OFFICIAL NAME: Republic of Nicaragua
DATE OF FORMATION: 1838
CAPITAL: Managua
POPULATION: 5.5 million
TOTAL AREA: 49,998 sq. miles
(129,494 sq. km)
DENSITY: 120 people per sq. mile

LANGUAGES: Spanish*, English Creole, Miskito
RELIGIONS: Roman Catholic 80%, Protestant Evangelical 17%, other 3%
ETHNIC MIX: Mestizo 69%, White 14%, Black 8%, Amerindian 5%, Zambo 4%
GOVERNMENT: Presidential system
CURRENCY: Córdoba oro = 100 centavos

Landlocked in the west of Africa, Niger is linked to the sea by the Niger River. It was ruled by one-party or military regimes until 1992, when a multiparty constitution was introduced.

GEOGRAPHY
The north and northeast regions are part of the Sahara. The Aïr Mountains in the center rise high above the desert. Savanna lies to the south.

CLIMATE
High temperatures persist for most of the year at around 95°F (35°C). The north is virtually rainless.

PEOPLE & SOCIETY
Considerable tensions exist between Tuareg nomads in the north and groups in the south. Tuareg have felt alienated from mainstream politics. A five-year rebellion by northern Tuareg ended in 1995 with a peace agreement. A sense of community and egalitarianism among the southern peoples helps to combat economic difficulties. Niger is largely Islamic. Women have limited rights, and restricted access to education.

THE ECONOMY
Niger has vast uranium deposits. Frequent droughts and the southwest expansion of the Sahara are problems.

INSIGHT: *Niger's name is derived from the Tuareg word* n'eghirren, *which means "flowing water"*

FACTFILE

OFFICIAL NAME: Republic of Niger
DATE OF FORMATION: 1960
CAPITAL: Niamey
POPULATION: 14 million
TOTAL AREA: 489,188 sq. miles (1,267,000 sq. km)
DENSITY: 29 people per sq. mile

LANGUAGES: Hausa, French*, other
RELIGIONS: Muslim 85%, traditional beliefs 14%, other 1%
ETHNIC MIX: Hausa 55%, Djerma and Songhai 21%, Peul 9%, Tuareg 9%, other 6%
GOVERNMENT: Presidential system
CURRENCY: CFA franc = 100 centimes

Nigeria

Lying in west Africa, Nigeria (a former UK colony) is now a federation of 36 states and the capital, Abuja. Dominated by military governments since 1966, democracy returned in 1999.

GEOGRAPHY

Coastal area of beaches, swamps, and lagoons gives way to rainforest, and then to savanna on the high plateaus. Semidesert to the north.

CLIMATE

The south is hot, rainy and humid for most of the year. The arid north has one very humid wet season. The Jos Plateau and highlands are cooler.

PEOPLE & SOCIETY

Some 250 ethnic groups: the largest are the Hausa, Yoruba, Ibo, and Fulani. Tensions between groups threaten national unity, and fierce intercommunal violence is common. The northern states have introduced *sharia* (Islamic law) for their majority Muslim populations. In the south, women are allowed economic independence; in the north they are restricted by conservative Islam.

THE ECONOMY

Nigeria has been overdependent on oil, its principal export, since the 1970s. Corruption is a serious issue.

INSIGHT: *Nigeria is Africa's most populous state – one in every seven Africans is Nigerian*

FACTFILE

OFFICIAL NAME: Federal Republic of Nigeria
DATE OF FORMATION: 1960
CAPITAL: Abuja
POPULATION: 132 million
TOTAL AREA: 356,667 sq. miles (923,768 sq. km)

DENSITY: 374 people per sq. mile
LANGUAGES: Hausa, English*, Yoruba, Ibo
RELIGIONS: Muslim 50%, Christian 40%, traditional beliefs 10%
ETHNIC MIX: Hausa 21%, Yoruba 21%, Ibo 18%, Fulani 11%, other 29%
GOVERNMENT: Presidential system
CURRENCY: Naira = 100 kobo

Norway

The Kingdom of Norway traces the rugged western coast of Scandinavia. Settlements are largely restricted to southern and coastal areas. Vast oil and gas revenues bring prosperity.

GEOGRAPHY
The western coast is indented with numerous fjords and features tens of thousands of islands. Mountains and plateaus cover most of the country.

CLIMATE
Mild coastal climate. Inland, weather is more extreme, with warm summers and cold, snowy winters.

PEOPLE & SOCIETY
Fairly homogeneous, with some recent refugees from the Bosnian conflict. There is a strong family tradition despite the high divorce rate. Fair-minded consensus promotes female equality, boosted by the generous child-care provision. Wealth is more evenly distributed than in most developed countries.

◆ **INSIGHT:** *Near Narvik, mainland Norway is only 4 miles (7 km) wide*

THE ECONOMY
Major European producer and exporter of oil and gas. Metal, engineering, and chemical industries.

2000m/6562ft
1000m/3281ft
500m/1640ft
200m/656ft
Sea Level

Hammerfest
Karasjok
Tromsø
Narvik
Bodø
Ålesund
Ørsta
Bergen Hønefoss
Stavanger
Sandnes
Kristiansand
Trondheim
Lillehammer
OSLO
Drammen Moss
Skien

Arctic Circle
Norwegian Sea
North Sea
Skagerrak
SWEDEN
FINLAND
RUSS. FED.

0   200 km
0   200 miles

FACTFILE
OFFICIAL NAME: Kingdom of Norway
DATE OF FORMATION: 1905
CAPITAL: Oslo
POPULATION: 4.6 million
TOTAL AREA: 125,181 sq. miles (324,220 sq. km)
DENSITY: 39 people per sq. mile

LANGUAGES: Norwegian* (Bokmål and Nynorsk), Sami
RELIGIONS: Evangelical Lutheran 89%, other 10%, Roman Catholic 1%
ETHNIC MIX: Norwegian 93%, other 6%, Sami 1%
GOVERNMENT: Parliamentary system
CURRENCY: Norwegian krone = 100 øre

Oman

Situated on the eastern coast of the Arabian Peninsula, Oman occupies a strategic position at the entrance to the Persian Gulf. It is the least developed Gulf state, despite modest oil exports.

 GEOGRAPHY
Mostly gravelly desert, with mountains in the north and south. Some narrow fertile coastal strips.

 CLIMATE
Blistering heat in the west. Summer temperatures often climb above 113°F (45°C). Southern uplands receive rains June–September.

 PEOPLE & SOCIETY
Urban drift has seen most Omanis move to northern towns. The majority are Ibadi Muslims who follow an appointed leader, the imam. Ibadism is not opposed to freedom for women, and a few women hold positions of authority. Baluchi from Pakistan are the largest group of foreign workers.

◆ **INSIGHT:** *Until the late 1980s, Oman was closed to all but business or official visitors*

 THE ECONOMY
Oil and gas account for most export revenue. Other exports include fish, animals, dates, and tomatoes. Foreigners work in all sectors.

- 2000m/6562ft
- 1000m/3281ft
- 500m/1640ft
- 200m/656ft
- Sea Level

Strait of Hormuz
Al Khaşab
Musandam
Peninsula
Gulf
of
Oman
UAE
Şuḩār
Al Khābūrah
Al Qābil
Bahlah
Maţrah ○ MUSCAT
Ar Rustāq Al Ḩadd
Şamad Şūr
Nazwā
SAUDI
ARABIA
24°
60°
Arabian
Sea
20°
Ar Rub' al Khālī
INDIAN
OCEAN
YEMEN
52°
56°
Şalālah

0 100 km
0 100 miles

 FACTFILE

OFFICIAL NAME: Sultanate of Oman
DATE OF FORMATION: 1951
CAPITAL: Muscat
POPULATION: 2.6 million
TOTAL AREA: 82,031 sq. miles (212,460 sq. km)
DENSITY: 32 people per sq. mile

LANGUAGES: Arabic*, Baluchi, other
RELIGIONS: Ibadi Muslim 75%, other Muslim and Hindu 25%
ETHNIC MIX: Arab 88%, Baluchi 4%, Persian 3%, Indian and Pakistani 3%, African 2%
GOVERNMENT: Monarchy
CURRENCY: Omani rial = 1000 baisa

Pakistan

Once a part of British India, Pakistan was created in 1947 in response to demands for an independent, largely Muslim state. Bangladesh (former East Pakistan) gained independence in 1971.

GEOGRAPHY

The floodplain of the Indus River dominates east and south. Hindu Kush mountains in the north. The west is semidesert plateau and mountains.

CLIMATE

Temperatures can soar to 122°F (50°C) in south and west, and fall to –4°F (–20°C) in the Hindu Kush.

PEOPLE & SOCIETY

Punjabis dominate government and the army. There are many tensions with minority groups, exacerbated by the vast gap between rich and poor. Strong family ties permeate all aspects of politics and business. Relations with India are very tense over the issue of Kashmir.

INSIGHT: *In 1988, Pakistan elected the first female prime minister in the Muslim world*

THE ECONOMY

Leading producer of cotton and rice, but unpredictable weather conditions often affect the crop. Oil and gas reserves. Aid for earthquake reconstruction and "war on terror."

FACTFILE

OFFICIAL NAME: Islamic Rep. of Pakistan
DATE OF FORMATION: 1947
CAPITAL: Islamabad
POPULATION: 158 million
TOTAL AREA: 310,401 sq. miles (803,940 sq. km)
DENSITY: 531 people per sq. mile

LANGUAGES: Punjabi, Sindhi, Pashtu, Urdu*, Baluchi, Brahui
RELIGIONS: Sunni Muslim 77%, Shi'a Muslim 20%, Hindu 2%, Christian 1%
ETHNIC MIX: Punjabi 50%, Pathan 15%, Sindhi 14%, other 14%, Mohajir 7%
GOVERNMENT: Presidential system
CURRENCY: Pakistani rupee = 100 paisa

Palau

The 300-island Palau archipelago (known locally as Belau) lies in the western Pacific Ocean. It achieved independence in 1994, and is gradually reducing its aid dependence.

GEOGRAPHY

Terrain varies from thickly forested mountains to limestone and coral reefs. Babeldaob, the largest island, is volcanic, with many rivers and waterfalls.

CLIMATE

Hot and wet. Little variation in daily and seasonal temperatures. February–April is the dry season.

PEOPLE & SOCIETY

Native Palauans are a mix of the original southeast Asian migrants and Pacific settlers. A modern influx from Asia has led to tension. 70% of the population live on the island-city of Koror, prompting the construction of a new capital on Babeldaob. Native culture is preserved on outer islands despite strong influence from the US and Japan. Modekngei is a blend of Christianity and local beliefs.

THE ECONOMY

Revenue from tourism and fishing licenses. Subsistence level. Main crops are coconuts and cassava.

INSIGHT: *Palau's reefs contain 1500 species of fish and 700 types of coral*

FACTFILE

OFFICIAL NAME: Republic of Palau
DATE OF FORMATION: 1994
CAPITAL: Koror
POPULATION: 20,303
TOTAL AREA: 177 sq. miles (458 sq. km)
DENSITY: 104 people per sq. mile

LANGUAGES: Palauan*, English*, Japanese, Angaur, Tobi, Sonsorolese
RELIGIONS: Christian 66%, Modekngei 34%
ETHNIC MIX: Palauan 74%, Filipino 16%, other 6%, Chinese and other Asian 4%
GOVERNMENT: Nonparty system
CURRENCY: US dollar = 100 cents

Panama

Panama is the southernmost country in Central America. The colossal Panama Canal (which was under US-control until 2000) links the Pacific and Atlantic Oceans.

GEOGRAPHY
Lowlands along both coasts, with savanna-covered plains and rolling hills. Mountainous interior. Swamps and rainforests in the east.

CLIMATE
Hot and humid, with heavy rainfall in the May–December wet season. Cooler at high altitudes.

PEOPLE & SOCIETY
A multiethnic society, dominated by people of Spanish origin. Amerindians live in remote areas. The Panama Canal and former US military bases (the last of which closed in 1999) have given society a cosmopolitan outlook, but Catholicism and the extended family remain strong. Crime is high; money-laundering, narcotics trafficking, and corruption are rife.

THE ECONOMY
Colón Free Trade Zone: second-largest in the world. Income from the canal. Earnings from merchant ships sailing under Panamanian flag. Banana and fish exports.

◆ **INSIGHT:** *The Panama Canal shortens the sea route between the east coast of the US and Japan by 3000 miles (4800 km)*

FACTFILE
OFFICIAL NAME: Republic of Panama
DATE OF FORMATION: 1903
CAPITAL: Panama City
POPULATION: 3.2 million
TOTAL AREA: 30,193 sq. miles (78,200 sq. km)
DENSITY: 109 people per sq. mile

LANGUAGES: English Creole, Spanish*, Amerindian and Chibchan languages
RELIGIONS: Roman Catholic 86%, other 8%, Protestant 6%
ETHNIC MIX: Mestizo 60%, White 14%, Black 12%, Amerindian 8%, other 6%
GOVERNMENT: Presidential system
CURRENCY: Balboa = 100 centésimos

Papua New Guinea

A former Australian colony, Papua New Guinea (PNG) occupies the eastern section of the island of New Guinea and several other island groups. Much of the country is isolated.

GEOGRAPHY
Mountainous and forested mainland, with broad, swampy river valleys. 40 active volcanoes in the north. Around 600 outer islands.

CLIMATE
Hot and humid in lowlands, cooling toward highlands, where snow can fall on highest peaks.

PEOPLE & SOCIETY
Around 750 language groups and even more tribes. The main social distinction is between lowlanders, who have frequent contact with the outside world, and the very isolated, but increasingly threatened, highlanders. Great tensions exist between highland tribes, and vendettas can often last several generations. The island of Bougainville has been granted autonomy and an eventual referendum on independence.

THE ECONOMY
Minerals: significant quantities of gold, copper, oil, and natural gas. High government spending almost led to national bankruptcy in 2002.

◆ **INSIGHT:** *PNG is home to the only known poisonous birds; contact with the feathers of some species of pitohui produce skin blisters*

FACTFILE
OFFICIAL NAME: Independent State of Papua New Guinea
DATE OF FORMATION: 1975
CAPITAL: Port Moresby
POPULATION: 5.9 million
TOTAL AREA: 178,703 sq. miles (462,840 sq. km)

DENSITY: 34 people per sq. mile
LANGUAGES: Pidgin English, Papuan, English*, Motu, c.750 native languages
RELIGIONS: Protestant 60%, Roman Catholic 37%, other 3%
ETHNIC MIX: Melanesian and mixed 100%
GOVERNMENT: Parliamentary system
CURRENCY: Kina = 100 toea

Paraguay

Landlocked in central South America, and once a Spanish colony, Paraguay's postindependence history has included periods of military rule. Free elections were held in 1993.

 GEOGRAPHY
The Paraguay River divides hilly and forested east from a flat alluvial plain with marsh and semidesert scrub land in the west.

 CLIMATE
Subtropical. The Gran Chaco is generally hotter and drier. All areas experience floods and droughts.

 PEOPLE & SOCIETY
Population mainly of mixed Spanish and native Guaraní origin. Most people are bilingual, though in rural areas Guaraní is more widely heard. Cattle-ranchers populate the Chaco, along with communities of the German-origin Mennonite Church. The army is politically active.

◆ **INSIGHT:** *The War of the Triple Alliance (1864–1870) killed almost 90% of Paraguay's male population*

$ THE ECONOMY
Agriculture: soybeans are the main export. Massive hydroelectric dams allow Paraguay to export electricity. Political instability deters foreign investment. Large informal economy. Corruption and smuggling.

BOLIVIA
BRAZIL
Gran Chaco
Paraguay
ARGENTINA
ASUNCIÓN
Lambaré
Pedro Juan Caballero
Concepción
Represa de Itaipú
Coronel Oviedo
Villarrica
Ciudad del Este
Pilar
Paraná
Encarnación

0   100 km
0   100 miles

1000m/3281ft
500m/1640ft
200m/656ft
Sea Level

📖 FACTFILE

OFFICIAL NAME: Republic of Paraguay
DATE OF FORMATION: 1811
CAPITAL: Asunción
POPULATION: 6.2 million
TOTAL AREA: 157,046 sq. miles (406,750 sq. km)
DENSITY: 40 people per sq. mile

LANGUAGES: Guaraní, Spanish*, German
RELIGIONS: Roman Catholic 96%, Protestant (including Mennonite) 4%
ETHNIC MIX: Mestizo 91%, other 7%, Amerindian 2%
GOVERNMENT: Presidential system
CURRENCY: Guaraní = 100 céntimos

Peru

Once the heart of the Inca empire, before the Spanish conquest in the 16th century, Peru lies on the Pacific coast of South America, just south of the equator.

 GEOGRAPHY
Coastal plain rises to Andes mountains. Uplands, dissected by fertile valleys, lie east of the Andes. Tropical forest in extreme east.

 CLIMATE
Coast is mainly arid. Middle slopes of the Andes are temperate; higher peaks are snow-covered. East is hot, humid, and very wet.

 PEOPLE & SOCIETY
Though populated mainly by Amerindians or mixed-race *mestizos*, society is dominated by a small group of Spanish descendants. Amerindians, and the small black community, suffer discrimination in towns, but access to information and political power are growing, with the first Amerindian president in 2001–2006. Clashes with left-wing militants killed almost 70,000 people between 1980 and 2000.

$ **THE ECONOMY**
Abundant mineral resources: notably copper and gold. Rich Pacific fish stocks. Leading coca producer.

 INSIGHT: *Lake Titicaca is the world's highest navigable lake*

PACIFIC OCEAN

4000m/13124ft
2000m/6562ft
500m/1640ft
Sea Level

0   200 km
0   200 miles

 FACTFILE

OFFICIAL NAME: Republic of Peru
DATE OF FORMATION: 1824
CAPITAL: Lima
POPULATION: 28 million
TOTAL AREA: 496,223 sq. miles (1,285,200 sq. km)
DENSITY: 57 people per sq. mile

LANGUAGES: Spanish*, Quechua*, Aymara
RELIGIONS: Roman Catholic 95%, other 5%
ETHNIC MIX: Amerindian 50%, Mestizo 40%, White 7%, other 3%
GOVERNMENT: Presidential system
CURRENCY: New sol = 100 céntimos

Philippines

Lying in the western Pacific Ocean, the Philippines is the world's second-largest archipelago. It comprises 7107 islands, of which 4600 are named and 1000 inhabited.

GEOGRAPHY
Larger islands are forested and mountainous. Over 20 active volcanoes. Frequent earthquakes.

CLIMATE
Tropical. Warm and humid all year round. Typhoons occur in the rainy season: June–October.

PEOPLE & SOCIETY
Over 100 ethnic groups; most are of Malay origin and Roman Catholic. The Church is a dominant cultural force; it opposes family-planning programs, despite the high population growth rate. The Chinese minority has been established for 400 years. Women play a prominent part in society. San Carlos University was founded in 1595 by the Spanish.

◆ **INSIGHT:** *Mass "People Power" demonstrations have brought down two presidents, in 1986 and 2001*

THE ECONOMY
Agricultural productivity is rising; coconuts, sugar, bananas, and pineapples are exported. Corruption and poor infrastructure limit growth.

2000m/6562ft
1000m/3281ft
500m/1640ft
200m/656ft
Sea Level

Babuyan Is.

PACIFIC OCEAN

Luzon

Philippine Sea

20°

16°

Angeles○ ○Cabanatuan

MANILA◉

Batangas○

Mindoro

○Legazpi City

South China Sea

12°

Panay

Calbayog

Samar

Palawan

Puerto Princesa○

Iloilo○ ○Bacolod

Negros

○Cebu

Butuan

Sulu Sea

Balabac Strait

○Zamboanga

○Iligan

○Davao

8°

116°

Sulu Archipelago

Mindanao

○General Santos

124°

4°

120°

Celebes Sea

0   200 km
0   200 miles

FACTFILE

OFFICIAL NAME: Rep. of the Philippines
DATE OF FORMATION: 1946
CAPITAL: Manila
POPULATION: 83.1 million
TOTAL AREA: 115,830 sq. miles (300,000 sq. km)
DENSITY: 722 people per sq. mile

LANGUAGES: Filipino*, Tagalog, Cebuano, Hiligaynon, other including English*
RELIGIONS: Roman Catholic 83%, Protestant 9%, Muslim 5%, other 3%
ETHNIC MIX: Tagalog 28%, Cebuano 13%, Ilocano 9%, Hiligaynon 8%, other 42%
GOVERNMENT: Presidential system
CURRENCY: Philippine peso = 100 centavos

Poland

Located in the heart of Europe, Poland has undergone massive social, economic, and political change since the collapse of communism in 1989, culminating with EU membership in 2004.

GEOGRAPHY

Lowlands, part of the North European Plain, cover most of the country. The Tatra mountains run along the southern border.

CLIMATE

Rainfall peaks during the hot summers. Cold winters with snow, especially in mountains.

PEOPLE & SOCIETY

Ethnic homogeneity masks a number of tensions. Secular liberals criticize the semiofficial status of the Roman Catholic Church, and emerging wealth disparities are resented by those unaffected by free-market reforms. The German minority in the west is growing more assertive.

◆ **INSIGHT:** *Poland was the second country in Europe to have a written constitution*

THE ECONOMY

Foreign investment reflects the country's large potential market. Rapid privatization is now slowing. High unemployment. Heavy industries dominate, though services growing.

FACTFILE

OFFICIAL NAME: Republic of Poland
DATE OF FORMATION: 1918
CAPITAL: Warsaw
POPULATION: 38.5 million
TOTAL AREA: 120,728 sq. miles (312,685 sq. km)
DENSITY: 328 people per sq. mile

LANGUAGES: Polish
RELIGIONS: Roman Catholic 93%, other and nonreligious 5%, Orthodox Christian 2%
ETHNIC MIX: Polish 97%, other 2%, Silesian 1%
GOVERNMENT: Parliamentary system
CURRENCY: Zloty = 100 groszy

Portugal

Portugal, with its long Atlantic coast, lies on the western side of the Iberian Peninsula, which it shares with Spain. It is the most westerly country on the European mainland.

 GEOGRAPHY

The Tagus River bisects the country roughly east to west, dividing mountainous north from lower and more undulating south.

CLIMATE

North is cool and moist. South is warmer with dry, mild winters.

 PEOPLE & SOCIETY

A homogeneous and stable society, which is losing some of its conservative traditions. History of immigration from former colonies, and recently from eastern Europe. Urban areas and the south are more socially liberal. The north is more responsive to traditional Roman Catholic values. Family ties remain important.

 INSIGHT: *Portugal is the world's leading producer of cork, which comes from the bark of the cork oak*

 THE ECONOMY

Agricultural economy declining: vegetables, fruits, and wine. Clothing and car exports. Strong banking and tourism sectors. High budget deficit.

```
1000m/3281ft
500m/1640ft
200m/656ft
Sea Level
```

 FACTFILE

OFFICIAL NAME: Republic of Portugal

DATE OF FORMATION: 1139

CAPITAL: Lisbon

POPULATION: 10.5 million

TOTAL AREA: 35,672 sq. miles (92,391 sq. km)

DENSITY: 296 people per sq. mile

LANGUAGES: Portuguese

RELIGIONS: Roman Catholic 97%, other 2%, Protestant 1%

ETHNIC MIX: Portuguese 98%, African and other 2%

GOVERNMENT: Parliamentary system

CURRENCY: Euro = 100 cents

Qatar

Projecting north from the Arabian Peninsula into the Gulf, Qatar was a founder member of OPEC. Its plentiful reserves of oil and gas make it one of the wealthiest states in the region.

GEOGRAPHY
Flat, semiarid desert with dunes and salt pans. Vegetation is limited to small patches of scrub.

CLIMATE
Hot and humid. Temperatures in summer can soar to over 104°F (40°C). Rainfall is rare.

PEOPLE & SOCIETY
Only one in five residents are native-born; the rest are guest workers from the Indian subcontinent, Iran, and north Africa. Qataris were once nomadic Bedouins, but since the advent of oil wealth around 90% now live in Doha and its suburbs. As a result, the north is dotted with abandoned villages. Women enjoy relative freedom; most wear the veil.

◆ **INSIGHT:** *There are twice as many men as women in Qatar*

THE ECONOMY
Steady supply of crude oil and huge gas reserves, plus related industries. Economy is heavily dependent on foreign workforce. All raw materials and most foods, except vegetables, are imported.

FACTFILE

OFFICIAL NAME: State of Qatar
DATE OF FORMATION: 1971
CAPITAL: Doha
POPULATION: 813,000
TOTAL AREA: 4416 sq. miles (11,437 sq. km)
DENSITY: 191 people per sq. mile

LANGUAGES: Arabic
RELIGIONS: Muslim (mainly Sunni) 95%, other 5%
ETHNIC MIX: Arab 40%, Indian 18%, Pakistani 18%, other 14%, Iranian 10%
GOVERNMENT: Monarchy
CURRENCY: Qatar riyal = 100 dirhams

Romania

Once dominated by Poles, Hungarians, and Ottomans, Romania has been slowly converting to a free-market economy since the overthrow of its communist regime in 1989.

GEOGRAPHY
Carpathian Mountains encircle the Transylvanian plateau. Wide plains to the south and east. Danube River forms southern border.

CLIMATE
Continental. Summers are hot and humid, winters are cold and snowy. Very heavy spring rains.

PEOPLE & SOCIETY
Romanians are ethnically distinct from their Slav and Hungarian (Magyar) neighbors. Hungarians are the largest minority and are based in Transylvania. They are protected by the influence of Hungary, unlike the Roma, who suffer from discrimination. The overall population is shrinking.

◆ **INSIGHT:** *In 2001, Romania became the last country in Europe to lift its ban on homosexuality*

THE ECONOMY
Pollution-spreading, outdated heavy industries and unmechanized agricultural sector. Exports of textiles and metals have led recovery from 1990s recession. EU membership in 2007. Privatization continues.

FACTFILE

OFFICIAL NAME: Romania
DATE OF FORMATION: 1878
CAPITAL: Bucharest
POPULATION: 21.7 million
TOTAL AREA: 91,699 sq. miles (237,500 sq. km)
DENSITY: 244 people per sq. mile

LANGUAGES: Romanian*, Hungarian
RELIGIONS: Romanian Orthodox 87%, Roman Catholic 5%, Protestant 4%, other 2%, Greek Orthodox 1%, Uniate 1%
ETHNIC MIX: Romanian 89%, Magyar 7%, Roma 2%, other 2%
GOVERNMENT: Presidential system
CURRENCY: Romanian leu

Russian Federation

The Russian Federation was the core of the old Soviet Union, which broke up in 1991. Russia is still the world's largest state. Its diversity is a source of both strength and problems.

GEOGRAPHY
The Ural Mountains divide the European steppes and forests from the tundra and forests of Siberia. South-central deserts and mountains.

CLIMATE
Continental in European Russia. Elsewhere climate ranges from sub-arctic to Mediterranean and hot desert.

PEOPLE & SOCIETY
Ethnic Russians make up around 80% of the population, but there are many minorities; 57 "nationalities" have territorial status, while a further 95 lack their own region. Most ethnic republics are concentrated in European Russia. There are a growing number of Muslims in Russia. The ongoing war with Chechnya highlights the potential for ethnic crisis. Wealth disparities, rising crime, and black-market activities have accompanied reforms.

INSIGHT: *The Trans-Siberian Railroad, which runs 5800 miles (9335 km) from Moscow to Vladivostok, is the longest in the world, passing through seven time zones*

FACTFILE
OFFICIAL NAME: Russian Federation
DATE OF FORMATION: 1480
CAPITAL: Moscow
POPULATION: 143 million
TOTAL AREA: 6,592,735 sq. miles (17,075,200 sq. km)
DENSITY: 22 people per sq. mile

LANGUAGES: Russian*, Tatar, Ukrainian, Chavash, other national languages
RELIGIONS: Orthodox Christian 75%, Muslim 14%, other 11%
ETHNIC MIX: Russian 80%, other 13%, Tatar 4%, Ukrainian 2%, Chavash 1%
GOVERNMENT: Presidential system
CURRENCY: Russian rouble = 100 kopeks

Russian Federation

THE ECONOMY

Lingering inefficiencies since transition to market economy sap Russia's obvious strengths: huge natural resources, in particular oil and gas, precious metals, timber, and hydrocarbons, which account for 80% of export earnings. High oil prices are driving economic growth and have allowed Russia to repay its Soviet-era debt. Important engineering, military, and scientific base. Tax evasion and corruption are widespread. Organized crime syndicates own huge areas of the economy, and the black market accounts for 40% of trade.

Rwanda

Rwanda lies just south of the equator in east central Africa, far from the nearest sea port. Since independence from France in 1962, ethnic tensions have dominated politics.

 GEOGRAPHY
A series of plateaus descend from the ridge of volcanic peaks in the west to the Akagera River on the eastern border. The Great Rift Valley also passes through this region.

CLIMATE
Tropical, though tempered by the altitude. Two wet seasons are separated by a dry season, from June to August. Heaviest rain in the west.

 PEOPLE & SOCIETY
For over 500 years the cattle-owning Tutsi minority were politically dominant over the land-owning Hutu. In 1959, violent revolt led to a reversal of the roles. Ethnic tensions are fierce; in the most recent violence, in 1994, over 800,000 people, mostly Tutsi, were massacred in an act of state-backed genocide; trials are ongoing. Rwandans live a subsistence existence.

THE ECONOMY
Rwanda has few resources, but if it could achieve lasting stability, it could become a key producer of coffee and tea. The potential from possible oil and gas reserves is offset by the high cost of transportation.

 INSIGHT: *Rwanda is the most densely populated country in mainland Africa*

 FACTFILE

OFFICIAL NAME: Republic of Rwanda
DATE OF FORMATION: 1962
CAPITAL: Kigali
POPULATION: 9 million
TOTAL AREA: 10,169 sq. miles (26,338 sq. km)
DENSITY: 934 people per sq. mile

LANGUAGES: Kinyarwanda*, French*, Kiswahili, English*
RELIGIONS: Catholic 56%, traditional beliefs 25%, Muslim 10%, Protestant 9%
ETHNIC MIX: Hutu 90%, Tutsi 9%, other (including Twa) 1%
GOVERNMENT: Presidential system
CURRENCY: Rwanda franc = 100 centimes

St. Kitts & Nevis

A popular Caribbean tourist destination, St. Kitts and Nevis lies in the northern part of the Leeward Island chain. Nevis is the less developed of the two islands.

GEOGRAPHY
Volcanic in origin, with forested, mountainous interiors. Nevis has hot and cold springs.

CLIMATE
Tropical, tempered by trade winds. Little seasonal variation in temperature. Moderate rainfall.

PEOPLE & SOCIETY
The majority of the population are descended from former African slaves. There are small numbers of Europeans, South Asians, and a community of Lebanese. Levels of emigration are high, and overseas remittances are an important source of national income. The government has pledged to retrain sugar workers. Native professionals and civil servants have largely replaced the former expatriate elite. The secessionist movement on Nevis remains an issue.

THE ECONOMY
Successful and still expanding tourist industry is vulnerable to downturns in US market. Once-key sugar industry closed down in 2005.

INSIGHT: *Nevis has been renowned as a spa since the 18th century, and is known as the "Queen of the Caribbean"*

0   5 km
0   5 miles

Dieppe Bay Town
St. Paul's
St Kitts
ATLANTIC
OCEAN
Cayon
17°20'
Old Road
62°50'   Town   Golden Rock Airport
●BASSETERRE
62°45'   62°35'
17°15'
Caribbean
Sea
62°40'   Newcastle
17°10'   *Nevis*
Charlestown   Zion
Bath

1000m/3281ft
500m/1640ft
200m/656ft
Sea Level

FACTFILE

OFFICIAL NAME: Federation of Saint Christopher and Nevis
DATE OF FORMATION: 1983
CAPITAL: Basseterre
POPULATION: 38,958
TOTAL AREA: 101 sq. miles (261 sq. km)
DENSITY: 280 people per sq. mile

LANGUAGES: English*, English Creole
RELIGIONS: Anglican 33%, Methodist 29%, other 22%, Moravian 9%, Roman Catholic 7%
ETHNIC MIX: Black 95%, mixed 3%, White 1%, other and Amerindian 1%
GOVERNMENT: Parliamentary system
CURRENCY: East Caribbean $ = 100 cents

St. Lucia

St. Lucia is one of the most beautiful of the Caribbean Windward Islands. Ruled by France and the UK at different times in its past, the island retains the character of both.

 GEOGRAPHY
Volcanic and mountainous, with some broad fertile valleys. The Pitons, ancient lava cones, rise from the sea on the forested west coast.

CLIMATE
Tropical, moderated by trade winds. May–October wet season brings daily warm showers. Rainfall is highest in the mountains.

PEOPLE & SOCIETY
Population is a tension-free mixture of descendants of Africans, Caribs, and Europeans. Family life and the Roman Catholic Church are important to most St. Lucians. In rural areas women often head the households, and run much of the farming. Plantation and hotel owners are the richest group. There is growing local resistance to overdevelopment of the island for tourism.

THE ECONOMY
Mainly agricultural, with some light industry. Bananas are biggest export. Successful tourist industry, but most resorts are foreign-owned.

INSIGHT: *St. Lucia has two Nobel laureates, the most per capita in the world*

Saint Lucia Channel
14°05′
Gros Islet
14°00′
CASTRIES
13°55′
Canaries
The Pitons
Praslin
ATLANTIC OCEAN
Soufrière
13°50′
Micoud
Caribbean Sea
13°45′
Vieux Fort
61°00′   60°55′

0   5 km
0   5 miles

500m/1640ft
200m/656ft
Sea Level

FACTFILE

OFFICIAL NAME: Saint Lucia
DATE OF FORMATION: 1979
CAPITAL: Castries
POPULATION: 166,312
TOTAL AREA: 239 sq. miles (620 sq. km)
DENSITY: 705 people per sq. mile

LANGUAGES: English*, French Creole
RELIGIONS: Roman Catholic 90%, other 10%
ETHNIC MIX: Black 83%, Mulatto (mixed race) 13%, Asian 3%, White 1%
GOVERNMENT: Parliamentary system
CURRENCY: East Caribbean $ = 100 cents

St. Vincent & the Grenadines

The islands of St. Vincent and the Grenadines form part of the Windward group in the Caribbean. St. Vincent is mostly volcanic, while the Grenadines are flat, mainly bare, coral reefs.

 GEOGRAPHY
St. Vincent is mountainous and forested, with one of two active volcanoes in the Caribbean, La Soufrière. The Grenadines are 32 islands and cays fringed by beaches.

CLIMATE
Tropical, with constant trade winds. Hurricanes are likely during July–November wet season.

 PEOPLE & SOCIETY
Population is racially diverse; intermarriage has reduced tensions. Society is informal and relaxed, but family life is strongly influenced by the Church. Locals fear that their traditional lifestyle is being threatened by the expanding tourist industry.

◆ **INSIGHT:** *The islands' precolonial inhabitants, the Carib, named them "Harioun" – home of the blessed*

$ THE ECONOMY
Dependent on agriculture and tourism. Bananas are the main cash crop. Tourism, targeted at the jet-set and cruise-ship markets, is concentrated on the Grenadines.

0	10 km
0	10 miles

1000m/3281ft
500m/1640ft
200m/656ft
Sea Level

La Soufrière ▲ 1234m
Chateaubelair
Georgetown
13°20'
St Vincent
KINGSTOWN
Arnos Vale
Airport
13°10'
Bequia
Caribbean Sea
Isle
à Quatre   *Baliceaux*
13°00'
Mustique
Canouan
12°50'
The Grenadines
Mayreau
61°10'
12°40'   ATLANTIC
Union I.   OCEAN
61°20'

📖 FACTFILE

OFFICIAL NAME: Saint Vincent and the Grenadines
DATE OF FORMATION: 1979
CAPITAL: Kingstown
POPULATION: 117,534
TOTAL AREA: 150 sq. miles (389 sq. km)

DENSITY: 897 people per sq. mile
LANGUAGES: English*, English Creole
RELIGIONS: Anglican 47%, Methodist 28%, Roman Catholic 13%, other 12%
ETHNIC MIX: Black 77%, Mulatto (mixed race) 16%, other 3%, Carib 3%, Asian 1%
GOVERNMENT: Parliamentary system
CURRENCY: East Caribbean $ = 100 cents

Samoa

The southern Pacific islands of Samoa gained independence from New Zealand in 1962. Four of the nine volcanic islands are inhabited – Apolima, Manono, Savai'i, and Upolu.

GEOGRAPHY

Comprises two large islands and seven smaller ones. The two largest islands have rainforested, mountainous interiors surrounded by coastal lowlands and coral reefs.

CLIMATE

Tropical, with high humidity. Cooler May–November. Hurricane season December–March.

PEOPLE & SOCIETY

Ethnic Samoans are the world's second-largest Polynesian group, after the Maoris. Their way of life is communal and formalized. Extended family groups own 80% of the land. Each family has an elected chief, who looks after its political and social interests. Large-scale migration to the US and New Zealand reflects the country's lack of jobs and the attractions of a Western lifestyle.

THE ECONOMY

Exports fish. Agricultural products include coconut cream, copra, and taro. Growth of the service sector: tourism and offshore banking. Dependent on aid and expatriate remittances. Rainforests are increasingly exploited for timber.

INSIGHT: *Samoa was named for the sacred (sa) chickens (moa) of Lu, son of Tagaloa, the god of creation*

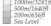

1000m/3281ft	
500m/1640ft	
200m/656ft	
Sea Level	

0   15 km
0   15 miles

FACTFILE

OFFICIAL NAME: Independent State of Samoa
DATE OF FORMATION: 1962
CAPITAL: Apia
POPULATION: 185,000
TOTAL AREA: 1104 sq. miles (2860 sq. km)

DENSITY: 169 people per sq. mile
LANGUAGES: Samoan*, English*
RELIGIONS: Christian 99%, other 1%
ETHNIC MIX: Polynesian 90%, Euronesian (mixed European and Polynesian) 9%, other 1%
GOVERNMENT: Parliamentary system
CURRENCY: Tala = 100 sene

San Marino

Perched on the slopes of Monte Titano in the Italian Appennino, San Marino has maintained its independence since the 4th century CE, but Italy effectively controls most of its affairs.

GEOGRAPHY
Distinctive limestone outcrop of Monte Titano dominates wooded hills and pastures near Italy's Adriatic coast.

CLIMATE
High altitude and sea breezes moderate a Mediterranean climate. Hot summers and cool, wet winters.

PEOPLE & SOCIETY
Territory is divided into nine "castles," or districts. Tightly knit society, with 16 centuries of tradition. Strict immigration rules require 30-year residence before applying for citizenship. Living standards are similar to those in northern Italy. About 20,000 Sammarinesi live abroad, most in Italy.

◆ **INSIGHT:** *Sales of postage stamps and coins contribute around 10% of the national income*

THE ECONOMY
Tourism provides over half of total government income. Lower tax rates than in Italy. Wine, cheese, olive oil, textiles, cement, ceramics, and building stone are exported. Italian infrastructure is a boon.

FACTFILE

OFFICIAL NAME: Republic of San Marino
DATE OF FORMATION: 1631
CAPITAL: San Marino
POPULATION: 28,880
TOTAL AREA: 23.6 sq. miles (61 sq. km)

DENSITY: 1203 people per sq. mile
LANGUAGES: Italian
RELIGIONS: Roman Catholic 93%, other and nonreligious 7%
ETHNIC MIX: Sammarinese 88%, Italian 10%, other 2%
GOVERNMENT: Parliamentary system
CURRENCY: Euro = 100 cents

São Tomé & Príncipe

A former Portuguese colony São Tomé and Príncipe lies off the west coast of Africa, comprising two main islands and the surrounding islets. Elections in 1991 ended 15 years of Marxism.

GEOGRAPHY
Islands scattered across the equator. São Tomé and Príncipe are heavily forested and mountainous.

CLIMATE
Hot and humid, but cooled by the Benguela Current. Plentiful rainfall.

PEOPLE & SOCIETY
Population is mostly black, though Portuguese culture pre-dominates. Blacks run the political parties. Society is well integrated and free of racial prejudice. Príncipe assumed autonomous status in 1995. There is a growing business class. Extended family offers main form of social security. One of Africa's highest aid-to-population ratios.

◆ **INSIGHT:** *The population is entirely of immigrant descent: the islands were uninhabited when colonized in 1470*

THE ECONOMY
Cocoa provides 90% of export earnings. Coconuts, pepper, and coffee are also farmed. Offshore oil may come onstream in 2007.

1000m/3281ft
500m/1640ft
200m/656ft
Sea Level

Príncipe Santo António
1°40'
Infante Dom Henrique
1°30'
Ilha Caroço
7°30'
1°20'
7°20'

0   20 km
0   20 miles

6°40'
Ilha das Cabras
6°30'
0°20'
SÃO TOMÉ
Santana
São Tomé
0°10'
Santa Cruz
Pôrto Alegre
Equator
Ilha das Rôlas
Gulf of Guinea

FACTFILE

OFFICIAL NAME: Democratic Republic of São Tomé and Príncipe
DATE OF FORMATION: 1975
CAPITAL: São Tomé
POPULATION: 187,410
TOTAL AREA: 386 sq. miles (1001 sq. km)
DENSITY: 505 people per sq. mile

LANGUAGES: Portuguese Creole, Portuguese*
RELIGIONS: Roman Catholic 84%, other 16%
ETHNIC MIX: Black 90%, Portuguese and Creole 10%
GOVERNMENT: Presidential system
CURRENCY: Dobra = 100 céntimos

Saudi Arabia

Occupying most of the Arabian Peninsula, Saudi Arabia covers an area the size of western Europe. It is the world's largest oil producer and has a major petrochemicals industry.

GEOGRAPHY
Mostly desert or semidesert plateau. Mountain ranges in the west run parallel to the Red Sea and drop steeply to a coastal plain.

CLIMATE
In summer, temperatures often soar above 118°F (48°C), but in winter they may fall below freezing. Rainfall is rare.

PEOPLE & SOCIETY
Most Saudis are Sunni Muslims who follow the strictly orthodox Wahhabi interpretation of Islam and embrace *sharia* (Islamic law) in their daily lives. Women are obliged to wear the veil, cannot hold driving licenses, and have no role in public life. The al-Sa'ud family have been absolutist rulers since 1932. With the support of the religious establishment, they control all political life.

THE ECONOMY
Vast oil and gas reserves. Other minerals: iron, gypsum, and limestone. Most people work in services sector.

◆ **INSIGHT:** *Over two million Muslims a year make the haj (pilgrimage) to the holy city of Mecca. Only practicing Muslims are allowed inside the city*

FACTFILE

OFFICIAL NAME: Kingdom of Saudi Arabia
DATE OF FORMATION: 1932
CAPITALS: Riyadh and Jiddah
POPULATION: 24.6 million
TOTAL AREA: 756,981 sq. miles (1,960,582 sq. km)

DENSITY: 30 people per sq. mile
LANGUAGES: Arabic
RELIGIONS: Sunni Muslim 85%, Shi'a Muslim 15%
ETHNIC MIX: Arab 90%, Afro-Asian 10%
GOVERNMENT: Monarchy
CURRENCY: Saudi riyal = 100 halalat

Senegal

Senegal's capital, Dakar, stands on the westernmost cape of Africa. After independence from France, Senegal became a single-party state. Multiparty elections were first held in 1981.

 GEOGRAPHY
Arid semidesert in the north. The south is mainly savanna bushland. Plains in the southeast.

 CLIMATE
Tropical, with humid rainy conditions June–October, and a drier season December–May. The coast is cooled by northern trade winds.

 PEOPLE & SOCIETY
Interethnic marriage has reduced ethnic tensions. Groups can be identified regionally. Dakar is a Wolof area, the Senegal River is dominated by the Toucouleur, and the Malinke mostly live in the east. The Diola (Jola) in Casamance have felt politically excluded, prompting a long-running secessionist struggle; a cease-fire has held since 2004. A large diaspora has raised global awareness of Senegalese culture and music.

$ **THE ECONOMY**
Good infrastructure, particularly the key port at Dakar. Development of tourism. Diminishing fish stocks. Potential for oil off Casamance.

◆ **INSIGHT:** *Senegal's name derives from the Zenega Berbers who invaded in the 1300s, bringing Islam with them*

 FACTFILE

OFFICIAL NAME: Republic of Senegal
DATE OF FORMATION: 1960
CAPITAL: Dakar
POPULATION: 11.7 million
TOTAL AREA: 75,749 sq. miles (196,190 sq. km)
DENSITY: 157 people per sq. mile

LANGUAGES: Wolof, Serer, Pulaar, Diola, Mandinka, Malinke, Soninke, French*
RELIGIONS: Sunni Muslim 90%, traditional beliefs 5%, Christian 5%
ETHNIC MIX: Wolof 43%, Serer 15%, other 14%, Peul 14%, Toucouleur 9%, Diola 5%
GOVERNMENT: Presidential system
CURRENCY: CFA franc = 100 centimes

The central and eastern rump of what was once Yugoslavia, Serbia was a pariah state until Slobodan Milosevic was ousted in 2000. Montenegro finally broke away from it in 2006.

GEOGRAPHY

Landlocked since secession of Montenegro. Fertile Danube plain in the north, rolling uplands in the center and southeast. Mountains in southwest.

CLIMATE

Continental in north, with wet springs and warm summers. Colder winters with heavy snow in south.

PEOPLE & SOCIETY

Serbs are Orthodox Christian, and their language uses the Cyrillic script. Muslim ethnic Albanians form a majority in Kosovo province, run by the UN since NATO intervened to end Serb oppression in 1999. Albanian nationalists are pushing for Kosovan independence. The Catholic Magyars (Hungarians) live mainly in Vojvodina.

◆ **INSIGHT:** *The medieval Serbian empire reached into northern Greece*

THE ECONOMY

Recovering from sanctions and 1999 NATO bombing. Strong industrial base. Foreign investment growing.

	2000m/6562ft
	1000m/3281ft
	500m/1640ft
	200m/656ft
	Sea Level

0   50 km
0   50 miles

FACTFILE

OFFICIAL NAME: Republic of Serbia
DATE OF FORMATION: 2006
CAPITAL: Belgrade
POPULATION: 9.7 million
TOTAL AREA: 34,116 sq. miles (88,361 sq. km)
DENSITY: 266 people per sq. mile

LANGUAGES: Serbo-Croat*, Albanian, Hungarian (Magyar)
RELIGIONS: Orthodox Christian 70%, Muslim 18%, other 7%, Catholic 5%
ETHNIC MIX: Serb 66%, Albanian 19%, other 9%, Magyar 4%, Bosniak 2%
GOVERNMENT: Parliamentary system
CURRENCY: Dinar = 100 para

Seychelles

The Seychelles comprises 115 islands in the Indian Ocean. Formerly a UK colony, multiparty elections were held in 1993 after 14 years as a one-party state.

GEOGRAPHY
Mostly low-lying coral atolls, but 40, including the largest, Mahé, are mountainous and are the only granitic midocean islands in the world.

CLIMATE
Tropical oceanic climate. Hot and humid. Rainy season December–May.

PEOPLE & SOCIETY
The islands were uninhabited when French settlers arrived in the 18th century. Today, the population is homogeneous – a result of inter-marriage between ethnic groups. Almost 90% of people live on Mahé. Living standards are among Africa's highest. Poverty is rare and the welfare system caters for all.

◆ **INSIGHT:** The Seychelles' unique species include the giant tortoise and the world's largest seed, the coco-de-mer

THE ECONOMY
Tourism is the main source of income, based on the appeal of beaches and exotic plants and animals. Tuna is fished and canned for export. There are virtually no mineral resources. All domestic requirements are imported.

FACTFILE
OFFICIAL NAME: Republic of Seychelles
DATE OF FORMATION: 1976
CAPITAL: Victoria
POPULATION: 81,188
TOTAL AREA: 176 sq. miles
(455 sq. km)
DENSITY: 781 people per sq. mile

LANGUAGES: Creole*, English*, French*
RELIGIONS: Roman Catholic 90%, Anglican 8%, other (including Muslim) 2%
ETHNIC MIX: Creole 89%, Indian 5%, other 4%, Chinese 2%
GOVERNMENT: Presidential system
CURRENCY: Seychelles rupee = 100 cents

Sierra Leone

The west African state of Sierra Leone achieved independence from the UK in 1961. Today, it is still trying to recover from a devastating civil war, and is one of the world's poorest nations.

GEOGRAPHY

Flat plain, running the length of the coast, stretches inland for 83 miles (133 km). Beyond, forests rise to highlands near neighboring Guinea in the northeast.

CLIMATE

Hot tropical weather, with very high rainfall and humidity. The dusty, northeastern *harmattan* wind blows November–April.

PEOPLE & SOCIETY

Mende and Temne are the major ethnic groups. Freetown's citizens are largely descended from slaves freed from Britain and the US, resulting in a strongly Anglicized Creole culture in the capital. The countryside is less developed. A brutal civil war broke out in 1991 and was not properly resolved until a 2001 peace agreement. Two million people were displaced.

THE ECONOMY

Diamonds are the key resource, though smuggling is rife. Cocoa and coffee are exported, though most people live by subsistence farming or are dependent on aid.

INSIGHT: *The British philanthropist Granville Sharp set up a settlement for freed slaves in Freetown in 1787*

FACTFILE

OFFICIAL NAME: Republic of Sierra Leone
DATE OF FORMATION: 1961
CAPITAL: Freetown
POPULATION: 5.5 million
TOTAL AREA: 27,698 sq. miles (71,740 sq. km)
DENSITY: 199 people per sq. mile

LANGUAGES: Mende, Temne, Krio, English*
RELIGIONS: Muslim 30%, traditional beliefs 30%, other 30%, Christian 10%
ETHNIC MIX: Mende 35%, Temne 32%, other 21%, Limba 8%, Kuranko 4%
GOVERNMENT: Presidential system
CURRENCY: Leone = 100 cents

Singapore

Linked to the southernmost tip of the Malay peninsula by a causeway, Singapore was established as a trading settlement in 1819. It is one of Asia's most important commercial centers.

GEOGRAPHY

Little remains of the original vegetation on Singapore Island. The other 54 much smaller islands are little more than swampy jungle.

CLIMATE

Equatorial. Hot and humid, with heavy rainfall all year round.

PEOPLE & SOCIETY

Dominated by the Chinese, who make up three-quarters of the community. The old English-speaking Straits Chinese and newer Mandarin-speakers are now well integrated. Malays are generally the poorest group. There is a significant foreign workforce. Society is highly regulated and government campaigns to improve public behavior are frequent. Crime is limited and punishment can be severe.

THE ECONOMY

Massive accumulated wealth is derived from success as an entrepôt and as a center of high-tech industries; Major producer of disk drives. Leads research in new biotechnologies. All food, energy, and water imported.

INSIGHT: *Chewing gum was banned outright from 1992 to 2004*

FACTFILE

OFFICIAL NAME: Republic of Singapore
DATE OF FORMATION: 1965
CAPITAL: Singapore
POPULATION: 4.3 million
TOTAL AREA: 250 sq. miles (648 sq. km)
DENSITY: 18,220 people per sq. mile

LANGUAGES: Mandarin*, Malay*, Tamil*, English*
RELIGIONS: Buddhist 55%, Taoist 22%, Muslim 16%, Hindu, Christian, Sikh 7%
ETHNIC MIX: Chinese 77%, Malay 14%, Indian 8%, other 1%
GOVERNMENT: Parliamentary system
CURRENCY: Singapore dollar = 100 cents

Slovakia

Landlocked in central Europe, Slovakia became an independent state in 1993. It is the less developed half of the former Czechoslovakia, with high levels of international debt.

 GEOGRAPHY
The Tatra Mountains stretch along the northern border with Poland. Southern lowlands include the fertile Danube plain.

 CLIMATE
Continental. Moderately warm summers and steady rainfall. Cold winters with heavy snowfalls.

 PEOPLE & SOCIETY
Slovaks are the largest and most dominant group. The largest minority, the Magyars, seek protection of their language and culture, and are backed by Hungary. Magyar parties exist in the political mainstream, and on occasion form part of the ruling coalition. Ethnic Czechs have dual citizenship. Roma are unrepresented and face significant discrimination. The rural eastern regions are least developed.

$ THE ECONOMY
Emphasis on heavy industry, especially cars. Strong growth in recent years. High unemployment. EU membership from 2004. Koruna linked to euro. Ongoing privatization plans.

◆ **INSIGHT:** *Bratislava was known as Pozsony when it served as the capital of Hungary from 1526 to 1784*

 FACTFILE

OFFICIAL NAME: Slovak Republic
DATE OF FORMATION: 1993
CAPITAL: Bratislava
POPULATION: 5.4 million
TOTAL AREA: 18,859 sq. miles (48,845 sq. km)
DENSITY: 285 people per sq. mile

LANGUAGES: Slovak*, Hungarian (Magyar), Czech
RELIGIONS: Roman Catholic 60%, other 22%, Atheist 10%, Protestant 8%
ETHNIC MIX: Slovak 86%, Magyar 10%, Roma 2%, Czech 1%, other 1%
GOVERNMENT: Parliamentary system
CURRENCY: Slovak koruna = 100 halierov

Slovenia

The northernmost of the former Yugoslav republics, Slovenia has close links with western Europe. Transition to independence in 1991 avoided the violence of the breakup of Yugoslavia.

GEOGRAPHY

Alpine terrain with hills and mountains. Forests cover almost half the country's area. There is a short coastline on the Adriatic Sea.

CLIMATE

Mediterranean climate on the small coastal strip. The alpine interior has continental extremes.

PEOPLE & SOCIETY

Slovenia's long historical association with western Europe, accounts for its "Alpine," rather than "Balkan," outlook, despite close similarities to other former Yugoslavs. The lack of sizable Serb or Croat minorities made for a relatively peaceful secession from Yugoslavia. There are small communities of Italians and Magyars (Hungarians) in the southwest and east respectively.

THE ECONOMY

Competitive manufacturing industry and healthy exports. First new EU member to join eurozone (in 2007). Inflation being reduced.

◆ **INSIGHT:** *Slovenia has the highest standard of living of any former Soviet bloc country*

FACTFILE

OFFICIAL NAME: Republic of Slovenia
DATE OF FORMATION: 1991
CAPITAL: Ljubljana
POPULATION: 2 million
TOTAL AREA: 7820 sq. miles (20,253 sq. km)
DENSITY: 256 people per sq. mile

LANGUAGES: Slovene*, Serbo-Croat
RELIGIONS: Roman Catholic 96%, other 3%, Muslim 1%
ETHNIC MIX: Slovene 83%, other 12%, Serb 2%, Croat 2%, Bosniak 1%
GOVERNMENT: Parliamentary system
CURRENCY: Tolar = 100 stotinov

Solomon Islands

The Solomons archipelago comprises several hundred coral reef islands scattered in the southwestern Pacific. Most of the population live on the six largest islands.

 ### GEOGRAPHY

The six largest islands are volcanic, mountainous, and thickly forested. Flat coastal plains provide the only cultivable land.

CLIMATE

Northern islands are hot and humid all year round; further south a cool season develops. November–April wet season brings cyclones.

PEOPLE & SOCIETY

Almost all Solomon Islanders are Melanesian. Tensions are regional; Guadalcanal natives (Isatabu) fought against immigrant Malaitan workers in the 1998–2000 conflict, displacing thousands and ruining the economy. In 2003 Australian-led peacekeepers arrived to restore the rule of law. Outlying islands have pressed for autonomy. Animist beliefs exist alongside Christianity.

THE ECONOMY

Main products are agricultural, though there are significant deposits of gold, copper, and bauxite. Civil conflict bankrupted the government, closed the main gold mine, and severed trade links.

INSIGHT: *The battle for Japanese-held Guadalcanal was the first major US offensive in the Pacific War during World War II*

FACTFILE

OFFICIAL NAME: Solomon Islands
DATE OF FORMATION: 1978
CAPITAL: Honiara
POPULATION: 478,000
TOTAL AREA: 10,985 sq. miles (28,450 sq. km)
DENSITY: 44 people per sq. mile

LANGUAGES: English*, Pidgin English, Melanesian Pidgin
RELIGIONS: Anglican 34%, Catholic 19%, other Protestant 38%, other 9%
ETHNIC MIX: Melanesian 94%, Polynesian 4%, other 2%
GOVERNMENT: Parliamentary system
CURRENCY: Solomon Is $ = 100 cents

Somalia

 A semiarid state occupying the Horn of Africa, Somalia was formed from the Italian and British colonies of Somaliland in 1960. The country descended into anarchy from 1991.

GEOGRAPHY

Highlands in the north, flatter scrub-covered land to the south. Coastal areas are more fertile.

CLIMATE

 Very dry, except for the north coast, which is hot and humid. The interior has among the world's highest average annual temperatures.

PEOPLE & SOCIETY

 The clan system forms the basis of all commercial, political, and social life. Most people are ethnic Somali. The minority Bantu are traditionally seen as socially inferior. The government collapsed in 1991, since when Somalia has lacked a strong central authority. Somaliland has declared independence while Puntland claims autonomy. Islamists now control Mogadishu and are challenging the power of the latest weak transitional government.

THE ECONOMY

Ongoing war. Every commodity, except arms, is in short supply. Piracy and banditry. Few natural strengths. Prone to drought. For the relatively stable Somaliland, trade is hampered by lack of international recognition.

◆ **INSIGHT:** *Until 1973 Somali was an unwritten language*

FACTFILE

OFFICIAL NAME: Somalia
DATE OF FORMATION: 1960
CAPITAL: Mogadishu
POPULATION: 8.2 million
TOTAL AREA: 246,199 sq. miles (637,657 sq. km)
DENSITY: 34 people per sq. mile

LANGUAGES: Somali*, Arabic*, English, Italian
RELIGIONS: Sunni Muslim 98%, Christian 2%
ETHNIC MIX: Somali 85%, other 15%
GOVERNMENT: Transitional regime
CURRENCY: Somali shilin = 100 senti

South Africa

South Africa is the southernmost nation on the African continent. After 80 years of white minority rule, the country held its first multiracial, multiparty elections in 1994.

GEOGRAPHY

Much of the interior is grassy *veld*. Desert in the west and far north. Mountains east, south, and west.

CLIMATE

Warm, temperate, and dry. Cape Town has a Mediterranean climate. Semiarid in the west.

PEOPLE & SOCIETY

The majority black population now dominates politically, but the minority white community still controls the economy. A small black middle class is growing, but unemployment among blacks is over 30%. Wealth disparities are widening. Over five million suffer from AIDS and the fight against it is hampered by social attitudes.

◆ **INSIGHT:** *Over the last century, South Africa has produced over half of the world's gold.*

THE ECONOMY

Africa's largest and most developed economy. Rich in mineral resources, particularly metals. Tourism largest foreign exchange earner. Wealth gap and AIDS epidemic worsening.

FACTFILE

OFFICIAL NAME: Republic of South Africa
DATE OF FORMATION: 1934
CAPITAL: Pretoria; Cape Town; Bloemfontein
POPULATION: 47.4 million
TOTAL AREA: 471,008 sq. miles (1,219,912 sq. km)
DENSITY: 101 people per sq. mile

LANGUAGES: English*, isiZulu*, isiXhosa*, 8 other languages* (including Afrikaans)
RELIGIONS: Christian 68%, animist and traditional beliefs 29%, other 3%
ETHNIC MIX: Black 79%, White 10%, Colored 9%, Asian 2%
GOVERNMENT: Presidential system
CURRENCY: Rand = 100 cents

Spain

Lodged between Europe, Africa, the North Atlantic, and the Mediterranean, Spain has occupied a pivotal global position since unification under Ferdinand and Isabella in 1492.

GEOGRAPHY
Mountain ranges in the north, center, and south, with a huge central plateau. Mediterranean lowlands. Verdant valleys in the northwest.

CLIMATE
Maritime in north. Hotter and drier in south. The central plateau has an extreme climate.

PEOPLE & SOCIETY
A vigorous ethnic regionalism, long suppressed under Franco's regime, now flourishes. There are now 17 autonomous regions. People remain churchgoing, though Roman Catholic teachings on social issues are often flouted. Spanish women are increasingly emancipated, with strong political representation.

◆ **INSIGHT:** *Over 3000 festivals and feasts take place each year in Spain*

THE ECONOMY
One of the fastest-growing economies in the West with a well-qualified workforce. There are few natural resources. Spain has one of the world's largest fishing fleets. Proximity to Africa makes it a target for illegal immigrants.

0	100 km
0	100 miles

Bay of Biscay

A Coruña · Gijón · Santander · Bilbao · San Sebastián
Vigo · León · Oviedo · Burgos · Vitoria · Logroño
Ourense · Palencia · Soria · Zaragoza · Lleida · Barcelona · Tarragona
PORTUGAL · Valladolid · Ávila · Tagus · Menorca
Leganés · **MADRID** · Mallorca · Palma · Islas Baleares
Fuenlabrada · Getafe · Albacete · Valencia
Badajoz · Ibiza · Alicante
Córdoba · Murcia · Cartagena
Huelva · Sevilla · Granada
Cádiz · Jerez de la Frontera · Málaga · Almería
Mediterranean Sea

FRANCE · ANDORRA · Pyrenees

■	2000m/6562ft
■	1000m/3281ft
■	500m/1640ft
■	200m/656ft
	Sea Level

📖 FACTFILE

OFFICIAL NAME: Kingdom of Spain
DATE OF FORMATION: 1492
CAPITAL: Madrid
POPULATION: 43.1 million
TOTAL AREA: 194,896 sq. miles (504,782 sq. km)
DENSITY: 224 people per sq. mile

LANGUAGES: Spanish*, Catalan*, Galician*, Basque*
RELIGIONS: Roman Catholic 96%, other 4%
ETHNIC MIX: Spanish 72%, Catalan 17%, Galician 6%, other 3%, Basque 2%
GOVERNMENT: Parliamentary system
CURRENCY: Euro = 100 cents

Sri Lanka

The teardrop-shaped island of Sri Lanka is separated from India by the Palk Strait. Civil war between the government and ethnic Tamil rebels – the Tamil Tigers – broke out in 1983.

GEOGRAPHY

The main island is dominated by rugged central highlands. Fertile northern plains are dissected by rivers. Much of the land is tropical jungle.

CLIMATE

Tropical, with breezes on the coast and cooler air in highlands. Northeast is driest and hottest.

PEOPLE & SOCIETY

The Sinhalese are mostly Buddhist, while Tamils are mostly Hindu. Tamils were the minority group favored by the British colonists. Majority-Sinhalese power since independence in 1948 fueled tensions, erupting into civil war in 1983. A peace deal was secured in 2002, with autonomy for the Tamil north and east, but in 2006 fighting escalated once again. Moors are the Muslim descendants of Arab traders.

THE ECONOMY

World's largest tea exporter. Civil war drained government funds. Insecurity continues to deter investors and tourists. Tsunami damage in 2004.

INSIGHT: *Sri Lanka elected the world's first woman prime minister in 1960*

FACTFILE

OFFICIAL NAME: Democratic Socialist Republic of Sri Lanka
DATE OF FORMATION: 1948
CAPITAL: Colombo
POPULATION: 20.7 million
TOTAL AREA: 25,332 sq. miles (65,610 sq. km)

DENSITY: 828 people per sq. mile
LANGUAGES: Sinhala*, Tamil*, English
RELIGIONS: Buddhist 69%, Hindu 15%, Muslim 8%, Christian 8%
ETHNIC MIX: Sinhalese 82%, Tamil 9%, Moor 8%, other 1%
GOVERNMENT: Parliamentary system
CURRENCY: Sri Lanka rupee = 100 cents

Sudan

The largest country in Africa, Sudan has undergone two civil wars between Arab north and black African south, while Darfur in the west now faces a terrible humanitarian crisis.

GEOGRAPHY
Lies within the upper Nile basin. Mostly arid plains, with marshes in the south. Highlands border the Red Sea in the northeast.

CLIMATE
North is hot, arid desert with constant dry winds. Rainy season ranging from two months in the center to eight in the south.

PEOPLE & SOCIETY
Two million people are nomads. Many ethnic and linguistic groups. Key social division is between Arabized Muslims in north, and mostly black African, largely Christian or animist peoples in the south. Attempts to impose Arab and Islamic values were the root cause of the 1983–2005 civil war. Ethnic violence by Arab militias in Darfur since 2004 has killed 300,000 people. Women's rights are restricted.

THE ECONOMY
Oil exports. Sesame is the major crop. Violence and drought hamper farming. Millions of people displaced.

INSIGHT: *Sudan's Sudd is the world's largest swamp*

FACTFILE
OFFICIAL NAME: Republic of the Sudan
DATE OF FORMATION: 1956
CAPITAL: Khartoum
POPULATION: 36.2 million
TOTAL AREA: 967,493 sq. miles (2,505,810 sq. km)
DENSITY: 37 people per sq. mile

LANGUAGES: Arabic*, African languages
RELIGIONS: Muslim 70%, Traditional beliefs 20%, Christian 9%, Other 1%
ETHNIC MIX: Black 59% (of which Beja and Dinka 7%), Arab 40%, other 1%
GOVERNMENT: Presidential system
CURRENCY: Sudanese pound or dinar = 100 piastres

Suriname

Suriname is a former Dutch colony on the north coast of South America. Democracy was restored in 1991, after almost 11 years of military rule. The Netherlands is still the main supplier of aid.

🌐 GEOGRAPHY

Mostly covered by tropical rainforest. Coastal plain rises to central plateaus and the Guiana Highlands.

☀ CLIMATE

Tropical. Hot and humid, but cooled by trade winds. High rainfall, especially in the interior.

👥 PEOPLE & SOCIETY

Independence provoked mass emigration: over 300,000 Surinamese live in the Netherlands. Of those left, over 90% live near the coast, the rest in scattered rainforest communities. Indigenous Amerindians only number a few thousand. *Bosnegers* – descended from runaway African slaves – fought the Creole-dominated government in the 1980s. Many South Asians and Javanese work in farming. Since return to civilian rule, each group has had a political party representing its interests.

💲 THE ECONOMY

Aluminum and bauxite are the leading exports. Rice and fruit are main cash crops, though Suriname is a net importer of food.

◆ INSIGHT: *Suriname was ceded to Holland by the English, in exchange for what is now New York state, in 1667*

📋 FACTFILE

OFFICIAL NAME: Republic of Suriname
DATE OF FORMATION: 1975
CAPITAL: Paramaribo
POPULATION: 499,000
TOTAL AREA: 63,039 sq. miles (163,270 sq. km)
DENSITY: 8 people per sq. mile

LANGUAGES: Sranan (creole), Dutch*, Javanese, Sarnami, Hindi, other
RELIGIONS: Christian 48%, Hindu 27%, Muslim 20%, traditional beliefs 5%
ETHNIC MIX: Creole 34%, South Asian 34%, Javanese 18%, Black 9%, other 5%
GOVERNMENT: Parliamentary system
CURRENCY: Surinamese $ = 100 cents

Swaziland

The tiny southern African kingdom of Swaziland is economically dependent on South Africa. The strong hereditary monarchy is being challenged by demands for a multiparty government.

GEOGRAPHY
Mainly high plateaus and mountains. Rolling grasslands and low scrub plains to the east. Pine forests on western border.

CLIMATE
Temperatures rise and rainfall declines as the land descends eastward, from high to low grassy *veld*.

PEOPLE & SOCIETY
One of Africa's most conservative states, though there is pressure from urban-based modernizers. Political system promotes Swazi tradition and is dominated by powerful monarchy. Women face discrimination. Swaziland has world's highest HIV infection rate: chastity is promoted to combat spread.

◆ **INSIGHT:** Polygamy is practiced in Swaziland – when King Sobhuza died in 1982, he left 100 widows

THE ECONOMY
Sugarcane is the main cash crop. Wood pulp and coal are also exported. Loss of workforce to AIDS, and high cost of health care.

FACTFILE

OFFICIAL NAME: Kingdom of Swaziland
DATE OF FORMATION: 1968
CAPITAL: Mbabane
POPULATION: 1 million
TOTAL AREA: 6704 sq. miles (17,363 sq. km)
DENSITY: 151 people per sq. mile

LANGUAGES: English*, siSwati*, isiZulu, Xitsonga
RELIGIONS: Christian 60%, traditional beliefs 40%
ETHNIC MIX: Swazi 97%, other 3%
GOVERNMENT: Monarchy
CURRENCY: Lilangeni = 100 cents

Sweden

The largest Scandinavian country in both population and area, Sweden has one of the world's most extensive welfare systems, and is among the leading proponents of equal rights for women.

GEOGRAPHY

Heavily forested, with many lakes. Northern plateau extends beyond the Arctic Circle. Southern lowlands are widely cultivated.

CLIMATE

Southern coasts warmed by Gulf Stream. Northern areas have more extreme continental climate.

PEOPLE & SOCIETY

The nuclear family forms the basis of society. Birth rates are rising, but marriages are declining and cohabitation is now common. The comprehensive welfare system was cut back during recession in the 1990s, but remains generous. Women are well represented at all levels. A 20,000-strong minority of Sámi lives in the far north. Most industries and the bulk of the population are based in and around the southern cities.

THE ECONOMY

Companies of global importance, including Volvo, Saab, SFK, Ericsson. Highly developed infra-structure. Up-to-date technology. Skilled labor force.

◆ INSIGHT:

Sweden has maintained a position of armed neutrality since 1815

FINLAND

Arctic Circle *Lapland*

NORWAY

Luleå

Umeå
Östersund

Gulf of Bothnia

Sundsvall

Uppsala

Västerås
Örebro
Vänern

STOCKHOLM
Norrköping

Trollhättan *Vättern* Linköping
Göteborg Jönköping
Borås

Gotland

Kattegat Öland
Helsingborg Karlskrona

Malmö *Baltic Sea*

1000m/3281ft
500m/1640ft
200m/656ft
Sea Level

0   100 km
0   100 miles

FACTFILE

OFFICIAL NAME: Kingdom of Sweden
DATE OF FORMATION: 1523
CAPITAL: Stockholm
POPULATION: 9 million
TOTAL AREA: 173,731 sq. miles (449,964 sq. km)
DENSITY: 57 people per sq. mile

LANGUAGES: Swedish*, Finnish, Sámi
RELIGIONS: Evangelical Lutheran 82%, other 13%, Roman Catholic 2%, Muslim 2%, Orthodox Christian 1%
ETHNIC MIX: Swedish 88%, recent immigrant 10%, Finnish and Sámi 2%
GOVERNMENT: Parliamentary system
CURRENCY: Swedish krona = 100 öre

Switzerland

One of the world's most prosperous countries, Switzerland lies at the center of Europe. It has managed to retain its neutral status through every major European conflict since 1815.

GEOGRAPHY

Mostly mountainous, with river valleys. The Alps cover 60% of its area; the Jura in the west cover 10%. Lowlands lie along the east–west axis.

CLIMATE

Most rain falls in the warm summer months. Winters are snowy, but milder and foggy away from the mountains. Avalanches are a problem.

PEOPLE & SOCIETY

Switzerland is composed of distinct German-Swiss, French-Swiss, and Italian-Swiss linguistic groups. Germans are in the majority and there is a 36,000-strong Romansch minority in the east. The country is divided into 26 autonomous cantons (states), each with control over housing and economic policy. Society is conservative; marriage is common but the divorce rate is above the EU average.

THE ECONOMY

Diversified economy relies on services – the banking sector manages one-third of the world's offshore private wealth – and specialized industries (engineering, watches, etc.).

INSIGHT: *Famed for its neutrality, Switzerland only became a member of the UN in 2002*

3000m/9843ft	
2000m/6562ft	
1000m/3281ft	
500m/1640ft	
200m/656ft	

0   50 km
0   50 miles

FACTFILE

OFFICIAL NAME: Swiss Confederation
DATE OF FORMATION: 1291
CAPITAL: Bern
POPULATION: 7.3 million
TOTAL AREA: 15,942 sq. miles (41,290 sq. km)
DENSITY: 475 people per sq. mile

LANGUAGES: German*, Swiss-German, French*, Italian*, Romansch
RELIGIONS: Roman Catholic 42%, Protestant 35%, other 19%, Muslim 4%
ETHNIC MIX: German 64%, French 20%, other 9%, Italian 6%, Romansch 1%
GOVERNMENT: Parliamentary system
CURRENCY: Franc = 100 rappen/centimes

Syria

Stretching from the eastern Mediterranean to the Tigris River, Syria's borders are regarded as an artificial creation of French colonial rule by many Syrians. Foreign affairs are turbulent.

GEOGRAPHY
A coastal plain is backed by a low range of hills. The Euphrates River cuts through a vast interior desert plateau.

CLIMATE
Mediterranean coastal climate. Inland areas are arid. In winter, snow is common on the mountains.

PEOPLE & SOCIETY
Most Syrians live within 60 miles (100 km) of the coast, where the largest cities are sited. 90% are Muslim, including the politically dominant Alawis. In the north and west are groups of Kurds, Armenians, and Turkic-speaking peoples. Some 435,000 Palestinian refugees live in Syrian camps. There is a growing gulf between rich and poor. Human rights are an issue, but women's rights are among the best in the Arab world.

THE ECONOMY
Crude oil, but exports declining. High defense spending. Agriculture is thriving: crops include cotton, fruit, wheat, and olives. Large public sector.

INSIGHT: *Syria is an ancient land; there are at least 3500 as yet unexcavated archaeological sites*

FACTFILE

OFFICIAL NAME: Syrian Arab Republic
DATE OF FORMATION: 1941
CAPITAL: Damascus
POPULATION: 19 million
TOTAL AREA: 71,498 sq. miles (184,180 sq. km)
DENSITY: 267 people per sq. mile

LANGUAGES: Arabic*, French, Kurdish, Armenian, Circassian, other
RELIGIONS: Sunni Muslim 74%, other Muslim 16%, Christian 10%
ETHNIC MIX: Arab 89%, Kurd 6%, other 3%, Armenian, Turkmen, Circassian 2%
GOVERNMENT: One-party state
CURRENCY: Syrian pound = 100 piastres

Taiwan

The island republic of Taiwan (formerly Formosa) lies 80 miles (130 km) off the southeast coast of mainland China. China still considers it to be a renegade province.

GEOGRAPHY
Mountain region covers two-thirds of the island. Highly fertile lowlands and coastal plains.

CLIMATE
Tropical monsoon. Hot and humid. Typhoons July–September. Snow falls in mountains in winter.

PEOPLE & SOCIETY
Most Taiwanese are Han Chinese, descendants of the 1644 migration of the Ming dynasty from the mainland. The modern republic was created in 1949, when the nationalist Kuomintang was expelled from the mainland following communist victory in the civil war. 100,000 emigrés established themselves as a ruling class. Initial resentment has subsided as a new, Taiwanese generation has taken over the reins of power. The aboriginal minority suffers discrimination.

THE ECONOMY
Successful economy based on small, adaptable manufacturing companies. Goods include televisions, mobile phones, and computer chips.

INSIGHT: *Taiwan lost its seat at the UN to Beijing in 1971: both claim to represent "China"*

FACTFILE

OFFICIAL NAME: Republic of China (ROC)

DATE OF FORMATION: 1949

CAPITAL: Taipei

POPULATION: 22.9 million

TOTAL AREA: 13,892 sq. miles (35,980 sq. km)

DENSITY: 1838 people per sq. mile

LANGUAGES: Amoy Chinese, Mandarin Chinese*, Hakka Chinese

RELIGIONS: Buddhist, Confucianist, and Taoist 93%, Christian 5%, other 2%

ETHNIC MIX: Indigenous Chinese 84%, mainland Chinese 14%, aboriginal 2%

GOVERNMENT: Presidential system

CURRENCY: Taiwan dollar = 100 cents

Tajikistan

Tajikistan lies landlocked on the western slopes of the Pamirs in central Asia. The Tajik language and traditions are similar to those of Iran, rather than to those of Turkic Uzbekistan.

GEOGRAPHY
Mainly mountainous: the bare slopes of the Pamir ranges cover most of the country. Small but fertile Fergana Valley in northwest.

CLIMATE
Continental extremes in the valleys. Bitterly cold winters in the mountains. Rainfall is low.

PEOPLE & SOCIETY
Unlike the other former Soviet "-stans," Tajikistan is dominated by a people of Persian (Iranian) rather than Turkic origin. The main ethnic conflict is with the Turkic Uzbek minority. Russians are discriminated against and most have left since independence. Civil war in the 1990s, between communists and Islamists, degraded the standard of living. Islamist militants are still active.

THE ECONOMY
Declining cotton revenue. Key resources are uranium and fast-flowing rivers which could provide hydroelectric power exports. Needs reforms to attract foreign investment.

 INSIGHT: *Carpet-making, an ancient tradition learned from Persia, is still a major source of revenue*

	4000m/13124ft
	3000m/9843ft
	2000m/6562ft
	1000m/3281ft
	500m/1640ft
	200m/656ft

UZBEKISTAN
Fergana Valley
70°
Khŭjand · Isfara
66° Ŭroteppa 72° 40° KYRGYZSTAN
Panjakent 74° CHINA
DUSHANBE
Norak P a m i r s 38°
Qŭrghonteppa Kŭlob
Farkhor · Khorugh
Amu Darya
AFGHANISTAN PAKISTAN

0   100 km
0   100 miles

FACTFILE
OFFICIAL NAME: Republic of Tajikistan
DATE OF FORMATION: 1991
CAPITAL: Dushanbe
POPULATION: 6.5 million
TOTAL AREA: 55,251 sq. miles (143,100 sq. km)

DENSITY: 118 people per sq. mile
LANGUAGES: Tajik*, Uzbek, Russian
RELIGIONS: Sunni Muslim 80%, other 15%, Shi'a Muslim 5%
ETHNIC MIX: Tajik 80%, Uzbek 15%, other 3%, Kyrgyz 1%, Russian 1%
GOVERNMENT: Presidential system
CURRENCY: Somoni = 100 diram

Tanzania

The east African state of Tanzania was formed in 1964 by the union of Tanganyika and the Zanzibar islands. A third of its area is game reserve or national park.

GEOGRAPHY
The mainland is mostly a high plateau lying to the east of the Great Rift Valley. Forested coastal plain. Highlands in the north and south.

CLIMATE
Tropical on the coast and Zanzibar. Semiarid on central plateau, semitemperate in the highlands. March–May rains.

PEOPLE & SOCIETY
99% of people belong to one of 120 small ethnic Bantu groups. Arabs, Asians, and Europeans make up the remaining population. Use of Kiswahili as the lingua franca has eliminated ethnic rivalries. The majority of Tanzanians are subsistence farmers.

◆ **INSIGHT:** *At 19,340 ft (5895 m), Kilimanjaro in northeast Tanzania is Africa's highest mountain*

THE ECONOMY
Heavily reliant on agriculture, including forestry and cattle. Cashew nuts, cotton, coffee, and cloves are cash crops. Tourism growing. Gold and diamonds are mined. Boom in nontraditional exports.

FACTFILE
OFFICIAL NAME: United Republic of Tanzania
DATE OF FORMATION: 1964
CAPITAL: Dodoma
POPULATION: 38.3 million
TOTAL AREA: 364,898 sq. miles (945,087 sq. km)

DENSITY: 112 people per sq. mile
LANGUAGES: Kiswahili*, English*, other
RELIGIONS: Muslim 33%, Christian 33%, traditional beliefs 30%, other 4%
ETHNIC MIX: Native African (over 120 tribes) 99%, European, Asian, Arab 1%
GOVERNMENT: Presidential system
CURRENCY: Tanzanian shilling = 100 cents

Thailand

Thailand lies at the heart of mainland southeast Asia. Continuing rapid industrialization has resulted in massive congestion in the capital and a serious depletion of natural resources.

GEOGRAPHY
One-third of the country is occupied by a low plateau, drained by tributaries of the Mekong River. Central plain is the most fertile area.

CLIMATE
Tropical. Hot, humid March–May; monsoon rains May–October; cooler season November–March.

PEOPLE & SOCIETY
Buddhism is a national binding force. The north and northeast are home to about 600,000 hill tribes-people, with their own languages. The Chinese minority is the most assimilated in the region. Islamist Malay rebels in the undeveloped far south are fighting for secession.

◆ **INSIGHT:** *Thailand, meaning "land of the free," is the only SE Asian nation never to have been colonized*

THE ECONOMY
Successful manufacturing. Gas reserves. Tsunami damage affected growth. Leading world exporter of rice and rubber. Sex tourism harms image.

FACTFILE
OFFICIAL NAME: Kingdom of Thailand
DATE OF FORMATION: 1238
CAPITAL: Bangkok
POPULATION: 64.2 million
TOTAL AREA: 198,455 sq. miles (514,000 sq. km)
DENSITY: 325 people per sq. mile

LANGUAGES: Thai*, Chinese, Malay, Khmer, Mon, Karen, Miao
RELIGIONS: Buddhist 95%, Muslim 4%, other (including Christian) 1%
ETHNIC MIX: Thai 83%, Chinese 12%, Malay 3%, Khmer and other 2%
GOVERNMENT: Military regime
CURRENCY: Baht = 100 satang

Togo

Togo lies sandwiched between Ghana and Benin in west Africa. General Eyadema ruled from 1967 until his death in 2005. The port of Lomé is an important entrepôt for west African trade.

GEOGRAPHY

Central forested region bounded by savanna lands to the north and south. Mountain range stretches southwest to northeast.

CLIMATE

Coast hot and humid; drier inland. Rainy season March–July, with heaviest falls in the west.

PEOPLE & SOCIETY

Harsh resentment between Ewe in the south and Kabye in the north. Kabye control military, but the north is undeveloped compared with the south. Extended family is important. Tribalism and nepotism are key factors in every-day life. Some ethnic groups, such as the Mina, have matriarchal societies.

◆ **INSIGHT:** *The "Nana Benz," the market-women of Lomé, control Togo's retail trade*

THE ECONOMY

Most people are farmers. Self-sufficient in basic foodstuffs. Main export crops are cotton, coffee, and cocoa. Togo's phosphate deposits have world's highest mineral content, though cadmium-rich phosphates are facing bans from importers.

(Map of Togo showing: BURKINA, Dapaong, BENIN, Sansanné-Mango, Kara, Tchamba, GHANA, Mono, Atakpamé, Kpalimé, Tsévié, Aného, LOMÉ, ATLANTIC OCEAN. Scale: 0 50 km / 0 50 miles. Elevation key: 500m/1640ft, 200m/656ft, Sea Level. Coordinates: 0°, 1°, 11°, 10°, 9°, 8°, 7°, 6°)

FACTFILE

OFFICIAL NAME: Republic of Togo
DATE OF FORMATION: 1960
CAPITAL: Lomé
POPULATION: 6.1 million
TOTAL AREA: 21,924 sq. miles (56,785 sq. km)
DENSITY: 290 people per sq. mile

LANGUAGES: Ewe, Kabye, Gurma, French*
RELIGIONS: Traditional beliefs 50%, Christian 35%, Muslim 15%
ETHNIC MIX: Ewe 46%, other African 41%, Kabye 12%, European 1%
GOVERNMENT: Presidential system
CURRENCY: CFA franc = 100 centimes

Tonga

Tonga is an archipelago of 170 islands in the South Pacific. Only 45 of these islands are inhabited. Politics is effectively controlled by the king, though calls for democracy are growing.

GEOGRAPHY

Easterly islands are generally low and fertile. Those in the west are higher and volcanic in origin.

CLIMATE

Tropical oceanic. Temperatures range between 68°F (20°C) and 86°F (30°C) all year round. Heavy rainfall, especially February–March.

PEOPLE & SOCIETY

Tonga is the last remaining Polynesian monarchy. All land belongs to the crown, but is administered by nobles who allot it to the common people. Respect for traditional values is high, though younger, Westernized Tongans are starting to question some attitudes. The first elected commoner became prime minister in 2006.

INSIGHT: *Unique in the Pacific, it was never brought under foreign rule*

THE ECONOMY

Cash crops are coconuts, vanilla, and squashes. Cassava, citrus fruits, yams, and breadfruit also cultivated. Tourism is increasingly important.

200m/656ft
Sea Level

Niuatoputapu
Tafahi
17°
18°
'Uta Vava'u
Vava'u Group
Neiafu
19°
PACIFIC
OCEAN
Ha'apai Group
Tofua
Pangai
Kotu Group
174°
20°
Nomuka Group
Otu Tolu Group
Tongatapu
21°
NUKU'ALOFA
'Eua
'Ohonua
Tongatapu Group
175°

0   100 km
0   100 miles

FACTFILE

OFFICIAL NAME: Kingdom of Tonga
DATE OF FORMATION: 1970
CAPITAL: Nuku'alofa
POPULATION: 112,422
TOTAL AREA: 289 sq. miles (748 sq. km)
DENSITY: 404 people per sq. mile

LANGUAGES: English*, Tongan*
RELIGIONS: Free Wesleyan 41%, other 29%, Roman Catholic 16%, Church of Jesus Christ of Latter-Day Saints 14%
ETHNIC MIX: Tongan 98%, other 2%
GOVERNMENT: Monarchy
CURRENCY: Pa'anga (Tongan dollar) = 100 seniti

Trinidad & Tobago

The two islands of the former UK colony of Trinidad and Tobago are the most southerly of the Caribbean Windward Islands, lying just 9 miles (15 km) off the coast of Venezuela.

GEOGRAPHY

Both islands are hilly and wooded. Trinidad has a rugged mountain range in the north, and swamps on its east and west coasts.

CLIMATE

Tropical, with July–December wet season. Escapes the region's hurricanes, which pass to the north.

PEOPLE & SOCIETY

Trinidad's East Indian community is the largest in the Caribbean and holds on to its Muslim and Hindu heritage. There are rising ethnic tensions with the predominantly Christian blacks; political parties are divided along race lines. Blacks form the majority on Tobago.

◆ **INSIGHT:** *Trinidad and Tobago is the birthplace of steel bands and Calypso music*

THE ECONOMY

Oil and gas exports. Associated industries: world's second-largest producer of methanol. Economic growth. Tourism is particularly strong on wildlife-rich Tobago.

FACTFILE

OFFICIAL NAME: Republic of Trinidad and Tobago

DATE OF FORMATION: 1962

CAPITAL: Port-of-Spain

POPULATION: 1.3 million

TOTAL AREA: 1980 sq. miles (5128 sq. km)

DENSITY: 656 people per sq. mile

LANGUAGES: English Creole, English*, Hindi, French, Spanish

RELIGIONS: Catholic 32%, Hindu 24%, Protestant 28%, other 9%, Muslim 7%

ETHNIC MIX: East Indian 40%, Black 40%, mixed 18%, White, Chinese 1%, other 1%

GOVERNMENT: Parliamentary system

CURRENCY: Trin. & Tob. dollar = 100 cents

Tunisia

Tunisia has traditionally been one of the more liberal Arab states, moving toward a multiparty democracy, but its government is now facing a challenge from Islamic fundamentalists.

GEOGRAPHY

Mountains in the north are surrounded by plains. Vast, low-lying salt pans in the center. To the south lies the Sahara Desert.

CLIMATE

Summer temperatures are high. The north is often wet and windy in winter. Far south is arid.

PEOPLE & SOCIETY

The population is almost entirely of Arab-Berber descent, with Jewish and Christian minorities. Many still live in extended family groups, in which three or four generations are represented. Women have better rights than in most other Arab countries and make up almost 30% of the total workforce. Politics, however, remains a male preserve. A low birth-rate is a result of a long-standing family planning policy.

THE ECONOMY

Well-diversified, despite limited resources. Oil and gas exports. Expanding manufacturing. Tourism. European investment.

◆ **INSIGHT:** *Tunisia was the center of trading empires from the 9th century BCE*

FACTFILE

OFFICIAL NAME: Republic of Tunisia
DATE OF FORMATION: 1956
CAPITAL: Tunis
POPULATION: 10.1 million
TOTAL AREA: 63,169 sq. miles
(163,610 sq. km)
DENSITY: 168 people per sq. mile

LANGUAGES: Arabic*, French
RELIGIONS: Muslim (mainly Sunni) 98%, Christian 1%, Jewish 1%
ETHNIC MIX: Arab and Berber 98%, Jewish 1%, European 1%
GOVERNMENT: Presidential system
CURRENCY: Tunisian dinar = 1000 millimes

Turkey

Lying partly in the region of eastern Thrace in Europe, but mostly in Asia, Turkey's position gives it significant influence in the Mediterranean, the Black Sea, and the Middle East.

GEOGRAPHY

Asian Turkey (Anatolia) is dominated by two mountain ranges, separated by a high, semidesert plateau. Coastal regions are fertile.

CLIMATE

Coast has a Mediterranean climate. Interior has cold, snowy winters and hot, dry summers.

PEOPLE & SOCIETY

The Turks are racially diverse. Many are refugees or descendants of refugees, often from the Balkans. However, the sense of national identity is strong. Turkey has close links with other Turkic states. Kurds, the largest minority, are based in the southeast; a violent campaign for greater autonomy has raged since 1984, with intermittent cease-fires. Tensions remain high.

THE ECONOMY

Liberalized economy, boosted by self-sufficient agriculture and strong textiles, tourism, and manufacturing sectors. Pipelines carry oil to Europe.

INSIGHT: *Turkey had two of the seven wonders of the ancient world: the tomb of King Mausolus at Halicarnassus (now Bodrum), and the temple of Artemis at Ephesus*

FACTFILE

OFFICIAL NAME: Republic of Turkey
DATE OF FORMATION: 1923
CAPITAL: Ankara
POPULATION: 73.2 million
TOTAL AREA: 301,382 sq. miles (780,580 sq. km)
DENSITY: 246 people per sq. mile

LANGUAGES: Turkish*, Kurdish, Arabic, Circassian, Armenian, Greek, other
RELIGIONS: Muslim (mainly Sunni) 99%, other 1%
ETHNIC MIX: Turkish 70%, Kurdish 20%, other 8%, Arab 2%
GOVERNMENT: Parliamentary system
CURRENCY: New Turkish lira = 100 kurus

Turkmenistan

Stretching from the Caspian Sea into the deserts of central Asia, Turkmenistan adjusted better than most former Soviet states to independence, but has since been run as a dictatorship.

GEOGRAPHY
Low Karakumy Desert covers 80% of the country. Mountains on southern border with Iran. Fertile Amu Darya Valley in north.

CLIMATE
Arid desert climate with extreme summer heat, but sub-freezing winter temperatures.

PEOPLE & SOCIETY
Before Russia annexed the area in 1884, the Turkmen were a largely nomadic tribal people. Today, the tribal unit remains strong, with population clustered around desert oases. Relations with Uzbek and Russian minorities have become tense in recent years due to the "Turkmenization" of government, education, and religion. Political uncertainty followed the sudden death of President Niyazov in December 2006.

THE ECONOMY
Cotton and gas are the main resources. Over-intensive farming of cotton has damaged the environment. Opening up to private investment.

INSIGHT: *President Niyazov created an elaborate personality cult, styling himself as Turkmenbashi – father of all Turkmen*

FACTFILE
OFFICIAL NAME: Turkmenistan
DATE OF FORMATION: 1991
CAPITAL: Aşgabat
POPULATION: 4.8 million
TOTAL AREA: 188,455 sq. miles (488,100 sq. km)
DENSITY: 25 people per sq. mile

LANGUAGES: Turkmen*, Uzbek, Russian, Kazakh, Tatar, other
RELIGIONS: Sunni Muslim 87%, Orthodox Christian 11%, other 2%
ETHNIC MIX: Turkmen 77%, Uzbek 9%, Russian 7%, other 5%, Kazakh 2%
GOVERNMENT: One-party state
CURRENCY: Manat = 100 tenge

Tuvalu

One of the world's smallest, most isolated states, Tuvalu lies in the central Pacific. The nine islands were linked to the Gilbert Islands (Kiribati) as a UK colony until independence.

GEOGRAPHY

A series of coral atolls, none more than 15 ft (4.6 m) above sea level. Poor soils restrict vegetation to bush, coconut palms, and breadfruit trees.

CLIMATE

Hot all year round. Heavy annual rainfall. Hurricane season brings many violent storms.

PEOPLE & SOCIETY

People are mostly Polynesian. Around half the population live on Funafuti, where government jobs are based. Life is communal and traditional. Most people live by subsistence farming, digging pits out of the coral to grow crops. Fresh water is precious due to frequent droughts.

◆ **INSIGHT:** *Tuvaluans have a reputation as excellent sailors, many work overseas on merchant ships*

THE ECONOMY

World's smallest sovereign economy. Fishing licenses sold mostly to foreign boats. Exports are few: copra, stamps, and clothes. Income from trust fund and the lease of .tv Internet suffix.

FACTFILE

OFFICIAL NAME: Tuvalu
DATE OF FORMATION: 1978
CAPITAL: Fongafale, on Funafuti Atoll
POPULATION: 11,636
TOTAL AREA: 10 sq. miles
(26 sq. km)
DENSITY: 1164 people per sq. mile

LANGUAGES: Tuvaluan, Kiribati, English*
RELIGIONS: Church of Tuvalu 97%, Baha'i 1%, Seventh-day Adventist 1%, other 1%
ETHNIC MIX: Polynesian 92%, other 6%, Kiribati 2%
GOVERNMENT: Nonparty system
CURRENCY: Australian dollar and Tuvaluan dollar = 100 cents each

Uganda

Landlocked in east Africa, Uganda has a history of ethnic strife. Under President Museveni, steps have been taken to restore peace and to rebuild the economy and democracy.

GEOGRAPHY

Predominantly a large plateau with the Ruwenzori mountain range and the Great Rift Valley in the west. Lake Victoria lies to the southeast. Vegetation is of savanna type.

CLIMATE

Altitude and the influence of the lakes modify the equatorial climate. Rain falls throughout the year; spring is the wettest period.

PEOPLE & SOCIETY

The predominantly rural population comprises some 13 main ethnic groups. President Museveni has worked hard to break down traditional ethnic animosities, but a noticeable north–south divide persists, with economic development focused in the south. Two decades of conflict against rebels in the north has killed thousands and left 80% of northerners as refugees.

THE ECONOMY

Coffee, tobacco, tea, and cotton. Oil exploration. Hydroelectric power is to be developed to reduce oil imports. Great potential from the country's underused mines.

◆ **INSIGHT:** *Lake Victoria is the world's third-largest lake*

3000m/9843ft
2000m/6562ft
1000m/3281ft
500m/1640ft

SUDAN
KENYA
Arua • Gulu
Albert Nile
DEM. REP. CONGO
Lake Albert
Lake Kyoga
Victoria Nile
Mbale
Tororo
Ruwenzori
Kabarole
Iganga
Jinja
Mubende
KAMPALA
Kasese
Entebbe
Equator
Masaka
Sese Is.
Lake Edward
Mbarara
Lake Victoria
Rukungrio
Kabale
TANZANIA
RWANDA

0   100 km
0   100 miles

FACTFILE

OFFICIAL NAME: Republic of Uganda
DATE OF FORMATION: 1962
CAPITAL: Kampala
POPULATION: 28.8 million
TOTAL AREA: 91,135 sq. miles (236,040 sq. km)
DENSITY: 374 people per sq. mile

LANGUAGES: Luganda, Nkole, Chiga, Lango, Acholi, Teso, Lugbara, English*
RELIGIONS: Catholic 38%, Protestant 33%, trad. beliefs 13%, Muslim 8%, other 8%
ETHNIC MIX: Baganda 17%, Banyakole 10%, Basoga 9%, Iteso 7%, other 57%
GOVERNMENT: Presidential system
CURRENCY: New Ug. shilling = 100 cents

Ukraine

The former "breadbasket of the Soviet Union," Ukraine lies on the northern coast of the Black Sea. Politics is divided between pro-Russian sentiments and assertive nationalism.

GEOGRAPHY
Mainly fertile steppes and forests. Carpathian Mountains in west, Crimean chain in south. Pripet Marshes in northwest.

CLIMATE
Mainly continental climate, with distinct seasons. Southern Crimea has Mediterranean climate.

PEOPLE & SOCIETY
Over 90% of people in the west are Ukrainian, but in cities in the east and south, and in Crimea, Russians form a majority. The government is wary of Crimean separatism. Tatars have been returning there since the Soviet Union's collapse and now comprise around 13% of the local population. Over five million people in Ukraine, Russia, and Belarus live in areas 'contaminated' by the 1986 Chernobyl nuclear disaster.

THE ECONOMY
Ukraine has 5% of global mineral reserves; metals account for around 40% of export earnings. Slow reform of land laws has held back the revival of agriculture. Political instability.

INSIGHT: *Ukraine means "on the border," referring to its historic position on the edge of the old Russian Empire*

FACTFILE
OFFICIAL NAME: Ukraine
DATE OF FORMATION: 1991
CAPITAL: Kiev
POPULATION: 46.5 million
TOTAL AREA: 223,089 sq. miles (603,700 sq. km)
DENSITY: 199 people per sq. mile

LANGUAGES: Ukrainian*, Russian, Tatar
RELIGIONS: Christian (mainly Orthodox) 95%, other 5%
ETHNIC MIX: Ukrainian 78%, Russian 17%, other 5%
GOVERNMENT: Presidential system
CURRENCY: Hryvna = 100 kopiykas

United Arab Emirates

Bordering the Gulf on the northern coast of the Arabian Peninsula, the seven states of the United Arab Emirates form the Arab world's only working federation.

 GEOGRAPHY

Mostly flat, semiarid desert with dunes, salt pans, and occasional oases. Cities are watered by extensive irrigation systems.

 CLIMATE

Summers are humid, despite minimal rainfall. Sand-laden *shamal* winds blow in winter and spring.

PEOPLE & SOCIETY

Emirians, who make up just a quarter of the population, are mostly Sunni Muslims of Bedouin descent, and largely city dwellers. In theory, women enjoy equal rights with men. Poverty is rare and there is no income tax. The 1970s oil boom encouraged the immigration of workers, mostly from Asia. Western expatriates are permitted a virtually unrestricted lifestyle. Islamism, however, is a growing force among the young.

THE ECONOMY

Major exporter of oil and natural gas. Dynamic Dubai has a free-trade zone and is a major financial center. Northern emirates are less developed. Most food and raw materials are imported, and water is scarce.

◆ **INSIGHT:** *Mina Jabal Ali, in Dubai, is the largest man-made port in the world*

500m/1640ft
200m/656ft
Sea Level

0   50 km
0   50 miles

DUBAI Emirate capital

 FACTFILE

OFFICIAL NAME: United Arab Emirates
DATE OF FORMATION: 1971
CAPITAL: Abu Dhabi
POPULATION: 4.5 million
TOTAL AREA: 32,000 sq. miles (82,880 sq. km)
DENSITY: 139 people per sq. mile

LANGUAGES: Arabic*, Farsi, Indian and Pakistani languages, English
RELIGIONS: Muslim (mainly Sunni) 96%, Christian, Hindu, and other 4%
ETHNIC MIX: Asian 60%, Emirian 25%, other Arab 12%, European 3%
GOVERNMENT: Monarchy
CURRENCY: UAE dirham = 100 fils

United Kingdom

Separated from continental Europe by the English Channel, the United Kingdom consists of Great Britain (England, Wales, and Scotland), a number of smaller islands, and Northern Ireland.

GEOGRAPHY

Rugged uplands dominate the landscape of Scotland, Wales, and northern England. All of the peaks in the United Kingdom over 4000 ft (1219 m) lie in highland Scotland. Known as the "backbone of England," the Pennine mountains run the length of northern England. Lowland England rises into several ranges of rolling hills, and there is an interconnected system of rivers and canals. Over 600 islands, mostly uninhabited, lie west and north of the Scottish mainland.

CLIMATE

Generally mild, temperate, and highly changeable. Rain is fairly well distributed throughout the year. The west is generally wetter than the east, and the south warmer than the north. Winter snow is common in upland areas.

PEOPLE & SOCIETY

The Welsh and Scottish nations remain recognizably distinct, and the creation of the Scottish Parliament and Welsh Assembly has given each country greater political autonomy. The future of devolved government in Northern Ireland remains problematic. People from other ethnic minorities, over half of whom were born in the UK, account for around 8% of the population. Asians and West Indians in most cities face deprivation and social stress; Asian women can be particularly isolated. In key areas such as policing, multiethnic recruitment has made little progress. Marriage is in decline. Over 40% of all births occur outside marriage, but most of them to cohabiting couples. Single-parent households account for almost a quarter of all families. Income inequality is greater now than in 1884 when records began.

FACTFILE

OFFICIAL NAME: United Kingdom of Great Britain and Northern Ireland

DATE OF FORMATION: 1707

CAPITAL: London

POPULATION: 59.7 million

TOTAL AREA: 94,525 sq. miles (244,820 sq. km)

DENSITY: 640 people per sq. mile

LANGUAGES: English*, Welsh*, other

RELIGIONS: Anglican 45%, other 39%, Catholic 9%, Presbyterian 4% Muslim 3%

ETHNIC MIX: White 92%, Asian 4%, Black 2%, mixed race 1%, other 1%

GOVERNMENT: Parliamentary system

CURRENCY: Pound sterling = 100 pence

United Kingdom

💲 THE ECONOMY

World leader in financial services, pharmaceuticals, and defense industries. Strong multinationals. Precision engineering and high-tech industries, including biotechnology and telecommunications. Energy sector based on declining North Sea oil and gas reserves. Innovative in computer software development. Flexible working practices. Success in controlling inflation. Decline of manufacturing sector, particularly heavy industries and car manufacture, matched by rise in financial and other services. High levels of government and consumer debt. Nonparticipation in euro threatens former status as EU's largest recipient of inward investment, and has prompted some major investors to close UK factories. The government is wary of adopting the currency fearing popular hostility to more European integration.

◆ **INSIGHT:** *The UK has no formal written constitution, but a stable government system based on Parliament, which originated as a check on royal power in the 13th century*

Orkney Is.

Outer Hebrides

Shetlands Is.
Lerwick
60°
2°

Stornoway
58°

Inverness

Aberdeen

Scotland

Inner Hebrides

Oban

Dundee

56°

Glasgow

Edinburgh

Newcastle upon Tyne

Londonderry

Northern Ireland

Belfast

Carlisle

Isle of Man

North Sea

IRELAND

Blackpool

Leeds

54°

Liverpool   Blackburn

Sheffield

Manchester

England

Derby

Norwich

Birmingham

Leicester

Cambridge

52°

Wales

Oxford

● LONDON

Swansea   *Thames*

Cardiff   Reading

Celtic Sea

Bristol

Southampton

Dover

8°   2°

Plymouth

Exeter

ATLANTIC OCEAN

50°

0°   2°

English Channel

6°   4°   2°

1000m/3281ft
500m/1640ft
200m/656ft
Sea Level

0   100 km
0   100 miles

United States of America

Stretching across the most temperate part of North America, and with many natural resources, the US is the world's leading economic power and third-largest country.

 GEOGRAPHY

The US has a varied topography. Forested mountains stretch from New England in the far northeast, giving way to lowlands and swamps in the extreme south. The central plains are dominated by the Mississippi–Missouri River system and the Great Lakes on the Canadian border. The Rocky Mountains in the west contain active volcanoes and drop to the coast across the earthquake-prone San Andreas Fault. The south-west is arid desert. Mountainous Alaska is mostly Arctic tundra.

CLIMATE

There are four main climatic zones. The north and east are continental and temperate, with heavy rainfall, warm summers, and cold winters. Florida and the Deep South are tropical and prone to hurricanes. The southwest is arid desert with searing summer heat and low rainfall. Southern California is Mediterranean, with hot summers and mild winters.

United States of America

◆ **INSIGHT:** The United States of America has the world's oldest constitution. Drafted in 1787, it has operated continuously ever since, albeit with numerous amendments

United States of America

◆ **INSIGHT:** By law, information collected in a United States census must remain confidential for 72 years

PEOPLE & SOCIETY

Though the demographic, economic, and cultural dominance of the whites is firmly entrenched after almost 400 years of settlement, the ethnic balance is rapidly shifting. The Hispanic community is now the largest single minority, and is predicted to account for 25% of the population by 2050. Despite its growing size, it struggles to compete socially with the better established, and more politically sensitive black community. The original native Amerindians, meanwhile, were dispossessed in the 19th century and are now among the poorest people. Constitutionally, state and religion are clearly separated. Conservative Christianity, however, is increasingly dominant politically. Living standards are high, but bad diet and insufficient exercise have left over a third of Americans clinically obese.

THE ECONOMY

World's largest economy: well-established engineering and high-tech industries, huge resource base, global spread of US culture. Manufacturing is in decline as jobs are lost to low-wage economies. Imports are increasing despite weak US dollar, which now faces competition from the euro as the leading global currency. In 2001 a record nine-year boom came to an end, bringing large corporations crashing down and raising unemployment to new highs, in a serious economic downturn. Recovery efforts focused on promoting consumer spending, the engine which drives the whole US economy. Taxes have been slashed along with interest rates. A concurrent increase in government spending, however, notably on defense, the "war on terror," and the 2003 invasion of Iraq, has seen a huge budget surplus slump to a record deficit.

FACTFILE

OFFICIAL NAME: United States of America
DATE OF FORMATION: 1776
CAPITAL: Washington D.C.
POPULATION: 298 million
TOTAL AREA: 3,717,792 sq. miles
(9,626,091 sq. km)
DENSITY: 84 people per sq. mile

LANGUAGES: English*, Spanish, other
RELIGIONS: Protestant 52%, Catholic 25%, other 19%, Muslim 2%, Jewish 2%
ETHNIC MIX: White 62%, Hispanic 13%, Black 13%, other 7%, Asian 4%, Native American 1%
GOVERNMENT: Presidential system
CURRENCY: US dollar = 100 cents

Uruguay

Situated in southeastern South America, Uruguay returned to civilian government in 1985, after 12 years of military rule. Most land is used for farming: Uruguay is a major wool exporter.

GEOGRAPHY

Low, rolling grasslands cover 80% of the country. Narrow coastal plain. Alluvial floodplain in south-west. Five rivers flow westward and drain into the Uruguay River.

CLIMATE

Temperate throughout the country. Warm summers, mild winters, and moderate rainfall.

PEOPLE & SOCIETY

Uruguayans are largely second- or third- generation Italians or Spaniards. Wealth derived from cattle ranching enabled the country to become the first welfare state in South America. Despite economic decline since the 1950s, a large, if less prosperous, middle class remains. Though a Roman Catholic country, Uruguay is liberal in its attitude to religion and all forms are tolerated.

THE ECONOMY

Wool, meat, and hides exported. Buoyant tourism. Return to economic growth after recession (1999–2002).

INSIGHT: *Uruguay's rich pastures are ideal for raising livestock; animal products bring in over 40% of export earnings*

200m/656ft Sea Level

0   100 km
0   100 miles

FACTFILE

OFFICIAL NAME: Eastern Republic of Uruguay
DATE OF FORMATION: 1828
CAPITAL: Montevideo
POPULATION: 3.5 million
TOTAL AREA: 68,039 sq. miles (176,220 sq. km)

DENSITY: 52 people per sq. mile
LANGUAGES: Spanish*
RELIGIONS: Roman Catholic 66%, other 30%, Jewish 2%, Protestant 2%
ETHNIC MIX: White 90%, Mestizo 6%, Black 4%
GOVERNMENT: Presidential system
CURRENCY: Urug. peso = 100 centésimos

Uzbekistan

Sharing what is left of the Aral Sea with its northern neighbor, Kazakhstan, Uzbekistan lies on the ancient Silk Road between Asia and Europe. It is the most populous central Asian republic.

GEOGRAPHY

Arid and semiarid plains in much of the west. Fertile, irrigated farmland in the east lies below the peaks of the western Pamirs.

CLIMATE

Harsh continental climate. Summers can be extremely hot and dry; winters are cold.

PEOPLE & SOCIETY

Complex ethnic makeup. Ex-communists are in firm control, but traditional social patterns based on clan, religion, and region have reemerged. Constitutional measures aim to control the influence of Islam: activities against Islamists have drawn international condemnation. Most people live in the fertile east. Birthrates are high, and the status of women continues to be low.

THE ECONOMY

Oil, gas, and coal. Rich mineral deposits: major producer of uranium and gold, with one of the world's largest gold mines. Cotton is a key export. Dependent on grain imports.

INSIGHT: *The Aral Sea has shrunk to less then half of the area it covered in the 1960s, due to diversion of rivers for irrigation*

FACTFILE

OFFICIAL NAME: Republic of Uzbekistan
DATE OF FORMATION: 1991
CAPITAL: Tashkent
POPULATION: 26.6 million
TOTAL AREA: 172,741 sq. miles (447,400 sq. km)
DENSITY: 154 people per sq. mile

LANGUAGES: Uzbek*, Russian, Tajik, Kazakh
RELIGIONS: Sunni Muslim 88%, Orthodox Christian 9%, other 3%
ETHNIC MIX: Uzbek 80%, other 6%, Russian 6%, Tajik 5%, Kazakh 3%
GOVERNMENT: Presidential system
CURRENCY: Som = 100 tiyin

Vanuatu

An archipelago of 82 islands and islets in the South Pacific, Vanuatu was ruled jointly by the UK and France from 1906 until independence in 1980. Politics is democratic but volatile.

GEOGRAPHY
Mountainous and volcanic, with coral beaches and dense rainforest. Cultivated land along the coasts.

CLIMATE
Tropical. Temperatures and rainfall decline from north to south.

PEOPLE & SOCIETY
Indigenous Melanesians form a majority. Ni-Vanuatu culture is traditional; local social and religious customs are strong, despite centuries of missionary influence. Subsistence farming and fishing are the main activities. 80% of the population live on the 12 main islands. Women have lower social status than men and payment of bride-price is common.

◆ **INSIGHT:** *With 105 indigenous tongues, Vanuatu has the world's highest per capita density of languages*

THE ECONOMY
Copra and cocoa exports are declining. Tourism is growing. Offshore banking rules have been tightened after international pressure.

FACTFILE

OFFICIAL NAME: Republic of Vanuatu
DATE OF FORMATION: 1980
CAPITAL: Port Vila
POPULATION: 211,000
TOTAL AREA: 4710 sq. miles (12,200 sq. km)
DENSITY: 45 people per sq. mile

LANGUAGES: Bislama*, English*, French*
RELIGIONS: Presbyterian 37%, other 25%, Anglican 15%, Roman Catholic 15%, traditional beliefs 8%
ETHNIC MIX: Melanesian 98%, European 1%, other 1%
GOVERNMENT: Parliamentary system
CURRENCY: Vatu = 100 centimes

Vatican City

The Vatican City, or Holy See, the seat of the Roman Catholic Church, is a walled enclave in the city of Rome, Italy. It is the world's smallest fully independent state.

GEOGRAPHY
The Vatican's territory includes ten other buildings in Rome, plus the papal residence. The Vatican Gardens cover half the City's area.

CLIMATE
Mild winters with regular rainfall. Hot, dry summers with occasional thunderstorms.

PEOPLE & SOCIETY
The Vatican has about 900 permanent inhabitants, including over 100 lay persons. It also employs thousands of lay staff. Citizenship can be acquired through stable residence and holding a position within the City. The reigning pope has supreme legislative and judicial powers, and holds office for life. Though the Vatican City is officially neutral, papal opinion has a great influence on the world's 1.1 billion Roman Catholics.

THE ECONOMY
Investments and voluntary contributions made by Catholics worldwide (known as Peter's Pence) are backed up by tourist revenue and the issue of Vatican stamps and coins.

◆ **INSIGHT:** *The Vatican City is the spiritual center for 17% of the world's population*

FACTFILE
OFFICIAL NAME: State of the Vatican City
DATE OF FORMATION: 1929
CAPITAL: Vatican City
POPULATION: 921
TOTAL AREA: 0.17 sq. miles (0.44 sq. km)
DENSITY: 5418 people per sq. mile

LANGUAGES: Italian*, Latin*
RELIGIONS: Roman Catholic 100%
ETHNIC MIX: Cardinals are from many nationalities, but Italians form the largest group. The current pope is from Germany.
GOVERNMENT: Papal state
CURRENCY: Euro = 100 cents

Venezuela

Lying on the southern shores of the Caribbean, Venezuela was the first of Spain's colonies to seek independence. Despite large oil reserves, many Venezuelans still live in poverty.

GEOGRAPHY

Andes Mountains and the Maracaibo lowlands in the northwest. Central grassy plains are drained by the Orinoco River system. Forested Guiana Highlands in the southeast.

CLIMATE

Tropical. Hot and humid. Uplands are cooler. Orinoco plains are alternately parched or flooded.

PEOPLE & SOCIETY

Venezuela is historically a "melting pot," with immigrants from Europe and all over Latin America. The few indigenous Amerindians live in remote areas. Venezuela has one of the most urbanized societies in the region, with most of its population living in the northern cities. President Chávez's left-wing rhetoric raises opposition within Venezuela from urban society, and from the US.

THE ECONOMY

Oil provides over 80% of export earnings. Vast reserves of coal, gold, and other minerals. Overmanned and often inefficient state sector. High inflation. Clampdown on tax evasion.

INSIGHT: *Venezuela's Angel Falls is the world's highest waterfall at 3210 ft (979 m)*

FACTFILE

OFFICIAL NAME: Bolivarian Republic of Venezuela

DATE OF FORMATION: 1830

CAPITAL: Caracas

POPULATION: 26.7 million

TOTAL AREA: 352,143 sq. miles (912,050 sq. km)

DENSITY: 78 people per sq. mile

LANGUAGES: Spanish*, native languages

RELIGIONS: Roman Catholic 89%, Protestant and other 11%

ETHNIC MIX: Mestizo 69%, White 20%, Black 9%, Amerindian 2%

GOVERNMENT: Presidential system

CURRENCY: Bolívar = 100 céntimos

Vietnam

Situated on the western edge of the South China Sea, Vietnam is run as a single-party Communist state. Since 1986 the regime has pursued a liberal economic policy known as *doi moi*.

GEOGRAPHY
A heavily forested mountain range separates the northern Red River delta lowlands from the Mekong River delta in the south.

CLIMATE
Cool winters in north; south is tropical, with even temperatures.

PEOPLE & SOCIETY
Ethnic Vietnamese dominate; the Chinese minority was viewed as a corrupt bourgeoisie by the victorious Communists after the war. Mountain-based minorities (*montagnards*) were also sidelined by the regime; tensions persist over the resettlement of the central highlands by lowlanders. Women play an active role in society.

INSIGHT: *The 1962–1975 Vietnam War was the longest conflict of the 20th century*

THE ECONOMY
The potential for continued strong growth rests on a diverse resource base (including gas reserves), an educated workforce, and strong light industries.

FACTFILE

OFFICIAL NAME: Socialist Republic of Vietnam
DATE OF FORMATION: 1976
CAPITAL: Hanoi
POPULATION: 84.2 million
TOTAL AREA: 127,243 sq. miles (329,560 sq. km)

DENSITY: 670 people per sq. mile
LANGUAGES: Vietnamese*, Chinese, other
RELIGIONS: Nonreligious 81%, Buddhist 9%, Christian 7%, other 3%
ETHNIC MIX: Vietnamese 86%, other 10%, Tay 2%, Thai 2%
GOVERNMENT: One-party state
CURRENCY: Dông = 10 hao = 100 xu

Yemen

Located in southern Arabia, Yemen was formerly two countries: the People's Democratic Republic of Yemen (south and east) and the Yemen Arab Republic (northwest), were united in 1990.

GEOGRAPHY

Mountainous west with a fertile strip along the Red Sea. Arid desert and mountains elsewhere.

CLIMATE

Desert climate, modified by altitude, which affects temperatures by as much as 54°F (30°C).

PEOPLE & SOCIETY
Yemenis are almost entirely of Arab and Bedouin descent. The majority are Sunni Muslims, of the Shafi sect. In rural areas and in the north, tribalism and Islamic orthodoxy are strong and most women wear the veil. Foreigners have been subject to sporadic attacks and kidnappings. Tension continues to exist between the south, led by the cosmopolitan city of Aden, and the more conservative north.

THE ECONOMY
Instability deters investment. Considerable oil and gas reserves. Agriculture is the largest employer: coffee, cotton, livestock, and fish.

◆ **INSIGHT:** *Mokha, on the Red Sea, gave its name to the first coffee beans exported to Europe in the 1600s*

3000m/9843ft
2000m/6562ft
1000m/3281ft
500m/1640ft
200m/656ft
Sea Level

0   100 km
0   100 miles

SAUDI ARABIA

OMAN

Ar Rub' al Khāli

Say'ūn

Sayhūt

16°

●SANA

Ash Shihr

52°

Red Sea

Al Hudaydah
Dhamār

Al Mukallā

Bayt al Faqīh

48°

Ta'izz

Al Mukhā
(Mokha)

Adan
(Aden)

Gulf of Aden

Suqutrā

Abd-Al-Kuri

12°

44°

52°

FACTFILE

OFFICIAL NAME: Republic of Yemen
DATE OF FORMATION: 1990
CAPITAL: Sana
POPULATION: 21 million
TOTAL AREA: 203,849 sq. miles (527,970 sq. km)
DENSITY: 97 people per sq. mile

LANGUAGES: Arabic*
RELIGIONS: Sunni Muslim 55%, Shi'a Muslim 42%, Christian, Hindu, and Jewish 3%
ETHNIC MIX: Arab 99%, Afro-Arab, Indian, Somali, and European 1%
GOVERNMENT: Presidential system
CURRENCY: Yemeni rial = 100 fils

Zambia

Bordered to the south by the Zambezi River, Zambia lies at the heart of southern Africa. In 1991, it made a peaceful transition from single-party rule to multiparty democracy.

 GEOGRAPHY
A high savanna plateau, broken by mountains in northeast. Vegetation mainly trees and scrub.

 CLIMATE
Tropical, with three seasons: cool and dry, hot and dry, and wet. Southwest is prone to drought.

 PEOPLE & SOCIETY
There are more than 70 different ethnic groups, but there are fewer ethnic tensions than in many African states. The largest group is the Bemba in the northeast. Other major groups are the Tonga in the south, the eastern Nyanja, and the Lozi in the west. There are also thousands of refugees, mostly from the DRC and Angola. A National Gender Policy was issued in 2000 to redress inequalities between the sexes. The standard of living has fallen in real terms since independence.

$ THE ECONOMY
After years of decline, world copper prices are rising and Zambia's output has increased. New agricultural exports have boomed: notably flowers.

◆ **INSIGHT:** *Spray from Musi-o-Tunya (Victoria Falls) can be seen up to 20 miles away*

■	1000m/3281ft
■	500m/1640ft
■	200m/656ft

L. Tanganyika
TANZANIA
L. Mweru
DEM. REP.
CONGO
Kasama
Mansa
MALAWI
ANGOLA
Chingola
Mufulira
Ndola
Kitwe
Luanshya
Chipata
Kabwe
Mongu
LUSAKA
MOZAMBIQUE
Kafue
Monze
Lake
Kariba
Choma
Zambezi
NAMIBIA
Livingstone
ZIMBABWE
Victoria
BOTSWANA
Falls

0   200 km
0   200 miles

 FACTFILE

OFFICIAL NAME: Republic of Zambia
DATE OF FORMATION: 1964
CAPITAL: Lusaka
POPULATION: 11.7 million
TOTAL AREA: 290,584 sq. miles (752,614 sq. km)
DENSITY: 41 people per sq. mile

LANGUAGES: Bemba, Tonga, Nyanja, Lozi, Lala-bisa, Nsenga, English*
RELIGIONS: Christian 63%, traditional beliefs 36%, Muslim and Hindu 1%
ETHNIC MIX: Bemba 34%, other 27%, Tonga 16%, Nyanja 14%, Lozi 9 %
GOVERNMENT: Presidential system
CURRENCY: Zamb. kwacha = 100 ngwee

Zimbabwe

Situated in southern Africa, Zimbabwe achieved independence from the UK in 1980. President Robert Mugabe, in power since then, has become increasingly authoritarian.

 GEOGRAPHY
High plateaus in center bordered by Zambezi River in the north and Limpopo in the south. Rivers crisscross central area.

 CLIMATE
Tropical, though moderated by the high altitude. Wet season November–March. Drought is common in the eastern highlands.

PEOPLE & SOCIETY
There are two main ethnic groups, Shona in the north and east, and Ndebele in the south. Shona outnumber Ndebele by four to one. Whites are generally far more affluent than blacks. Government efforts to redress this imbalance have become increasingly more aggressive. Economic mismanagement and international isolation has destroyed the economy and prices have rocketed.

THE ECONOMY
The broad-based economy is undermined by drought, budget deficits, unemployment, and massive inflation. Food is increasingly scarce.

 INSIGHT: *The city of Great Zimbabwe, after which the country is named, was built in the 8th century, near Masvingo*

 FACTFILE

OFFICIAL NAME: Republic of Zimbabwe
DATE OF FORMATION: 1980
CAPITAL: Harare
POPULATION: 13 million
TOTAL AREA: 150,803 sq. miles (390,580 sq. km)
DENSITY: 87 people per sq. mile

LANGUAGES: Shona, isiNdebele, English*
RELIGIONS: Syncretic Christian/ traditional beliefs 50%, Christian 25%, traditional beliefs 24%, other 1%
ETHNIC MIX: Shona 71%, Ndebele 16%, other African 11%, White 1%, Asian 1%
GOVERNMENT: Presidential system
CURRENCY: Zimbabwe $ = 100 cents

Overseas territories

Despite the rapid process of global decolonization since World War II, around eight million people in more than 50 territories around the world continue to live under the protection of France, Australia, Denmark, the Netherlands, Norway, New Zealand, the UK, or the USA. These remnants of former colonial empires may have persisted for economic, strategic, or political reasons and are administered by the protecting country in a variety of ways.

AUSTRALIA

Australia's overseas territories have not been an issue since Papua New Guinea became independent in 1975. Consequently there is no overriding policy toward them.
Norfolk Island is inhabited by descendants of the HMS *Bounty* mutineers and more recent Australian migrants. Phosphate is mined on Christmas Island.

ASHMORE & CARTIER IS. *Ref: 124 A3*

STATUS: External territory
CLAIMED: 1931
CAPITAL: Not applicable
POPULATION: None
AREA: 2 sq miles (5.2 sq km)

CHRISTMAS ISLAND *Ref: 123 E5*

STATUS: External territory
CLAIMED: 1958
CAPITAL: The Settlement
POPULATION: 1493
AREA: 52 sq miles (135 sq km)

COCOS ISLANDS *Ref: 123 D5*

STATUS: External territory
CLAIMED: 1955
CAPITAL: Not applicable
POPULATION: 574
AREA: 5.5 sq miles (14 sq km)

CORAL SEA ISLANDS *Ref: 126 B4*

STATUS: External territory
CLAIMED: 1969
CAPITAL: Not applicable
POPULATION: 8 (Meteorologists)
AREA: 1.2 sq miles (3 sq km)

HEARD & MCDONALD IS. *Ref: 123 C7*

STATUS: External territory
CLAIMED: 1947
CAPITAL: Not applicable
POPULATION: None
AREA: 161 sq miles (417 sq km)

NORFOLK ISLAND *Ref: 124 D4*

STATUS: External territory
CLAIMED: 1774
CAPITAL: Kingston
POPULATION: 1828
AREA: 13 sq miles (34 sq km)

DENMARK

The Faeroe Islands have been under Danish administration since Queen Margreth I of Denmark inherited Norway in 1380. The Home Rule Act of 1948 gave the Faeroese control over all their internal affairs. Greenland first came under Danish rule in 1380. Denmark remains responsible for the island's foreign affairs.

FAEROE ISLANDS *Ref: 65 F5*

STATUS: External territory
CLAIMED: 1380
CAPITAL: Tórshavn
POPULATION: 47,246
AREA: 540 sq miles (1399 sq km)

GREENLAND *Ref: 64 D3*

STATUS: External territory
CLAIMED: 1380
CAPITAL: Nuuk
POPULATION: 56,361
AREA: 840,000 sq miles (2,175,500 sq km)

FRANCE

France has developed economic
ties with its *Territoires d'Outre–Mer*,
thereby stressing interdependence
over independence. Overseas
départements, officially part of
France, have their own governments.
Territorial *collectivités* and overseas
territoires have varying degrees
of autonomy.

CLIPPERTON ISLAND *Ref: 135 F3*

STATUS: Dependency of
French Polynesia
CLAIMED: 1935
CAPITAL: Not applicable
POPULATION: None
AREA: 2.7 sq miles (7 sq km)

FRENCH GUIANA *Ref: 41 H3*

STATUS: Overseas department
CLAIMED: 1817
CAPITAL: Cayenne
POPULATION: 199,509
AREA: 35,135 sq miles
(91,000 sq km)

FRENCH POLYNESIA *Ref: 127 H4*

STATUS: Overseas country
CLAIMED: 1843
CAPITAL: Papeete
POPULATION: 260,000
AREA: 1608 sq miles (4165 sq km)

GUADELOUPE *Ref: 37 G4*

STATUS: Overseas department
CLAIMED: 1635
CAPITAL: Basse-Terre
POPULATION: 452,000
AREA: 687 sq miles (1780 sq km)

MARTINIQUE *Ref: 37 G4*

STATUS: Overseas department
CLAIMED: 1635
CAPITAL: Fort-de-France
POPULATION: 397,000
AREA: 425 sq miles (1100 sq km)

MAYOTTE *Ref: 61 G2*

STATUS: Territorial collectivity
CLAIMED: 1843
CAPITAL: Mamoudzou
POPULATION: 201,234
AREA: 144 sq miles (374 sq km)

NEW CALEDONIA *Ref: 126 D5*

STATUS: Overseas territory
CLAIMED: 1853
CAPITAL: Nouméa
POPULATION: 241,000
AREA: 7347 sq miles (19,100 sq km)

RÉUNION *Ref: 61 H4*

STATUS: Overseas department
CLAIMED: 1638
CAPITAL: Saint-Denis
POPULATION: 796,000
AREA: 970 sq miles (2500 sq km)

Overseas territories

ST PIERRE & MIQUELON
Ref: 21 G4
STATUS: Territorial collectivity
CLAIMED: 1604
CAPITAL: Saint-Pierre
POPULATION: 7026
AREA: 93 sq miles (242 sq km)

WALLIS & FUTUNA
Ref: 127 E4
STATUS: Overseas territory
CLAIMED: 1842
CAPITAL: Matā'Utu
POPULATION: 16,025
AREA: 106 sq miles (274 sq km)

NETHERLANDS

The country's two remaining
territories were formerly part
of the Dutch West Indies. Both
are now self-governing, but the
Netherlands remains responsible
for their defense.

ARUBA *Ref: 37 E5*

STATUS: Autonomous part
of the Netherlands
CLAIMED: 1634
CAPITAL: Oranjestad
POPULATION: 71,891
AREA: 75 sq miles (194 sq km)

NETHERLANDS ANTILLES *Ref: 37 E5*

STATUS: Autonomous part
of the Netherlands
CLAIMED: 1816
CAPITAL: Willemstad
POPULATION: 184,000
AREA: 371 sq miles (960 sq km)

NEW ZEALAND

New Zealand's government has
no desire to retain any overseas
territories. However, the
economic weakness of Tokelau, Niue, and
the Cook Islands has forced it
to remain responsible for their
foreign policy and defense.

COOK ISLANDS *Ref: 127 G4*

STATUS: Associated
territory
CLAIMED: 1901
CAPITAL: Avarua
POPULATION: 21,388
AREA: 91 sq miles (235 sq km)

NIUE *Ref: 127 F5*

STATUS: Associated
territory
CLAIMED: 1901
CAPITAL: Alofi
POPULATION: 2166
AREA: 102 sq miles (264 sq km)

TOKELAU *Ref: 127 F3*
STATUS: Dependent territory
CLAIMED: 1926
CAPITAL: Not applicable
POPULATION: 1392
AREA: 4 sq miles (10 sq km)

NORWAY

In 1920, 41 nations signed the
Spits-bergen treaty recognizing
Norwegian sovereignty over
Svalbard. There is a NATO base
on Jan Mayen. Bouvet Island
is a nature reserve.

BOUVET ISLAND *Ref: 49 D7*
STATUS: Dependency
CLAIMED: 1928
CAPITAL: Not applicable
POPULATION: None
AREA: 22 sq miles (58 sq km)

JAN MAYEN *Ref: 65 F3*
STATUS: Dependency
CLAIMED: 1929
CAPITAL: Not applicable
POPULATION: None
AREA: 147 sq miles (381 sq km)

PETER I. ISLAND *Ref: 136 A3*
STATUS: Dependency
CLAIMED: 1931
CAPITAL: Not applicable
POPULATION: None
AREA: 69 sq miles (180 sq km)

SVALBARD *Ref: 65 F2*
STATUS: Dependency CLAIMED: 1920
CAPITAL: Longyearbyen
POPULATION: 2701
AREA: 24,289 sq miles (62,906 sq km)

UNITED KINGDOM

The UK has the largest number of overseas territories. These are locally governed by a mixture of elected representatives and appointed officials.

ANGUILLA *Ref: 37 G3*

STATUS: Dependent territory
CLAIMED: 1650
CAPITAL: The Valley
POPULATION: 13,477
AREA: 37 sq miles (96 sq km)

ASCENSION ISLAND *Ref: 49 C5*
STATUS: Dependency of St Helena
CLAIMED: 1673
CAPITAL: Georgetown
POPULATION: 1177
AREA: 34 sq miles (88 sq km)

BERMUDA *Ref: 17 E6*

STATUS: Crown colony
CLAIMED: 1612
CAPITAL: Hamilton
POPULATION: 65,773
AREA: 20 sq miles (53 sq km)

BRITISH INDIAN OCEAN TERRITORY *Ref: 122 C4*

STATUS: Dependent territory
CLAIMED: 1814
CAPITAL: Diego Garcia
POPULATION: 4000
AREA: 23 sq miles (60 sq km)

BRITISH VIRGIN IS. *Ref: 37 F3*

STATUS: Dependent territory
CLAIMED: 1672
CAPITAL: Road Town
POPULATION: 23,098
AREA: 59 sq miles (153 sq km)

CAYMAN ISLANDS *Ref: 36 B3*

STATUS: Dependent territory
CLAIMED: 1670
CAPITAL: George Town
POPULATION: 45,436
AREA: 100 sq miles (259 sq km)

FALKLAND ISLANDS *Ref: 47 D7*

STATUS: Dependent territory
CLAIMED: 1832
CAPITAL: Stanley
POPULATION: 2967
AREA: 4699 sq miles (12,173 sq km)

Overseas territories

GIBRALTAR *Ref: 74 D5*

STATUS: Crown colony
CLAIMED: 1713
CAPITAL: Gibraltar
POPULATION: 27,928
AREA: 2.5 sq miles (6.5 sq km)

GUERNSEY *Ref: 71 D8*

STATUS: Crown dependency
CLAIMED: 1066
CAPITAL: St. Peter Port
POPULATION: 65,409
AREA: 25 sq miles (65 sq km)

ISLE OF MAN *Ref: 71 C5*

STATUS: Crown dependency
CLAIMED: 1765
CAPITAL: Douglas
POPULATION: 75,441
AREA: 221 sq miles (572 sq km)

JERSEY *Ref: 71 D8*

STATUS: Crown dependency
CLAIMED: 1066
CAPITAL: St. Helier
POPULATION: 91,084
AREA: 45 sq miles (116 sq km)

MONTSERRAT *Ref: 37 G4*

STATUS: Dependent
territory
CLAIMED: 1632
CAPITAL: Plymouth (uninhabitable)
POPULATION: 9439
AREA: 40 sq miles (102 sq km)

PITCAIRN ISLANDS *Ref: 125 G4*

STATUS: Dependent
territory
CLAIMED: 1887
CAPITAL: Adamstown POPULATION: 45
AREA: 18 sq miles (47 sq km)

ST HELENA *Ref: 49 D5*

STATUS: Dependent territory
CLAIMED: 1673
CAPITAL: Jamestown
POPULATION: 4299
AREA: 47 sq miles (122 sq km)

SOUTH GEORGIA & THE SANDWICH ISLANDS *Ref: 49 C7*

STATUS: Dependent territory
CLAIMED: 1775 CAPITAL: Not applicable
POPULATION: None
AREA: 1387 sq miles (3592 sq km)

TRISTAN DA CUNHA *Ref: 49 D6*

STATUS: Dependency of St. Helena
CLAIMED: 1612 CAPITAL: Edinburgh
POPULATION: 276
AREA: 38 sq miles (98 sq km)

TURKS & CAICOS ISLANDS *Ref: 37 E2*

STATUS: Dependent territory
CLAIMED: 1766
CAPITAL: Cockburn Town
POPULATION: 21,152
AREA: 166 sq miles (430 sq km)

UNITED STATES

US Commonwealth territories
are self-governing incorporated
territories that are an integral part
of the US. Unincorporated territories
have varying degrees of autonomy.

AMERICAN SAMOA *Ref: 127 F4*

STATUS: Unincorporated
territory
CLAIMED: 1900
CAPITAL: Pago Pago
POPULATION: 57,794
AREA: 75 sq miles (195 sq km)

BAKER & HOWLAND ISLANDS
Ref: 127 E2
STATUS: Unincorporated territory
CAPITAL: Not applicable
CLAIMED: 1856 POPULATION: None
AREA: 0.5 sq miles (1.4 sq km)

GUAM *Ref: 126 B1*

STATUS: Unincorporated territory
CLAIMED: 1898
CAPITAL: Hagåtña
POPULATION: 172,000
AREA: 212 sq miles (549 sq km)

JARVIS ISLAND *Ref: 127 G2*
STATUS: Unincorporated territory
CLAIMED: 1856
CAPITAL: Not applicable
POPULATION: None
AREA: 1.7 sq miles (4.5 sq km)

JOHNSTON ATOLL *Ref: 125 E1*
STATUS: Unincorporated territory
CLAIMED: 1858
CAPITAL: Not applicable
POPULATION: None
AREA: 1 sq miles (2.8 sq km)

KINGMAN REEF *Ref: 127 F2*
STATUS: Administered territory
CLAIMED: 1856
CAPITAL: Not applicable
POPULATION: None
AREA: 0.4 sq miles (1 sq km)

MIDWAY ISLANDS *Ref: 134 D2*
STATUS: Administered territory
CLAIMED: 1867
CAPITAL: Not applicable
POPULATION: None
AREA: 2 sq miles (5.2 sq km)

NAVASSA ISLAND *Ref: 36 D3*
STATUS: Unincorporated territory
CLAIMED: 1856 CAPITAL: Not applicable
POPULATION: None
AREA: 2 sq miles (5.2 sq km)

NORTHERN MARIANA ISLANDS
Ref: 124 C1

STATUS: Commonwealth territory
CLAIMED: 1947
CAPITAL: Saipan POPULATION: 82,459
AREA: 177 sq miles (457 sq km)

PALMYRA ATOLL *Ref: 127 G2*
STATUS: Unincorporated territory
CLAIMED: 1898 CAPITAL: Not applicable
POPULATION: None
AREA: 5 sq miles (12 sq km)

PUERTO RICO *Ref: 37 F3*

STATUS: Commonwealth territory
CLAIMED: 1898
CAPITAL: San Juan
POPULATION: 4 million
AREA: 3515 sq miles (9104 sq km)

VIRGIN ISLANDS *Ref: 37 F3*

STATUS: Unincorporated territory
CLAIMED: 1917
CAPITAL: Charlotte Amalie
POPULATION: 108,605
AREA: 137 sq miles (355 sq km)

WAKE ISLAND *Ref: 124 D1*
STATUS: Unincorporated territory
CLAIMED: 1898
CAPITAL: Not applicable
POPULATION: 200
AREA: 2.5 sq miles (6.5 sq km)

International organizations

This listing provides acronym definitions for the main international organizations concerned with worldwide economics, trade, and defense, plus an indication of membership.

ASEAN

Association of Southeast Asian Nations
ESTABLISHED: 1967
MEMBERS: Brunei, Cambodia, Indonesia, Laos, Malaysia, Myanmar, Philippines, Singapore, Thailand, Vietnam

CIS

Commonwealth of Independent States
ESTABLISHED: 1991
MEMBERS: Arm., Az., Belarus, Georgia, Kaz., Kyrgy., Mold., Russia, Tajik., Ukraine, Uzbek.

COMM

The Commonwealth
ESTABLISHED: 1931; evolved out of the British Empire. Formerly known as the British Commonwealth of Nations.
MEMBERS: 53

EU

European Union
ESTABLISHED: 1965; formerly known as EEC (European Economic Community) and EC (Economic Community)
MEMBERS: Austria, Belg., Cyprus, Czech Rep., Denmark, Est., Fin., Fr., Ger., Greece, Hung., Ireland, Italy, Lat., Lith., Lux., Malta, Neth., Pol., Port., Slvka., Slvna., Spain, Swed., UK

G8

Group of 8
ESTABLISHED: 1994
MEMBERS: Canada, France, Germany, Italy, Japan, Russia, UK, US

IMF

International Monetary Fund
(UN agency)
ESTABLISHED: 1945 MEMBERS: 184

NAFTA

North American Free Trade Agreement
ESTABLISHED: 1994
MEMBERS: Canada, Mexico, US

NATO

North Atlantic Treaty Organization
ESTABLISHED: 1949 MEMBERS: Belg., Bulg., Canada, Czech Rep., Denmark, Est., France, Ger., Greece, Hung., Iceland, Italy, Lat., Lith., Lux., Neth., Norway, Poland, Port., Rom., Slovakia, Slovenia, Spain, Turkey, UK, US

OPEC

Organization of Petroleum Exporting Countries
ESTABLISHED: 1960
MEMBERS: Algeria, Indonesia, Iran, Iraq, Kuwait, Libya, Nigeria, Qatar, Saudi Arabia, United Arab Emirates, Venezuela

UN

United Nations
ESTABLISHED: 1945 MEMBERS: 192; all nations are represented, except Taiwan. The Vatican City has "observer status" only.

WTO

World Trade Organization
ESTABLISHED: 1995
MEMBERS: 146

Abbreviations

This glossary provides a comprehensive guide to the abbreviations used in this atlas.

abbrev. abbreviation
Afgh. Afghanistan
Amh. Amharic
anc. ancient
Ar. Arabic
Arm. Armenia / Armenian
Aus. Austria
Aust. Australia
Az. Azerbaijan

Bas. Basque
Bel. Belorussian
Belg. Belgium / Belgian
Bos. & Herz. Bosnia & Herzegovina
Bul. Bulgarian
Bulg. Bulgaria
Bur. Burmese

C Central
C. Cape
Cam. Cambodian
Cast. Castilian
Chin. Chinese
Cord. Cordillera (Sp. mts.)
Cz. Czech
Czech Rep. Czech Republic

D.C. District of Columbia
Dan. Danish
Dominican Rep. Dominican Republic

E East
Emb. Embalse
Eng. English
Eq. Guinea Equatorial Guinea
Est. Estonia / Estonian

Faer. Faeroese
Fin. Finland / Finnish
Flem. Flemish
Fr. France / French

Geo. Georgia
Geor. Georgian
Ger. Germany / German
Gk. Greek

Heb. Hebrew
Hung. Hungary / Hungarian

I. Island
Ind. Indonesia, Indonesian
Is. Islands
It. Italian

Kaz. Kazakhstan / Kazakh
Kep. Kepulauan (Ind. island group)
Kir. Kirghiz
Kor. Korean
Kurd. Kurdish
Kyrgy. Kyrgyzstan

L. Lake, Lago
Lat. Latvia
Latv. Latvian
Leb. Lebanon
Liech. Liechtenstein
Lith. Lithuania / Lithuanian
Lux. Luxembourg

m meters
Mac. Macedonia
Med. Sea Mediterranean Sea
Mon. Montenegro
Mold. Moldova
Mt. Mount / Mountain
Mts. Mountains

N North
N. Korea North Korea
Neth. Netherlands
NW Northwest
NZ New Zealand

P. Pulau (Ind. island)
Peg. Pegunungan (Ind. mountain range)
Per. Persian
Pol. Poland / Polish

Port. Portugal, Portuguese
prev. previously
R. River, Rio, Río
Res. Reservoir
Rom. Romania / Romanian
Rus. Russian
Russ. Fed. Russian Federation

S South
S. Korea South Korea
SA South Africa
SCr. Serbian and Croatian
Serb. Serbia
Slvka. Slovakia
Slvna. Slovenia
Som. Somali
Sp. Spanish
St, St. Saint
Str. Strait
Swed. Swedish
Switz. Switzerland
Tajik. Tajikistan
Th. Thai
Turk. Turkish
Turkm. Turkmen
Turkmen. Turkmenistan

U.A.E. United Arab Emirates
UK United Kingdom
Ukr. Ukrainian
Urug. Uruguayan
US United States of America
Uzb. Uzbek
Uzbek. Uzbekistan

var. variant
Vdkhr. Vodokhranilishche (Rus. reservoir)
Vdskh. Vodoskhovyshche (Ukr. reservoir)
Ven. Venezuela

W West
W. Sahara Western Sahara
Wel. Welsh

Yugo. Yugoslavia

Zamb. Zambian

Al Başrah Iraq *var.* Basra 102 C4

Al Baydā' Libya 53 G2

Albert, Lake *lake* Uganda/Dem. Rep. Congo 59 E5

Alberta *province* Canada 19 E4

Albi France 73 C6

Albuquerque New Mexico, USA 28 D2

Alcácer do Sal Portugal 74 C4

Aldabra Group *island group* Seychelles 61 G2

Aleg Mauritania 56 C3

Aleksandriya *see* Oleksandriya

Aleksandropol' *see* Gyumri

Aleksinac Serbia 82 E4

Alençon France 72 B3

Alessandria Italy 78 B2

Ålesund Norway 67 A5

Aleutian Basin *undersea feature* Bering Sea 134 D1

Aleutian Islands *islands* Alaska, USA 18 A3

Aleutian Trench *undersea feature* Pacific Ocean 134 D1

Alexander Island *island* Antarctica 136 A3

Alexandra New Zealand 133 B7

Alexandretta *see* İskenderun

Alexandria Egypt 54 B1

Alexandria Louisiana, USA 30 B3

Alexandroúpoli Greece 86 D3

Al Fāshir *see* El Fasher

Alföld *see* Great Hungarian Plain

Algarve *region* Portugal 74 C4

Algeciras Spain 74 D5

Algeria *country* N Africa 52-53

Alghero Italy 79 A5

Algiers *capital of* Algeria 52 D1

Al Ḥasakah Syria 100 D2

Al Ḥudaydah Yemen 103 B7

Al Ḥufūf Saudi Arabia 103 C5

Alicante Spain *Cat.* Alacant 75 F4

Alice Springs Australia 130 A4

Al Jawf Saudi Arabia 102 B4

Al Jazirah *region* Iraq/Syria 100 E2

Al Jizah *see* El Giza

Al Karak Jordan 101 B6

Al Khalīl *see* Hebron

Al Khārijah *see* El Khârga

Al Khums Libya 53 F2

Al Khurţūm *see* Khartoum

Alkmaar Netherlands 68 C2

Al Kufrah Libya 53 H4

Al Lādhiqīyah Syria *Eng.* Latakia 100 B3

Allahābād India 117 E4

Allenstein *see* Olsztyn

Allentown Pennsylvania, USA 23 F4

Alma-Ata *capital of* Kazakhstan *Rus./Kaz.* Almaty 96 C5

Al Madīnah Saudi Arabia *Eng.* Medina 102 A5

Al Mafraq Jordan 101 B5

Almalyk Uzbekistan *Uzb.* Olmaliq 105 E2

Al Manāmah *see* Manama

Al Marj Libya 53 G2

Almaty *see* Alma-Ata

Al Mawşil Iraq *Eng.* Mosul 102 B3

Almelo Netherlands 68 E3

Almería Spain 75 E5

Al Mukallā Yemen 103 C7

Alofi *capital of* Niue 127 F5

Alor, Kepulauan *island group* Indonesia 121 E5

Alps *mountain range* C Europe 62 D4

Al Qāhirah *see* Cairo

Al Qāmishlī Syria *var.* Kamishli 100 E1

Al Qunayţirah Syria 100 B4

Altai Mountains *mountain range* C Asia 108 C2

Altamura Italy 79 E5

Altar, Desierto de *Desert* Mexico/USA *var.* Sonoran Desert 32 A1

Altay China 108 D2

Altay Mongolia 108 D2

Altun Shan *mountain range* China 108 C3

Alturas California, USA 26 B4

Alytus Lithuania *Pol.* Olita 89 B5

Amadeus, Lake *seasonal lake* Australia 129 E5

Amakusa-nada *island group* Japan 113 A6

Amami-Ō-shima *island* Japan 113 A8

Amarillo Texas, USA 29 E2

Amazon *river* South America 38 C3

Amazon Basin *region* C South America 42 D2

Ambanja Madagascar 61 G2

Ambarchik Russian Federation 97 G2

Ambato Ecuador 40 A4

Amboasary Madagascar 61 F4

Ambon Indonesia 121 F4

Ambositra Madagascar 61 G3

Ambriz Angola 60 B1

Amdo China 108 C4

Ameland *island* Netherlands 68 D1

American Falls Reservoir *Reservoir* Idaho, USA 26 E4

American Samoa *external territory* USA, Pacific Ocean 127 F4

Amersfoort Netherlands 68 D3

Amga *river* Russian Federation 95 F2

Amindivi Islands *island group* India 114 C2

Amirante Islands *island group* Seychelles 61 H1

Amman *capital of* Jordan 101 B5

Ammassalik Greenland *var.* Angmagssalik 64 D4

Ammochostos *see* Gazimağusa

Āmol Iran 102 C3

Amorgós *island* Greece 87 D6

Amritsar India 116 D2

Amsterdam *capital of* Netherlands 68 C3

Amsterdam Island *island* French Southern and Antarctic Territories 123 C6

Am Timan Chad 58 C3

Amu Darya *river* C Asia 104 D3

Amundsen Gulf *sea feature* Canada 19 E2

Amundsen Plain *undersea feature* Pacific Ocean 136 B4

Amundsen Sea Antarctica 97 C4

Amur *river* E Asia 97 G4 107 E1

Anabar *river* Russian Federation 95 E2

Anadolu Dağları *see* Doğu Karadeniz Dağlarıı

Anadyr' Russian Federation 97 H1

Anápolis Brazil 43 F4

Anatolia *region* SE Europe 85 G3

Anchorage Alaska, USA 18 C3

Ancona Italy 78 C3

Andalucía *region* Spain 74 D4

Andaman Islands *island group* India 115 H2 119 A5

Andaman Sea Indian Ocean 122 D3

Andes *mountain range* South America 39 B6

Andijon Uzbekistan *Rus.* Andizhan 105 F2

Andizhan *see* Andijon

Andorra *country* SW Europe 73 B6

Andorra la Vella *capital of* Andorra 73 B6

Ándros *island* Greece 87 D5

Andros Island *island* Bahamas 36 C1

Angara *river* C Asia 95 D3

Ángel de la Guarda, Isla *island* Mexico 32 B2

Angel Falls *see* Salto Ángel

Angeles Philippines 121 E1

Ángel, Salto *waterfall* Venezuela *Eng.* Angel Falls 41 F2

Ångermanälven *river* Sweden 66 C4

Angers France 72 B4

Anglesey *island* Wales, UK 71 C5

Angmagssalik *see* Ammassalik

Angola *country* C Africa 60

Angola Basin *undersea feature* Atlantic Ocean 49 D6

Angora *see* Ankara

Angoulême France 73 B5

Angren Uzbekistan 105 E2

Anguilla *external territory* UK, West Indies 37

Anhui *province* China *var.* Anhwei, Wan 111 C5

Anhwei *see* Anhui

Anjouan *island* Comoros 61 F2

Ankara *capital of* Turkey *prev.* Angora 98 C3

Annaba Algeria 53 E1

An Nafūd *desert region* Saudi Arabia 102 B4

An Najaf Iraq *var.* Najaf 102 B4

Annapolis Maryland, USA 23 F4

Ann Arbor Michigan, USA 22 C3

Annecy France 73 D5

Anshan China 110 D4

Ansongo Mali 57 E3

Antakya Turkey *var.* Hatay 98 D4

Antalaha Madagascar 61 G2

Antalya Turkey *prev.* Adalia 98 B4

Antalya, Gulf of *see* Antalya Körfezi

Antalya Körfezi *sea feature* Mediterranean Sea *Eng.* Gulf of Antalya, *var.* Gulf of Adalia 98 B4

Antananarivo *capital of* Madagascar *prev.* Tananarive 61 G3

Antarctica 136

Antarctic Peninsula *peninsula* Antarctica 136 A2

Antequera Spain 74 D5

Anticosti, Île d' *island* Canada 21 F3

Antigua *island* Antigua & Barbuda 37 G3

Antigua & Barbuda *country* West Indies 37

Anti-Lebanon *mountains* Lebanon/Syria 100 B3

Antipodes Islands *island group* New Zealand124 D5

Antofagasta Chile 46 B2

Antsirañana Madagascar 61 G2

Antsohihy Madagascar 61 G2

Antwerp *see* Antwerpen

Antwerpen Belgium *Eng.* Antwerp 69 C5

Anyang China 110 C4

Aoga-shima *island* Japan 113 D6

Aomori Japan 112 D3

Aoraki *peak* New Zealand *var.* Cook, Mount 133 B6

Aosta Italy 78 A2

Aoukâr *Plateau* Mauritania 56 D3

Apeldoorn Netherlands 68 D3

Apennines *see* Appennino

Apia *capital of* Samoa 127 F4

Appalachian Mountains *mountain range* E USA 17 D5

Appennino *mountain range* Italy *Eng.* Apennines 78 C4

Apure *river* Venezuela 40 D2

Aqaba *see* Al 'Aqabah

Aqaba, Gulf of *sea feature* Red Sea *Ar.* Khalīj al 'Aqabah 101 A8

'Aqabah, Khalīj al *see* Aqaba, Gulf of

Āqchah Afghanistan *var.* Āqcheh 104 D3

Āqcheh *see* Āqchah

Arabian Basin *undersea feature* Indian Ocean 122 B3

Arabian Peninsula *peninsula* Asia 85 H5 94 B5 103 C5

Arabian Sea Indian Ocean 122 B3

Aracaju Brazil 43 H3

Arad Romania 90 B4

Arafura Sea Asia/Australasia 126 A4

Araguaia *river* Brazil 43 F3

Arāk Iran 102 C3

Araks see Aras

Arak's see Aras

Aral Sea inland sea Kazakhstan/Uzbekistan 94 C3

Araouane Mali 57 E2

Ararat, Mount peak Turkey var. Great Ararat, Turk. Büyükağrı Dağı 94 F3

Aras river SW Asia Arm. Arak's, Per. Rūd-e Aras, Rus. Araks, Turk. Aras Nehri 99 G3

Aras Nehri see Aras

Arauca Colombia 40 C2

Arauca river Colombia/Venezuela 40 C2

Arbil Iraq Kurd. Hawlēr 102 B3

Arctic Ocean 18-19 137

Arda river Bulgaria/Greece 86 C3

Ardabīl Iran 102 C3

Ardennes region W Europe 69 D7

Arendal Norway 67 A6

Arensburg see Kuressaare

Arequipa Peru 42 B4

Arezzo Italy 78 C3

Argentina country S South America 46-47

Argentine Basin undersea feature Atlantic Ocean 49 B7

Argun river China/Russian Federation 95 E3

Århus Denmark 67 A7

Arica Chile 46 B1

Arizona state USA 28 B2

Arkansas state USA 30 B1

Arkansas river C USA 17 C5

Arkhangel'sk Russian Federation 92 C3 96 C2

Arles France 73 D6

Arlington Texas, USA 29 G3

Arlington Virginia, USA 23 E4

Arlon Belgium 69 D8

Armenia country SW Asia 99 G2

Armenia Colombia 40 B3

Armidale Australia 131 D5

Arnhem Netherlands 68 D4

Arnhem Land region Australia 128 E2

Arno river Italy 78 B3

Arran island Scotland, UK 70 C4

Ar Raqqah Syria 100 C2

Arras France 72 C3

Ar Riyāḍ see Riyadh

Ar Rub 'al Khālī desert Asia Eng. Empty Quarter, Great Sandy Desert 103 C6

Ar Rustāq Oman var. Rostak 103 D5

Artesia New Mexico, USA 28 D3

Artigas Uruguay 44 B4

Aru, Kepulauan island group Indonesia 121 G5

Arua Uganda 55 B6

Aruba external territory Netherlands, West Indies 37 E5

Arusha Tanzania 55 C7

Asad, Buḥayrat al Lake Syria Eng. Lake Assad 100 C2

Asadābād Afghanistan 105 E4

Asahikawa Japan 112 D2

Asamankese Ghana 57 E5

Ascension island Atlantic Ocean 49 C5

Ascoli Piceno Italy 78 C4

Aseb Eritrea var. Assab 54 D4

Ashburton New Zealand 133 C6

Asheville North Carolina, USA 31 E1

Aşgabat capital of Turkmenistan prev. Ashkhabad, Poltoratsk 104 C3

Ashkhabad see Aşgabat

Ashmore and Cartier Islands Australian external territory Indian Ocean 124 A3

Ash Shāriqah see Sharjah

Asia 94-95 106-107

Asmara capital of Eritrea Amh. Asmera 54 C4

Asmera see Asmara

Assab see Aseb

As Salt Jordan var. Salt 101 B5

Assamakka Niger 57 F2

Assen Netherlands 68 E2

Assad, Lake see Asad, Buḥayrat al

As Sulayyil Saudi Arabia 103 B6

As Suwaydā' Syria 101 B5

Astana country capital Kazakhstan prev. Akmola, Akmolinsk, Tselinograd, Kaz. Aqmola. 96 C4

Astoria Oregon, USA 26 A2

Astrakhan' Russian Federation 93 B7

Astypálaia island Greece 87 D6

Asunción capital of Paraguay 44 B3

Aswân Egypt 54 B2

Asyût Egypt 54 B2

Atacama Desert desert Chile 46 B2

Atamyrat prev. Kerki. Turkmenistan 104 D3

Aţâr Mauritania 56 C2

Atbara Sudan 54 C3

Athabasca, Lake lake Canada 19 F4

Athens capital of Greece Gk. Athína, prev. Athínai 87 C5

Athens Georgia, USA 31 E2

Athina see Athens

Athínai see Athens

Athlone Ireland 71 B5

Ati Chad 58 C3

Atlanta Georgia, USA 30 D2

Atlantic City New Jersey, USA 23 F4

Atlantic Ocean 48-49

Atlantic-Indian Basin undersea feature Indian Ocean 136 B1

Atlantic-Indian Ridge undersea feature Atlantic Ocean 49 D7

Atlas Mountains mountain range Morocco 52 C2

Aţ Ţafīlah Jordan 101 B6

Aţ Ţā'if Saudi Arabia 102 B6

Attapu Laos 119 E5

Attawapiskat Canada 20 C3

Attawapiskat *river* Canada 20 B3

Attu Island *island* Alaska, USA 18 A2

Auch France 73 B6

Auckland New Zealand 132 D3

Auckland Islands *island group* New Zealand124 D5

Augsburg Germany 77 C6

Augusta Australia 129 B7

Augusta Georgia, USA 31 E2

Augusta Maine, USA 23 G2

Aurillac France 73 C5

Aurora Colorado, USA 24 D4

Aurora Illinois, USA 22 B3

Aussig *see* Ústí nad Labem

Austin Texas, USA 29 G4

Australasia 124-125

Australes, Îles *island group* French Polynesia 125 F4

Austral Fracture Zone *tectonic feature* Pacific Ocean 125 H4

Australia *country* Pacific Ocean 124

Australian Alps Australia 131 D7

Australian Capital Territory *territory* Australia *abbrev.* A.C.T. *131* D6

Austria *country* C Europe 77

Auxerre France 72 C4

Avarua *capital of* Cook Islands 127 G5

Aveiro Portugal 74 C2

Avignon France 73 D6

Ávila Spain 74 D2

Avilés Spain 74 D1

Awbārī Libya 53 F3

Axel Heiberg Island *island* Canada 19 F1

Axios *see* Vardar

Ayacucho Peru 42 B4

Aydarko'l Ko'li *lake* Uzbekistan *var.* Aydarkül 104 D2

Aydarkül *see* Aydarko'l Ko'li

Aydın Turkey 98 A3

Ayer's Rock *see* Uluru

Ayr Scotland, UK 70 C4

Ayutthaya Thailand 119 C5

Ayvalık Turkey 98 A3

Azaouâd *desert* Mali 57 E2

A'zāz Syria 100 B2

Azerbaijan *country* SW Asia 99 G2

Azores *islands* Portugal, Atlantic Ocean 48 C3

Azov, Sea of Black Sea *Ukr.* Azovs'ke More, *Rus.* Azovskoye More 93 A6 91 G4

Azovs'ke More *see* Azov, Sea of

Azovskoye More *see* Azov, Sea of

Azul Argentina 46 D4

Azur, Côte d' *coastal region* France 73 E6

Az Zarqā' Jordan 101 B5

Az Zāwiyah Libya 53 F2

B

Baalbek Lebanon *var.* Ba'labakk 100 B4

Babeldaob *Island* Palau 124 B2

Babruysk Belarus *Rus.* Bobruysk 89 D6

Babuyan Channel *channel* Philippines 121 E1

Bacan, Pulau *island* Indonesia 121 F4

Bačka Topola Serbia 82 D3

Bacău Romania 90 C4

Badajoz Spain 74 C4

Baden Switzerland 77 E6

Bādiyat ash Shām *see* Syrian Desert

Baffin Bay *sea feature* Atlantic Ocean 48 B1

Baffin Island *island* Canada 19 G2

Bafing *river* Africa 56 C3

Bafoussam Cameroon 58 B4

Bagdad *see* Baghdad

Bagé Brazil 44 C4

Baghdad *capital of* Iraq *var.* Bagdad, *Ar.* Baghdād 102 B3

Baghdād *see* Baghdad

Baghlān Afghanistan 105 E3

Bagoé *river* Côte d'Ivoire/Mali 56 D4

Baguio Philippines 121 E1

Bahamas *country* West Indies, Atlantic Ocean 36

Baharden *see* Baharly

Baharly Turkmenistan *prev.* Baharden, Bäherden, Bakharden, Bakherden 104 B3

Bahāwalpur Pakistan 116 C3

Bäherden *see* Baharly

Bahia Blanca Argentina 47 C5

Bahía, Islas de la *islands* Honduras 34 D2

Bahir Dar Ethiopia 54 C4

Bahrain *country* SW Asia 103 C5

Baia Mare Romania 90 B3

Baikal, Lake *see* Baykal, Ozero

Bairiki *capital of* Kiribati 127 E2

Baja Hungary 81 C7

Baja California *peninsula* Mexico *Eng.* Lower California 32 B2

Bajo Nuevo *island* Colombia 35 F2

Baker Oregon, USA 26 C3

Baker & Howland Islands *external territory* USA, Pacific Ocean 125 E2

Bakersfield California, USA 27 C7

Bakharden *see* Baharly

Bakherden *see* Baharly

Bākhtarān *see* Kermānshāh

Bakı *see* Baku

Baku *capital of* Azerbaijan *Az.* Bakı, *var.* Baky 99 H2

Baky *see* Baku

Balabac Strait *sea feature* South China Sea/Sulu Sea 120 D2

Ba'labakk *see* Baalbek

Balakovo Russian Federation 93 C6

Bālā Morghāb Afghanistan 104 D4

Balaton *lake* Hungary *var.* Lake Balaton, *Ger.* Plattensee 81 C7

Balaton, Lake *see* Balaton

Balbina, Represa *Reservoir* Brazil 42 D2

Baleares, Islas *island group* Spain *Eng.* Balearic Islands 75 H3

Balearic Islands *see* Baleares, Islas

Bali *island* Indonesia 120 D5

Balıkesir Turkey 98 A3

Balikpapan Indonesia 120 D4

Balkanabat Turkmenistan *prev.* Nebitdag 104 B2

Balkan Mountains *mountain range* Bulgaria *Bul.* Stara Planina 86 C2

Balkhash Kazakhstan 96 C5

Balkhash, Lake *see* Balkhash, Ozero

Balkhash, Ozero *lake* Kazakhstan *Eng.* Lake Balkhash 94 C3

Ballarat Australia 131 C7

Balsas *river* Mexico 33 E5

Bălţi Moldova 90 D3

Baltic Port *see* Paldiski

Baltic Sea Atlantic Ocean 67 C7

Baltimore Maryland, USA 23 F4

Baltischport *see* Paldiski

Baltiski *see* Paldiski

Bamako *capital of* Mali 56 D3

Bambari Central African Republic 58 D4

Bamenda Cameroon 58 B4

Banaba *island* Kiribati *prev.* Ocean Island 127 E2

Bandaaceh Indonesia 120 A3

Banda, Laut *see* Banda Sea

Banda Sea *sea feature* Pacific Ocean *Ind.* Laut Banda 121 F4

Bandar-e ʻAbbās Iran 102 D4

Bandar-e Būshehr Iran 102 C4

Bandar Lampung Indonesia *prev.* Tanjungkarang 120 C4

Bandar Seri Begawan *capital of* Brunei 120 D3

Bandon Oregon, USA 26 A3

Bandundu Dem. Rep. Congo 59 C6

Bandung Indonesia 120 C5

Bangalore India 114 D2

Banggai, Kepulauan *island group* Indonesia 121 E4

Banghāzī Libya *Eng.* Benghazi 53 G2

Bangka, Palau *island* Indonesia 120 C4

Bangkok *capital of* Thailand *Th.* Krung Thep 119 C5

Bangladesh *country* S Asia 117

Bangor Northern Ireland, UK 71 B5

Bangor Maine, USA 23 G2

Bangui *capital of* Central African Republic 59 C5

Bani *river* Mali 56 D3

Banī Suwayf *see* Beni Suef

Banja Luka Bosnia & Herzegovina 82 B3

Banjarmasin Indonesia 120 D4

Banjul *capital of* Gambia 56 B3

Banks Island *island* Canada 19 E2

Banks Islands *island group* Vanuatu, Pacific Ocean 126 D4

Banks Peninsula *peninsula* New Zealand 133 C6

Banks Strait *sea feature* Tasman Sea 131 C7

Banská Bystrica Slovakia *Ger.* Neusohl, *Hung.* Besztercebánya 81 C6

Bantry Bay *sea feature* Ireland 71 A6

Banyo Cameroon 58 B4

Banzare Seamounts *undersea feature* Indian Ocean 123 C7

Baotou China 109 F3

Baranavichy Belarus *Rus.* Baranovichi, *Pol.* Baranowicze 89 C6

Baranovichi *see* Baranavichy

Baranowicze *see* Baranavichy

Barbados *country* West Indies 37 H4

Barbuda *island* Antigua & Barbuda 37 G3

Barcaldine Australia 130 C4

Barcelona Spain 75 G2

Barcelona Venezuela 41 E1

Barcolod City Philippines 121 E2

Bareilly India 117 E3

Barentsburg Svalbard 65 F2

Barentsøya *island* Svalbard 65 G2

Barents Sea Arctic Ocean 137 H5

Bari Italy 79 E5

Barinas Venezuela 40 D2

Barisan, Pegunungan *mountains* Indonesia 120 B4

Barkly Tableland *plateau* Australia 130 B3

Barlavento, Ilhas de *island group* Cape Verde *var.* Windward Islands 56 A2

Bar-le-Duc France 72 D3

Barlee, Lake *lake* Australia 129 B 5

Barlee Range *mountain range* Australia 128 B4

Barnaul Russian Federation 96 D4

Barnstaple England, UK 71 C7

Barquisimeto Venezuela 40 D1

Barra *island* Scotland, UK 70 B3

Barranquilla Colombia 40 B1

Barrier Range *mountain range* Australia 131 C5

Barrow *river* Ireland 71 B6

Barstow California, USA 27 C7

Bartang *river* Tajikistan 105 F3

Bartica Guyana 41 G2

Baruun-Urt Mongolia 109 F2

Barwon River *river* Australia 131 D5

Barysaw Belarus *Rus.* Borisov 89 D5

Basarabeasca Moldova 90 D4

Basel Switzerland 77 B6

Basra *see* Al Başrah

Bassein Myanmar 118 A4

Basse-Terre *capital of* Guadeloupe 37 G4

Basseterre *capital of* St Kitts & Nevis 37 G3

Bass Strait *sea feature* Australia 131 C7

Bastia *Corse,* France 73 E7

Bastogne Belgium 69 D7

Bata Equatorial Guinea 58 A5

Batangas Philippines 121 E2

Bătdâmbâng Cambodia 119 D5

Bath England, UK 71 D6

Bathurst Canada 21 F4

Bathurst Island *island* Australia 128 D2

Bathurst Island *island* Canada 19 F2

Bāţin, Wādī al *dry watercourse* Asia 102 C4

Batman Turkey *var.* Iluh 99 E4

Batna Algeria 53 E1

Baton Rouge Louisiana, USA 30 B3

Batticaloa Sri Lanka 115 E3

Bat'umi Georgia 99 F2

Bauru Brazil 44 D2

Bavarian Alps *mountains* Austria/Germany 77 C6

Bayamo Cuba 36 C2

Bayan Har Shan *mountain range* China 108 D4

Bayanhongor Mongolia 108 D2

Bay City Michigan, USA 22 C3

Baydhabo Somalia 55 D6

Baykal, Ozero *lake* Russian Federation *Eng.* Lake Baikal 95 E3

Bayonne France 73 A6

Bayramaly Turkmenistan 104 C3

Bayrūt *see* Beirut

Beaufort Sea Arctic Ocean 137 F2

Beaufort West South Africa 60 D5

Beaumont Texas, USA 29 H4

Beauvais France 72 C3

Béchar Algeria 52 C2

Be'ér Sheva' Israel 101 A6

Beijing *capital of* China *var.* Peking 110 C4

Beira Mozambique 61 E3

Beirut *capital of* Lebanon *var.* Beyrouth, Bayrūt 100 B4

Beja Portugal 74 C4

Béjaïa Algeria 53 E1

Bek-Budi *see* Karshi

Békéscsaba Hungary 81 D7

Belarus *country* E Europe *var.* Belorusia 89

Belau *see* Palau

Belcher Islands *islands* Canada 20 C2

Belém Brazil 43 F2

Belfast Northern Ireland, UK 71 B5

Belfort France 72 E4

Belgaum India 114 C1

Belgium *country* W Europe 69

Belgorod Russian Federation 93 A5

Belgrade *capital of* Serbia *SCr.* Beograd 82 D3

Belitung, Pulau *island* Indonesia 120 C4

Belize *country* Central America 34

Belize City Belize 34 C1

Belle Île *island* France 72 A4

Belle Isle, Strait of *sea feature* Canada 21 G3

Bellevue Washington, USA 26 B2

Bellingham Washington, USA 26 B1

Bellingshausen Sea Antarctica 136 A3

Bello Colombia 40 B2

Bellville South Africa 60 C5

Belmopan *capital of* Belize 34 C1

Belo Horizonte Brazil 45 F1

Belorussia *see* Belarus

Belostok *see* Białystok

Beloye More Arctic Ocean *Eng.* White Sea 63 F1

Belyy, Ostrov *island* Russian Federation 137 H4

Bend Oregon, USA 26 B3

Bendery *see* Tighina

Bendigo Australia 131 C7

Benevento Italy 79 D5

Bengal, Bay of *sea feature* Indian Ocean 122 D3

Bengbu China 111 D5

Benghazi *see* Banghāzī

Bengkulu Indonesia 120 B4

Benguela Angola 60 B2

Beni *river* Bolivia 42 C4

Benidorm Spain 75 F4

Beni Mellal Morocco 52 C2

Benin *country* N Africa *prev.* Dahomey 57

Benin, Bight of *sea feature* W Africa 57 F5

Benin City Nigeria 57 F5

Beni Suef Egypt *var.* Banī Suwayf 54 B1

Ben Nevis *mountain* Scotland, UK 70 C3

Benue *river* Cameroon/Nigeria 57 G4

Beograd *see* Belgrade

Berat Albania 83 D6

Berbera Somalia 54 D4

Berbérati Central African Republic 58 C5

Berdyans'k Ukraine 91 G4

Bereket Turkmenistan *prev.* Gazandzhyk, *var.* Kazandzhik, *Turkm.* Gazanjyk 104 C3

Berezina *see* Byerazino

Bergamo Italy 78 B2

Bergen Norway 67 A5

Bergse Maas *river* Netherlands 68 D4

Bering Sea Pacific Ocean 134 D1

Bering Strait *sea feature* Bering Sea/Chukchi Sea 134 D1

Berkeley California, USA 27 B6

Berlin *capital of* Germany 76 D3

Bermejo *river* Argentina 46 D2

Bermuda *external territory* UK, Atlantic Ocean 48 B3

Bern *capital of* Switzerland *Fr.* Berne 77 B7

Berne *see* Bern
Berner Alpen *mountain range* Switzerland 77 B7
Bertoua Cameroon 59 B5
Besançon France 72 D4
Besztercebánya *see* Banská Bystrica
Bethlehem West Bank 101 A5
Beyrouth *see* Beirut
Béziers France 73 C6
Bezmein *see* Abadan
Bhamo Myanmar 118 B2
Bhāvnagar India 116 C4
Bhôpal India 116 D4
Bhutan *country* S Asia 117
Biak, Pulau *island* Indonesia 121 G4
Białystok Poland *Rus.* Belostok 80 E3
Biel Switzerland 77 B7
Bielefeld Germany 76 B4
Bielitz-Biala *see* Bielsko-Biała
Bielsko-Biała Poland *Ger.* Bielitz-Biala 81 C5
Bié Plateau *upland* Angola 51 C6
Bighorn Mountains *mountains* C USA 24 C2
Bignona Senegal 56 B3
Big Spring Texas, USA 29 E3
Bihać Bosnia & Herzegovina 82 B3
Bihār *state* India 117 F3
Bijelo Polje Montenegro 82 D4
Bikāner India 116 C3
Bila Tserkva Ukraine 91 E2
Bilbao Spain 75 E1
Billings Montana, USA 24 C2
Bilma, Grand Erg de *desert* Niger 57 G3
Biloela Australia 130 D4
Biloxi Mississippi, USA 30 C3
Biltine Chad 58 D3
Binghamton New York, USA 23 F3
Birāk Libya 53 F3
Birātnagar Nepal 117 F3
Birmingham England, UK 71 D6

Birmingham Alabama, USA 30 D2
Bir Mogreïn Mauritania 56 C1
Birsen *see* Biržai
Biržai Lithuania *Ger.* Birsen 88 C4
Biscay, Bay of *sea feature* Atlantic Ocean 62 C4
Bishkek *capital of* Kyrgyzstan *prev.* Frunze, Pishpek 95 F4
Bishop California, USA 27 C6
Biskra Algeria 53 E2
Bismarck North Dakota, USA 25 E2
Bismarck Archipelago *island group* Papua New Guinea 126 B3
Bismarck Sea *sea* Pacific Ocean 124 B2
Bissau *capital of* Guinea-Bissau 56 B4
Bitola Macedonia 83 E6
Bitterroot Range *mountains* NW USA 26 D2
Biwa-ko *lake* Japan 113 C5
Bizerte Tunisia 53 E1
Bjelovar Croatia 82 B2
Bjørnøya *Island* N Norway *Eng.* Bear Island 65 G3
Black Drin *river* Albania/Macedonia 83 D5
Black Forest *see* Schwarzwald
Black Hills *mountains* C USA 24 D3
Blackpool England, UK 71 D5
Black River *river* China/Vietnam 118 D3
Black Sea Asia/Europe 63 F4
Black Volta *river* Ghana/Côte d'Ivoire 57 E4
Blackwater *river* Ireland 71 A6
Blagoevgrad Bulgaria 86 C3
Blagoveshchensk Russian Federation 97 G4
Blanca, Bahía *sea feature* Argentina 39 D5
Blanche, Lake *lake* Australia 131 B5
Blantyre Malawi 61 E2

Blenheim New Zealand 133 D5
Blida Algeria 52 D1
Bloemfontein South Africa 60 D4
Blois France 72 C4
Bloomington Indiana, USA 22 C4
Bluefields Nicaragua 35 E3
Blue Mountains *mountains* W USA 26 C2
Blue Nile *river* Ethiopia/Sudan 54 C4
Blumenau Brazil 44 D3
Bo Sierra Leone 56 C4
Boa Vista Brazil 42 D1
Boa Vista *island* Cape Verde 56 A3
Bobo-Dioulasso Burkina 56 D4
Bobruysk *see* Babruysk
Boca de la Serpiente *see* Serpent's Mouth, The
Bochum Germany 76 B4
Bodø Norway 66 C3
Bodrum Turkey 98 A4
Bogor Indonesia 120 C5
Bogotá *capital of* Colombia 40 B3
Bo Hai *sea feature* Yellow Sea 110 D4
Bohemian Forest *region* Germany 77 D5
Bohol Sea *Sea* Philippines 121 E2
Boise Idaho, USA 26 D3
Boké Guinea 56 C4
Bokhara *see* Buxoro
Bol Chad 58 B3
Bolivia *country* C South America 42-43
Bologna Italy 78 C3
Bolton England, UK 71 D5
Bolzano Italy *Ger.* Bozen 78 C2
Boma Dem. Rep. Congo 59 B7
Bombay *see* Mumbai
Bomu *river* Central African Republic/Dem. Rep. Congo 59 D5
Bongo, Massif des *upland* Central African Republic 58 D4

Bongor Chad 58 C3

Bonn Germany 76 B4

Boosaaso Somalia 54 E4

Borås Sweden 67 B7

Bordeaux France 73 B5

Borger Texas, USA 29 E2

Borisov see Barysaw

Borlänge Sweden 67 C6

Borneo *island* SE Asia 120-121

Bornholm *island* Denmark 67 C8

Bosanski Šamac Bosnia & Herzegovina 82 C3

Bosna *river* Bosnia & Herzegovina 82 C3

Bosna I Hercegovina, Federacija Admin. region *republic* Bosnia and Herzegovina 82 C4

Bosnia & Herzegovina *country* SE Europe 82-83

Bosporus *sea feature* Turkey *Turk.* İstanbul Boğazı 98 B2

Bossangoa Central African Republic 58 C4

Bosten Hu *Lake* China 108 C3

Boston Massachusetts, USA 23 G3

Bothnia, Gulf of *sea feature* Baltic Sea 67 C5

Botoşani Romania 90 C3

Botswana *country* southern Africa 60

Bouar Central African Republic 58 C4

Bougainville Island *island* Papua New Guinea 126 C3

Bougouni Mali 56 D4

Boulder Colorado, USA 24 C4

Boulogne-sur-Mer France 72 C2

Bourges France 72 C4

Bourgogne *region* France *Eng.* Burgundy 72 D4

Bourke Australia 131 C5

Bournemouth England, UK 71 D7

Bouvet Island *external territory* Norway, Atlantic Ocean 49 D7

Bowen Australia 130 D3

Bowling Green Kentucky, USA 22 C5

Bozeman Montana, USA 24 B2

Bozen see Bolzano

Brač *island* Croatia 82 B4

Bradford England, UK 71 D5

Braga Portugal 74 C2

Bragança Portugal 74 C2

Brahmaputra *river* Asia 117 G3

Brăila Romania 90 D4

Brainerd Minnesota, USA 25 F2

Brandon Canada 19 F5

Brasília *capital of* Brazil 43 F4

Braşov Romania 90 C4

Bratislava *capital of* Slovakia *Ger.* Pressburg, *Hung.* Pozsony 81 C6

Bratsk Russian Federation 97 E4

Braunau am Inn Austria 77 D6

Braunschweig Germany *Eng.* Brunswick 76 C4

Brazil *country* South America 42-43

Brazil Basin *undersea feature* Atlantic Ocean 49 C5

Brazilian Highlands *upland* Brazil 43 G4

Brazos *river* SW USA 29 G3

Brazzaville *capital of* Congo 59 B6

Brecon Beacons *hills* Wales, UK 71 C6

Breda Netherlands 68 C4

Bregenz Austria 77 B7

Bremen Germany 76 B3

Bremerhaven Germany 76 B3

Brescia Italy 78 B2

Breslau see Wrocław

Brest Belarus *Pol.* Brześć nad Bugiem, *prev.* Brześć Litewski, *Rus.* Brest-Litovsk 89 B6

Brest France 72 A3

Brest-Litovsk see Brest

Bretagne *region* France *Eng.* Brittany 72 A3

Brezhnev see Naberezhnyye Chelny

Bria Central African Republic 58 D4

Bridgetown *capital of* Barbados 37 H4

Brig Switzerland 77 B5

Brighton England, UK 71 E7

Brindisi Italy 79 E5

Brisbane Australia 131 E5

Bristol England, UK 71 D6

British Columbia *province* Canada 18-19

British Indian Ocean Territory *external territory* UK, Indian Ocean 122 C4

British Isles *islands* W Europe 70-71

British Virgin Islands *external territory* UK, West Indies 37

Brittany see Bretagne

Brno Czech Republic *Ger.* Brünn 81 B5

Broken Arrow Oklahoma, USA 29 G1

Broken Hill Australia 131 B6

Broken Ridge *undersea feature* Indian Ocean 123 D6

Bromberg see Bydgoszcz

Brooks Range *mountains* Alaska, USA 18 D2

Brookton Australia 129 B6

Broome Australia 128 C3

Brownfield Texas, USA 29 E2

Brownsville Texas, USA 29 G5

Bruges see Brugge

Brugge Belgium *Fr.* Bruges 69 A5

Brunei *country* E Asia 120 D3

Brünn see Brno

Brunswick Georgia, USA 31 E3

Brunswick see Braunschweig

Brusa see Bursa

Brussel see Brussels

Brussels *capital of* Belgium *Fr.* Bruxelles, *Flem.* Brussel 69 C6

Brüx see Most

Bruxelles see Brussels

Bryan Texas, USA 29 G3

Bryansk Russian Federation 93 A5 96 A2

Brześć Litewski see Brest

Brześć nad Bugiem see Brest

Canberra *capital of* Australia 131 D6
Cancún Mexico 33 H3
Caniapiscau *river* Canada 21 E2
Caniapiscau, Réservoir *Reservoir* Canada 21 E3
Canik Dağları *mountains* Turkey 98 D2
Çankırı Turkey 98 C2
Cannes France 73 D6
Canoas Brazil 44 D4
Canterbury England, UK 71 E6
Canterbury Bight *sea feature* Pacific Ocean 133 C6
Canterbury Plains *plain* New Zealand 133 B6
Cân Tho Vietnam 119 D6
Canton Ohio, USA 22 D4
Canton *see* Guangzhou
Cape Basin *undersea feature* Atlantic Ocean 49 D6
Cape Town South Africa 60 C5
Cape Verde *country* Atlantic Ocean 56 A2
Cape Verde Basin *undersea feature* Atlantic Ocean 48 C4
Cape York Peninsula *peninsula* Australia 124 B3
Cap-Haïtien Haiti 36 D3
Capri, Isola di *island* Italy 79 D5
Caquetá *river* Colombia 40 C4
CAR *see* Central African Republic
Caracas *capital of* Venezuela 40 D1
Carazinho Brazil 44 D4
Carbondale Illinois, USA 22 B5
Carcassonne France 73 C6
Cardiff Wales, UK 71 C6
Cardigan Bay *sea feature* Wales, UK 71 C6
Carey, Lake *lake* Australia 129 C5
Caribbean Sea Atlantic Ocean 36-37
Carlisle England, UK 70 D4
Carlsbad New Mexico, USA 28 D3
Carlsberg Ridge *undersea feature* Indian Ocean 122 B4

Carnarvon Australia 128 A5
Carnegie, Lake *lake* Australia 129 C5
Carolina Brazil 43 F3
Caroline Island *see* Millennium Island
Caroline Islands *island group* Micronesia 126 B1
Caroni *river* Venezuela 41 F2
Carpathian Mountains *mountain range* E Europe *var.* Carpathians 63 E4
Carpathians *see* Carpathian Mountains
Carpaţii Meridionali *mountain range* Romania *Eng.* South Carpathians, Transylvanian Alps 90 B4
Carpentaria, Gulf of *sea feature* Australia 130 B2
Carson City Nevada, USA 27 B5
Cartagena Colombia 40 B1
Cartagena Spain 75 F4
Cartago Costa Rica 35 E4
Cartwright Canada 21 G2
Carúpano Venezuela 41 F1
Casablanca Morocco 52 C2
Casa Grande Arizona, USA 28 B3
Cascade Range *mountain range* Canada/USA 26 B2
Cascais Portugal 74 B3
Casper Wyoming, USA 24 C3
Caspian Sea *inland sea* Asia/Europe 94 B4
Castellón de la Plana Spain 75 F3
Castelo Branco Portugal 74 C3
Castries *capital of* St Lucia 37 G4
Castro Chile 47 B6
Cat Island *island* Bahamas 36 D1
Catania Italy 79 D7
Catanzaro Italy 79 D6
Cauca *river* Colombia 40 B2
Caucasus *mountains* Asia/Europe 93 A7
Caura *river* Venezuela 41 E2

Caviana, Ilha *island* Brazil 43 F1
Cawnpore *see* Kānpur
Caxias do Sul Brazil 44 D4
Cayenne *capital of* French Guiana 41 H3
Cayman Islands *external territory* UK, West Indies 36
Cebu Philippines 121 E2
Cedar Rapids Iowa, USA 25 G3
Cedros, Isla *island* Mexico 32 A2
Ceduna Australia 131 A6
Cefalù Italy 79 C6
Celebes *see* Sulawesi
Celebes Sea Pacific Ocean *Ind.* Laut Sulawesi 134 B3
Celje Slovenia 77 E7
Central African Republic *country* C Africa *abbrev.* CAR 58-59
Central, Cordillera *mountain range* Philippines 121 E1
Central Makrān Range *mountains* Pakistan 116 A3
Central Pacific Basin *undersea feature* Pacific Ocean 125 E1
Central Russian Upland *upland* Russian Federation 94 B3
Central Siberian Plateau *see* Srednesibirskoye Ploskogor'ye
Central Siberian Uplands *see* Srednesibirskoye Ploskogor'ye
Central, Sistema *mountain range* Spain 74 D3
Cephalonia *see* Kefallonia
Ceram Sea *Sea* Indonesia 121 F4
Cernăuţi *see* Chernivtsi
Cēsis Latvia *Ger.* Wenden 88 C3
České Budějovice Czech Republic *Ger.* Budweis 81 B5
Ceuta *external territory* Spain, N Africa 52 C1
Cévennes *mountains* France 73 C6
Ceylon *see* Sri Lanka
Ceylon Plain *undersea feature* Indian Ocean 122 C4
Chad *country* C Africa 58
Chad, Lake *lake* C Africa 58 B3

Chāgai Hills *mountains* Pakistan 116 A2

Chagos-Laccadive Plateau *undersea feature* Indian Ocean 122 C4

Chagos Trench *undersea feature* Indian Ocean 122 C4

Chalkída Greece 87 C5

Challenger Deep *undersea feature* Pacific Ocean 134 B3

Châlons-en-Champagne France 72 D3

Chambéry France 73 D5

Champaign Illinois, USA 22 B4

Chañaral Chile 46 B2

Chandīgarh India 116 D2

Chang, Ko *island* Thailand 119 C5

Changchun China 110 D3

Chang Jiang *river* China *var.* Yangtze 111 B6

Changsha China 111 C6

Chaniá Greece 87 C7

Channel Islands *island group* California, USA 27 B8

Channel Islands *islands* UK 71 D8

Channel-Port-aux-Basques Canada 21 G4

Channel Tunnel France/UK 71 E7

Chapala, Lago de *lake* Mexico 32 D4

Chardzhev *see* Türkmenabat

Chardzhou *see* Türkmenabat

Chari *river* C Africa 58 C3

Chārīkār Afghanistan 105 E4

Chärjew *see* Türkmenabat

Charleroi Belgium 69 C6

Charleston South Carolina, USA 31 F2

Charleston West Virginia, USA 22 D5

Charleville Australia 130 C4

Charlotte North Carolina, USA 31 F1

Charlotte Amalie *capital of* Virgin Islands 37 F3

Charlottesville Virginia, USA 23 E5

Charlottetown Canada 21 G4

Charters Towers Australia 130 D3

Chartres France 72 C3

Châteauroux France 72 C4

Chatham Islands *islands* New Zealand 134 D4

Chattanooga Tennessee, USA 30 D1

Chauk Myanmar 118 A3

Chaves Portugal 74 C2

Cheboksary Russian Federation 93 C5

Cheboygan Michigan, USA 22 C2

Chech, Erg *desert* Algeria/Mali 56 D1

Che-chiang *see* Zhejiang

Cheju-do *island* South Korea 111 E5

Cheju Strait *sea feature* South Korea 111 E5

Chekiang *see* Zhejiang

Cheleken *see* Hazar

Chelyabinsk Russian Federation 96 C3

Chemnitz Germany *prev.* Karl-Marx-Stadt 76 D4

Chenāb *river* Pakistan 116 C2

Chengdu China 111 B5

Chennai India *prev.* Madras 115 E2

Cherbourg France 72 B3

Cherepovets Russian Federation 92 B4

Cherkasy Ukraine 91 E2

Cherkessk Russian Federation 93 A7

Chernigov *see* Chernihiv

Chernihiv Ukraine *Rus.* Chernigov 91 E1

Chernivtsi Ukraine *Rus.* Chernovtsy, *Rom.* Cernăuţi 90 C3

Chernobyl' *see* Chornobyl'

Chernovtsy *see* Chernivtsi

Chernyakhovsk Kaliningrad, Russian Federation 88 B4

Chesapeake Bay *sea feature* USA 23 F5

Chester England, UK 71 D5

Cheyenne Wyoming, USA 24 D4

Chiang-hsi *see* Jiangxi

Chiang Mai Thailand 118 B4

Chiang-su *see* Jiangsu

Chiba Japan 113 D5

Chicago Illinois, USA 22 B3

Chiclayo Peru 42 A3

Chico California, USA 27 B5

Chicoutimi Canada 21 E4

Chifeng China 109 F2

Chihli *see* Hebei

Chihuahua Mexico 32 C2

Chile *country* S South America 46–47

Chile Basin *undersea feature* Pacific Ocean 135 G4

Chile Chico Chile 47 B6

Chile Rise *undersea feature* Pacific Ocean 135 G4

Chi-lin *see* Jilin

Chillán Chile 46 B4

Chiloé, Isla de *island* Chile 47 B6

Chimborazo *peak* Ecuador 38 A3

Chimbote Peru 42 A3

Chimkent *see* Shymkent

Chimoio Mozambique 61 E3

China *country* E Asia 108–109

Chinandega Nicaragua 34 C3

Chindwin *river* Myanmar 118 A2

Chinghai *see* Qinghai

Chingola Zambia 60 D2

Chinook Trough *undersea feature* Pacific Ocean 134 D1

Chíos Greece 87 D5

Chíos *island* Greece *prev.* Khíos 87 D5

Chirchik Uzbekistan *Uzb.* Chirchiq 105 E2

Chirchiq *see* Chirchik

Chiriquí, Golfo de *sea feature* Panama 35 F5

Chişinău *capital of* Moldova, *var.* Kishinev 90 D3

Chita Russian Federation 97 F4

Chitré Panama 35 F5

Comoros *country* Indian Ocean 61

Conakry *capital of* Guinea 56 C4

Concepción Chile 47 B5

Concepción Paraguay 44 B2

Conchos *river* Mexico 32 C2

Concord New Hampshire, USA 22 G2

Concordia E Argentina 46 D3

Congo *country* C Africa 59

Congo *river* C Africa *var.* Zaire 51 C5

Congo Basin *drainage basin* C Africa 59 C5

Congo, Democratic Republic of *country* C Africa 59

Connecticut *state* USA 23 G3

Constance, Lake *river* C Europe 77 B6

Constantine Algeria 53 E1

Constantinople *see* İstanbul

Constanţa Romania 90 D5

Coober Pedy Australia 131 A5

Cook, Mount *see* Aoraki

Cook Islands *external territory* New Zealand, Pacific Ocean 127 G4

Cook Strait *sea feature* New Zealand 133 D5

Cooktown Australia 130 D2

Cooma Australia 131 D7

Coos Bay Oregon, USA 26 A3

Cootamundra Australia 131 D6

Copenhagen *capital of* Denmark 67 B7

Copiapó Chile 46 B3

Coppermine *see* Kugluktuk

Coquimbo Chile 46 B3

Corabia Romania 90 B5

Coral Sea Pacific Ocean 130 E3

Coral Sea Islands *external territory* Australia, Coral Sea 130 E3

Corantijn *see* Courantyne

Cordillera Cantábrica *mountain range* Spain 74 D1

Córdoba Argentina 46 C3

Córdoba Spain 74 D4

Cordova Alaska, USA 18 D3

Corfu *see* Kérkyra

Corinth *see* Kórinthos

Corinth, Gulf of *see* Korinthiakós Kólpos

Corinto Nicaragua 34 C3

Cork Ireland 71 B6

Corner Brook Canada 21 G3

Coro Venezuela 40 D1

Coronel Oviedo Paraguay 44 C2

Corpus Christi Texas, USA 29 G5

Corrib, Lough *lake* Ireland 71 A5

Corrientes Argentina 46 D3

Corse *island* France *Eng.* Corsica 73 E7 84 D2

Corsica *see* Corse

Çorum Turkey 98 D2

Corvallis Oregon, USA 26 A3

Cosenza Italy 79 D6

Costa Blanca *coastal region* Spain 75 F4

Costa Brava *coastal region* Spain 75 H2

Costa Rica *country* Central America 34-35

Côte d'Ivoire *country* W Africa *Eng.* Ivory Coast 56 D4

Cottbus Germany 76 D4

Council Bluffs Iowa, USA 25 F4

Courantyne *river* Guyana /Suriname *var.* Corantijn 41 G3

Courland Lagoon *sea feature* Baltic Sea 88 B4

Coventry England, UK 71 D6

Covilhã Portugal 74 C3

Cowan, Lake *lake* Australia 129 C6

Cozumel, Isla de *island* Mexico 33 H3

Cracow *see* Kraków

Craiova Romania 90 B5

Cremona Italy 78 B2

Cres *island* Croatia 82 A3

Crescent City California, USA 26 A4

Crete *see* Kríti

Crete, Sea of Mediterranean Sea *Gk.* Kritikó Pélagos 87 D7

Crimea *see* Krym

Cristóbal Panama 48 A4

Croatia *country* SE Europe 82

Croker Island *island* Australia 128 E2

Crotone Italy 79 E6

Crozet Basin *undersea feature* Indian Ocean 123 B6

Crozet Islands *island group* Indian Ocean 123 B7

Crystal Brook Australia 131 B6

Cuanza *river* Angola 60 B2

Cuba *country* West Indies 36

Cubango *see* Okavango

Cúcuta Colombia 40 C2

Cuenca Ecuador 40 A5

Cuenca Spain 75 E3

Cuernavaca Mexico 33 E4

Cuiabá Brazil 43 E4

Culiacán Mexico 32 C3

Cumaná Venezuela 41 E1

Cumberland Maryland, USA 23 E4

Cunene *river* Angola/Namibia 60 B3

Cunnamulla Australia 131 C5

Curicó Chile 46 B4

Curitiba Brazil 44 D3

Cusco Peru *prev.* Cuzco 42 B4

Cuttack India 117 F5

Cuxhaven Germany 76 B3

Cuyuni *river* Guyana/Venezuela 41 F2

Cuzco *see* Cusco

Cyclades *see* Kykládes

Cymru *see* Wales

Cyprus *country* Mediterranean Sea 98 C5

Czechoslovakia *see* Czech Republic *or* Slovakia

Czech Republic *country* C Europe 80-81

Częstochowa Poland *Ger.* Tschenstochau 80 C4

Człuchów Poland 80 C3

D

Dacca *see* Dhaka
Dagden *see* Hiiumaa
Dagö *see* Hiiumaa
Dagupan Philippines 121 E1
Da Hinggan Ling *mountain range* China *Eng.* Great Khingan Range 109 G1
Dahomey *see* Benin
Dakar *capital of* Senegal 56 B3
Đakovo Croatia 82 C3
Dalain Hob China 108 D3
Dalaman Turkey 98 B4
Dalandzadgad Mongolia 109 E3
Đa Lat Vietnam 119 E5
Dalby Australia 131 D5
Dalian China 110 D4
Dallas Texas, USA 29 G3
Dalmacija *region* Croatia 82 B4
Daly Waters Australia 128 E3
Damān India 116 C5
Damas *see* Damascus
Damascus Syria *var.* Esh Sham, *Fr.* Damas, *Ar.* Dimashq 100 B4
Dampier Australia 128 B4
Damxung China 108 C5
Đa Năng Vietnam 119 E4
Dandong China 110 D4
Daneborg Greenland 65 E3
Danghara Tajikistan 105 E3
Danmarksstraedet *see* Denmark Strait
Danube *river* C Europe 63 E4
Danville Virginia, USA 23 E5
Danzig *see* Gdańsk
Danzig, Gulf of 76 C2 *Gulf* Poland 80 C2
Dar'ā Syria 101 B5
Dardanelles *sea feature* Turkey *Turk.* Çanakkale Boğazı 98 A2
Dar es Salaam Tanzania 55 C7
Darfur *Cultural region* Sudan 54 A4
Darhan Mongolia 109 E2
Darien, Gulf of *sea feature* Caribbean Sea 35 G5

Darling *river* Australia 131 C6
Darmstadt Germany 77 B5
Darnah Libya 53 H2
Dartmoor *region* England, UK 71 C7
Dartmouth Canada 21 F4
Darwin Australia 128 D2
Dashhowuz *see* Daşoguz
Daşoguz Turkmenistan *prev.* Tashauz, *Turkm.* Dashhowuz 104 C2
Datong China 110 C4
Daugava *see* Western Dvina
Daugavpils Latvia *Ger.* Dünaburg, *Rus.* Dvinsk 88 D4
Dāvangere India 114 D2
Davao Philippines 121 F3
Davao Gulf *gulf* Philippines 121 F3
Davenport Iowa, USA 25 G3
David Panama 35 E5
Davie Ridge *undersea feature* Indian Ocean 123 A5
Davis Sea Indian Ocean 136 D3
Davis Strait *sea feature* Atlantic Ocean 64 C3
Dayr az Zawr Syria 100 D3
Dayton Ohio, USA 22 C4
Daytona Beach Florida, USA 31 F4
Dead Sea *salt lake* SW Asia *Ar.* Al Bahr al Mayyit, Bahrat Lūt, *Heb.* Yam HaMelah 101 B5
Death Valley *valley* W USA 27 C6
Deatnu *river* Finland/Norway 66 D2
Debrecen Hungary *prev.* Debreczen, *Ger.* Debreczin 81 D6
Debreczen *see* Debrecen
Debreczin *see* Debrecen
Decatur Illinois, USA 22 B4
Deccan *plateau* India 106 B3 115 D1
Děčín Czech Republic *Ger.* Tetschen 80 B4
Dej Romania 90 B4
Delaware *state* USA 23 F4
Delémont Switzerland 77 A7

Delft Netherlands 68 C4
Delfzijl Netherlands 68 E1
Delhi India 116 D3
Del Rio Texas, USA 29 F4
Demchok *disputed region* China/India *var.* Dêmqog 108 B3
Demopolis Alabama, USA 30 C2
Dêmqog *see* Demchok
Denali *see* Mount McKinley
Denham Australia 129 A5
Den Helder Netherlands 68 C2
Denizli Turkey 98 B4
Denmark *country* NW Europe 67
Denmark Strait *sea feature* Greenland/Iceland *var.* Danmarksstraedet 65 D4
Denpasar Indonesia 120 D5
Denton Texas, USA 29 G2
Denver Colorado, USA 24 D4
Dera Ghāzi Khān Pakistan 116 C2
Derby England, UK 71 D6
Derg, Lough *lake* Ireland 71 B6
Desē Ethiopia 54 C4
Deseado *river* Argentina 47 C6
Des Moines Iowa, USA 25 F3
Despoto Planina *see* Rhodope Mountains
Dessau Germany 76 D4
Detroit Michigan, USA 22 D3
Deutschendorf *see* Poprad
Deva Romania 90 B4
Deventer Netherlands 68 D3
Devollit, Lumi i *river* Albania 83 D6
Devon Island *island* Canada 19 F2
Devonport Tasmania, Australia 131 C8
Dezfūl Iran 102 C3
Dhaka *capital of* Bangladesh *var.* Dacca 117 G4
Dhanbād India 117 F4
Dhrepanon, Ákra *see* Drépano, Akrotírio

Diamantina Fracture Zone *tectonic feature* Indian Ocean 123 E6

Dickinson North Dakota, USA 24 D2

Diekirch Luxembourg 69 D7

Dieppe France 72 C3

Digul *River* Indonesia 121 H5

Dijon France 72 D4

Dikson Taymyrskiy (Dolgano-Nenetskiy) Russian Federation 137 H4

Dili *capital of* East Timor 121 F5

Dilling Sudan 54 B4

Dilolo Dem. Rep. Congo 59 D8

Dimashq *see* Damascus

Dimitrovo *see* Pernik

Dinant Belgium 69 C7

Dinaric Alps *mountains* Bosnia & Herzegovina/Croatia 82 B4

Diourbel Senegal 56 B3

Dirē Dawa Ethiopia 55 D5

Dirk Hartog Island *island* Australia 129 A5

Disappointment, Lake *salt lake* Australia 128 C4

Dispur India 117 G3

Divinópolis Brazil 45 D4

Diyarbakır Turkey 99 E4

Dkaraganda *see* Zhezkazgan

Djambala Congo 59 B6

Djibouti *country* E Africa 54

Djibouti *capital of* Djibouti *var.* Jibuti 54 D4

Dnieper *river* E Europe 63 F4

Dniester *river* Moldova/Ukraine 90 D3

Dnipropetrovs'k Ukraine 91 F3

Dobele Latvia *Ger.* Doblen 88 C3

Doberai, Jazirah *Peninsula* Indonesia 121 G4

Doblen *see* Dobele

Doboj Bosnia & Herzegovina 82 C3

Dobrich Bulgaria 86 E1

Dodecanese *see* Dodekánisa

Dodekánisa *islands* Greece *Eng.* Dodecanese 87 E6

Dodge City Kansas, USA 25 E5

Dodoma *capital of* Tanzania 55 C7

Doğu Karadeniz Dağları *mountains* Turkey *var.* Anadolu Dağları 99 E2

Doha *capital of* Qatar *Ar.* Ad Dawhah 103 C5

Dolisie Congo 59 B6

Dolomites *see* Dolomitiche, Alpi

Dolomitiche, Alpi *mountains* Italy *Eng.* Dolomites 78 C2

Dolores Argentina 46 D4

Dolores Hidalgo Mexico 33 E4

Dominica *country* West Indies 37

Dominican Republic *country* West Indies 37

Don *river* Russian Federation 93 B6 96 A3

Donegal Bay *sea feature* Ireland 71 A5

Donets *river* Russian Federation/Ukraine 93 A6

Donets'k Ukraine 91 G3

Dongguan China 111 C6

Dongola Sudan 54 B3

Donostia *see* San Sebastián

Dordogne *river* France 73 B5

Dordrecht Netherlands 68 C4

Dorpat *see* Tartu

Dortmund Germany 76 B4

Dothan Alabama, USA 30 D3

Douai France 72 D3

Douala Cameroon 59 A5

Douglas UK 71 C5

Douglas Arizona, USA 28 C3

Dourados Brazil 44 C2

Douro *river* Portugal/Spain *Sp.* Duero 74 C2

Dover England, UK 71 E7

Dover Delaware, USA 23 F4

Drakensberg *mountain range* Lesotho/South Africa 60 D5

Drake Passage *sea feature* Atlantic Ocean/Pacific Ocean 39 C8

Dráma Greece 86 C3

Drammen Norway 67 B6

Drau *river* C Europe *var.* Drava 77 D7 82 C3

Drava *river* C Europe *var.* Drau 81 C7

Drépano, Akrotírio *coastal feature* Greece *var.* Dhrepanon Ákra 86 C4

Dresden Germany 76 D4

Drina *river* Bosnia & Herzegovina/Serbia 82 D4

Drobeta-Turnu Severin Romania *prev.* Turnu Severin 90 B4

Dronning Maud Land *region* Antarctica 137 B1

Druskieniki *see* Druskininkai

Druskininkai Lithuania *Pol.* Druskieniki 89 B5

Dubayy United Arab Emirates 103 D5

Dubăsari Moldova 90 D3

Dubawnt *river* Canada 19 F4

Dubbo Australia 131 D6

Dublin *capital of* Ireland 71 B5

Dubrovnik Croatia 83 C5

Dubuque Iowa, USA 25 G3

Duero *river* Portugal/Spain *Port.* Douro 74 D2

Dugi Otok *island* Croatia 82 A4

Duisburg Germany 76 A4

Dulan China 108 D4

Duluth Minnesota, USA 25 F2

Dumfries Scotland, UK 70 C4

Düna *see* Western Dvina

Dünaburg *see* Daugavpils

Dundalk Ireland 71 B5

Dundee Scotland, UK 70 D3

Dunedin New Zealand 133 B7

Dunkerque France *Eng.* Dunkirk 72 C2

Dunkirk *see* Dunkerque

Duqm Oman 103 E6

Durango Mexico 32 D3

Durango Colorado, USA 24 C5

Durazno Uruguay 44 C5

Durban South Africa 60 E4

Durham North Carolina, USA 31 F1

Durrës Albania 83 C5

Dushanbe *capital of* Tajikistan *var.* Dyushambe, *prev.* Stalinabad 105 E3
Düsseldorf Germany 76 A4
Dutch Harbor Alaska, USA 18 B3
Dutch West Indies *see* Netherland Antilles
Dvinsk *see* Daugavpils
Dyushambe *see* Dushanbe
Dzaudzhikau *see* Vladikavkaz
Dzhalal-Abad Kyrgyzstan *Kir.* Jalal-Abad 105 F2
Dzhambul *see* Taraz
Dzhezkazgan *see* Zhezkazgan
Dzvina *see* Western Dvina

— **E** —

Eagle Pass Texas, USA 29 F4
East Cape *coastal feature* New Zealand 132 E2
East China Sea Pacific Ocean 111 E5
Easter Fracture Zone *tectonic feature* Pacific Ocean 135 G4
Easter Island *island* Pacific Ocean 135 F4
Eastern Ghats *mountain range* India 117 B5
Eastern Sierra Madre *see* Sierra Madre Oriental
East Falkland *island* Falkland Islands 47 D7
East Indiaman Ridge *undersea feature* Indian Ocean 23 D5
East Indies *island group* Asia 122 E4
East London South Africa 60 D5
Eastmain *river* Canada 20 D3
East Pacific Rise *undersea feature* Pacific Ocean 135 F4
East Siberian Sea *see* Vostochno-Sibirskoye More
East St Louis Illinois, USA 22 B4
East Timor *country* SE Asia 121

East Novaya Zemlya Trench *var.* Novaya Zemlya Trench. *Undersea feature* Kara Sea 137 H4
Eau Claire Wisconsin, USA 22 A2
Ebolowa Cameroon 59 B5
Ebro *river* Spain 75 F2
Ecuador *country* NW South America 40
Ede Netherlands 68 D3
Ede Nigeria 57 F4
Edgeoya *island* Svalbard 65 G2
Edinburgh Scotland, UK 70 C4
Edirne Turkey 98 A2
Edmonton Canada 19 E5
Edward, Lake *lake* Uganda/Dem. Rep. Congo 59 E6
Edwards Plateau *upland* S USA 29 F4
Efate *Island* Vanuatu *prev.* Sandwich Island 124 D4
Effingham Illinois, USA 22 B4
Eforie-Sud Romania 90 D5
Egadi, Isole *island group* Italy 79 B6
Ege Denizi *see* Aegean Sea
Eger *see* Ohře
Egypt *country* NE Africa 54
Eighty Mile Beach *beach* Australia 128 C3
Eindhoven Netherlands 69 D5
Eisenstadt Austria 77 E6
Eivissa *see* Ibiza
Elat Israel 101 A7
Elazig Turkey 99 E3
Elba, Isola d' *island* Italy 78 B4
Elbasan Albania 83 D6
Elbe *river* Czech Republic/Germany 81 B5
Elbing *see* Elbląg
Elbląg Poland *Ger.* Elbing 80 D2
El'brus *peak* Russian Federation 93 A7
El Calafate Argentina *var.* Calafate 47 B7
Elche Spain *Cat.* Elx 75 F4
Elda Spain 75 F4

Eldoret Kenya 55 C6
Eleuthera *island* Bahamas 36 C1
El Fasher Sudan *var.* Al Fāshir 54 A4
El Geneina Sudan 54 A4
Elgin Scotland, UK 70 C3
El Giza Egypt *var.* Al Jīzah 54 B1
El Hank *cliff* Mauritania 56 D1
Elista Russian Federation 93 B6
El Khalil *see* Hebron
El Khārga Egypt *var.* Al Khārijah 54 B2
Elko Nevada, USA 27 D5
Ellensburg Washington, USA 26 B2
Ellesmere Island *island* Canada 19 F1
Ellsworth Land *region* Antarctica 136 A3
El Minya Egypt 54 B2
Elmira New York, USA 23 E3
El Mreyyé *desert* Mauritania 56 D2
El Obeid Sudan 54 B4
El Paso Texas, USA 28 D3
El Puerto de Santa María Spain 74 D5
El Qâhira *see* Cairo
El Salvador *country* Central America 34
Eltanin Fracture Zone *tectonic feature* Pacific Ocean 135 E5
El Tigre Venezuela 41 E2
Elx *see* Elche
Ely Nevada USA 27 D5
Emden Germany 76 B3
Emerald Australia 130 D4
Emmen Netherlands 68 E2
Empty Quarter *see* Ar Rub' al Khali
Ems *river* Germany/Netherlands 76 B3
Encarnación Paraguay 44 C3
Enderbury Island *atoll* Kiribati 136 C2
Enderby Land *region* Antarctica 136 C2

Enderby Plain *undersea feature* Indian Ocean 123 B7

England *national region* UK 70-71

English Channel *sea feature* Atlantic Ocean 71 D7

Enguri *river* Georgia *Rus.* Inguri 99 F1

Enid Oklahoma, USA 29 F1

Ennedi *plateau* Chad 58 D2

Enns *river* Austria 77 D6

Enschede Netherlands 68 E3

Ensenada Mexico 32 A1

Entebbe Uganda 55 B6

Enugu Nigeria 57 G5

Eolie, Isole *island group* Italy *Eng.* Lipari Islands, *var.* Aeolian Islands 79 D6

Eperies *see* Prešov

Eperjes *see* Prešov

Épinal France 72 E4

Equatorial Guinea *country* W Africa 59

Erdenet Mongolia 109 E2

Erechim Brazil 44 D3

Erenhot China 109 F2

Erevan *see* Yerevan

Ereğli Turkey 98 C4

Erfurt Germany 76 C4

Erie Pennsylvania, USA 22 D3

Erie, Lake *lake* Canada/USA 17 D5

Eritrea *country* E Africa 54

Erivan *see* Yerevan

Erlangen Germany 77 C5

Ernākulam India 114 D3

Er Rachidia Morocco 52 C2

Erzerum *see* Erzurum

Erzgebirge *mountain range* Czech Republic/Germany *var* Krušné Hory 77 D5

Erzincan Turkey 99 E3

Erzurum Turkey *prev.* Erzerum 99 F3

Esbjerg Denmark 67 A7

Esch-sur-Alzette Luxembourg 69 D8

Escuintla Guatemala 34 B2

Eşfahān Iran 102 C3

Esh Sham *see* Damascus

Eskişehir Turkey 98 B3

Esmeraldas Ecuador 40 A4

Esperance Australia 129 C6

Espíritu Santo *island* Vanuatu 124 D3

Espoo Finland 67 D6

Esquel Argentina 47 B6

Essaouira Morocco 52 B2

Essen Germany 76 A4

Essequibo *river* Guyana 41 G3

Estelí Nicaragua 34 D3

Estevan Canada 19 F5

Estonia *country* E Europe 88 D2

Ethiopia *country* E Africa 54-55

Ethiopian Highlands *upland* E Africa 50 D4

Etna, Mount *peak* Sicily, Italy 79 D7

Etosha Pan *salt basin* Namibia 60 C3

Eucla Australia 129 D6

Eugene Oregon, USA 26 A3

Eugene Washington, USA 26 B1

Euphrates *river* SW Asia 102 C4

Europe 62-63

Evansville Indiana, USA 22 B5

Everest, Mount *peak* China/Nepal 108 B5

Everett Washington, USA 26 B1

Everglades, The *wetlands* Florida, USA 31 F5

Évvoia *island* Greece 87 C5

Exeter England, UK 71 C7

Exmoor *region* England, UK 71 C7

Exmouth Australia 128 A4

Exmouth Gulf *gulf* Australia 128 A4

Exmouth Plateau *undersea feature* Indian Ocean 123 E5

Eyre North, Lake *salt lake* Australia 131 B5

Eyre Peninsula *peninsula* Australia 131 A6

Eyre South, Lake *salt lake* Australia 131 B5

— F —

Fada-N'gourma Burkina 57 E4

Faeroe Islands *external territory* Denmark, Atlantic Ocean *Faer.* Føroyar, *Dan.* Færøerne 65 F5

Færøerne *see* Faeroe Islands

Faguibine, Lac *lake* Mali 57 E3

Fairbanks Alaska, USA 18 D3

Fairlie New Zealand 133 B6

Faisalābād Pakistan 116 C2

Faizabad *see* Feyzābād

Falkland Islands *external territory* UK, Atlantic Ocean 47 D7

Fallon Nevada, USA 27 C5

Falun Sweden 67 C6

Famagusta *see* Gazimağusa

Farafangana Madagascar 61 G4

Farāh Afghanistan 104 C5

Farasān, Jazā'ir *island group* Saudi Arabia 103 B6

Farewell, Cape *headland* New Zealand 132 C4

Farewell, Cape *see* Nunap Isua

Farghona *see* Farg'ona

Farg'ona Uzbekistan *prev.* Novyy Margilan, *Uzb.* Faghona 105 F2

Fargo North Dakota, USA 25 E2

Farkhor Tajikistan 105 E3

Farmington New Mexico, USA 28 C1

Faro Portugal 74 C4

Farquhar Group *island group* Seychelles 61 G2

Farvel, Cape *see* Nunap Isua

Faxaflói *bay* Iceland 64 D5

Faya Chad 58 C2

Fayetteville Arkansas, USA 30 A1

Fayetteville North Carolina, USA 31 F1

Fdérik Mauritania 56 C1

Fear, Cape *coastal feature* North Carolina, USA 31 G2

Fehmarn *island* Germany 76 C2

Fehmarn Belt *sea feature* Germany 76 C2

Feira de Santana Brazil 43 G3

Fellin *see* Viljandi

Fénérive *see* Fenoarivo

Fengtien *see* Liaoning

Fenoarivo Madagascar *prev.* Fénérive 61 G3

Fens, The *wetland* England, UK 71 E6

Fergana *see* Farg'ona

Ferrara Italy 78 C3

Ferrol Spain 74 C1

Fès Morocco *Eng.* Fez 52 C2

Feyzābād Afghanistan *var.* Faizabad 105 E3

Fez *see* Fès

Fianarantsoa Madagascar 61 G3

Fier Albania 83 D6

Figueira da Foz Portugal 74 C3

Figueres Spain 75 G2

Figuig Morocco 52 D2

Fiji *country* Pacific Ocean 127

Finland *country* N Europe 66-67

Finland, Gulf of *sea feature* Baltic Sea 67 E6

Fiordland *physical region* New Zealand 133 A7

Firenze Italy *Eng.* Florence 78 C3

Fishguard Wales, UK 71 C6

Fitzroy *river* Australia 128 C3

Fitzroy Crossing Australia 128 D3

Fiume *see* Rijeka

Flagstaff Arizona, USA 28 B2

Flanders *region* Belgium 69 A5

Flensburg Germany 76 B2

Flinders Island *island* Australia 131 C7

Flinders Ranges *mountain range* Australia 131 B6

Flinders River *river* Australia 130 C3

Flin Flon Canada 19 F5

Flint Michigan, USA 22 C3

Flint Island *island* Kiribati 127 H4

Florence Alabama, USA 30 C2

Florence South Carolina, USA 31 F2

Florence *see* Firenze

Florencia Colombia 40 B3

Flores Guatemala 34 B1

Flores *island* Indonesia 121 E5

Flores, Laut *see* Flores Sea

Flores Sea Pacific Ocean *Ind.* Laut Flores 121 E5

Florianópolis Brazil 44 B3

Florida *state* USA 31 E4

Florida, Straits of *sea feature* Bahamas/USA 31 F5 36 B1

Florida Keys *island chain* Florida, USA 31 F5

Flórina Greece 86 B3

Flushing *see* Vlissingen

Foča Bosnia & Herzegovina 82 C4

Focşani Romania 90 C4

Foggia Italy 79 D5

Fogo *island* Cape Verde 56 A3

Foligno Italy 78 C4

Fongafale *capital of* Tuvalu 127 E3

Fonseca, Gulf of *sea feature* El Salvador/Honduras 34 C3

Forlì Italy 78 C3

Formentera *island* Spain 75 G4

Former Yugoslav Republic of Macedonia *see* Macedonia

Formosa Argentina 46 D2

Formosa *see* Taiwan

Formosa Strait *see* Taiwan Strait

Fóroyar *see* Faeroe Islands

Fortaleza Brazil 43 H2

Fortescue River *river* Australia 128 B4

Fort Collins Colorado, USA 24 D4

Fort-de-France *capital of* Martinique 37 G4

Forth *river* Scotland, UK 70 C4

Forth, Firth of *inlet* Scotland, UK 70 D4

Fort Lauderdale Florida, USA 31 F5

Fort McMurray Canada 19 F4

Fort Myers Florida, USA 31 E4

Fort Peck Lake *lake* Montana, USA 24 C1

Fort Saint John Canada 19 E4

Fort Smith Canada 19 E4

Fort Smith Arkansas, USA 30 A1

Fort Wayne Indiana, USA 22 C4

Fort William Scotland, UK 70 C3

Fort Worth Texas, USA 29 G3

Foveaux Strait *sea feature* New Zealand 133 A7

Fox Glacier New Zealand 133 B6

Franca Brazil 45 E1

France *country* W Europe 72-73

Francistown Botswana 60 D3

Frankfort Kentucky, USA 22 C5

Frankfurt *see* Frankfurt am Main

Frankfurt am Main Germany *Eng.* Frankfurt 77 B5

Frankfurt an der Oder Germany 76 D5

Fränkische Alb *mountains* Germany 77 C6

Frantsa-Iosifa, Zemlya *islands* Russian Federation *Eng.* Franz Josef Land 137 G2

Franz Josef Land *see* Frantsa-Iosifa, Zemlya

Fraser Island *island* Australia 130 E4

Frauenburg *see* Saldus

Fray Bentos Uruguay 44 B5

Fredericksburg Virginia, USA 23 E4

Fredericton Canada 21 F4

Frederikshavn Denmark 67 B7

Fredrikstad Norway 67 B6

Freeport Bahamas 36 C1

Freeport Texas, USA 29 G4

Freetown *capital of* Sierra Leone 56 C4

Freiburg im Breisgau Germany 77 B6

Fremantle Australia 129 B6

French Guiana *external territory* France, N South America 41

French Polynesia *external territory* France, Pacific Ocean 135 E3

French Southern and Antarctic Territories *French overseas territory* Indian Ocean *Fr.* Terres Australes et Antarctiques Françaises 123 C7

Fresnillo Mexico 32 D1

Fresno California, USA 27 B6

Frome, Lake *salt lake* Australia 131 B5

Frunze *see* Bishkek

Fu-chien *see* Fujian

Fuerte Olimpo Paraguay 44 B1

Fuerteventura *island* Spain 52 A3

Fuhkien *see* Fujian

Fujian *province* China *var.* Fu-chien, Fuhkien, Fukien, Min 111 D6

Fukien *see* Fujian

Fukui Japan 113 C5

Fukuoka Japan 113 A6

Fukushima Japan 112 D4

Fulda Germany 77 C5

Fünfkirchen *see* Pécs

Fushun China 110 D3

Furnas, Represa de *Reservoir* Brazil 45 E1

Fuxin China 110 D3

Fujian China *prev.* Linchuan 111 D6

FYR Macedonia *see* Macedonia

G

Gaalkacyo Somalia 55 E5

Gabès Tunisia 53 E2

Gabon *country* W Africa 59

Gaborone *capital of* Botswana 60 D4

Gabrovo Bulgaria 86 D2

Gadsden Alabama, USA 30 D2

Gaeta, Golfo di *sea feature* Italy 79 C5

Gafsa Tunisia 53 E2

Gagnoa Côte d'Ivoire 56 D5

Gagra Georgia 99 E1

Gairdner, Lake *lake* Australia 131 B6

Galapagos Fracture Zone *tectonic feature* Pacific Ocean 135 F3

Galapagos Islands *islands* Ecuador, Pacific Ocean *var.* Tortoise Islands, *Sp.* Archipiélago de Colón 135 G3

Galapagos Rise *undersea feature* Pacific Ocean 135 G3

Galaţi Romania 90 D4

Galesburg Illinois, USA 22 B4

Galicia *region* Spain 74 C1

Galilee, Sea of *see* Tiberias, Lake

Galle Sri Lanka 115 E4

Gallego Rise *undersea feature* Pacific Ocean 135 F3

Gallipoli Italy 79 E5

Gällivare Sweden 66 D3

Gallup New Mexico, USA 28 C2

Galveston Texas, USA 29 G4

Galway Ireland 71 A5

Gambia *country* W Africa 56

Gambia *River* Africa 56 C3

Gambier, Îles *island group* French Polynesia 135 E4

Gan *see* Gansu

Gan *see* Jiangxi

Gäncä Azerbaijan *Rus.* Gyandzha, *prev.* Kirovabad, Yelisavetpol 99 G2

Gand *see* Gent

Gander Canada 21 H3

Gandia Spain 75 F3

Ganges *river* S Asia 116 F4

Ganges Fan *Undersea feature* Bay of Bengal 122 D3

Ganges, Mouths of the *wetlands* Bangladesh/India 117 G4

Gangtok India 117 G3

Gansu *province* China *var.* Gan, Kansu 111 B5

Gao Mali 57 E3

Gaoual Guinea 56 C4

Gar China 108 A4

Garagum Kanaly *canal* Turkmenistan *prev.* Karakumskiy Kanal 104 C3

Garagum *desert* Turkmenistan *var.* Kara Kum, Karakumy 104 C2

Garda, Lago di *lake* Italy 78 B2

Gardíz Afghanistan 105 E4

Garissa Kenya 55 C6

Garmo Peak *see* Communism Peak

Garonne *river* France 73 B5

Garoowe Somalia 55 E5

Garoua Cameroon 58 B4

Gary Indiana, USA 22 B3

Gaspé Canada 21 F4

Gastonia North Carolina, USA 31 E1

Gävle Sweden 67 C5

Gaya India 117 F4

Gaza Gaza Strip 101 A6

Gazandzhyk *see* Bereket

Gazanjyk *see* Bereket

Gaza Strip *disputed territory* SW Asia 101 A6

Gaziantep Turkey *prev.* Aintab 98 D4

Gazimağusa Cyprus *var.* Famagusta *Gk.* Ammochostos 98 C5

Gdańsk Poland *Ger.* Danzig 80 C2

Gdingen *see* Gdynia

Gdynia Poland *Ger.* Gdingen 80 C2

Gedaref Sudan 54 C4

Geelong Australia 131 C7

Gëkdepe *see* Gökdepe

Gemena Dem. Rep. Congo 59 C5

General Eugenio A. Garay Paraguay 44 A1

General Santos Philippines 121 F3

Geneva *see* Genève

Geneva, Lake *lake* France/Switzerland *Fr.* Lac Léman, *var.* Le Léman, *Ger.* Genfer See 77 A7

Genève Switzerland *Eng.*
Geneva 77 A7
Genfer See *see* Geneva, Lake
Genhe China 109 F1
Genk Belgium 69 D5
Genoa *see* Genova
Genoa Italy *see* Genoa 78 B3
Genova, Golfo di *sea feature*
Italy 78 B3
Gent Belgium *Fr.* Gand, *Eng.*
Ghent 69 B5
Geok-Tepe *see* Gökdepe
George South Africa 60 D5
George V Land *physical region*
Antarctica 136 C4
Georgenburg *see* Jurbarkas
George Town *capital of*
Cayman Islands 36 B3
Georgetown *capital of* Guyana
41 G2
George Town Malaysia 120 B3
Georgia *country* SW Asia 99 F2
Georgia *state* 31 E3
Gera Germany 76 C4
Geraldton Australia 129 A5
Gereshk Afghanistan 104 D5
Germany *country* W Europe
76–77
Gerona *see* Girona
Getafe Spain 75 E3
Gettysburg Pennsylvania, USA
23 E4
Gevgelija Macedonia 83 E6
Ghana *country* W Africa 57
Ghanzi Botswana 60 C3
Ghardaïa Algeria 52 D2
Gharyān Libya 53 F2
Ghaznī Afghanistan 105 E4
Ghent *see* Gent
Gibraltar *external territory* UK,
SW Europe 74 D5
Gibson Desert *desert region*
Australia 128 C4
Gijón Spain *var.* Xixón 74 D1
Gilbert Islands *see* Tungaru
Gilbert River *river* Australia
130 C3
Gillette Wyoming, USA 24 C3
Gingin Australia 129 B6

Girin *see* Jilin
Girne Cyprus *var.* Kyrenia
98 C5
Girona Spain *var.* Gerona 75 G2
Gisborne New Zealand 132 E3
Giurgiu Romania 90 C5
Gjirokastër Albania 83 D6
Gjøvik Norway 67 B5
Glasgow Scotland, UK 70 C4
Gleiwitz *see* Gliwice
Glendale Arizona, USA 28 B2
Glendive Montana, USA 24 D2
Gliwice Poland *Ger.* Gleiwitz
81 C5
Gloucester England, UK 71 D6
Glubokoye *see* Hlybokaye
Gobi *desert* China/Mongolia
108 D3
Godāvari *river* India 106 D3
115 E1
Godoy Cruz Argentina 46 B4
Godthåb *see* Nuuk
Godwin Austin, Mount *see* K2
Goiânia Brazil 43 F4
Gökdepe Turkmenistan *prev.*
Geok-Tepe, *prev.* Gēkdepe
104 B3
Golan Heights *disputed
territory* SW Asia 100 B4
Gold Coast *coastal region*
Australia 131 E5
Goldingen *see* Kuldīga
Golmud China 108 D4
Gómez Palacio Mexico 32 D3
Gonaïves Haiti 36 D3
Gonder Ethiopia 54 C4
Gongola *river* Nigeria 57 G4
Good Hope, Cape of *coastal
feature* South Africa 60 C5
Goondiwindi Australia 131 D5
Goose Lake *lake* W USA 26 B4
Goré Chad 58 C4
Gorē Ethiopia 55 C5
Gore New Zealand 133 B7
Gorgān Iran 102 D3
Gorki *see* Horki
Gor'kiy *see* Nizhniy Novgorod

Gorlovka *see* Horlivka
Gorontalo Indonesia 121 E4
Gorzów Wielkopolski Poland
Ger. Landsberg 80 B3
Gospić Croatia 82 B3
Gosford Australia 131 D6
Gostivar Macedonia 83 D5
Göteborg Sweden 67 B7
Gotel Mountains *mountain
range* Nigeria 57 G4
Gotland *island* Sweden 67 C7
Gotō-rettō *island group* Japan
113 A6
Göttingen Germany 76 C4
Gouda Netherlands 68 C4
Gough Island *external territory*
UK, Atlantic Ocean 49 D7
Gouin, Réservoir *Reservoir*
Canada 20 D4
Gouré Niger 57 G3
Governador Valadares Brazil
43 G4 45 F1
Goví Altayn Nuruu *mountain
range* Mongolia 109 E3
Gozo *island* Malta 79 C7
Grafton Australia 131 E5
Grampian Mountains *mountains*
Scotland, UK 70 C4
Granada Nicaragua 34 D3
Granada Spain 75 E4
Gran Canaria *island* Spain
52 A3
Gran Chaco *region* C South
America 38 C4 44 A2 46 D2
Grand Bahama *island* Bahamas
36 C1
Grand Banks *undersea feature*
Atlantic Ocean 48 B3
Grand Canyon *valley* SW USA
28 B1
Grande, Rio *river* Brazil 45 E1
Grande, Rio *River* Mexico/USA
17 B6
Grande Comore *island*
Comoros 61 F2
Grande Prairie Canada 19 E4
Grand Erg Occidental *desert
region* Algeria 52 D2
Grand Erg Oriental *desert
region* Algeria/Tunisia 53 E3

Grand Falls Canada 21 G3

Grand Forks North Dakota, USA 25 E1

Grand Junction Colorado, USA 24 C4

Grand Rapids Michigan, USA 22 C3

Graudenz see Grudziądz

Graz Austria 77 E7

Great Abaco island Bahamas 36 C1

Great Ararat see Ararat, Mount

Great Australian Bight sea feature Australia 129 D6

Great Barrier Island island N NZ 132 D2

Great Barrier Reef coral reef Coral Sea 130 C4

Great Basin region USA 26 D4

Great Bear Lake lake Canada 19 E4

Great Dividing Range mountain range Australia 130-131

Great Exhibition Bay inlet New Zealand132 C1

Greater Antarctica region Antarctica 136 C3

Greater Antilles island group West Indies 36 C3

Great Exuma Island island Bahamas 36 C2

Great Falls Montana, USA 24 B1

Great Hungarian Plain plain SE Europe Hung. Alföld 81 D7

Great Inagua island Bahamas 36 D2

Great Khingan Range see Da Hinggan Ling

Great Lakes, The lakes N America see Erie, Huron, Michigan, Ontario, Superior 17 C5

Great Nicobar island India 115 H3

Great Plain of China region China 106 E2

Great Plains region N America 16-17 C5

Great Rift Valley valley E Africa/SW Asia 55 C6

Great Salt Desert see Kavir, Dasht-e

Great Salt Lake salt lake Utah, USA 24 B3

Great Sand Sea desert region Egypt/Libya 53 H3

Great Sandy Desert desert Australia 128 C4

Great Sandy Desert see Ar Rub' al Khali

Great Slave Lake lake Canada 19 E4

Great Victoria Desert desert Australia 129 C5

Greece country SE Europe 86-87

Green Bay Wisconsin, USA 22 B2

Greenland external territory Denmark, Atlantic Ocean var. Grønland 64

Greenland Sea Atlantic Ocean 65 F2

Greenock Scotland, UK 70 C4

Greensboro North Carolina, USA 31 F1

Greenville South Carolina, USA 31 E2

Greifswald Germany 76 D2

Gregory Range mountain range Australia 130 C3

Grenada country West Indies 37 G5

Grenoble France 73 D5

Greymouth New Zealand 133 B5

Grey Range mountain range Australia 124 B4

Grimsby England, UK 71 E5

Groningen Netherlands 68 E1

Grønland see Greenland

Groote Eylandt island Australia 130 B2

Grootfontein Namibia 60 C3

Grosseto Italy 78 B4

Grosskanizsa see Nagykanizsa

Groznyy Russian Federation 93 B7 96 A4

Grudziądz Poland Ger. Graudenz 80 C3

Grünberg in Schlesien see Zielona Góra

Guadalajara Mexico 32 D4

Guadalcanal island Solomon Islands 124 C3

Guadalquivir river Spain 74 D4

Guadeloupe external territory France, West Indies 37 G4

Guadiana river Portugal/Spain 74 C4

Gualeguaychú Argentina 46 D4

Guam external territory USA, Pacific Ocean 126 B1

Guanare Venezuela 40 D1

Guanare river Venezuela 40 D2

Guangdong province China var. Kuang-tung, Kwangtung, Yue 111 C6

Guangxi autonomous region China var. Kwangsi 111 B6

Guangzhou China Eng. Canton 111 C6

Guantánamo Cuba 36 D3

Guaporé River Bolivia/Brazil 32 D3

Guarapuava Brazil 44 D3

Guatemala country Central America 34

Guatemala Basin undersea feature Pacific Ocean 135 G3

Guatemala City capital of Guatemala 34 B2

Guaviare river Colombia 40 D3

Guayaquil Ecuador 40 A4

Guayaquil, Golfo do sea feature Ecuador/Peru 40 A5

Guernsey island Channel Islands 71 D8

Güney Dogu Toroslar mountain range SE Turkey 99 F3

Guiana Highlands upland N South America 38 C2

Guider Cameroon 58 B4

Guimarães Portugal 74 C2

Guinea country W Africa 56

Guinea, Gulf of sea feature Atlantic Ocean 49 D5

Guinea-Bissau country W Africa 56

Guiyang China 111 B6

Guizhou *province* China *var.*
Kuei-chou, Kweichow, Qian
111 B6

Gujarāt *state* India 116 C4

Gujrānwāla Pakistan116 C2

Gujrāt Pakistan 116 C2

Gulf, The *sea feature* Arabian
Sea *var.* Persian Gulf
122 B2

Gulfport Mississippi, USA 30 C3

Gulu Uganda 55 B6

Gumbinnen see Gusev

Gunnbjørn Fjeld
mountain Greenland 64 D4

Gurbantünggüt Shamo *desert*
China 108 C2

Guri, Embalse de *Reservoir*
Venezuela 41 E2

Gusau Nigeria 57 F3

Gusev Kaliningrad, Russian
Federation *prev.* Gumbinnen
88 B4

Gushgy see Serhetabat

Guwāhāti India 117 G3

Guyana *country* NE South
America 41

Gwalior India 116 D3

Gyandzha see Gäncä

Gyangzê China 108 C5

Győr Hungary *Ger.* Raab 81 C6

Gyumri Armenia *Rus.* Kumayri,
prev. Leninakan,
Aleksandropol '99 F2

Gyzylarbat see Serdar

H

Ha'apai Group *islands* Tonga
127 F5

Haapsalu Estonia *Ger.* Hapsal
88 C2

Haarlem Netherlands
68 C3

Haast New Zealand 133 B6

Hachijō-jima *island* Japan
113 D5

Hachinohe Japan 112 D3

Hadejia *river* Nigeria
57 G3

Ḩaḑramawt *Mountain range*
Yemen 103 C7

Hagåtña Guam 126 B1

Hague, The see 's-Gravenhage

Haicheng China 110 D4

Haifa Israel *Heb.* Hefa 85 G4

Ḩā'il Saudi Arabia 102 B4

Hailar China 109 F1

Hainan *island* China *var.*
Hainan Dao 106 D3 111 C8

Hainan *province* China *var.*
Qiong 111 C7

Hainan Dao see Hainan Dao

Hai Phong Vietnam 118 D3

Haiti *country* West Indies 36

Hajdarken see Khaydarkan

Hakodate Japan 112 D3

Ḩalab Syria 100 B2

Ḩalāniyāt, Juzur al *Island group*
Oman 103 D6

Halden Norway 67 B6

Halfmoon Bay New Zealand
133 A7

Halifax Canada 21 F4

Halle Germany 76 C4

Hallein Austria 77 D7

Halls Creek Australia 128 D3

Halmahera, Pulau *island*
Indonesia 121 F3

Halmahera Sea *Sea* Indonesia
121 F4

Halmstad Sweden 67 B7

Hamada Japan 113 B5

Hamadān Iran 102 C3

Ḩamāh Syria 100 B3

Hamamatsu Japan 113 C5

Hamar Norway 67 B5

Hamburg Germany 76 C3

Hämeenlinna Finland 67 D5

HaMelaḩ, Yam see Dead Sea

Hamersley Range *mountain
range* Australia 128 B4

Hamhŭng North Korea 110 E4

Hami China 108 C3

Hamilton Canada 20 D5

Hamilton New Zealand 132 D3

Hamm Germany 76 B4

Hammerfest Norway 66 D2

Handan China 110 C4

HaNegev *desert region* Israel
Eng. Negev 101 A6

Hangayn Nuruu *mountain
range* Mongolia 108 D2

Hangzhou China 111 D5

Hannover Germany *Eng.*
Hanover 76 B4

Hanoi *capital* of Vietnam 118
D3

Hanover see Hannover

Hanzhong China 111 B5

Hapsal see Haapsalu

Ḩaraḍ Yemen 103 C5

Harare *capital* of Zimbabwe
61 E3

Harbin China 110 E3

Hargeysa Somalia 55 D5

Hari *river* Indonesia 120 B4

Harīrūd *river* C Asia 104 D4

Harper Liberia 56 D5

Harrisburg Pennsylvania, USA
23 E4

Harstad Norway 66 C2

Hartford Connecticut, USA
23 G3

Har Us Nuur *lake* Mongolia
108 C2

Hasselt Belgium 69 D5

Hastings New Zealand 132 E4

Hastings Nebraska, USA
24 E4

Hatay see Antakya

Hatteras, Cape *coastal feature*
North Carolina, USA 31 G1

Hattiesburg Mississippi, USA
30 C3

Hat Yai Thailand 119 C7

Haugesund Norway 67 A6

Hauraki Gulf *gulf* New Zealand
132 D2

Havana *capital* of Cuba *Sp.* La
Habana 36 B2

Havelock North Carolina, USA
31 G1

Havre Montana, USA 24 C1

Havre-Saint-Pierre Canada
21 F3

Hawaii *state* USA 135 E2

Hawaiian Islands *islands* USA
125 F1

Hawaiian Ridge *undersea feature* Pacific Ocean 134 D2

Hawera New Zealand 132 D4

Hawke Bay *bay* New Zealand 132 E4

Hawlēr *see* Arbīl

Hawthorne Nevada, USA 27 C6

Hay River Canada 19 E4

Hays Kansas, USA 25 E4

Hazar Turkmenistan *prev.* Cheleken 104 A2

Heard & McDonald Islands *islands* Indian Ocean 123 C7

Hebei *province* China *var.* Hopeh, Hopei, Ji; *prev.* Chihli 110 C4

Hebron West Bank *var.* Al Khalīl, El Khalīl, *Heb.* Ḥevron 101 D7

Heerenveen Netherlands 68 D2

Heerlen Netherlands 69 D6

Hefa Israel *prev.* Haifa 101 A5

Hefei China 111 D5

Hei *see* Heilongjiang

Heidelberg Germany 77 B5

Heilbronn Germany 77 B5

Heilongjiang *province* China *var.* Hei, Hei-lung-chiang 110 D3

Hei-lung-chiang *see* Heilongjiang

Helena Montana, USA 24 B2

Hells Canyon *valley* Idaho/Oregon USA 26 C3

Helmand *river* Afghanistan 104 C5

Helmond Netherlands 69 D5

Helsingborg Sweden 67 B7

Helsinki *capital of* Finland 67 D6

Henan *province* China *var.* Honan, Yu 111 C5

Hengduan Shan *mountain range* China 111 A6

Hengelo Netherlands 68 E3

Hengyang China 111 C6

Henzada Myanmar 118 A4

Herāt Afghanistan 104 C4

Hermansverk Norway 67 A5

Hermosillo Mexico 32 B2

Herning Denmark 67 A7

Heywood Islands *island group* Australia 128 C3

Hiiumaa *island* Estonia *Ger.* Dagden, *Swed.* Dagö 88 C2

Hildesheim Germany 76 C4

Hilversum Netherlands 68 C3

Himalayas *mountain range* S Asia 106 B2

Himora Ethiopia 54 C4

Ḥimṣ Syria 100 B3

Hinchinbrook Island *island* Australia 130 D3

Hindu Kush *mountain range* C Asia 105 E4

Hiroshima Japan 113 B5

Hitachi Japan 112 D4

Hjørring Denmark 67 A7

Hlybokaye Belarus *Rus.* Glubokoye 89 D5

Hobart Tasmania 131 C8

Hobbs New Mexico, USA 29 E3

Hồ Chí Minh Vietnam *var.* Ho Chi Minh City, *prev.* Saigon 119 E6

Ho Chi Minh City *see* Hồ Chí Minh

Hodeida *see* Al Ḥudaydah

Hoek van Holland Netherlands 68 B4

Hoggar *see* Ahaggar

Hohe Tauern *mountain range* Austria 77 C7

Hohhot China 109 F3

Hokitika New Zealand 133 B5

Hokkaidō *island* Japan 112 D2

Holguín Cuba 36 C2

Holland *see* Netherlands

Hollabrunn Austria 77 E6

Holon Israel 101 A5

Holyhead Wales, UK 71 C5

Hombori Mopti, Mali 57 E3

Homyel' Belarus *Rus.* Gomel' 89 E7

Honan *see* Henan

Honduras *country* Central America 34-35

Honduras, Gulf of *sea feature* Caribbean Sea 34 C2

Hønefoss Norway 67 B6

Hông Gai Vietnam 118 E3

Hong Kong China *var.* Xianggang 111 C6

Honiara *capital of* Solomon Islands 126 C3

Honshū *island* Japan 112 D3

Hoorn Netherlands 68 C2

Hopa Turkey 99 E2

Hopedale Canada 21 F2

Hopeh *see* Hebei

Hopei *see* Hebei

Hopkinsville Kentucky, USA 22 B5

Horki Belarus *Rus.* Gorki 89 E5

Horlivka Ukraine *Rus.* Gorlovka 90 G3

Horn, Cape *see* Hornos, Cabo

Hornos, Cabo *Eng* Cape Horn *coastal feature* Chile 47 C8

Horsham Australia 131 C7

Hospitalet *see* L'Hospitalet de Llobregat

Hot Springs Arkansas, USA 30 B2

Houston Texas, USA 29 G4

Hovd Mongolia 108 C2

Hövsgöl Nuur *lake* Mongolia 108 D1

Hradec Králové Czech Republic *Ger.* Königgrätz 81 B5

Hrodna Belarus *Rus.* Grodno 89 B5

Huacho Peru 42 A3

Huainan China 111 D5

Huambo Angola 60 B2

Huancayo Peru 42 B3

Huang He *river* China *Eng.* Yellow River 110 C4

Huánuco Peru 42 B3

Huaraz Peru 42 B3

Hubei *province* China 111 C5

Hubli India 114 C2

Hudson *river* NE USA 23 F3

Hudson Bay *sea feature* Canada 16 C4

Hudson Strait *sea feature* Canada 19 H3

Huê Vietnam 118 E4

Huehuetenango Guatemala 34 B2

Huelva Spain 74 C4

Huesca Spain 75 F2

Hughenden Australia 130 C4

Hull *see* Kingston upon Hull

Hulun Nur *lake* China 109 F1

Humboldt *river* W USA 27 C5

Hunan *province* China *var.* Xiang 111 C6

Hungarian Plain *plain* C Europe 85 H2

Hungary *country* C Europe 81

Huntington Beach California, USA 27 C8

Huntington West Virginia, USA 22 D5

Huntsville Alabama, USA 30 D2

Hurghada Egypt 54 B2

Huron, Lake *lake* Canada/USA 22 D2

Hurunui *river* New Zealand 133 C5

Húsavík Iceland 65 E4

Huvadhu Atoll *island* Maldives 114 C5

Hvar *island* Croatia 82 B4

Hyargas Nuur *lake* Mongolia 108 D2

Hyderābād India 114 D1 116 B3

Hyères, Îles d' *islands* France 73 D6

I

Iaşi Romania 90 D3

Ibadan Nigeria 57 F4

Ibagué Colombia 40 B3

Ibarra Ecuador 40 A4

Iberian Peninsula *peninsula* SW Europe 84 B3

Ibérico, Sistema *Mountain range* Spain 75 F2

Ibiza *island* Spain *Cat.* Eivissa 75 G4

Ica Peru 42 B4

İçel *see* Mersin

Iceland *country* Atlantic Ocean 65 E4

Idaho *state* USA 26

Idaho Falls Idaho, USA 26 E3

Idfu Egypt 54 B2

Idlib Syria 100 B2

Ieper Belgium *Fr.* Ypres 69 A6

Ifôghas, Adrar des *upland* Mali *var.* Adrar des Iforas 57 F2

Iforas, Adrar des *see* Ifôghas, Adrar des

Iglau *see* Jihlava

Iglesias Italy 79 A5

Iguaçu *River* Argentina/Brazil 44 C3

Iguidi, 'Erg *Desert* Algeria/Mauritania 56 D1

Ihosy Madagascar 61 G4

Iisalmi Finland 66 E4

IJssel *river* Netherlands 68 D3

IJsselmeer *lake* Netherlands *prev.* Zuider Zee 68 D2

Ikaria *island* Greece 87 D5

Iki *island* Japan 113 A6

Ilagan Philippines 121 E1

Ilebo Dem. Rep. Congo 59 C6

Ili *River* China/Kazakhstan 94 D3

Iligan Philippines 121 F2

Illapel Chile 46 B3

Illinois *state* USA 22 B4

Iloilo Philippines 121 E2

Ilorin Nigeria 57 F4

İluh *see* Batman

Imatra Finland 67 E5

Imperatriz Brazil 43 F2

Impfondo Congo 59 C5

Imphāl India 117 H4

Independence Missouri, USA 25 F4

India *country* S Asia 114–115, 116-117

Indian Ocean 122-123

Indiana *state* USA 22 C4

Indianapolis Indiana, USA 22 C4

Indigirka *river* Russian Federation 95 F2

Indonesia *country* SE Asia 120-121

Indonesian Borneo *see* Kalimantan

Indore India 116 D4

Indus *river* S Asia 116 C1

Indus Cone *see.* Indus Fan

Indus Fan *var.* Indus Cone. *Undersea feature* Arabian Sea 122 B3

Indus, Mouths of the *wetlands* Pakistan 116 B4

Ingolstadt Germany 77 C6

Inguri *see* Enguri

Inhambane Mozambique 61 E4

Inn *river* C Europe 77 D6

Innaanganeq *headland* Greenland 64 C1

Inner Islands *islands* Seychelles 61 H1

Inner Mongolia *autonomous region* China 109 F3

Innsbruck Austria 77 C7

I-n-Sâkâne, Erg *Desert* Mali 57 F2

I-n-Salah Algeria 52 D3

Insein Myanmar 118 B4

Inukjuak Canada 20 D2

Inuvik Canada 19 E3

Invercargill New Zealand 133 A7

Inverness Scotland, UK 70 C3

Investigator Ridge *undersea feature* Indian Ocean 122 D4

Ioánnina Greece 86 A4

Iónia Nisiá *island group* Greece *Eng.* Ionian Islands 87 A5

Ionian Islands *see* Iónia Nisiá

Ionian Sea Mediterranean Sea 87 A6

Íos *island* Greece 87 D6

Iowa *state* USA 25 F3

Ipoh Malaysia 120 B3

Ipswich England, UK 71 E6

Iqaluit Canada 19 H3

Iquique Chile 46 B1

Iquitos Peru 42 B2

Irákleio Greece 87 D7

Iran *country* SW Asia 102-103

Iranian Plateau *upland* Iran 102 D4

Irapuato Mexico 33 E4

Iraq *country* SW Asia 102

Jihlava Czech Republic *Ger.* Iglau 81 B5

Jilin *province* China *var.* Chi-lin, Girin, Ji, Kirin 110 E3

Jilin China 110 E3

Jīma Ethiopia 55 C5

Jin *see* Shanxi

Jinan China 111 C4

Jingdezhen China 111 D5

Jinhua China 111 D5

Jining China 109 F3

Jinotega Nicaragua 34 D3

Jinsha Jiang *river* China 108 D5

Jinzhou China 110 D4

Jīzān Saudi Arabia 103 B6

João Pessoa Brazil 43 H3

Jodhpur India 116 C3

Joensuu Finland 67 E5

Johannesburg South Africa 60 D4

Johnston Atoll *US unincorporated territory* Pacific Ocean 125 E1

Johor Bahru Malaysia 120 C3

Joinville Brazil 44 D3

Joliet Illinois, USA 22 B3

Jönköping Sweden 67 B7

Jonquière Canada 21 E4

Jordan *country* SW Asia 100-101

Jordan *river* SW Asia 101 B5

Joseph Bonaparte Gulf *gulf* Australia 128 D2

Jos Plateau *upland* Nigeria 57 G4

Juan Fernandez, Islas *islands* Chile 46 A4

Juàzeiro Brazil 43 G3

Juàzeiro do Norte Brazil 43 G3

Juba Sudan 55 B5

Júcar *river* Spain 75 E3

Judenburg Austria 77 D7

Juigalpa Nicaragua 34 D3

Juiz de Fora Brazil 43 G5 45 F2

Juneau Alaska, USA 18 D4

Junín Argentina 46 D4

Jura *mountains* France/Switzerland 77 A7

Jura *island* Scotland, UK 70 B4

Jurbarkas Lithuania *Ger.* Jurburg, *var.* Georgenburg 88 B4

Jurburg *see* Jurbarkas

Juruá *river* Brazil/Peru 42 C2

Juticalpa Honduras 34 D2

Jutland *see* Jylland

Juventud, Isla de la *island* Cuba 36 B2

Jylland *peninsula* Denmark *Eng.* Jutland 67 A7

Jyväskylä Finland 67 D5

───────── K ─────────

K2 *peak* China/Pakistan *Eng.* Mount Godwin Austen 116 D1

Kaachka *see* Kaka

Kaakhka *see* Kaka

Kabale Uganda 55 B6

Kabinda Dem. Rep. Congo 59 D7

Kābol *see* Kabul

Kabul *capital of* Afghanistan *Per.* Kabol 105 E4

Kachch, Gulf of *sea feature* Arabian Sea 116 B4

Kachch, Rann of *wetland* India/Pakistan *var.* Rann of Kutch 116 B4

Kadugli Sudan 54 B4

Kaduna Nigeria 57 G4

Kaédi Mauritania 56 C3

Kâghet *Physical region* Mauritania 56 D1

Kagoshima Japan 113 A6

Kahramanmaraş Turkey *var.* Marash, Maraş 98 D4

Kai, Kepulauan *island group* Indonesia 121 G4

Kaifeng China 111 C5

Kaikohe New Zealand 132 C2

Kaikoura New Zealand 133 C5

Kainji Reservoir *Reservoir* Nigeria 57 F4

Kairouan Tunisia 53 E1

Kaiserslautern Germany 77 B5

Kaitaia New Zealand 132 C2

Kajaani Finland 66 E4

Kaka Turkmenistan *prev.* Kaahka, *var.* Kaachka 104 D3

Kakhovka Ukraine 91 F4

Kakhovs'ka Vodoskhovyshche *Reservoir* Ukraine 91 F3

Kalahari Desert *desert* southern Africa 60 C4

Kalamariá Greece 86 C3

Kalámata Greece 87 B6

Kalāt Afghanistan 104 D5

Kalbarri Australia 129 A5

Kalemie Dem. Rep. Congo 59 E7

Kalgoorlie Australia 129 C6

Kalimantan *geopolitical region* Indonesia *Eng.* Indonesian Borneo 120 D4

Kaliningrad *external territory* Russian Federation 96 A2

Kaliningrad Kaliningrad, Russian Federation *prev.* Königsberg 88 A4

Kalinkavichy Belarus *Rus.* Kalinkovichi 89 D7

Kalinkovichi *see* Kalinkavichy

Kalisch *see* Kalisz

Kalispell Montana, USA 24 B1

Kalisz Poland *Ger.* Kalisch 80 C4

Kalmar Sweden 67 C7

Kalpeni Island *island* India 114 C3

Kama *river* Russian Federation 92 D4

Kamchatka *peninsula* Russian Federation 97 H3

Kamchiya *river* Bulgaria 86 E2

Kamina Dem. Rep. Congo 59 D7

Kamishli *see* Al Qāmishlī

Kamloops Canada 19 E5

Kampala *capital of* Uganda 55 B6

Kâmpóng Cham Cambodia 119 D6

Kâmpóng Chhnăng Cambodia 119 D5

Kâmpóng Saôm Cambodia 119 D6

Kâmpôt Cambodia 119 D6

Kampuchea *see* Cambodia

Kermadec Trench *undersea feature* Pacific Ocean 125 E4

Kermān Iran *var.* Kirman 102 D4

Kermānshāh Iran *prev.* Bākhtarān 102 C3

Kerulen *river* China/Mongolia 109 E2

Ketchikan Alaska, USA 18 D4

Key West Florida, USA 31 E5

Khabarovsk Russian Federation 97 G4

Khanka, Lake *lake* China/Russian Federation 110 E3

Khankendy *see* Xankändi

Kharkiv Ukraine *Rus.* Khar'kov 91 G2

Khar'kov *see* Kharkiv

Khartoum *capital of* Sudan *var.* Al Khurṭūm 54 B4

Khāsh Iran 102 E4

Khaskovo Bulgaria 86 D2

Khaydarkan Kyrgyzstan *var.* Khaydarken, Hajdarken 105 E2

Khaydarken *see* Khaydarkan

Kherson Ukraine 91 E4

Kheta *river* Russian Federation 94 D2

Khios *see* Chios

Khirbet el 'Aujā et Tahtā West Bank 101 D6

Khmel 'nyts'kyy Ukraine 90 D2

Khodzhent *see* Khŭjand

Khojend *see* Khŭjand

Khokand *see* Qo'qon

Kholm Afghanistan 105 E3

Khon Kaen Thailand 118 C4

Khorog *see* Khorugh

Khorugh Tajikistan *Rus.* Khorog 105 F3

Khouribga Morocco 52 C2

Khudzhand *see* Khŭjand

Khŭjand Tajikistan *var.* Khodzhent, Khojend, *Rus.* Khudzhand *prev.* Leninabad 105 E2

Khulna Bangladesh 117 G4

Khvoy Iran 102 B3

Kiangsi *see* Jiangxi

Kiangsu *see* Jiangsu

Kičevo Macedonia 83 D5

Kiel Germany 76 C2

Kielce Poland 80 D4

Kiev *capital of* Ukraine *Ukr.* Kyyiv 91 E2

Kiffa Mauritania 56 C3

Kigali *capital of* Rwanda 55 B6

Kigoma Tanzania 55 B7

Kikládhes *see* Kyklades

Kikwit Dem. Rep. Congo 59 C6

Kilimanjaro *peak* Tanzania 55 C7

Kilkis Greece 86 B3

Killarney Ireland 71 A6

Kimberley South Africa 60 D4

Kimberley Plateau *upland* Australia 128 D3

Kindia Guinea 56 C4

Kindu Dem. Rep. Congo 59 D6

King Island *island* Australia 131 C7

Kingisepp *see* Kuressaare

Kingman Reef *external territory* USA, Pacific Ocean 125 F2

King Sound *sound* Australia 128 C3

Kingsport Tennessee, USA 31 E1

Kingsville Texas, USA 29 G5

Kingston Canada 20 C5

Kingston *capital of* Jamaica 36 C3

Kingston upon Hull England, UK *var.* Hull 71 E5

Kingstown St Vincent & The Grenadines 36 G4

King William Island *island* Canada 19 F3

Kinneret, Yam *see* Tiberius, Lake

Kinshasa *capital of* Dem. Rep. Congo *prev.* Léopoldville 59 B6

Kirghizia *see* Kyrgyzstan

Kiribati *country* Pacific Ocean 127

Kirin *see* Jilin

Kiritimati *island* Kiribati *var.* Christmas Island 127 G2

Kirkenes Norway 66 E2

Kirklareli Turkey 98 A2

Kirksville Missouri, USA 25 F4

Kirkūk Iraq 102 B3

Kirkwall Scotland, UK 70 C2

Kirman *see* Kermān

Kirov Russian Federation 92 C4 96 B3

Kirovabad *see* Gäncä

Kirovakan *see* Vanadzor

Kirovohrad Ukraine 91 E3

Kiruna Sweden 66 C3

Kisangani Dem. Rep. Congo *prev.* Stanleyville 59 D5

Kishinev *see* Chişinău

Kismaayo Somalia 55 D6

Kisumu Kenya 55 C6

Kitakyūshū Japan 113 A5

Kitami Japan 112 D2

Kitchener Canada 20 C5

Kitwe Zambia 56 D2

Kivu, Lake *lake* Rwanda/Dem. Rep. Congo 55 B6 59 E6

Kızıl Irmak *river* Turkey 98 C2

Kizyl-Arvat *see* Serdar

Kladno Czech Republic 81 A5

Klagenfurt Austria 77 D7

Klaipėda Lithuania *Ger.* Memel 88 B4

Klamath Falls Oregon, USA 26 B4

Klang Malaysia *var.* Kelang 120 B2

Ključ Bosnia & Herzegovina 82 B3

Knin Croatia 82 B4

Knoxville Tennessee, USA 31 E1

Knud Rasmussen Land *region* Greenland 64 D1

Kōbe Japan 113 C5

Koblenz Germany 77 B5

Kobryn Belarus 89 B6

Kocaeli *see* İzmit

Kočani Macedonia 83 E5

Kōchi Japan 113 B6

Kochi *see* Cochin

Kodiak Alaska, USA 18 C3

Kodiak Island *island* Alaska, USA 18 C3

Koedoes *see* Kudus

Krung Thep see Bangkok
Kruševac Serbia 83 E4
Krušné Hory see Erzgebirge
Krychaw Belarus *Rus.* Krichev 89 E6
Kryms'kyy Pivostriv *peninsula* Ukraine *var.* Crimea 90 F4
Kryvyy Rih Ukraine *Rus.* Krivoy Rog 91 E3
Kuala Lumpur *capital of* Malaysia 120 B3
Kuala Terengganu Malaysia 120 B3
Kuang-tung see Guangdong
Kuantan Malaysia 120 C3
Kuba see Quba
Kuching Malaysia 120 C3
Kuçovë Albania *prev.* Qyteti Stalin 83 D6
Kudus Indonesia *prev.* Koedoes 120 D5
Kuei-chou see China Guizhou
Kuglutuk Canada *prev.* Coppermine 19 E3
Kuito Angola 60 C2
Kuldīga Latvia *Ger.* Goldingen 88 B3
Kullorsuaq Greenland 64 C2
Kŭlob Tajikistan *Rus.* Kulyab 105 E3
Kulyab see Kŭlob
Kum see Qom
Kuma *river* Russian Federation 93 B7
Kumamoto Japan 113 B6
Kumanovo Macedonia 83 E5
Kumasi Ghana 57 E5
Kumayri see Gyumri 99 F2
Kumo Nigeria 57 G4
Kumon Range *mountain range* Myanmar 118 B1
Kunashir *island* Japan/Russian Federation (disputed) 112 E1
Kunduz see Kondoz
Kunja-Urgenč see Köneürgench
Kunlun Mountains see Kunlun Shan
Kunlun Shan *mountain range* China *Eng.* Kunlun Mountains 106 B4

Kunming China 111 B6
Kununurra Australia 128 D3
Kupang Indonesia 120 E5
Kür see Kura
Kura *river* Azerbaijan/Georgia *Az.* Kür 99 G2
Kurashiki Japan 113 B5
Kurdistan *region* Turkey 99 F4
Küre Dağları *mountains* Turkey 98 C2
Kuressaare Estonia *prev.* Kingissepp, *Ger.* Arensburg 88 C2
Kurgan-Tyube see Qürghonteppa
Kurile Islands *islands* Pacific Ocean 112 E2
Kurile Trench *undersea feature* Pacific Ocean 134 C2
Kurnool India 114 C1
Kushiro Japan 112 E2
Kushka see Serhetabat
Kustanay see Kostanay
Kütahya Turkey *prev.* Kutaiah 98 B3
Kutaiah see Kütahya
K'ut'aisi Georgia 99 F2
Kutch, Rann of see Kachch, Rann of
Kuujjuaq Canada 21 E2
Kuujjuarapik Canada 20 D2
Kuusamo Finland 66 E3
Kuwait *country* SW Asia 102 C4
Kuwait City *capital of* Kuwait 102 C4
Kuytun China 108 C2
Kvitøya *island* Svalbard 65 G1
Kwangju South Korea 111 E4
Kwango *river* Dem. Rep. Congo 59 C7
Kwangtung see Guangdong
Kweichow see Guizhou
Kykládes *island group* Greece *prev.* Kikládhes, *Eng.* Cyclades 87 D6
Kyrenia see Girne
Kyrgyzstan *country* C Asia *var.* Kirghizia 105
Kýthira *island* Greece 87 B6

Kyushu-Palau Ridge *undersea feature* Pacific Ocean 124 B1
Kyyiv see Kiev
Kyyivs'ke Vodoskhovyshche *Reservoir* Ukraine 91 E1
Kyōto Japan 113 C5
Kyūshū *island* Japan 113 B6
Kyzylorda Kazakhstan 96 B5

L

Laâyoune Western Sahara 52 B3
Labé Guinea 56 C4
Laborca see Laborec
Laborec *river* Slovakia *Hung.* Laborca 81 E5
Labrador *region* Canada 21 F2
Labrador Sea Atlantic Ocean 64 B5
Laccadive Islands see Lakshadweep
La Ceiba Honduras 34 D2
Lachlan River *river* Australia 131 C6
La Coruña see A Coruña
La Crosse Wisconsin, USA 22 A2
Ladoga, Lake see Ladozhskoye Ozero
Ladozhskoye Ozero *lake* Russian Federation *Eng.* Lake Ladoga 92 B3
Ladysmith Wisconsin, USA 22 A2
Lae Papua New Guinea 126 B3
La Esperanza Honduras 34 C2
Lafayette Louisiana, USA 30 B3
Laghouat Algeria 52 D2
Lagos Nigeria 57 F5
Lagos Portugal 74 C4
Lagouira Western Sahara 52 A4
La Grande Oregon, USA 26 C3
La Habana see Havana
Lahore Pakistan 116 C2
Laï Chad 58 C4
Laila see Laylá
Lajes Brazil 44 D3
Lake Charles Louisiana, USA 30 B3

Lake District *region* England, UK 71 C5

Lakewood Colorado, USA 24 D4

Lakshadweep *island group* India *Eng.* Laccadive Islands 114 B2

La Ligua Chile 46 B4

La Louvière Belgium 69 B6

Lambaré Paraguay 44 B3

Lambaréné Gabon 59 B6

Lamia Greece 86 B4

Lancaster England, UK 71 D5

Lancaster California, USA 27 C7

Lancaster Sound *sea feature* Canada 19 F2

Landsberg *see* Gorzów Wielkopolski

Land's End *coastal feature* England, UK 71 C7

Landshut Germany 77 D6

Lang Son Vietnam 118 D3

Länkäran Azerbaijan *Rus.* Lenkoran' 99 H3

Lansing Michigan, USA 22 C3

Lanzarote *island* Spain 52 B3

Lanzhou China 110 B4

Laon France 72 D3

La Oroya Peru 42 B3

Laos *country* SE Asia 118

La Palma *island* Spain 52 A3

La Paz *capital* of Bolivia 42 C4

La Paz Mexico 32 B3

La Pérouse Strait *sea feature* Japan 112 D1

Lapland *region* N Europe 66 C3

La Plata Argentina 46 D4

Lappeenranta Finland 67 E5

Laptev Sea *see* Laptevykh, More

Laptevykh, More Arctic Ocean *Eng.* Laptev Sea 97 F2

L'Aquila Italy 78 C4

Laramie Wyoming, USA 24 C4

Laredo Texas, USA 29 F5

La Rioja Argentina 46 C3

Lárisa Greece 86 B4

Lárkána Pakistan 116 B3

Larnaca Cyprus *var.* Larnaka, Larnax 98 C5

Larnaka *see* Larnaca

Larnax *see* Larnaca

La Rochelle France 72 B4

La Roche-sur-Yon France 72 B4

La Romana Dominican Republic 36 E3

Las Cruces New Mexico, USA 28 D3

Las Piedras Uruguay 44 C5

La Serena Chile 46 B3

La Spezia Italy 78 B3

Las Tablas Panama 35 F5

Las Vegas Nevada, USA 27 D7

Latakia *see* Al Lādhiqīyah

Latvia *country* NE Europe 88

Launceston Tasmania 131 C8

Laurentian Basin *see* Canada Basin

Laurentian Mountains *upland* Canada 16 D4

Lausanne Switzerland 77 A7

Laut, Pulau *prev.* Laoet. *Island* Indonesia 120 D4

Laval France 72 B4

Lawton Oklahoma, USA 29 F2

Laylá Saudi Arabia 103 C5

Lazarev Sea *sea* Antarctica 136 B2

Lebanon *country* SW Asia 100-101

Lebu Chile 47 B5

Lecce Italy 79 E5

Leduc Canada 19 E5

Leeds England, UK 71 D5

Leeuwarden Netherlands 68 D1

Leeward Islands *see* Sotavento, Ilhas de

Lefkáda *island* Greece *prev.* Levkás 87 A5

Lefkoşa *see* Nicosia

Lefkosia *see* Nicosia

Legaspi *see* Legazpi City

Legazpi City Philippines *var.* Legaspi 120 E2

Legnica Poland *Ger.* Liegnitz 80 B4

Le Havre France 72 B3

Leicester England, UK 71 D6

Leiden Netherlands 68 C3

Leipzig Germany 76 D4

Lek *river* Netherlands 68 C4

Le Léman *see* Geneva, Lake

Lelystad Netherlands 68 D3

Léman, Lac *see* Geneva, Lake

Le Mans France 72 B4

Lemesos *see* Limassol

Lemnos *see* Límnos

Lena *river* Russian Federation 97 F3

Leninabad *see* Khŭjand

Leninakan *see* Gyumri

Leningrad *see* St Petersburg

Leninsk *see* Türkmenabat

Lenkoran' *see* Länkäran

León Mexico 33 E4

León Nicaragua 34 C3

León Spain 74 D1

Léopoldville *see* Kinshasa

Lepel' *see* Lyepyel'

Le Puy France 73 C5

Lérida *see* Lleida

Lerwick Scotland, UK 70 D1

Lesbos *see* Lésvos

Leshan China 111 B5

Leskovac Serbia 82 E4

Lesotho *country* southern Africa 60

Lesser Antarctica *region* Antarctica 134 B3

Lesser Antilles *island group* West Indies 37 G4

Lésvos *island* Greece *Eng.* Lesbos 86 D4

Lethbridge Canada 19 E5

Leti, Kepulauan *island group* Indonesia 121 F5

Leuven Belgium 69 C6

Leverkusen Germany 76 A4

Levin New Zealand 132 D4

Levkás *see* Lefkáda

Lewis *island* Scotland, UK 70 B2

Lewiston Idaho, USA 26 C2

Lewiston Maine, USA 23 G2

Lexington Kentucky, USA 22 C5

Lower California *see* Baja California
Lower Hutt New Zealand
Loxa *see* Loksa
Loyauté, Îles *island group* New Caledonia 126 D5
Loznica Serbia 82 C3
Lu *see* Shandong
Luanda *capital of* Angola 60 B1
Luanshya Zambia 60 D2
Lubango Angola 60 B2
Lubbock Texas, USA 29 E2
Lübeck Germany 76 C3
Lublin Poland *Rus.* Lyublin 80 E4
Lubny Ukraine 91 F2
Lubumbashi Dem. Rep. Congo 59 E8
Lucapa Angola 60 C1
Lucena Philippines 120 E2
Lučenec Slovakia *Hung.* Losonc, *Ger.* Losontz 81 D6
Lucerne *see* Luzern
Lucknow India 117 E3
Lüderitz Namibia 60 C4
Ludhiāna India 116 D2
Lugano Switzerland 77 B7
Lugo Spain 74 C1
Luhans'k Ukraine 91 H3
Luleå Sweden 66 D4
Lumsden New Zealand 133 A7
Lüneburg Germany 76 C3
Luninyets Belarus 89 C6
Luoyang *var.* Honan, Lo-yang. China 110 C4
Lusaka *capital of* Zambia 60 D2
Lushnjë Albania 83 D6
Lūt, Baḥrat *see* Dead Sea
Luts'k Ukraine 90 C1
Luxembourg *country* W Europe 69 D8
Luxembourg *capital of* Luxembourg 69 D8
Luxor Egypt 54 B2
Luzern Switzerland *Fr.* Lucerne 77 B7
Luzon *island* Philippines 121 E1

Luzon Strait *sea feature* Philippines/Taiwan 107 E3
L'viv Ukraine *Rus.* L'vov 90 C2
L'vov *see* L'viv
Lyepyel' Belarus *Rus.* Lepel' 89 D7
Lyon France 73 D5
Lyublin *see* Lublin

— **M** —

Ma'ān Jordan 101 B6
Maas *see* Meuse
Maastricht Netherlands 69 D6
Macao *external territory* Portugal, E Asia *var.* Macau 111 C7
Macapá Brazil 43 F1
Macau *see* Macao
Macdonnell Ranges *mountains* Australia 130 A4
Macedonia *country* SE Europe officially Former Yugoslav Republic of Macedonia, *abbrev.* FYR Macedonia 83
Maceió Brazil 43 H3
Machala Ecuador 40 A5
Mackay Australia 130 D4
Mackay, Lake *lake* Australia 128 D4
Mackenzie *river* Canada 19 E4
Mackenzie Bay *sea feature* Atlantic Ocean 136 D3
Macleod, Lake *lake* Australia 128 A4
Mâcon France 72 D5
Macon Georgia, USA 31 E2
Madagascar *country* Indian Ocean 61
Madagascar Basin *undersea feature* Indian Ocean 123 B5
Madagascar Plateau *undersea feature* Indian Ocean 123 A6
Madang Papua New Guinea 126 B3
Madeira *river* Bolivia/Brazil 42 D2
Madeira *island group* Portugal 52 A2

Madhya Pradesh *state* India 117 E4
Madison Wisconsin, USA 22 B3
Madiun *prev.* Madioen. Indonesia 120 D5
Madona Latvia *Ger.* Modohn 88 D3
Madras *see* Chennai
Madre de Dios *river* Bolivia/Peru 42 C3
Madrid *capital of* Spain 75 E3
Madurai India 114 D3
Magadan Russian Federation 97 G3
Magallanes *see* Punta Arenas
Magallanes, Estrecho de *see* Magellan, Strait of
Magdalena *river* Colombia 40 B2
Magdeburg Germany 76 C4
Magelang Indonesia 120 C5
Magellan, Strait of *sea feature* S South America *Sp.* Estrecho de Magallanes 47 B8
Maggiore, Lake *lake* Italy/Switzerland 78 B2
Mahajanga Madagascar 61 G3
Mahalapye Botswana 60 D4
Mahanādi *river* India 117 F5
Mahārāshtra *state* India 116 D5
Mahé *island* Seychelles 61 H1
Mahilyow Belarus *Rus.* Mogilëv 89 E6
Mährisch-Ostrau *see* Ostrava
Maicao Colombia 40 C1
Maiduguri Nigeria 57 H4
Maimana *see* Meymaneh
Maine *state* USA 23 G1
Maine, Gulf of *gulf* USA 23 G2
Mainz Germany 77 B5
Maio *island* Cape Verde 56 A3
Maíz, Islas del *islands* Nicaragua 35 E3
Majorca *see* Mallorca
Majuro *island* Marshall Islands 126 D1
Makarska Croatia 82 B4
Makarov Basin *undersea feature* Arctic Ocean 137 G3

Makassar Indonesia *prev.*
Ujungpandang 121 E4
Makassar Strait *strait* Indonesia
120 D4
Makeyevka *see* Makiyivka
Makhachkala Russian
Federation 93 B7 96 A4
Makiyivka Ukraine *Rus.*
Makeyevka 91 G5
Makkah Saudi Arabia *Eng.*
Mecca 103 A5
Makkovik Canada 21 F2
Malabo *capital of* Equatorial
Guinea 59 A5
Maladzyechna Belarus *Rus.*
Molodechno, *Pol.*
Molodeczno 89 C5
Málaga Spain 74 D5
Malakal Sudan 55 B5
Malang Indonesia 120 D5
Malanje Angola 60 C2
Malatya Turkey 99 E3
Malawi *country* southern
Africa 61
Malay Peninsula *peninsula*
Malaysia/Thailand 119 D8
Malaysia *country* Asia 120
Malden Island *atoll* Kiribati
125 F2
Maldives *country* Indian Ocean
114 C4
Male' *capital of* Maldives
114 C4
Malekula *island* Vanuatu 124 D3
Mali *country* W Africa 57
Malindi Kenya 55 C7
Mallorca *island* Spain *Eng.*
Majorca 75 H3
Malmö Sweden 67 B7
Malta *country* Mediterranean
Sea 79 C8
Malta Montana, USA 24 C1
Malta Channel *sea feature*
Mediterranean Sea 79 C7
Maluku *island group*
Indonesia *var.* Moluccas
107 E4 121 F4

Maluku, Laut Pacific Ocean
Eng. Molucca Sea 121 F4
Mamberamo *river* Indonesia
121 H4
Mamoudzou *capital of*
Mayotte 61 G2
Man, Isle of *island* UK 71 C5
Manado Indonesia 121 F3
Managua *capital of* Nicaragua
34 D3
Manama *capital of* Bahrain *Ar.*
Al Manāmah 103 C5
Mananjary Madagascar 61 G3
Manaus Brazil 42 D2
Manchester England, UK 71 D5
Manchester New Hampshire,
USA 23 G2
Manchurian Plain *plain* E Asia
107 F2
Mandalay Myanmar 118 B3
Mangalia Romania 90 D5
Mangalore India 114 C2
Manicouagan, Réservoir
Reservoir Canada 21 E3
Manihiki *atoll* Cook Islands
125 F3
Maniitsoq Greenland 64 C3
Manila *capital of* Philippines
121 E1
Manisa Turkey *prev.* Saruhan
98 A3
Manitoba *province* Canada
19 G4
Manizales Colombia 40 B3
Manjimup Australia 129 B7
Mannar Sri Lanka 115 E3
Mannar, Gulf of *sea feature*
Indian Ocean 114 D3
Mannheim Germany 77 B5
Manono Dem. Rep. Congo
59 E7
Mansel Island *island* Canada
20 C1
Mansfield Ohio, USA 22 D4
Manta Ecuador 40 A4
Mantes-la-Jolie France 72 C3
Mantova Italy *Eng.* Mantua
78 B2
Mantua *see* Mantova
Manurewa New Zealand 132 D3

Manzhouli China 109 F1
Mao Chad 58 B3
Maoke, Pegunungan
mountains Indonesia
121 H4
Maputo *capital of*
Mozambique 61 E4
Mar, Serra do *mountains* Brazil
38 D4
Maracaibo Venezuela 40 C1
Maracaibo, Lago de *inlet*
Venezuela 40 C1
Maracay Venezuela 40 D1
Maradi Niger 57 F3
Marāgheh Iran 102 C3
Marajó, Ilha de *island* Brazil
43 F2
Marañón *river* Peru 42 B2
Maraş *see* Kahramanmaraş
Marash *see* Kahramanmaraş
Marbella Spain 74 D5
Marble Bar Australia 128 B4
Mar Chiquita, Laguna *salt lake*
Argentina 46 C3
Mardān Pakistan 116 C1
Mar del Plata Argentina
47 D5
Mardin Turkey 99 E4
Margarita, Isla de *island*
Venezuela 41 E1
Mārgow, Dasht-e- *desert*
Afghanistan 104 C5
Mariana Trench *undersea*
feature Pacific Ocean 124 B1
126 B1
Marias, Islas *islands* Mexico
32 C4
Maribor Slovenia 77 E7
Marie Byrd Land *region*
Antarctica 136 B4
Mariehamn Finland 67 D6
Marijampolė Lithuania *prev.*
Kapsukas 88 B4
Marília Brazil 44 D2
Maringá Brazil 44 D2
Marion, Lake *lake* South
Carolina, USA 31 F2
Mariscal Estigarribia Paraguay
44 B2
Maritsa *river* SE Europe 86 D3

Mariupol' Ukraine *prev.*
Shdanov 91 G3

Marka Somalia 55 D6

Marmara, Sea of *see* Marmara
Denizi

Marmara Denizi Turkey *Eng.*
Sea of Marmara 98 B2

Marne *river* France 72 D3

Marotiri *Island group* French
Polynesia 125 F4

Maroua Cameroon 58 B3

Marowijne *river* French
Guiana/Suriname 41 H3

Marquesas Fracture Zone
tectonic feature Pacific Ocean
125 G3

Marquesas Islands *island group*
French Polynesia *Fr.* Îles
Marquises 125 F4

Marquette Michigan, USA
22 B1

Marquisas, Îles *see* Marquesas
Islands

Marrakech Morocco *Eng.*
Marrakesh 52 C2

Marrawah Australia 131 C8

Marree Australia 131 B5

Marsala Italy 79 C6

Marseille France 73 D6

Marshall Islands *country* Pacific
Ocean 126-127

Martin Slovakia *prev.*
Turčiansky Svätý Martin, *Ger.*
Sankt Martin, *Hung.*
Turócszentmárton 81 C5

Martinique *external territory*
France, West Indies 37

Mary Turkmenistan *prev.* Merv
104 C3

Maryborough Australia 131 E5

Maryland *state* USA 23 F4

Masai Steppe *grassland*
Tanzania 55 C7

Mascarene Basin *undersea
feature* Indian Ocean 123 B5

Mascarene Islands *island group*
Indian Ocean 61 H4

Mascarene Plain *undersea
feature* Indian Ocean 123 B5

Mascarene Plateau *undersea
feature* Indian Ocean 123 B5

Maseru *capital of* Lesotho
60 D4

Mas-ha Bank 101 D6

Mashhad Iran *var.* Meshed 100
E3

Masindi Uganda 55 B6

Maşīrah, Jazīrat *Island* Oman
103 E6

Maşīrah, Khalīj *bay* Oman
103 E6

Mason City Iowa, USA 25 F3

Masqaţ *see* Muscat

Massachusetts *state* USA
23 G3

Massawa Eritrea 54 C4

Massif Central *upland* France
73 C5

Massoukou Gabon 59 B6

Masterton New Zealand
133 D5

Matadi Dem. Rep. Congo 59 B7

Matagalpa Nicaragua 34 D3

Matamoros Mexico 33 E2

Matanzas Cuba 36 B2

Matara Sri Lanka 115 E4

Mataram Indonesia 120 D5

Mataró Spain 75 G2

Mato Grosso *upland* Brazil
43 E3

Matosinhos Portugal 74 C2

Matsue Japan 113 B5

Matsuyama Japan 113 B5

Matterhorn *peak*
Italy/Switzerland 77 B7

Maturín Venezuela 41 E1

Maun Botswana 60 D3

Mauritania *country* W Africa 56

Mauritius *country* Indian
Ocean 61 H4 123 B5

Mayaguana *island* Bahamas
36 D2

Mayfield New Zealand 133 C6

Mayotte *external territory*
France, Indian Ocean 61 G2

Mayyit, Al Baḥr al *see* Dead Sea

Mazār-e Sharīf Afghanistan
104 D3

Mazatlán Mexico 32 C3

Mažeikiai Lithuania 88 B3

Mazury *region* Poland 80 D3

Mazyr Belarus *Rus.* Mozyr'
89 D7

Mbabane *capital of* Swaziland
61 E4

Mbaké Senegal 56 B3

Mbala Zambia 61 E1

Mbale Uganda 55 C6

Mbandaka Dem. Rep. Congo
59 C5

Mbeya Tanzania 55 B8

Mbuji-Mayi Dem. Rep. Congo
59 D7

McKinley, Mount *peak* Alaska,
USA *var.* Denali 18 C3

Mead, Lake *lake* SW USA
28 A1

Mecca *see* Makkah

Mechelen Belgium 69 C5

Mecklenburger Bucht *bay*
Germany 76 C2

Medan Indonesia 120 B3

Medellín Colombia 40 B2

Médenine Tunisia 53 F2

Medford Oregon, USA 26 A4

Medina *see* Al Madīnah

Mediterranean Sea Atlantic
Ocean 84-85

Meekatharra Australia 129 B5

Meerut India 116 D3

Megísti *island* Greece 98 B4

Mek'elē Ethiopia 54 C4

Mekong *river* SE Asia 106 C3

Mekong, Mouths of the
wetlands Vietnam 119 D6

Melanesia *region* Pacific Ocean
126 C3

Melanesian Basin *undersea
feature* Pacific Ocean 134 C4

Melbourne Australia 131 C7

Melbourne Florida, USA 31 F4

Melghir, Chott *Salt lake* Algeria
53 E2

Melilla *external territory* Spain,
N Africa 52 C1

Melitopol' Ukraine 91 F4

Melo Uruguay 44 C4

Melville Island *island* Australia
128 E2

Melville Island *island* Canada 19 E2

Memel *see* Klaipėda

Memel *see* Neman

Memphis Tennessee, USA 30 C1

Mendaña Fracture Zone *tectonic feature* Pacific Ocean 135 G3

Mende France 73 C6

Mendeleyev Ridge *undersea feature* Arctic Ocean 137 G2

Mendocino Fracture Zone *tectonic feature* Pacific Ocean 134 D2

Mendoza Argentina 46 B4

Menengiyn Tal *plain* Mongolia 109 F2

Menongue Angola 60 C2

Menorca *island* Spain *Eng.* Minorca 75 H3

Metairie Louisiana, USA 30 C3

Mentawai, Kepulauan *island group* Indonesia 120 B4

Meppel Netherlands 68 D2

Merced California, USA 27 B6

Mercedes Uruguay 44 B5

Mergui Myanmar 119 B5

Mergui Archipelago *island chain* Myanmar 119 B6

Mérida Mexico 33 H3

Mérida Spain 74 D3

Mérida Venezuela 40 C2

Meridian Mississippi, USA 30 C2

Merredin Australia 129 B6

Mersin Turkey *var.* İçel 98 C4

Meru Kenya 55 C6

Merv *see* Mary

Mesa Arizona, USA 28 B2

Meshed *see* Mashhad

Messina Italy 79 D6

Messina, Stretto di *sea feature* Ionian Sea/Tyrrhenian Sea 79 D7

Mestre Italy 78 C2

Meta *river* Colombia/Venezuela 40 C2

Metković Croatia 82 C4

Metz France 72 E3

Meuse *river* W Europe *var.* Maas 72 D3

Mexicali Mexico 32 A1

Mexico *country* North America 32-33

México, Golfo de *see* Mexico, Gulf of

Mexico, Gulf of *sea feature* Atlantic Ocean/Caribbean Sea 48 A4

Mexico City *capital of* Mexico *Sp.* Ciudad de México 33 E4

Meymaneh Afghanistan *var.* Maimana 104 D4

Mezen' *river* Russian Federation 92 D3

Miami Florida, USA 31 F5

Miami Beach Florida, USA 31 F5

Mianyang China 111 B5

Michigan *state* USA 22 C2

Michigan, Lake *lake* USA 17 C5

Micronesia *country* Pacific Ocean 126 B2

Micronesia *region* Pacific Ocean 126

Mid Atlantic Ridge *undersea feature* Atlantic Ocean 48 B4

Middelburg South Africa 60 D5

Middle Andaman *island* India 115 G2

Middlesbrough England, UK 71 D5

Mid-Indian Basin *undersea feature* Indian Ocean 122 C4

Mid-Indian Ridge *undersea feature* Indian Ocean 123 C5

Midland Texas, USA 29 E3

Mid-Pacific Mountains *var.* Mid-Pacific Seamounts. *Undersea feature* Pacific Ocean 124 C1

Mid-Pacific Seamounts *see* Mid-Pacific Mountains

Midway Islands *US territory* Pacific Ocean 134 D2

Mikhaylovka Russian Federation 93 B6

Milagro Ecuador 40 A4

Milan *see* Milano

Milano Italy *Eng.* Milan 78 B2

Mildura Australia 131 C6

Millennium Island *island* Kiribati *prev.* Caroline Island 127 H3

Miles Australia 131 D5

Miles City Montana, USA 24 C2

Milford Haven Wales, UK 71 C6

Milford Sound New Zealand 133 E6

Milford Sound *inlet* New Zealand 133 A6

Milos *island* Greece 87 C6

Milwaukee Wisconsin, USA 22 B3

Min *see* Fujian

Minatitlán Mexico 33 G4

Minch, The *Strait* Scotland, UK 70 C3

Mindanao *island* Philippines 121 F2

Mindoro *island* Philippines 121 E2

Mindoro Strait *sea feature* South China Sea/Sulu Sea 121 E2

Mingäçevir Azerbaijan *Rus.* Mingechaur 99 G2

Mingechaur *see* Mingäçevir

Minho *river* Portugal/Spain *Sp.* Miño 74 C2

Minicoy Island *island* India 114 C3

Minneapolis Minnesota, USA 23 F2

Minnesota *state* USA 25 F2

Miño *river* Portugal/Spain *Port.* Minho 74 C1

Minorca *see* Menorca

Minot North Dakota, USA 24 D1

Minā' Qābūs Oman 122 B3

Minsk *capital of* Belarus 89 C5

Minto *lake* Canada 20 D2

Miranda de Ebro Spain 75 E1

Mirim, Lake *see* Mirim Lagoon

Mirim Lagoon *lagoon* Brazil/Uruguay *var.* Mirim, Lake 44 C5

Mirtóo Pelagos *sea feature* Mediterranean Sea 87 C6

Miskitos Cayos *islands* Nicaragua 35 E2

Miskolc Hungary 81 D6

Mişrātah Libya 53 F2

Mississippi *state* USA 30 C2

Mississippi *river* USA 16 C5

Mississippi Delta *wetlands* USA 30 C4

Missoula Montana, USA 24 B2

Missouri *state* USA 25 G4

Missouri *river* USA 17 C5

Mistassini, Lake *lake* Canada 20 D3

Mitau *see* Jelgava

Mitchell S Dakota, USA 25 E3

Mitchell River *river* Australia 130 C3

Mitilíni Greece 86 D4

Mito Japan 112 D4

Mitumba, Monts *Mountain range* Dem. Rep. Congo 59 E7

Miyazaki Japan 113 B6

Mjøsa *lake* Norway 67 B5

Mljet *island* Croatia 83 C5

Mmabatho South Africa 60 D4

Mo Norway 66 C3

Mobile Alabama, USA 30 C3

Moçambique Mozambique 61 F2

Mocímboa da Praia Mozambique 61 F2

Mocoa Colombia 40 B4

Mocuba Mozambique 61 E3

Modena Italy 78 B3

Modesto California, USA 27 B6

Modohn *see* Madona

Modriča Bosnia & Herzegovina 82 C3

Mogadiscio *see* Mogadishu

Mogadishu *capital of* Somalia *Som.* Muqdisho, *It.* Mogadiscio 55 D6

Mogilëv *see* Mahilyow

Mohéli *island* Comoros 61 F2

Mo i Rana Norway 66 C3

Mojave California, USA 27 C7

Mojave Desert *desert* W USA 27 C7

Moldavia *see* Moldova

Molde Norway 67 A5

Moldova *country* E Europe *var.* Moldavia 90

Molodechno *see* Maladzyechna

Molodeczno *see* Maladzyechna

Molotov *see* Perm'

Moluccas *see* Maluku

Molucca Sea *see* Maluku, Laut

Mombasa Kenya 55 C7

Monaco *country* W Europe 73 E6

Monclova Mexico 33 E2

Moncton Canada 21 F4

Mongo Chad 58 C3

Mongolia *country* NE Asia 108-109

Monroe Louisiana, USA 30 B2

Monrovia *capital of* Liberia 56 C5

Mons Belgium 69 B6

Montague Seamount *undersea feature* Atlantic Ocean 45 H1

Montana *state* USA 24 C2

Montauban France 73 C6

Mont Blanc *peak* France/Italy 62 D4

Mont-de-Marsan France 72 B6

Monte Cristi Dominican Republic 37 E3

Montego Bay Jamaica 36 C3

Montenegro *Country* SE Europe 83 D5

Monterey California, USA 27 B6

Montería Colombia 40 B2

Montero Bolivia 42 D4

Monterrey Mexico 33 E2

Montes Claros Brazil 43 G4

Montevideo *capital of* Uruguay 44 C5

Montgomery Alabama, USA 30 D2

Monthey Switzerland 77 A7

Montpelier Vermont, USA 23 F2

Montpellier France 73 C6

Montréal Canada 21 E4

Montserrat *external territory* UK, West Indies 37

Monywa Myanmar 118 A3

Monza Italy 78 B2

Moora Australia 129 B6

Moore, Lake *lake* Australia 129 B6

Moorhead Minnesota, USA 25 E2

Moosonee Canada 20 C3

Mopti Mali 57 E3

Morava *river* C Europe 82 E4

Moravská Ostrava *see* Ostrava

Moray Firth *inlet* Scotland, UK 70 C3

Moree Australia 131 D5

Morelia Mexico 33 E4

Morena, Sierra *mountain range* Spain 74 D4

Morghāb *river* Afghanistan/Turkmenistan 104 D3

Morioka Japan 112 D3

Mornington Abyssal Plain *undersea feature* Pacific Ocean 135 G5

Morocco *country* N Africa 52

Morogoro Tanzania 55 C7

Mörön Mongolia 108 D2

Morondava Madagascar 61 F3

Moroni *capital of* Comoros 61 F2

Morotai, Pulau *island* Indonesia 121 F3

Morova *river* Poland 80 C6

Morris Jesup, Kap *headland* Greenland 65 E1

Moscow *capital of* Russian Federation *Rus.* Moskva 92 B4 96 B2

Mosel *river* W Europe *Fr.* Moselle 77 E3

Moselle *river* W Europe *Ger.* Mosel 72 E4

Mosgiel New Zealand 133 B7

Moshi Tanzania 55 C7

Moskva *see* Moscow

Mosquito Coast *coastal region* Nicaragua 35 E3

Moss Norway 67 B6

Mossendjo Congo 59 B6

Mossoró Brazil 43 H2

Most Czech Republic *Ger.* Brüx 80 A4

N

Napier New Zealand 132 E4

Naples see Napoli

Napo *river* Ecuador/Peru 42 B2

Napoli Italy *Eng.* Naples 79 D5

Narbonne France 73 C6

Nares Strait *sea feature* Canada/Greenland 64 C1

Narew *river* Poland 80 E3

Narmada *river* India 116 D4

Narva Estonia 88 E2

Narva *river* Estonia/Russian Federation 88 E2

Narva Bay *sea feature* Gulf of Finland *Est.* Narva Laht, *Rus.* Narvskiy Zaliv 88 E2

Narva Laht see Narva Bay

Narvik Norway 66 C3

Narvskiy Zaliv see Narva Bay

Naryn Kyrgyzstan 105 G2

Näshik India 116 C5

Nashville Tennessee, USA 30 D1

Nâşir, Buḥeiret see Nasser, Lake

Nassau *capital of* Bahamas 36 C1

Nasser, Lake *reservoir* Egypt *var.* Nâşir, Buheiret 54 B2

Natal Brazil 43 H3

Natal Basin *Undersea feature* Indian Ocean 123 A5

Natitingou Benin 57 E4

Naturaliste Plateau *undersea feature* Indian Ocean 123 E6

Nauru *country* Pacific Ocean 126 D3

Navapolatsk Belarus *Rus.* Novopolotsk 89 D5

Navassa Island *external territory* USA, West Indies 36 D3

Navoiy Uzbekistan *Uzb.* Nawoly 104 D2

Nawābshāh Pakistan 116 B3

Nawoly see Navoiy

Naxçıvan Azerbaijan *Rus.* Nakhichevan' 99 G3

Náxos *island* Greece 87 D6

Nazareth see Nazaret

Nazca Peru 42 B4

Nazerat Israel *Eng.* Nazareth 101 A5

Nazrēt Ethiopia 55 C5

Nazwá Oman 103 E5

N'Dalatando Angola 60 B2

Ndélé Central African Republic 58 C4

N'Djamena *capital of* Chad 58 B3

Ndola Zambia 60 D2

Nebitdag see Balkanabat

Nebraska *state* USA 24-25 E3

Neches *river* S USA 29 H3

Neckar *river* Germany 77 B5

Necochea Argentina 47 D5

Neftezavodsk see Seýdi

Negēlē Ethiopia 55 C5

Negev see HaNegev

Negro, Rio *river* Argentina 47 C5

Negro, Rio *river* Brazil/Uruguay 44 C4

Negro, Rio *river* N South America 40 C1

Neiva Colombia 40 B3

Nellore India 115 E2

Neman *river* NE Europe *Bel.* Nyoman, *Lith.* Nemunas, *Ger.* Memel, *Pol.* Niemen 88 B4

Nemunas see Neman

Nemuro Japan 112 E2

Nepal *country* S Asia 117

Neris *river* Belarus/Lithuania *Bel.* Viliya, *Pol.* Wilja 88 C4

Ness, Loch *lake* Scotland, UK 70 C1

Netherlands *country* W Europe *var.* Holland 68-69

Netherlands Antilles *external territory* Netherlands, West Indies *prev.* Dutch West Indies 37 E5

Netze see Noteć

Neubrandenburg Germany 76 D3

Neuchâtel, Lac de *lake* Switzerland 77 A7

Neumünster Germany 76 C2

Neuquén Argentina 47 C5

Neusiedler See *lake* Austria/Hungary 77 E6

Neusohl see Banská Bystrica

Neutra see Nitra

Nevada *state* USA 26-27

Nevers France 72 C4

Nevşehir Turkey 98 C3

New Amsterdam Guyana 41 G2

Newark New Jersey, USA 23 F3

New Britain *island* Papua New Guinea 126 B3

New Brunswick *province* Canada 21 F4

New Caledonia *external territory* France, Pacific Ocean 126 C5

New Caledonia *island* Pacific Ocean 124 D3

New Caledonia Basin *undersea feature* Pacific Ocean 124 D4

Newcastle Australia 131 D6

Newcastle upon Tyne England, UK 70 D4

New Delhi *capital of* India 116 D3

Newfoundland & Labrador *province* Canada 21 F2

Newfoundland *island* Canada 21 G3

Newfoundland Basin *undersea feature* Atlantic Ocean 48 B3

New Georgia Islands *island group* Solomon Is 126 C3

New Guinea *island* Pacific Ocean 126 B3

New Hampshire *state* USA 23 G2

New Haven Connecticut, USA 23 G3

New Ireland *island* Papua New Guinea 126 C3

New Jersey *state* USA 23 F4

Newman Australia 128 B4

New Mexico *state* USA 28-29

New Orleans Louisiana, USA 30 C3

New Plymouth New Zealand 132 D3

Newport Oregon, USA 26 A3

Newport News Virginia, USA 23 F5

North Uist *island* Scotland, UK 70 B3

Northwest Territories *territory* Canada 19 E3

Norway *country* N Europe 66-67

Norwegian Sea Arctic Ocean 137 G5

Norwich England, UK 71 E6

Noteć *river* Poland *Ger.* Netze 80 C3

Nottingham England, UK 71 D6

Nottingham Island *island* Hudson Strait 20 D1

Nouâdhibou Mauritania 56 B2

Nouakchott *capital of* Mauritania 56 B2

Nouméa *capital of* New Caledonia 126 D5

Nova Gradiška Croatia 82 C3

Nova Iguaçu Brazil 43 F5 45 F2

Novara Italy 78 B2

Nova Scotia *province* Canada 21 F4

Novaya Zemlya *islands* Russian Federation 137 H4

Novaya Zemlya Trench *see* East Novaya Zemlya Trench

Novi Sad Serbia 82 D3

Novokuznetsk Russian Federation *prev.* Stalinsk 96 D4

Novopolotsk *see* Navapolatsk

Novosibirsk Russian Federation 96 D4

Novosibirskiye Ostrova *islands* Russian Federation *Eng.* New Siberian Islands 95 F1

Novo Urgench *see* Urgench

Novyy Margilan *see* Farg'ona

Nsanje Malawi 61 E3

Nsawam Ghana 57 E5

Nubian Desert *desert* Sudan 54 B3

Nu'eima West Bank 101 D7

Nuevo Laredo Mexico 33 E2

Nuku'alofa *capital of* Tonga 127 F5

Nukus Uzbekistan 104 C2

Nullarbor Plain *region* Australia 129 D6

Nunap Isua Island *coastal region* Greenland *var.* Uummannaruaq *Dan.* Kap Farvel 64 C5

Nunavut *Territory* Canada 19 F3

Nunivak Island *island* Alaska, USA 18 B2

Nuoro Italy 79 A5

Nuremberg *see* Nürnberg

Nürnberg Germany *Eng.* Nuremberg 77 C5

Nusa Tenggara *islands* East Timor / Indonesia 120 E5

Nuuk Greenland *var.* Godthåb 64 C4

Nyainqêntanglha Shan *mountain range* China 108 D5

Nyala Sudan 54 A4

Nyasa, Lake *lake* E Africa 51 D5

Nyeri Kenya 51 C6

Nyima China 108 C4

Nyíregyháza Hungary 81 E6

Nyitra *see* Nitra

Nykøbing Denmark 67 B8

Nyköping Sweden 67 C6

Nyngan Australia 131 D6

Nyoman *see* Neman

O

Oakland California, USA 27 B6

Oakley Kansas, USA 25 E4

Oamaru New Zealand 133 B7

Oaxaca Mexico 33 F5

Ob' *river* Russian Federation 96 D4

Oban Scotland, UK 70 C4

Obihiro Japan 112 D2

Obo Central African Republic 58 D4

Oceania 124-125

Ocean Island *see* Banaba

Oceanside California, USA 27 C8

Ochamchira *see* Och'amch'ire

Och'amch'ire Georgia *Rus.* Ochamchira 99 E1

Ödenburg *see* Sopron

Odense Denmark 67 B7

Oder *river* C Europe 80 C4

Odesa Ukraine *Rus.* Odessa 91 E4

Odessa *see* Odesa

Odessa Texas, USA 29 E3

Odienné Côte d'Ivoire 56 D4

Oesel *see* Saaremaa

Ofanto *river* Italy 79 D5

Offenbach Germany 77 B5

Ogadēn *plateau* Ethiopia 55 D5

Ogallala Nebraska, USA 24 D4

Ogbomosho Nigeria 57 F4

Ogden Utah, USA 24 B3

Ogdensburg New York, USA 23 F2

Oger *see* Ogre

Ogre Latvia *Ger.* Oger 88 C3

Ogulin Croatia 82 B3

Ohio *state* USA 22 D4

Ohio *river* N USA 22 B5

Ohrid Macedonia 83 D6

Ohrid, Lake *lake* Albania/Macedonia 83 D6

Ohře *river* Czech Republic/ Germany *Ger.* Eger 81 A5

Ōita Japan 113 B6

Okavango *river var.* Cubango southern Africa 60 C3

Okavango Delta *wetland* Botswana 60 C3

Okayama Japan 113 B5

Okazaki Japan 113 C5

Okeechobee, Lake *lake* Florida, USA 31 F4

Okhotsk Russian Federation 97 G3

Okhotsk, Sea of Pacific Ocean 134 C1

Okinawa *island* Japan 113 A8

Oki-shotō *island group* Japan 113 B5

Oklahoma *state* USA 29 F1

Oklahoma City Oklahoma, USA 29 F2

Okushiri-tō *island* Japan 112 C2

Oyem Gabon 59 B5
Oyo Nigeria 57 F4
Ozark Plateau *plain* Arkansas/Missouri, USA 25 G5
Ózd Hungary 81 D6

P

Paamiut Greenland 64 B4
Pachuca Mexico 33 E4
Pacific-Antarctic Ridge *undersea feature* Pacific Ocean 136 B5
Pacific Ocean 134-135
Padang Indonesia 120 B4
Paderborn Germany 76 B4
Padova Italy *Eng.* Padua 78 C2
Padre Island *island* Texas, USA 29 G5
Padua *see* Padova
Paducah Kentucky, USA 22 B5
Paeroa Waikato, New Zealand 132 D3
Pafos *see* Paphos
Pag *island* Croatia 82 A3
Pago Pago *capital of* American Samoa 127 F4
Paide Estonia *Ger.* Weissenstein 88 D2
Paihia New Zealand 132 D2
Painted Desert *desert* SW USA 28 C1
País Valenciano *cultural region* Spain 75 F3
Pakistan *country* S Asia 116
Pakokku Myanmar 118 A3
Palagruža *island* Croatia 83 B5
Palau *country* Pacific Ocean *var.* Belau 124 B2 126
Palawan *island* Philippines 121 E2
Palawan Passage *passage* Philippines 121 E2
Paldiski Estonia *prev.* Baltiski, *Eng.* Baltic Port, *Ger.* Baltischport 88 C2
Palembang Indonesia 120 C4
Palencia Spain 74 D2
Palermo Italy 79 C6

Palikir *capital of* Micronesia 126 C2
Palioúri, Akrotírio *coastal feature* Greece *var.* Akra Kanestron 86 C4
Palk Strait *sea feature* India/Sri Lanka 115 E3
Palliser, Cape *headland* New Zealand 133 D5
Palm Springs California, USA 27 D8
Palma Spain 75 G3
Palmer Land *physical region* Antarctica 136 A3
Palmerston North New Zealand 132 D4
Palmyra *see* Tudmur
Palmyra Atoll *external territory* USA, Pacific Ocean 125 F2
Palu Indonesia 121 E4
Pamir *river* Afghanistan/Tajikistan 105 F3
Pamirs *mountains* Tajikistan 105 F3
Pampa Texas, USA 29 E2
Pampas *region* South America 46 C4
Pamplona Spain *var.* Iruña 75 F1
Panaji India 114 C2
Panama *country* Central America 35
Panamá, Golfo de *sea feature* Panama 35 F5
Panama Canal *canal* Panama 35 F4
Panama City *capital of* Panama 35 F5
Panama City Florida, USA 30 D3
Pančevo Serbia 82 D3
Panevėžys Lithuania 88 C4
Pantanal *region* Brazil 38 C4
Pantelleria *island* Italy 79 B7
Papeete *capital of* French Polynesia 127 H4
Paphos Cyprus *var.* Pafos 98 C5
Papua *province* Indonesia *prev.* Irian Jaya 121 H4
Papua New Guinea *country* Pacific Ocean 126

Paracel Islands *disputed territory* Asia 120 D1
Paragua *river* Venezuela 41 E3
Paraguay *country* South America 44
Paraguay *river* C South America 38 C4 44 B2
Parakou Benin 57 F4
Paramaribo *capital of* Suriname 41 G2
Paraná Argentina 46 D4
Paraná *river* C South America 46 D3
Paranaíba Brazil 43 G2
Paraparaumu New Zealand 132 D4
Pardubice Czech Republic *Ger.* Pardubitz 81 B5
Pardubitz *see* Pardubice
Parepare Indonesia 121 E4
Paris *capital of* France 72 C3
Paris Texas, USA 29 G2
Parma Italy 78 B3
Pärnu Estonia *Rus.* Pyarnu, *prev.* Pernov, *Ger.* Pernau 88 C2
Páros *island* Greece 87 D6
Pasadena California, USA 27 C7
Pasadena Texas, USA 29 G4
Passo Fundo Brazil 44 D3
Pasto Colombia 40 B4
Patagonia *region* S South America 47 C6
Patna India 117 F3
Patos, Lagoa dos *lagoon* Brazil 44 D4
Pátra Greece 87 B5
Pattani Thailand 119 C7
Pattaya Thailand 119 C5
Patuca *river* Honduras 34 D2
Pau France 73 B6
Pavlodar Kazakhstan 96 C4
Pavlograd *see* Pavlohrad
Pavlohrad Ukraine *Rus.* Pavlograd 91 G3
Paysandú Uruguay 44 B4
Pazardzhik Bulgaria *prev.* Tatar Pazardzhik 86 C2
Pearl *river* SE USA 30 C3

Pishpek *see* Bishkek
Pistyan *see* Piešťany
Pitcairn Islands *external territory* UK, Pacific Ocean 125 G4
Piteå Sweden 66 D4
Pitești Romania 90 C4
Pittsburgh Pennsylvania, USA 23 E4
Piura Peru 42 A2
Pivdennyy Bug *river* Ukraine 91 E3
Plasencia Spain 74 D3
Plata, Río de la *river* Argentina/Uruguay *var.* River Plate 44 B5 46 D4
Plate, River *see* **Plata, Río de la**
Platte *river* C USA 25 E4
Plattensee *see* Balaton
Plenty, Bay of *bay* New Zealand 132 E3
Pleven Bulgaria 86 C1
Płock Poland 80 D3
Ploiești Romania 90 C4
Plovdiv Bulgaria *Gk.* Philippopolis 86 C2
Plungė Lithuania 88 B4
Plymouth *capital of* Montserrat 37 G3
Plymouth England, UK 71 C7
Plzeň Czech Republic *Ger.* Pilsen 81 A5
Po *river* Italy 78 B2
Pocatello Idaho, USA 26 E4
Po Delta *wetland* Italy 78 C3
Podgorica *capital of* Montenegro 83 C5
Pohnpei Island *island* Micronesia 126 C2
Pointe-Noire Congo 59 B6
Poitiers France 72 B4
Poland *country* E Europe 80-81
Polatsk Belarus 89 D5
Pol-e Khomri Afghanistan 105 E4
Poltava Ukraine 91 F2
Poltoratsk *see* Aşgabat
Polynesia *region* Pacific Ocean 127

Pomeranian Bay *bay* Germany/Poland 80 B2
Pompano Beach Florida, USA 31 F5
Ponca City Oklahoma, USA 29 G1
Pondicherry India 115 E2
Ponta Grossa Brazil 44 D2
Pontevedra Spain 74 C1
Pontianak Indonesia 120 C4
Poona *see* Pune
Poopó, Lake *lake* Bolivia 42 C5
Popayán Colombia 40 B3
Poprad Slovakia *Ger.* Deutschendorf 81 D5
Porbandar India 116 B4
Pori Finland 67 D5
Porsgrunn Norway 67 B6
Portalegre Portugal 74 C3
Port Angeles Washington, USA 26 A1
Port Arthur Texas, USA 29 H4
Port Augusta Australia 131 B6
Port-au-Prince *capital of* Haiti 36 D3
Port Blair India 115 G2
Port Douglas Australia 130 D3
Port Elizabeth South Africa 60 D5
Port-Gentil Gabon 59 A6
Port Harcourt Nigeria 57 F5
Port Hardy Canada 18 D5
Port Hedland Australia 128 B4
Portland Australia 131 B7
Portland Maine, USA 23 G2
Portland Oregon, USA 26 B2
Port Lincoln Australia 131 A6
Port Louis *capital of* Mauritius 61 H4
Port Macquarie Australia 131 E6
Port Moresby *capital of* Papua New Guinea 126 B3
Porto Portugal *Eng.* Oporto 74 C2
Porto Alegre Sao Tome and Principe 44 D4
Port-of-Spain *capital of* Trinidad & Tobago 37 G5

Porto-Novo *capital of* Benin 57 F5
Porto Velho Brazil 42 C3
Portoviejo Ecuador 40 A4
Port Said Egypt 54 B1
Portsmouth England, UK 71 D7
Port Sudan Sudan 54 C3
Portugal *country* SW Europe 74
Port-Vila *capital of* Vanuatu 126 D5
Porvenir Chile 47 B7
Posadas Argentina 46 E3
Posen *see* Poznań
Pöstyén *see* Piešťany
Potenza S Italy 79 D5
P'ot'i Georgia 99 E2
Potosí Bolivia 42 C5
Potsdam Germany 76 D4
Póvoa de Varzim Portugal 74 C2
Powder *river* N USA 24 C2
Powell, Lake *lake* SW USA 24 B5
Poza Rica Mexico 33 F4
Poznań Poland *Ger.* Posen 80 C3
Pozo Colorado Paraguay 44 B2
Pozsony *see* Bratislava
Prag *see* Prague
Prague *capital of* Czech Republic *Cz.* Praha, *Ger.* Prag 81 B5
Praha *see* Prague
Praia *capital of* Cape Verde 56 A3
Prato Italy 78 B3
Pratt Kansas, USA 25 E5
Preschau *see* Prešov
Prescott Arizona, USA 28 B2
Presidente Prudente Brazil 44 D2
Prešov Slovakia *Ger.* Eperies, *var.* Preschau, *Hung.* Eperjes 81 D5
Prespa, Lake *lake* SE Europe 83 D6 86 A3
Presque Isle Maine, USA 23 G1
Pressburg *see* Bratislava
Preston England, UK 71 D5

Pretoria *see* Tshwane

Préveza Greece 86 A4

Prijedor Bosnia & Herzegovina 82 B3

Prilep Macedonia 83 E5

Prince Albert Canada 19 F5

Prince Edward Island *province* Canada 21 F4

Prince Edward Islands *island group* South Africa 123 A7

Prince George Canada 19 E5

Prince of Wales Island *island* Canada 19 F2

Prince Rupert Canada 18 D4

Princess Charlotte Bay *bay* Australia 130 C2

Princess Elizabeth Land *region* Antarctica 136 C3

Príncipe *island* Sao Tome & Principe 59 A5

Pripet *river* Belarus/Ukraine 90 C1

Pripet Marshes *wetlands* Belarus/Ukraine 90 C1

Priština Serbia 83 D5

Prizren Serbia 83 D5

Prome Myanmar 118 A4

Prossnitz *see* Prostějov

Prostějov Czech Republic *Ger.* Prossnitz 81 C5

Provence *region* France 73 D6

Providence Rhode Island, USA 23 G3

Providencia, Isla de *island* Colombia 35 E3

Provo Utah, USA 24 B4

Prudhoe Bay Alaska, USA 18 D2

Przheval'sk *see* Karakol

Pskov Russian Federation 92 A4

Pskov, Lake *lake* Estonia/Russian Federation *Est.* Pihkva Järv, *Rus.* Pskovskoye Ozero 88 D3

Pskovskoye Ozero *see* Pskov, Lake

Ptich' *see* Ptsich

Ptsich *river* Belarus *Rus.* Ptich' 89 D6

Pucallpa Peru 42 B3

Puebla Mexico 33 F4

Pueblo Colorado, USA 22 D4

Puerto Aisén Chile 47 B6

Puerto Barrios Guatemala 34 C2

Puerto Carreño Colombia 40 D2

Puerto Cortés Honduras 34 C2

Puerto Deseado Argentina 47 C6

Puerto Maldonado Peru 42 C4

Puerto Montt Chile 47 B5

Puerto Natales Chile 47 B7

Puerto Plata Dominican Republic 37 E3

Puerto Princesa Philippines 120 E2

Puerto Rico *external territory* USA, West Indies 37 F3

Puerto San Julián Argentina 47 C7

Puerto Suárez Bolivia 42 D4

Puerto Vallarta Mexico 32 D4

Pula Croatia 82 A3

Pune India *prev.* Poona 114 C1

Puno Peru 42 C4

Punta Arenas Chile *prev.* Magallanes 47 B7

Puntarenas Costa Rica 34 D4

Purmerend Netherlands 68 C3

Purus *river* Brazil/Peru 42 C3

Pusan South Korea 110 E4

Putrajaya *capital of* Malaysia 120 B3

Putumayo *river* NW South America 38 B3

Pyapon Myanmar 118 B4

Pyarnu *see* Pärnu

Pyinmana *capital of* Myanmar 118 B3

Pyongyang *capital of* North Korea 110 E4

Pyramid Lake *lake* Nevada, USA 27 C5

Pyrenees *mountain range* SW Europe 62 C4

Q

Qaanaaq Greenland *var.* Thule 64 D1

Qābatiya West Bank 101 D7

Qaidam Pendi *basin* China 108 D4

Qalqīlya West Bank 101 D7

Qamdo China 108 D5

Qandahār *see* Kandahār

Qaqortoq Greenland 64 C4

Qara Qum *see* Karakumy

Qarshi *see* Karshi

Qasigiannguit Greenland 64 C3

Qatar *country* SW Asia 103 D5

Qattara Depression *see* Qaṭṭâra, Monkhafad el

Qaṭṭâra, Monkhafad el *desert basin* Egypt *Eng.* Qattara Depression 54 A1

Qena Egypt 54 B2

Qeqertarsuaq Greenland 64 B3

Qeqertarsuaq *island* Greenland 64 B3

Qian *see* Guizhou

Qilian Shan *mountain range* China 108 A4

Qimusseriarsuaq *bay* Greenland 64 C2

Qingdao China 110 D4

Qinghai *province* China *var.* Chinghai, Koko Nor, Qing, Tsinghai 108 D4

Qinghai Hu *lake* China *var.* Koko Nor 108 D4

Qingzang Gaoyuan *plateau* China *Eng.* Plateau of Tibet 110 A4

Qiong *see* Hainan

Qiqihar China 110 D3

Qira China 108 B4

Qitai China 108 C3

Qom Iran *var.* Kum 102 C3

Qondūz *river* Afghanistan 105 E4

Qondūz *see* Kondoz

Qo'qon Uzbekistan *prev.* Kokand, *var.* Khokand, 105 E2

Quba Azerbaijan *Rus.* Kuba 99 H2

Québec Canada 21 E4
Québec *province* Canada 20 D3
Queen Charlotte Islands *islands* Canada 18 D4
Queen Charlotte Sound *sea feature* Canada 18 D5
Queen Elizabeth Islands *islands* Canada 19 F1
Queensland *state* Australia 130 C4
Queenstown New Zealand 133 B6
Quelimane Mozambique 61 E3
Querétaro Mexico 33 E4
Quetta Pakistan 116 B2
Quezaltenango Guatemala 34 B2
Quibdó Colombia 40 B3
Quimper France 72 A3
Qui Nhon Vietnam 119 E5
Qing *see* Qinghai
Quito *capital of* Ecuador 40 A4
Qürghonteppa Tajikistan *Rus.* Kurgan–Tynbe 105 E3
Qyteti Stalin *see* Kuçovë

R

Raab *see* Győr
Raab *see* Rába
Rába *river* Austria/Hungary *Ger.* Raab 81 C7
Rabat *capital of* Morocco 52 C2
Race, Cape *coastal feature* Canada 21 H4
Rach Gia Vietnam 119 D6
Radom Poland 80 D4
Radviliškis Lithuania 88 C4
Ragusa Italy 79 D7
Rahīmyār Khān Pakistan 116 C3
Raipur India 117 E5
Rājahmundry India 115 E1
Rājasthān *state* India 116 C3
Rājkot India 116 C4
Rājshāhi Bangladesh 117 G4

Rakaia *river* New Zealand 133 C6
Rakvere Estonia *Ger.* Wesenberg 88 D2
Raleigh North Carolina, USA 31 F1
Ralik Chain *islands* Marshall Islands 126 D1
Râmnicu Vâlcea Romania *prev.* Rimnicu Vîlcea 90 B4
Ramallah West Bank 101 D7
Ramree Island *island* Myanmar 118 A3
Rancagua Chile 46 B4
Rānchi India 117 F4
Randers Denmark 67 A7
Rangiora New Zealand 133 C6
Rangitikei *river* New Zealand 132 D4
Rangoon *capital of* Myanmar *Bur.* Yangon 118 B4
Rankin Inlet Canada 19 G3
Rapid City South Dakota, USA 24 D3
Rarotonga *island* Cook Islands 127 G5
Rasht Iran 102 C3
Ratak Chain *islands* Marshall Islands 126 D1
Ratchaburi Thailand 119 C5
Rat Islands *island group* Alaska, USA 18 A2
Raukumara Range *mountain range* New Zealand 132 E3
Rauma Finland 67 D5
Ravenna Italy 78 C3
Rāwalpindi Pakistan 116 C1
Rawson Argentina 47 C6
Razgrad Bulgaria 86 D1
Reading England, UK 71 D6
Rebecca, Lake *lake* Australia 129 C6
Rebun-tō *island* Japan 112 D1
Rechytsa Belarus 89 D7
Recife Brazil 43 H3
Recklinghausen Germany 76 G4
Red Deer Canada 19 E5
Redding California, USA 27 B5
Red River *river* S USA 30 B3

Red River *river* China/ Vietnam 118
Red Sea Indian Ocean 122 A3
Reefton New Zealand 133 C5
Regensburg Germany 77 C5
Reggane Algeria 52 D3
Reggio di Calabria Italy 79 D6
Reggio nell' Emilia Italy 78 B3
Regina Canada 19 F5
Rehoboth Namibia 60 C4
Reichenberg *see* Liberec
Reid Australia 129 D6
Reims France *Eng.* Rheims 72 D3
Reindeer Lake *lake* Canada 17 C4
Reni Ukraine 90 D4
Rennes France 72 B3
Reno Nevada, USA 27 B5
Resistencia Argentina 46 D3
Reşiţa Romania 90 B4
Resolute Canada 19 F2
Réunion *external territory* France, Indian Ocean 123 B5
Reus Spain 75 G2
Reutlingen Germany 77 B6
Reval *see* Tallinn
Revel *see* Tallinn
Revillagigedo, Islas *island* Mexico 32 B4
Rey, Isla del *island* Panama 35 F5
Reykjavík *capital of* Iceland 65 E5
Reynosa Mexico 33 E2
Rēzekne Latvia *Ger.* Rossitten, *Rus.* Rezhitsa 88 D4
Rezhitsa *see* Rēzekne
Rheims *see* Reims
Rhine *river* W Europe 62 D4
Rhode Island *state* USA 23 G3
Rhodes *see* Ródos
Rhodope Mountains *mountain range* Bulgaria/Greece *Gk.* Orosirá Rodópis, *Bul.* Despoto Planina 86 C3
Rhône *river* France/Switzerland 62 C4
Ribeirão Preto Brazil 45 E1

Riberalta Bolivia 42 C3
Rîbniţa Moldova 90 D3
Richfield Utah, USA 24 B4
Richland Washington, USA 24 C2
Richmond Kentucky, USA 22 C5
Richmond New Zealand 133 C5
Richmond Virginia, USA 23 E5
Richmond Range *mountain range* New Zealand 133 C5
Ricobayo, Embalse de *reservoir* Spain 74 D2
Riga *capital* of Latvia *Latv.* Rīga 88 C3
Riga, Gulf of *sea feature* Baltic Sea 88 C3
Riihimäki Finland 67 D5
Rijeka Croatia *It.* Fiume 82 A3
Rimah, Wādī ar *dry watercourse* Saudi Arabia 103 B5
Rimini Italy 78 C3
Rîmnicu Vîlcea *see* Râmnicu Vâlcea
Riobamba Ecuador 40 A4
Rio Branco Brazil 42 C3
Río Cuarto Argentina 46 C4
Rio de Janeiro Brazil 45 F2
Río Gallegos Argentina 47 C7
Rio Grande Brazil 44 D4
Rio Grande *river* N America 16 B6
Rio Grande Rise *undersea feature* Atlantic Ocean 49 C6
Río Verde Mexico 33 E3
Rishiri-tō *island* Japan 112 D1
Rivas Nicaragua 34 D3
Rivera Uruguay 44 C4
Riverside California, USA 27 C8
Riverton New Zealand 133 A7
Rivne Ukraine *Rus.* Rovno 90 C2
Riyadh *capital* of Saudi Arabia *Ar.* Ar Riyāḍ 103 C5
Rize Turkey 99 E2
Rkiz Mauritania 56 C3
Road Town *capital* of British Virgin Islands 37 F3
Roanne France 73 D5
Roanoke Virginia, USA 23 E5
Roanoke *river* SE USA 31 G1

Robinson Range *mountain range* Australia 129 B5
Rochester Minnesota, USA 25 F3
Rochester New York, USA 23 E3
Rockford Illinois, USA 22 B3
Rockhampton Australia 130 D4
Rock Island Illinois, USA 22 B3
Rock Springs Wyoming, USA 24 C3
Rockstone Guyana 41 G2
Rocky Mountains *mountain range* Canada/USA 18-19 D4
Rodez France 73 C6
Ródhos *see* Ródos
Ródos *island* Greece *var.* Ródhos, *Eng.* Rhodes 87 E6
Ródos Greece *Eng.* Rhodes 87 E6
Rodosto *see* Tekirdağ
Roeselare Belgium 69 A5
Roma Australia 131 D5
Roma *see* Rome
Romania *country* SE Europe 90
Rome *capital* of Italy *It.* Roma 78 C4
Rome Georgia, USA 30 D2
Rønne Denmark 67 B8
Ronne Ice Shelf *ice feature* Antarctica 136 B3
Roosendaal Netherlands 68 C4
Rosario Argentina 46 D4
Roseau *capital* of Dominica 37 G4
Rosenau *see* Rožňava
Rositten *see* Rēzekne
Ross Ice Shelf *ice feature* Antarctica 136 B4
Ross Sea Antarctica 136 B4
Rostak *see* Ar Rustāq
Rostock Germany 76 C2
Rostov-na-Donu Russian Federation 96 A3
Roswell New Mexico, USA 28 D2
Rotorua New Zealand 132 D3
Rotorua, Lake *lake* New Zealand 132 D3

Rotterdam Netherlands 68 C4
Rouen France 72 C3
Rovaniemi Finland 66 D3
Rovno *see* Rivne
Rovuma *river* Mozambique/Tanzania 61 F2
Roxas City Philippines 121 E2
Rožňava Slovakia *Ger.* Rosenau, *Hung.* Rozsnyó 81 D6
Rozsnyó *see* Rožňava
Ruatoria New Zealand 132 E3
Ruawai New Zealand 132 D2
Rudnyy Kazakhstan 96 C4
Rudolf, Lake *see* Lake Turkana
Rügen *headland* Germany 76 D2
Rukwa, Lake *lake* Tanzania 55 B7
Rumbek Sudan 55 B5
Rundu Namibia 60 C3
Ruoqiang China 108 C3
Ruse Bulgaria 86 D1
Russian Federation *country* Europe/Asia 92-93 96-97
Rust'avi Georgia 99 F2
Rutland Vermont, USA 23 F2
Rutög China 108 B4
Rwanda *country* C Africa 55
Ryazan' Russian Federation 93 B5 96 B3
Rybinskoye Vodokhranilishche *Reservoir* Russian Federation *Eng.* Rybinsk Reservoir 92 B4
Rybnik Poland 81 C5
Ryūkyū-rettō *island group* Japan 113 A8
Ryukyu Trench *Undersea feature* East China Sea 134 B2
Rzeszów Poland 81 E5**Saale** *river* Germany 76 C4

S

Saarbrücken Germany 77 A5
Saare *see* Saaremaa
Saaremaa *island* Estonia *var.* Saare, Sarema, *Ger.* Ösel, *var.* Oesel 88 C2
Šabac Serbia 82 C3

Sabadell Spain 75 G2
Sabah *cultural region* Borneo 120 D3
Sab'atayn, Ramlat as *desert* Yemen 103 C7
Sabhā Libya 53 F3
Sabzevār Iran 102 D3
Sacramento California, USA 27 B6
Şa'dah Yemen 103 B6
Sado *island* Japan 112 C4
Safi Morocco 52 B2
Saginaw Michigan, USA 22 C3
Sahara *desert* N Africa 50 B3
Sahel *region* W Africa 50 B3
Saïda Lebanon *anc.* Sidon 100 B4
Saidpur Bangladesh 117 G3
Saigon *see* Hồ Chi Minh
Saimaa *lake* Finland 67 E5
Saint-Brieuc France 72 A3
Saint Catherines Canada 20 D5
Saint-Chamond France 73 D5
St Christopher & Nevis *see* St Kitts & Nevis
St Cloud Minnesota, USA 25 F2
St-Denis *capital of* Réunion 61 H4
Saintes France 72 B5
Saint-Étienne France 73 D5
Saint George Australia 131 D5
St. George's *capital of* Grenada 37 G5
St Helena *external territory* UK, Atlantic Ocean 49 D5
St Helier *capital* Jersey 71 D8
Saint-Jean, Lake *lake* Canada 21 E4
Saint John Canada 21 F4
St John's *country capital* Antigua and Barbuda 37 G3
Saint John's Canada 21 H3
St Joseph Missouri, USA 25 F4
St Kitts & Nevis *country* West Indies *var.* St Christopher & Nevis 37
St.-Laurent-du-Maroni French Guiana 41 H2

Saint Lawrence *river* Canada 21 E4
Saint Lawrence, Gulf of *sea feature* Canada 21 F3
St. Lawrence Island *island* Alaska, USA 18 C2
Saint-Lô France 73 B3
Saint Louis Senegal 56 B3
St Louis Missouri, USA 25 G4
St Lucia *country* West Indies 37
Saint-Malo France 72 B3
Saint-Nazaire France 72 B4
Saint Paul Minnesota, USA 25 F2
St-Paul, Île *island* French Southern and Antarctic Territories 123 D6
St Peter Port *capital of* Guernsey 71 D8
St Petersburg Russian Federation *Rus.* Sankt-Peterburg, *prev.* Leningrad, Petrograd 92 B3 96 B2
St Petersburg Florida, USA 31 E4
Saint Pierre & Miquelon *external territory* France, Atlantic Ocean 21 G4
St Vincent, Cape *see* São Vicente, Cabo de
St Vincent & The Grenadines *country* West Indies 37
Saipan *island country capital* Northern Mariana Islands 124 B1
Sakākah Saudi Arabia 102 B4
Sakakawea, Lake *lake* North Dakota, USA 24 D2
Sakarya *see* Adapazarı
Sakhalin *island* Russian Federation 97 H4
Sal *island* Cape Verde 56 A2
Salado *river* Argentina 46 C3
Şalālah Oman 103 D6
Salamanca Spain 74 D2
Sala y Gómez *island* Chile, Pacific Ocean 135 H4
Saldus Latvia *Ger.* Frauenburg 88 B3
Salekhard Russian Federation 96 D3

Salem India 114 D2
Salem Oregon, USA 26 A3
Salerno Italy 79 D5
Salerno, Golfo di *sea feature* Italy 79 D5
Salihorsk Belarus *Rus.* Soligorsk 89 C6
Salima Malawi 61 E2
Salinas California, USA 27 B6
Salisbury England, UK 71 D7
Salisbury Island *island* Canada 20 D1
Salonica *see* Thessaloníki
Salso *river* Italy 79 C7
Salt *see* As Salt
Salta Argentina 46 C2
Saltillo Mexico 33 E2
Salt Lake City Utah, USA 24 B4
Salto Uruguay 44 B4
Salton Sea *lake* California, USA 27 D8
Salvador Brazil 43 G4
Salween *river* SE Asia 111 A6
Salzburg Austria 77 D6
Salzgitter Germany 76 C4
Samara Russian Federation 93 C6 96 B3
Samarinda Indonesia 121 E4
Samarkand Uzbekistan 104 D2
Sambre *river* Belgium 69 B7
Samoa *country* Pacific Ocean 127 F4
Samobor Croatia 82 B3
Sámos *island* Greece 87 D5
Samothrace *see* Samothráki
Samothráki *island* Greece *Eng.* Samothrace 86 D3
Samsun Turkey 98 D2
Samui, Ko *island group* Thailand 119 C6
San *river* Poland 81 E5
Saña Peru 42 A3
Sana *capital of* Yemen *var.* Şan'ā' 103 B7
Sanandaj Sinneh. Iran 102 C3
San Andrés, Isla de *island* Colombia 35 E3
San Angelo Texas, USA 29 F3
San Antonio Chile 46 B4

San Antonio Texas, USA 29 F4
San Antonio *river* S USA 29 G4
San Antonio Oeste Argentina 47 C5
Sanāw Yemen 103 C6
San Bernardino California, USA 27 C7
San Carlos Uruguay 44 C5
San Carlos de Bariloche Argentina 47 B5
San Clemente Island *island* W USA 27 C8
San Cristóbal Venezuela 40 C2
San Diego California, USA 27 C8
Sandwich Island *see* Efate
San Fernando Trinidad & Tobago 37 G5
San Fernando Venezuela 40 D2
San Fernando de Noronha *island* Brazil 43 H2
San Francisco California, USA 27 B6
Sangir, Kepulauan *island group* Indonesia 121 F3
San Ignacio Belize 34 C1
San Joaquin Valley *valley* W USA 27 B6
San José *capital of* Costa Rica 34 D4
San Jose California, USA 27 B6
San José del Guaviare Colombia 40 C3
San Juan Argentina 46 B3
San Juan *river* Costa Rica/Nicaragua 34 D4
San Juan *capital of* Puerto Rico 37 F3
San Juan Bautista Paraguay 44 B3
San Juan de los Morros Venezuela 40 D1
Sankt Martin *see* Martin
Sankt-Peterburg *see* St Petersburg
Sankt Pölten Austria 77 E6
Şanlıurfa Turkey *prev.* Urfa 98 E4
San Lorenzo Honduras 34 C3
San Luis Potosí Mexico 33 E3

San Marino *country* S Europe 78 C3
San Matías, Golfo *sea feature* Argentina 39 C6
San Miguel El Salvador 34 C3
San Miguel de Tucumán Argentina 46 C3
San Nicolas Island *island* W USA 27 B8
San Pedro Sula Honduras 34 C2
San Remo Italy 78 A3
San Salvador *capital of* El Salvador 34 C3
San Salvador de Jujuy Argentina 46 C2
San Sebastián Spain *Bas. Donostia* 75 E1
Santa Ana El Salvador 34 B2
Santa Ana California, USA 27 C8
Santa Barbara California, USA 27 B7
Santa Catalina Island *island* W USA 27 C8
Santa Clara Cuba 36 B2
Santa Cruz Bolivia 42 D4
Santa Cruz California, USA 27 B6
Santa Cruz Islands *island group* Solomon Islands 126 C4
Santa Fe Argentina 46 D3
Santa Fe New Mexico, USA 28 D2
Santa Maria Brazil 44 C4
Santa Marta Colombia 40 C1
Santander Spain 75 E1
Santanilla, Islas *islands* Honduras 35 E1
Santarém Brazil 43 E2
Santarém Portugal 74 C3
Santaren Channel *Channel* Bahamas 36 C2
Santa Rosa Argentina 47 C4
Santa Rosa California, USA 27 A6
Santa Rosa de Copán Honduras 34 C2
Santa Rosa Island *island* W USA 27 B8
Santiago *island* Cape Verde 56 A3

Santiago *capital of* Chile 46 B4
Santiago Dominican Republic 37 E3
Santiago Panama 35 F5
Santiago de Compostela Spain 74 C1
Santiago de Cuba Cuba 36 C3
Santiago del Estero Argentina 46 C3
Santo Antão *island* Cape Verde 56 A2
Santo Domingo *capital of* Dominican Republic 37 E3
Santo Domingo de los Colorados Ecuador 40 A4
Santorini *island* Greece 87 D6
Santos Brazil 45 E2
São Borja Brazil 44 C3
São Francisco *river* Brazil 43 G3
São José do Rio Preto Brazil 45 D1
São Luís Brazil 43 G2
São Nicolau *island* Cape Verde 56 A2
Saône *river* France 72 D4
São Paulo Brazil 43 F5 45 E2
São Tomé *capital of* Sao Tome & Principe 59 A5
São Tomé *island* Sao Tome & Principe 59 A5
Sao Tome & Principe *country* W Africa 59
São Vincente *island* Cape Verde 56 A2
São Vicente, Cabo de *coastal feature* Portugal *Eng.* Cape St Vincent 74 B4
Sapele Nigeria 57 F5
Sapporo Japan 112 D2
Saragossa *see* Zaragoza
Sarajevo *capital of* Bosnia & Herzegovina 82 C4
Sarandë Albania 83 D6
Saransk Russian Federation 93 B5
Saratov Russian Federation 93 B6
Sarawak *state* Malaysia 120 D3

Sardegna *island* Italy *Eng.*
Sardinia 79 A5
Sardinia *see* Sardegna
Sarema *see* Saaremaa
Sargasso Sea Atlantic Ocean
48 B4
Sargodha Pakistan 116 C2
Sarh Chad 58 C4
Sāri Iran 102 D3
Saruhan *see* Manisa
Sasebo Japan 113 A6
Saskatchewan *province*
Canada 19 F5
Saskatchewan *river* Canada
19 F5
Saskatoon Canada 19 F5
Sassandra *River* Côte d'Ivoire 56
D5
Sassari Italy 79 A5
Satu Mare Romania 90 B3
Saudi Arabia *country* SW Asia
102-103
Sault Sainte Marie Canada
20 C4
Sault Sainte Marie Michigan,
USA 22 C1
Saurimo Angola 60 C2
Sava *river* SE Europe 82 C3
Savannah Georgia, USA
31 F3
Savannah *river* SE USA 31 E2
Savissivik Greenland 64 C2
Savona Italy 78 A3
Savu Sea *sea* Indonesia 120 E5
Şawqirah Oman 103 D6
Saýat Turkmenistan 104 D3
Sayhūt Yemen 103 D7
Saynshand Mongolia 109 E2
Say 'ūn Yemen 103 C6
Scandinavia *geophysical region*
Europe 48 D2
Schaffhausen Switzerland
77 B6
Schaulen *see* Šiauliai
Schefferville Canada 21 E2
Scheldt *river* W Europe 69 B5
Schiermonnikoog *island*
Netherlands 68 D1
Schneidemühl *see* Piła

Schwäbische Alb *mountains*
Germany 77 B6
Schwarzwald *Forested*
mountain region Germany
Eng. Black Forest 77 B6
Schwerin Germany 76 C3
Scilly, Isles of *islands* UK 71 B7
Scotia Sea Atlantic Ocean
136 A1
Scotland *national region* UK 70
Scottsbluff Nebraska, USA
24 D3
Scottsdale Arizona, USA 28 B2
Scranton Pennsylvania, USA
23 F3
Scutari, Lake *lake*
Albania/Montenegro 83 C5
Seddon New Zealand 133 C5
Seattle Washington, USA 26 B2
Ségou Mali 56 D3
Segovia Spain 75 E2
Segura *river* Spain 75 E4
Seikan Tunnel *tunnel* Japan
112 D3
Seinäjoki Finland 67 D5
Seine *river* France 72 C3
Selfoss Iceland 65 E5
Semara *see* Smara
Semarang Indonesia 120 D4
Semipalatinsk Kazakhstan 96
D4
Sendai Japan 112 D4
Senegal *country* W Africa 56
Senegal *river* Africa 56 C3
Sên, Stœng *river* Cambodia
119 D5
Seoul *capital of* South Korea
Kor. Sŏul 110 E4
Sept-Iles Canada 21 F3
Seraing Belgium 69 D6
Seram, Pulau *island* Indonesia
121 F4
Serbia *country* SE Europe
82 D3
Serdar Turkmenistan *prev.*
Gyzylarbat, *prev.* Kizyl-Arvat
104 B2
Serhetabat Turkmenistan *prev.*
Gushgy, Kushka
104 C4

Serov Russian Federation 96 C3
Serpent's Mouth, The *sea*
feature Trinidad &
Tobago/Venezuela *Sp.* Boca
de la Serpiente 41 F1
Serra do Mar *mountains* Brazil
44 D3
Sérres Greece 86 C3
Setesdal *valley* Norway 67 A6
Sétif Algeria 53 E1
Setúbal Portugal 74 C4
Seul, Lake *lake* Canada 20 A3
Sevana Lich *lake* Armenia
99 G2
Sevastopol' Ukraine 91 F5
Severn *river* Canada 20 B3
Severn *river* England/Wales, UK
71 D6
Severnaya Dvina *river* Russian
Federation *Eng.* Northern
Dvina 92 C3
Severnaya Zemlya *island group*
Russian Federation 137 H3
Sevilla Spain *Eng.* Seville
74 D4
Seville *see* Sevilla
Seychelles *country* Indian
Ocean 61 122 B4
Seydhisfjördhur Iceland 65 E4
Seýdi Turkmenistan *prev.*
Neftezavodsk 104 D2
Seyhan *see* Adana
Sfax Tunisia 53 F2
's-Gravenhage *capital of*
Netherlands *Eng.* The Hague
68 B3
Shaan *see* Shaanxi
Shaanxi *province* China *var.*
Shaan, Shan-hsi, Shaanxi
Sheng, Shenshi, Shensi
111 C5
Shaanxi Sheng *see* Shaanxi
Shache China 108 A3
Shackleton Ice Shelf *ice feature*
Antarctica 136 D3
Shandong *province* China *var.*
Lu, Shantung 110 D4
Shanghai China 111 D5
Shangrao China 111 D6
Shan-hsi *see* Shaanxi
Shannon *river* Ireland 71 B5

Surat Thani Thailand 119 C6

Sûre *river* W Europe 69 D7

Surfers Paradise Australia 131 E5

Surinam *see* Suriname

Suriname *country* NE South America *var.* Surinam 41

Surkhob *river* Tajikistan 105 E3

Surt Libya *var.* Sidra 53 G2

Surt, Khalij *sea feature* Mediterranean Sea *Eng.* Gulf of Sirte, Gulf of Sidra 85 E4

Surtsey *island* S Iceland 65 E5

Susanville California, USA 27 B5

Suways, Qanât as *see* Suez Canal

Suva *capital of* Fiji 127 E4

Svalbard *external territory* Norway, Arctic Ocean 65 G2

Svay Riëng Cambodia 119 D6

Sverdlovsk *see* Yekaterinburg

Svetlogorsk *see* Svyetlahorsk

Svyataya Anna Trough *undersea feature* Kara Sea 137 H4

Svyetlahorsk Belarus *Rus.* Svetlogorsk 89 D6

Swakopmund Namibia 60 B3

Swansea Wales, UK 71 C6

Swaziland *country* southern Africa 61

Sweden *country* N Europe 66-67

Sweetwater Texas, USA 29 F3

Swindon England, UK 71 D6

Switzerland *country* C Europe 77

Sydney Australia 131 D6

Sydney Canada 21 G4

Syeverodonets'k Ukraine 91 G1

Syktyvkar Russian Federation 92 D4 96 C3

Sylhet Bangladesh 117 G4

Syracuse *see* Siracusa

Syracuse New York, USA 23 E3

Syr Darya *river* C Asia 104 D1

Syria *country* SW Asia 100-101

Syrian Desert *desert* SW Asia *Ar.* Bādiyat ash Shām 101 C5

Szczecin Poland *Ger.* Stettin 80 B3

Szczeciński, Zalew *bay* Germany/Poland 80 A2

Szechwan *see* Sichuan

Szeged Hungary *Ger.* Szegedin 81 D7

Szegedin *see* Szeged

Székesfehérvár Hungary *Ger.* Stuhlweissenburg 81 C6

Szekszárd Hungary 81 C7

Szolnok Hungary 81 D6

Szombathely Hungary *Ger.* Steinamanger 81 B6

T

Tabariya, Bahrat *see* Tiberius, Lake

Tábor Czech Republic 81 B5

Tabora Tanzania 55 B7

Tabriz Iran 102 C2

Tabuaeran *island* Kiribati 127 G2

Tabūk Saudi Arabia 102 A4

Tacloban Philippines 120 F2

Tacna Peru 42 C4

Tacoma Washington, USA 26 B2

Tacuarembó Uruguay 44 C4

Tadmur *see* Tudmur

Taegu South Korea 110 E4

Taejŏn South Korea 110 E4

Tafassâsset, Ténéré du *desert* Niger 57 G2

Taguatinga Brazil 43 F3

Tagus *river* Portugal/Spain *Port.* Tejo, *Sp.* Tajo 74 C3

Tahiti *island* French Polynesia 127 H5

Tahoe, Lake *lake* W USA 27 B5

Tahoua Niger 57 F3

T'aichung Taiwan 111D6

Taieri 129 New Zealand 133 B7

Taihape New Zealand 132 D4

T'ainan Taiwan 111 D6

Taipei *capital of* Taiwan 111 D6

Taiping Malaysia 120 B3

Taiwan *country* E Asia *prev.* Formosa 111

Taiwan Strait *sea feature* East China Sea/South China Sea *var.* Formosa Strait 111 D7

Taiyuan China 110 C4

Ta'izz Yemen 103 B7

Tajikistan *country* C Asia 105

Tajo *see* Tagus

Takapuna New Zealand 132 D2

Takla Makan *see* Taklimakan Shamo

Taklimakan Shamo *desert region* China *var.* Takla Makan 108 B3

Talamanca, Cordillera de *mountains* Costa Rica 35 E4

Talas Kyrgyzstan 105 F2

Talaud, Kepulauan *island group* Indonesia 121 F3

Talca Chile 46 B4

Talcahuano Chile 46 B4

Taldykoigan Kazakhstan 96 C5

Tallahassee Florida, USA 30 D3

Tallinn *capital of* Estonia *prev.* Revel, *Ger.* Reval, *Rus.* Tallin 88 D2

Talsen *see* Talsi

Talsi Latvia *Ger.* Talsen 88 B3

Tamale Ghana 57 E4

Tamanrasset Algeria 53 E4

Tambo Australia 130 C4

Tambov Russian Federation 93 B5

Tamil Nādu *state* India 114 D2

Tampa Florida, USA 31 E4

Tampere Finland 67 D5

Tampico Mexico 33 F3

Tamworth Australia 131 D6

Tanami Desert *desert* Australia 128 E3

Tananarive *see* Antananarivo

Tanega-shima *island* Japan 113 B7

Tanga Tanzania 55 C7

Tanganyika, Lake *lake* E Africa 51 D5

Tanger Morocco *var.* Tangiers 52 C1

Tanggula Shan *mountain range* China 108 C4

Tangiers see Tanger
Tangra Yumco lake China 108 B5
Tangshan China 110 D4
Tanimbar Islands see Tanimbar, Kepulauan
Tanimbar, Kepulauan island group Indonesia Eng. Tanimbar Islands 121 F5
Tanjungkarang see Bandar Lampung
Tan-Tan Morocco 52 B3
Tanzania country E Africa 55
Taoudenni Mali 57 E2
Tapa Estonia Ger. Taps 88 D2
Tapachula Mexico 33 G5
Tapajós river Brazil 43 E2
Taps see Tapa
Ṭarābulus see Tripoli, Lebanon
Ṭarābulus al-Gharb see Tripoli, Libya
Taranto Italy 79 E5
Taranto, Golfo di sea feature Mediterranean Sea 79 E5
Tarapoto Peru 42 B2
Tarawa island Kiribati 127 E2
Taraz Kazakhstan prev. Dzhambul, Zhambyl 96 C5
Tarbes France 73 B6
Tarcoola Australia 131 A5
Târgovişte Romania prev. Tîrgovişte 90 C4
Târgu Mureş Romania prev. Tîrgu Mureş 90 C4
Tarija Bolivia 42 C5
Tarim Basin basin China 108 B3
Tarim He river China 108 B3
Tarn river France 73 C6
Tarnów Poland 81 D5
Tarragona Spain 75 G2
Tarsus Turkey 98 D4
Tartu Estonia prev. Yur'yev, var. Yurev, Ger. Dorpat 88 D3
Ṭarţūs Syria 100 B3
Tashauz see Daşoguz
Tashkent capital of Uzbekistan var. Taškent, Uzb. Toshkent 105 E2
Taškent see Tashkent

Tasman Bay inlet New Zealand 132 C4
Tasmania state Australia 131 C8
Tasman Basin undersea feature Tasman Sea 124 D5
Tasman Plateau undersea feature Pacific Ocean 124 C5
Tasman Sea Pacific Ocean 134 C4
Tassili-n-Ajjer desert plateau Algeria 53 E4
Tatabánya Hungary 81 C6
Tatar Pazardzhik see Pazardzhik
Taubaté Brazil 43 F5 45 E2
Taumarunui New Zealand 132 D3
Taunggyi Myanmar 118 B3
Taunton England, UK 71 D7
Taupo New Zealand 132 D3
Taupo, Lake lake New Zealand 132 D3
Tauragé Lithuania 88 B4
Tauranga New Zealand 132 D3
Taurus Mountains mountain range Turkey see Toros Dağları 94 D4
Tavoy Myanmar 119 B5
Tawau Malaysia 120 D3
Taymyr, Ozero lake Russian Federation 97 E2
Taymyr, Poluostrov peninsula Russian Federation Eng. Taymyr Peninsula 97 E2
Taymyr Peninsula see Taymyr, Poluostrov
Tbilisi capital of Georgia Geor. T'bilisi, prev. Tiflis 99 F2
Te Anau New Zealand 133 A7
Te Anau, Lake lake New Zealand 133 A7
Tedzhen see Tejen
Tegal Indonesia 120 C5
Tegucigalpa capital of Honduras 34 C2
Teheran see Tehrān
Tehrān capital of Iran prev. Teheran 102 C3
Tehuacán Mexico 33 F4

Tehuantepec, Golfo de sea feature Mexico 33 G5
Tejen Turkmenistan prev. Tedzhen 104 C3
Tejo see Tagus
Te Kao New Zealand 131 C1
Tekirdağ Turkey It. Rodosto 98 A2
Te Kuiti Waikato, New Zealand 132 D3
Tel Aviv-Yafo Israel 101 A5
Teles Pires river Brazil 43 E3
Tell Atlas plateau Africa 84 C3
Telschen see Telšiai
Telšiai Lithuania Ger. Telschen 88 B4
Temuco Chile 47 B5
Ténéré physical region Niger 57 G2
Tenerife island Spain 52 A3
Tennant Creek Australia 130 A3
Tennessee state USA 30 D1
Tennessee river SE USA 31 C1
Tepelenë Albania 83 D6
Tepic Mexico 32 D4
Teplice Czech Republic Ger. Teplitz, prev. Teplice-Šanov, Ger. Teplitz-Schönau 80 A4
Teplice-Šanov see Teplice
Teplitz see Teplice
Teplitz-Schönau see Teplice
Teraina island Kiribati 127 G2
Teresina Brazil 43 G2
Termez Uzbekistan 105 E3
Terneuzen Netherlands 69 B5
Terni Italy 78 C4
Ternopil' Ukraine Rus. Ternopol' 90 C2
Ternopol' see Ternopil'
Terrassa Spain 75 G2
Terre Haute Indiana, USA 22 B4
Terres Australes et Antarctiques Françaises see French Southern and Antarctic Territories
Terschelling island Netherlands 68 C1
Teruel Spain 75 F3
Teseney Eritrea 54 C4

Tessalit Mali 57 E2

Tete Mozambique 61 E3

Tétouan Morocco 52 C1

Tetovo Macedonia 83 D5

Tetschen see Děčín

Tevere river Italy 78 C4

Texas state USA 28-29 F3

Texarkana Arkansas, USA 30 A2

Texas City Texas, USA 29 G4

Texel island Netherlands 68 C2

Thailand country SE Asia 118-119

Thailand, Gulf of sea feature South China Sea 119 C6

Thames river England, UK 71 D6

Thar Desert desert India/Pakistan 116 C3

Tharthār, Buḩayrat ath lake Iraq 102 B3

Thásos island Greece 86 C3

Thaton Myanmar 118 B4

Theiss see Tisza

Thermaic Gulf see Thermaïkós Kólpos

Thermaïkós Kólpos sea feature Greece Eng. Thermaic Gulf 86 B4

Thessaloníki Greece var. Salonica 86 B3

The Valley dependent territory capital Anguilla 37 G5

Thimphu capital of Bhutan 117 G3

Thionville France 72 E3

Thompson Canada 19 F4

Thorn see Toruń

Thorshavn see Tórshavn

Thracian Sea Greece Gk. Thrakikó Pélagos 86 D3

Thrakikó Pélagos see Thracian Sea

Three Kings Islands island group New Zealand 132 C1

Thule see Qaanaaq

Thunder Bay Canada 20 B4

Thuner See lake Switzerland 77 B7

Thurso Scotland, UK 70 C2

Tianjin China var. Tientsin 110 D4

Tiberias, Lake lake Israel var. Sea of Galilee, Heb. Yam Kinneret, Ar. Bahrat Tabariya 101 B5

Tibesti mountains Chad/Libya 50 C3

Tibet autonomous region China Chin. Xizang 108 C5

Tibet, Plateau of see Qingzang Gaoyuan

Tienen Belgium 69 C6

Tien Shan mountain range C Asia 105 G2

Tientsin see Tianjin

Tierra del Fuego island Argentina/Chile 47 C8

Tiflis see Tbilisi

Tighina Moldova prev. Bendery 90 D4

Tigris river SW Asia 94 B4

Tijuana Mexico 32 A1

Tiki Basin undersea feature Pacific Ocean 135 E3

Tiksi Russian Federation 97 F2

Tilburg Netherlands 68 C4

Timaru New Zealand 133 B6

Timișoara Romania 90 A4

Timmins Canada 20 C4

Timor island Indonesia 121 F5

Timor Sea Indian Ocean 121 F5

Tindouf Algeria 52 B3

Tinos island Greece 87 D5

Tirana capital of Albania 83 D6

Tiraspol Moldova 90 D4

Târgoviște see Târgoviște

Tirgu Mureș see Târgu Mureș

Tirol region Austria var. Tyrol 77 C7

Tiruchchirāppalli India 114 D3

Tisa see Tisza

Tisza river E Europe Ger. Theiss, Cz./Rom./SCr. Tisa 81 D6

Titicaca, Lake lake Bolivia/Peru 42 C4

Tlemcen Algeria 52 D2

Toamasina Madagascar 61 G3

Toba, Danau lake Indonesia 120 B3

Tobago island Trinidad and Tobago 37 G5

Toba Kākar Range mountains Pakistan 116 B2

Tobruk see Ţubruq

Tocantins river Brazil 43 F3

Tocopilla Chile 46 B2

Togo country W Africa 57 E4

Tokat Turkey 98 D3

Tokelau external territory New Zealand, Pacific Ocean 127 F3

Tokmak Kyrgyzstan 105 F2

Tokuno-shima island Japan 113 A8

Tokushima Japan 113 B5

Tokyo capital of Japan 113 D5

Toledo Spain 75 E3

Toledo Ohio, USA 22 C3

Toledo Bend Reservoir Reservoir S USA 29 H3

Toliara Madagascar 61 F4

Tol'yatti prev. Stavropol' Russian Federation 93 C5

Tomakomai Japan 112 D2

Tombouctou Mali 57 E3

Tombua Angola 60 B2

Tomini, Gul of sea feature Indonesia 121 E4

Tomsk Russian Federation 96 D4

Tonga country Pacific Ocean 127

Tongatapu island Tonga 125 E3

Tongking, Gulf of sea feature South China Sea var. Gulf of Tonkin 111 B7

Tongliao China 109 G2

Tongtian He river China 108 C4

Tonkin, Gulf of see Tongking, Gulf of

Tônle Kông river Cambodia/Vietnam 118 E5

Tônlé Sap lake Cambodia 119 D5

Tonopah Nevada, USA 27 C6

Toowoomba Australia 131 D5

Topeka Kansas, USA 25 F4

Top Springs Australia 130 A3

Torino Italy Eng. Turin 78 A2

Tornio Finland 66 D4

Tornionjoki *river* Finland/Sweden 66 D3

Toronto Canada 20 D5

Toros Dağları *mountain range* Turkey *Eng.* Taurus Mountains 98 C4

Torre del Greco Italy 79 D5

Torrens, Lake *lake* Australia 131 B5

Torreón Mexico 32 D2

Torres Strait *sea feature* Arafura Sea/Coral Sea 126 B4

Torrington Wyoming, USA 24 D3

Tórshavn *capital of* Faeroe Islands *Dan.* Thorshavn 65 F5

To'rtko'l Uzbekistan *prev.* Petroaleksandrovsk, Turtkul', *Uzb.* Türtkül 104 C2

Tortoise Islands *see* Galapagos Islands

Tortosa Spain 75 F2

Toruń Poland *Ger.* Thorn 80 C3

Toscana *region* Italy *Eng.* Tuscany 78 B3

Toscano, Arcipelago *island group* Italy 78 B4

Toshkent *see* Tashkent

Tottori Japan 113 B5

Touggourt Algeria 53 E2

Toulon France 73 D6

Toulouse France 73 B6

Toungoo Myanmar 118 B4

Tournai Belgium 69 B6

Tours France 72 C4

Townsville Australia 130 D3

Toyama Japan 112 C4

Tozeur Tunisia 53 E2

Trâblous *see* Tripoli, Lebanon

Trabzon Turkey *Eng.* Trebizond 99 E2

Tralee Ireland 71 A6

Trang Thailand 119 C7

Transantarctic Mountains *mountain range* Antarctica 136 B3

Transylvania *region* Romania 90 B3

Transylvanian Alps *see* Carpaţii Meridionali

Trapani Italy 79 C6

Traralgon Australia 131 C7

Trasimeno, Lago *Lake* Italy 78 C4

Traverse City Michigan, USA 22 C2

Travis, Lake *lake* Texas, USA 29 F4

Trebinje Bosnia & Herzegovina 83 C5

Trebizond *see* Trabzon

Trelew Argentina 47 C6

Trenčín Slovakia *Ger.* Trentschin *Hung.* Trencsén 81 C6

Trencsén *see* Trenčín

Trento Italy *Ger.* Trient 78 C2

Trenton New Jersey, USA 23 F4

Trentschin *see* Trenčín

Tres Arroyos Argentina 47 D5

Treviso Italy 78 C2

Trient *see* Trento

Trieste Italy 78 D2

Tríkala Greece 86 B4

Trincomalee Sri Lanka 115 E3

Trindade *external territory* Brazil, Atlantic Ocean 49 C6

Trinidad Bolivia 42 C4

Trinidad Uruguay 44 B5

Trinidad *island* Trinidad & Tobago 38 C2

Trinidad & Tobago *country* West Indies 37 G5

Tripoli Greece 87 B5

Tripoli Lebanon *var.* Trâblous, Ţarābulus 100 B4

Tripoli *capital of* Libya *Ar.* Ţarābulus al-Gharb 53 F2

Tristan da Cunha *external territory* UK, Atlantic Ocean 49 D6

Trivandrum India 114 D3

Trnava Slovakia *Ger.* Tyrnau, *Hung.* Nagyszombat 81 C6

Trois-Rivières Canada 21 E4

Trollhättan Sweden 67 B6

Tromsø Norway 66 C2

Trondheim Norway 66 B4

Trondheimsfjorden *inlet* Norway 66 B4

Troyes France 72 D4

Trujillo Honduras 34 D2

Trujillo Peru 42 A3

Tsarigrad *see* İstanbul

Tschenstochau *see* Częstochowa

Tselinograd *see* Astana

Tsetserleg Mongolia 108 D2

Tshikapa Dem. Rep. Congo 59 C7

Tshwane *capital of* South Africa *prev.* Pretoria 60 D4

Tsinghai *see* Qinghai

Tsumeb Namibia 60 C3

Tsushima *island* Japan 113 A5

Tuamotu Fracture Zone *tectonic feature* Pacific Ocean 125 H3

Tuamotu Islands *island group* French Polynesia 125 G3

Tubmanburg Liberia 56 C4

Ţubruq Libya *Eng.* Tobruk 53 H2

Tucson Arizona, USA 28 B3

Tucupita Venezuela 41 F1

Tucurui, Represa de *Reservoir* Brazil 43 F2

Tudmur Syria *var.* Tadmur, *Eng.* Palmyra 100 C3

Tuguegarao Philippines 121 E1

Tuktoyaktuk Canada 137 D2

Tula Russian Federation 93 B5 96 A3

Tulancingo Mexico 33 E4

Tulcán Ecuador 40 B4

Tulcea Romania 90 D4

Tülkarm West Bank 101 D7

Tully Australia 130 D3

Tulsa Oklahoma, USA 29 G1

Tundzha *river* Bulgaria 86 D2

Tungaru *island group* Kiribati *prev.* Gilbert Islands 127 E2

Tunis *capital of* Tunisia 53 F1

Tunisia *country* N Africa 53 F2

Tunja Colombia 40 C2

Tupiza Bolivia 42 C5

Turan Lowland *lowland* Turkmenistan/Uzbekistan *var.* Turan Plain, *Rus.* Turanskaya Nizmennost' 104 C2

Turan Plain *see* Turan Lowland

Turanskaya Nizmennost' *see* Turan Lowland

Turčianský Svätý Martin *see* Martin

Turin *see* Torino

Turkana, Lake *lake* Ethiopia/Kenya *var.* Lake Rudolf 50 D4 55 C5

Turkey *country* SW Asia 98-99

Türkmenabat Turkmenistan *prev.* Chardzhev, *prev.* Chardzhou, *prev.* Leninsk, *Turkm.* Chärjew 104 D3

Türkmenbaşy Turkmenistan *prev.* Krasnovodsk 104 A2

Turkmenistan *country* C Asia 104

Turks & Caicos Islands *external territory* UK, West Indies 37

Turku Finland 67 D5

Turnagain, Cape *headland* New Zealand 132 E4

Turnhout Belgium 69 C5

Turnu Severin *see* Drobeta-Turnu Severin

Turócszentmárton *see* Martin

Turpan China 108 C3

Turtkul' *see* To'rtko'l

Türtkül *see* To'rtko'l

Tuscany *see* Toscana

Tuvalu *country* Pacific Ocean 127

Tuxtla Mexico 33 G5

Tuz Gölü *lake* Turkey 98 C3

Tuzla Bosnia & Herz. 82 C3

Tver' Russian Federation 92 B4

Twin Falls Idaho, USA 26 D4

Tyler Texas, USA 29 G3

Tyre *see* Soûr

Tyrnau *see* Trnava

Tyrol *see* Tirol

Tyrrhenian Sea Mediterranean Sea 78 C6

Tyup Kyrgyzstan 105 G2

Tziá *island* Greece *prev.* Kéa 87 C5

U

Ubangi *river* C Africa 59 C5

Uberaba Brazil 43 F5 45 E1

Uberlândia Brazil 43 F5 45 E1

Ubon Ratchathani Thailand 119 D5

Ucayali *river* Peru 42 B3

Uchkuduk Uzbekistan *Uzb.* Uchqudúq 104 D2

Uchqudúq *see* Uchkuduk

Udine Italy 78 C2

Udon Thani Thailand 118 C4

Uele *river* Dem. Rep. Congo 58 D5

Ufa Russian Federation 96 B3

Uganda *country* E Africa 55

Uíge Angola 60 B1

Ujungpandang *see* Makassar

Ukhta Russian Federation 92 D4

Ukiah California, USA 27 A5

Ukmergė Lithuania 88 C4

Ukraine *country* E Europe 90-91

Ulaanbaatar *see* Ulan Bator

Ulaangom Mongolia 108 C2

Ulan Bator *capital of* Mongolia *var.* Ulaanbaatar 109 E2

Ulan-Ude Russian Federation 97 E4

Ullapool Scotland, UK 70 C3

Ulm Germany 77 C6

Ulster *region* Ireland/UK 71 B5

Ulungur Hu *lake* China 108 C2

Uluru *peak* Australia *var.* Ayers Rock 129 E5

Ul'yanovsk Russian Federation 93 C5

Umeå Sweden 66 D4

Umnak Island *island* Alaska, USA 18 B3

Una *river* Bosnia & Herzegovina/Croatia 82 B3

Unalaska Island *island* Alaska, USA 18 B3

Ungava, Péninsule d' *peninsula* Canada 20 D1

Ungava Bay *sea feature* Canada 21 E1

United Arab Emirates *country* SW Asia 103 D5

United Kingdom *country* NW Europe 70-71

United States of America *country* North America 16-17

Uppsala Sweden 67 C6

Ural *river* Kazakhstan/Russian Federation 96 B4

Ural Mountains *mountain range* Russian Federation *var.* Ural'skiy Khrebet, *Rus.* Ural'skiye Gory 92-93

Ural'sk Kazakhstan 96 B3

Ural'skiy Khrebet *see* Ural Mountains

Ural'skiye Gory *see* Ural Mountains

Urfa *see* Şanlıurfa

Urganch *see* Urgench

Urgench Uzbekistan *prev.* Novo Urgench, *Uzb.* Urganch 104 C2

Uroševac Serbia 83 D5

Üroteppa Tajikistan 105 E2

Uruapan Mexico 33 E4

Uruguaiana Brazil 44 B4

Uruguay *country* SE South America 44

Uruguay *river* S South America 46 D3

Urumchi *see* Ürümqi

Ürümqi China *prev.* Urumchi 108 C3

Usa *river* Russian Federation 92 D3

Uşak Turkey *prev.* Ushak 98 B3

Ushak *see* Uşak

Ushuaia Argentina 47 C8

Ust'-Chaun Russian Federation 97 G1

Ustica, Isola de *island* Italy 79 C6

Ústí nad Labem Czech Republic *Ger.* Aussig 80 A4

Ust'-Kamchatsk Russian Federation 97 H2

Ust'-Kamenogorsk Kazakhstan 96 D5